Everybody's San Francisco Cookbook

Recipes Celebrating the City's Best Ethnic Cooking

Charles Lemos

Good Life Publications — San Francisco

EVERYBODY'S SAN FRANCISCO COOKBOOK

ISBN 1-886776-01-6

A Good Life Publications Book/February 1998

Cover design by Big Fish Books, San Francisco.
Cover illustrations by Paula Pangaro.
Interior design and illustrations by Nancy Lee.
Edited by Sharon Silva.
Additional editing, research, testing, and support provided by many people, including Beverly Cambron, Jeremy Chipman, Rose Cremin, Elizabeth Davis, Suzanne Joyal, Benny Mart, and Sean Vitali.
Restaurant recipes courtesy of the restaurants.

First edition.
Printed in Canada on recycled paper.

Good Life Publications
580 Washington St. #306
San Francisco, California 94111
(415) 989-1844
(888) 989-GOOD
(415) 989-3122 fax
info@goodlifebooks.com

SPECIAL SALES
Good Life books are available at bulk discounts for conventions, corporate gifts, fundraising sales premiums, and sales promotions. Special editions, including custom covers, excerpts of existing guides, and corporate imprints, can be created for large orders. For more information, contact Good Life Publications, (888) 989-GOOD.

Table of contents

For my mother, Frinet, my grandmother Aura, and my uncle, Luis, who taught me much about life.

Introduction

I was lucky to have grown up surrounded by good cooks and therefore good food. As a young child in Colombia, our lunches were long, elaborate, rather formal affairs. As a teenager in New York, I began cooking with my mother, helping her with our daily meals and with her menus for entertaining.

Thus, began my long apprenticeship as a cook. My mother taught me the patience and basic techniques required, as well as the flair indispensable to presentation. In time, I took over the daily cooking for our family, although my mother retained control of her true culinary love, baking and desserts. During summer visits to Colombia, my great aunt Carlina, a robust woman with a jovial demeanor, taught me the intricacies of Colombian, French, and Spanish cooking.

By the time I arrived as a student at Stanford University, I was a good cook but still a novice and very Eurocentric. It was in the Bay Area that I discovered Asia. I had been to Chinese and Indonesian restaurants before I came to the West Coast, but that was more or less the extent of my exposure to Asian cuisines. Soon enough, though, I was captivated by them, and the wealth of Asian restaurants and markets close to where I lived encouraged me to experiment and practice.

My professional career as a cook began haphazardly while I was at Stanford. A classmate, Mary White, needed to host a reception for Stanford's Bolivar Center for Latin American Studies. She couldn't afford a caterer, so she asked me to cater it. Another classmate, Jennifer Sparigen, introduced me to Robert and Sally Freelen. At the time, Robert Freelen was Stanford's Vice President for Public Affairs. Before I knew it, I was in charge of official university receptions hosted by the Public Affairs office. Sally is a great cook and was a terrific boss. She expanded my repertoire, taught me new techniques, allowed me to be creative, and showed me how to throw a party for 500 people without breaking a sweat. My cooking also benefitted from occasional stints with outside caterers, especially Susan Kemp of SKS Party Planners of Los Altos.

As I grew older, I began to travel the world, sometimes with friends and sometimes alone. On these journeys, I always pursued my love of exotic and authentic gastronomy, regularly seeking out cooks in the restaurants and homes I visited. I watched them in the kitchen, and I took note of their use of spices and flavorings. I have tried to remain faithful to the lessons of the many people who shared their knowledge with me.

This book had its genesis in one splendid year at Glenwood Manor, a large house in Atherton where I shared digs with five remarkable young men attending Stanford's Graduate School of Business. Over the course of 12 months, Aneel Bhusri, Steve Chan, Tom Frangione, Martin Romo, Jeff Samberg, and I became the closest of friends and threw many parties. The house, with its great kitchen and spacious grounds, lent itself to entertaining. We had a few gatherings of more than two hundred people and many more more intimate ones. My housemates were all enthusiastic learners. Their constant requests for written recipes are what led to this cookbook, a very personal yet eclectic collection of recipes that reflect my interests and tastes in the foods of the world.

But it is to my publisher Peter Massik to whom I am most deeply indebted for the existence of this book. His tireless efforts and never-ending joy of cooking has made it a reality. He tested many of the recipes that appear here, and his feedback was instrumental in refining its character. Not only was he inquisitive about particular dishes, but he was also curious about the ingredients and where to get them. This led to the glossary and the provisions list.

The San Francisco Bay Area is a wonderful place to live. It shelters a bounty of cultures, and this diversity, this intersection of different traditions, enhances our lives immeasurably. Indeed, few areas of the globe can claim such varied culinary offerings within such a small region. So go out, explore the ethnic markets, and get down to some of the best cooking on the planet.

List of Recipes

China

India

Italy

Japan

Latin America

The Middle East

Morocco

Southeast Asia

Spain

China

There is no doubt that China possesses one of the world's most distinctive and distinguished cuisines. The country's sheer size has produced significant regional variations, but four basic cuisines predominate: Canton and southern China, Sichuan and western China, Shanghai and eastern China, and Beijing and northern China. Of these, the Cantonese kitchen is by far the most commonly encountered in Chinese restaurants in America, especially in San Francisco.

The classic Cantonese stove-top method is stir-frying, the quick cooking of finely cut meats and/or vegetables over high heat, a technique developed in response to a scarcity of wood for fuel. Cantonese cooks use a variety of bean sauces, in particular one made from salted black beans that seasons everything from pork and chicken to vegetables and seafood. But the highlight of Cantonese cuisine is dim sum, countless small dishes—steamed and fried dumplings, meat-filled buns, tiny spareribs, parchment chicken, custard tartlets—consumed at midday with tea.

In the past two decades, the spicy cuisine of Sichuan (and to a lesser extent Hunan) has been enthusiastically embraced by American diners. The fare of this inland province is characterized by a generous use of chilies (a relatively recent arrival in China) and of fagara, more commonly known as Sichuan pepper. While stir-frying is common, so is smoking, marinating, and braising, and poultry, pork, and freshwater fish are the primary protein sources.

The cuisines of Beijing and Shanghai are encountered more infrequently in the United States. The former, sometimes called mandarin cuisine, relies more on wheat and millet than on rice, and northern cooks have access to far fewer vegetables than their counterparts in more temperate climates. Poultry, freshwater fish, and lamb are favored, and soybeans are a major crop and important protein source. Grilling, steaming, and hot pot cooking are popular, and garlic and thick soybean pastes are prevalent seasonings.

Because the lower Yangtze is a major rice-producing area, rice appears in many guises in Shanghai cooking: as the basis of the wine used in the making of such dishes as drunken chicken and drunken spareribs, in poultry stuffings, and as the staple starch of the everyday meal. Braising is a favored cooking technique, producing the famed red-cooked dishes—meats bathed in a soy bath—of the region, and sweet sauces, built on honey or crystal sugar, are traditional fare.

Chinese dishes, which are generally low in fat because only small amounts of meat and little cooking oil are used, deliver the full range of flavors: sweet, sour, hot, bitter, and salty. Cooks arrive at these characteristic tastes in part through the use of many different seasonings; among the most common are soy sauce, various bean pastes, five-spice powder, sugar, rice vinegar, and tangerine peel. But for Chinese cooks it is paramount that fresh, top-quality vegetables and other ingredients be used whenever possible, and they resist masking their fine flavors with a heavy dose of herbs, spices, and other seasonings. In this regard, Chinese cooking can be seen as the inspiration for California cuisine, where fresh ingredients are allowed to shine over any seasoning.

If you don't already own them, consider purchasing three specialty cookware items to streamline your Chinese cooking. The first is the wok, a deep, usually round-bottomed pan that permits stir-frying over high heat in a minimum amount of oil. The second is the bamboo steamer, which can be placed over boiling water in a wok or other pan. (If you plan on doing a lot of steaming, buy two or three bamboo steamers, as they stack for efficient cooking.) The third is the clay pot, with its unglazed exterior, glazed interior, and lid. It can be placed directly over the heat and is an ideal vessel for braising.

Wok or Skillet?

If you do not already own a wok, consider buying one if you have a gas stove. (Woks for electric stoves have flat bottoms, making them virtually a skillet anyway, albeit with deep sides.) A wok's flared sides and rounded bottom make it ideal for stir-frying, as they distribute the heat evenly, permit ingredients to be stirred and tossed vigorously without spilling them, and allow a minimum of oil to be used. A skillet, in contrast, with its flat bottom, means that more oil is needed because of the greater cooking surface always in contact with the heat. In addition, any added moisture cooks away more quickly in a skillet, again due to the larger cooking surface.

Suggested Menus

Cantonese Dinner

This meal is typical of those eaten in many San Francisco Chinese restaurants. All of the dishes are easy to prepare. Keep in mind, however, that while you can ready many ingredients in advance, most of the dishes involve a quick, last-minute stir-fry. Follow the lead of Chinese cooks and insist on high-quality fresh ingredients.

Winter Melon Soup
Shrimp with Black Bean Sauce
Beef and Asparagus with Oyster Sauce
Bok Choy with Mushrooms
Cantonese Seafood and Vegetables with Noodles
Steamed Rice

Hot and Spicy Dinner

Here is a meal that is more typical of the food served in so-called Hunan-Sichuan Chinese restaurants. Again, most of the dishes are easy to prepare, but aside from prep work, the cooking will have to be done quickly just before service. Most of the ingredients are readily available, but if you choose to make your own sauces and condiments, you should do so in advance, as some will need to sit.

Hot-and-Sour Soup
Smoked Sea Bass
Kung Pao Chicken
Beef in Chili-Hoisin Sauce
Eggplant with Ginger and Garlic
Steamed Rice

Basic Sauces and Condiments

Most of these sauces can be purchased, but it is nice to make your own versions.

Sweet-and-Sour Dipping Sauce

••

¼ cup cold water

¼ cup rice vinegar

3 tbs sugar

1 tbs soy sauce

¼-inch-piece fresh ginger, peeled and minced

1 clove garlic, minced

2 tbs apricot jam

½ tsp cornstarch

¼ cup warm water

In a nonreactive bowl, combine the cold water, vinegar, sugar, and soy sauce. Stir well to dissolve the sugar, then stir in the ginger and garlic. Transfer the mixture to a small saucepan and bring to a simmer. Stir in the apricot jam, mixing well; do not allow to boil.

In a small bowl, dissolve the cornstarch in the warm water, add to the vinegar mixture, and bring to a boil. As soon as it boils, remove from the heat. Let cool before serving. Store any unused sauce in a tightly capped container in the refrigerator for up to 1 week.

Makes about ⅔ cup.

Garlic-Chili Oil

••

½ cup peanut oil

3 cloves garlic, thinly sliced

5 dried chilies, chopped

¼ cup Asian sesame oil

2 dried red chilies, left whole

In a saucepan, heat the peanut oil over medium heat. When it is hot, add the garlic and the chopped chilies and cook for 2 minutes, shaking the pan occasionally to prevent sticking. Remove from the heat, cover, and let cool.

Add the sesame oil and let stand for 1 hour, then strain through a fine-mesh sieve into a storage container. Add the whole chilies, cover tightly, and store in a cool, dark place.

Makes about ¾ cup.

Plum Sauce

· ·

2 cups plum preserves

½ cup apricot preserves

1 tbs cornstarch

½ cup warm water

½ cup rice vinegar

2 cloves garlic, minced

½ tsp ground ginger

½ tsp salt

In a medium bowl, combine the plum and apricot preserves. Set aside. In a small bowl, dissolve the cornstarch in the warm water. Set aside.

In a small saucepan, bring the vinegar to a boil. Add the garlic, ginger, salt, and combined preserves, mixing well. Reduce the heat to low and cook, stirring frequently to help melt the preserves, for about 5 minutes. Stir in the reserved cornstarch mixture and cook, stirring often, until the sauce thickens, about 2 minutes. It should still be slightly runny. Remove from the heat, let cool, and serve. Store any unused sauce in the refrigerator in a tightly covered container for up to 2 weeks.

Makes about 2 ½ cups.

Hot Mustard Sauce

· ·

3 tbs hot water

1 tbs rice vinegar

¼ cup dry mustard

1 tsp Asian sesame oil

In a small bowl, combine the hot water and rice vinegar. Stir in the mustard, mixing well. Add the sesame oil and stir until smooth. Let stand for 1 hour before using.

Makes about ½ cup.

Preserved Cabbage

1 daikon, 1½ lb, peeled

1 head green cabbage, 2 lb, leaves separated

1 cup kosher salt

5 carrots, cut into matchsticks

Marinade:

2-inch-piece fresh ginger, peeled and cut up

1¼ cups water

10 red serrano chilies, seeded if desired

12 cloves garlic

½ cup sesame seeds, toasted (page 227)

¼ cup Shaoxing wine

¼ cup soy sauce

½ tsp Sichuan peppercorns, lightly crushed

½ cup rice vinegar

The seasoned cabbage should sit for at least 4 days before serving, to marry the flavors. It makes the ideal accompaniment to Smoked Sea Bass (page 24).

Using a mandoline (French slicer) or a sharp knife, cut the daikon into paper-thin slices. Place in a large bowl with the cabbage leaves. Sprinkle with the kosher salt and let stand for a least 1 hour or for up to 3 hours. The salt will leach the water from the vegetables. Using your hands, tightly squeeze all the moisture out of the cabbage and daikon, then rinse under cold running water and squeeze dry. Set aside along with the carrots.

To make the marinade, process the ginger in a small food processor until finely chopped. Add ¼ cup of the water and process to combine. Strain the mixture through a fine-mesh sieve, pushing against the ginger with the back of a spoon to extract all the juice. Set aside.

Again in the food processor, process the serrano chilies (include the seeds for extra heat) and garlic cloves until finely chopped. Add the strained ginger water, sesame seeds, wine, soy sauce, Sichuan peppercorns, and vinegar and process to blend well. Set the marinade aside.

On a work surface, place a layer of the cabbage leaves. Douse them with the marinade and then top with a layer of daikon. Douse again with some marinade and sprinkle with a few carrot matchsticks. Repeat the process. Roll up the layered vegetables and slice across the roll—like sushi—to make pieces about 1½ inches wide. Repeat until all the vegetables are used up.

Pack the rolls into a sterilized canning jar, drizzling any remaining marinade over them. Cap tightly. Store in the refrigerator for at least 4 days before serving. The cabbage will keep for about 4 weeks.

Makes about 4 cups.

Spicy Almonds

3 tbs corn oil

1 tsp chili oil

⅔ cup sugar

2 cups blanched almonds

½ tsp Sichuan peppercorns

1 tsp red pepper flakes

1 tsp salt

This makes a great dim sum dish or snack.

In a heavy saucepan or skillet, heat the corn and chili oils over high heat. When the oil is hot, add the sugar and mix well with a wooden spoon. As soon as the sugar starts to darken and caramelize, add the almonds. Mix well to coat the almonds. Reduce the heat to medium and continue to cook, stirring, until the sugar has completely caramelized. Remove from the heat and toss in the peppercorns, pepper flakes, and salt. Mix well. Serve warm or at room temperature.

Makes about 2 cups.

Fried Tofu

1 package (14 oz) Chinese-style firm tofu

2 tbs peanut oil (more if using a skillet instead of a wok)

Sweet-and-Sour Dipping Sauce (page 16) or Plum Sauce (page 17)

Drain the tofu. Wrap it in paper towels and place on a plate. Put a second plate on top, and then rest a 1-lb weight (a can of food, for example) on the plate. Let stand for 30 minutes to press out excess moisture.

Unwrap the tofu and transfer to a cutting board. Cut into small squares. In a wok or deep skillet, heat the peanut oil over high heat. When it is hot, add the tofu squares and stir-fry until puffy and golden, 6 to 8 minutes. Serve with one of the sauces.

Makes 4 servings.

Tea-Smoked Eggs

6 eggs

1 tbs kosher salt, plus extra for serving

3 tbs soy sauce

2 star anise

1 cup brewed Earl Grey tea

Place the eggs in a saucepan, add cold water to cover, and bring just to a boil. Reduce the heat to low and boil very gently for 15 minutes. Remove from the heat, cover, and let stand for 15 minutes.

Remove the eggs from the pan and let cool. Discard the water. Using the back of a spoon, tap the shells of the eggs to crackle the entire surface.

Combine the 1 tbs salt, soy sauce, anise, and tea in the saucepan. Return the eggs to the pan and add enough water to cover the eggs. Bring to a boil, remove from the heat, cover, and let stand overnight. Peel and serve with salt.

Makes 6 servings.

Pearl Balls

1 cup glutinous rice

6 dried black mushrooms or black fungus

1-inch-piece fresh ginger, peeled and chopped

2 cloves garlic

12 water chestnuts, cut in half

2 green onions, cut into thirds

2 fresh cilantro sprigs

1½ lb ground pork

2 tbs soy sauce

2 eggs

1 tsp oyster sauce

lettuce or bok choy leaves

Plum Sauce (page 17)

Place the rice in a bowl with cold water to cover and let stand for 4 hours. Drain and pat dry with a kitchen towel, then place in a shallow bowl.

Meanwhile, soak the mushrooms or fungus in warm water to cover for 30 minutes to 1 hour. Drain and cut off the tough stems.

In a food processor, combine the mushrooms or fungus, ginger, garlic, water chestnuts, green onions, and cilantro. Process until finely chopped. Add the pork, soy sauce, eggs, and oyster sauce and process until blended.

Form the pork mixture into small balls about 1 inch in diameter. Roll them in the rice, coating them evenly and completely. Set the balls on a baking sheet lined with waxed paper. Refrigerate for 1 hour.

Line 1 large or 2 smaller bamboo steamers with lettuce or bok choy leaves, and arrange the rice-coated balls on the leaves. Place the steamer(s) over boiling water and steam until the rice coating is tender and the meat filling is fully cooked, about 30 minutes. Serve with the sauce for dipping.

Makes about 50 meatballs.

Drunken Chicken

1 chicken, 3½ to 4 lb

chicken broth to cover

2 green onions, cut into 2-inch pieces

3 thin slices peeled fresh ginger

1 tsp kosher salt

white pepper to taste

¾ cup Shaoxing wine

This dish requires the use of a Chinese clay pot. Remember, if your pot is new or has not been used in awhile, you need to cure it before you begin cooking (page 21). Otherwise, it may crack when it is over the heat.

Place the chicken, breast side up, in a clay pot. Pour in the broth just to cover and add the green onions, ginger, salt, and pepper. Cover and bring to a boil over medium heat. Reduce the heat to low and simmer the chicken just until the juices run clear when a thigh joint is pierced, about 1¼ hours. Remove from the heat and let cool completely in the broth.

Remove the chicken from the pot (strain the broth and reserve for another use). Cut up the chicken into large pieces and then, using a heavy cleaver, chop the chicken into small pieces on the bone. Place the pieces in a bowl and douse with the wine. Marinate for at least 30 minutes or for up to 3 hours in the refrigerator. Serve cold.

Makes 8 servings.

Steamed Pork Dumplings

....

Siu Mai

½-inch-piece ginger, peeled

3 cloves garlic

2 green onions, cut into thirds

1 lb pork loin, cut into small strips

¼ lb pork fat, diced

1 tsp salt

2 tbs soy sauce

1 tbs Shaoxing wine

1 tbs cornstarch

1 tbs Asian sesame oil

1 package (1 lb) wonton wrappers

lettuce or bok choy leaves

chili oil, soy sauce, and rice vinegar for dipping or a dipping sauce (pages 16 to 17)

If you don't want to use pork fat in this recipe, you can substitute lard or solid vegetable shortening, or skip the fat but use a fattier cut of pork such as pork butt. It adds flavor and holds the mixture together.

In a food processor, combine the ginger, garlic, and green onions. Add the strips of pork, a few at a time, and process to grind. Once you have ground all the pork loin, add the pork fat, salt, soy sauce, wine, cornstarch, and sesame oil. Process until well blended. Transfer to a bowl and refrigerate for 2 hours.

To make the dumplings, put a heaping teaspoon of the pork mixture in the center of a wonton wrapper. (Keep the remaining wrappers covered with a lightly dampened towel to prevent them from drying out.) Lift up the sides of the wrapper and, with a thumb and index finger, gently squeeze the wrapper at the point just above the filling. Your dumpling will look like a money bag. Repeat with the remaining filling.

Line 1 large or 2 smaller bamboo steamers with lettuce or bok choy leaves, and arrange the dumplings on the leaves. Place the steamer(s) over boiling water and steam until the filling is cooked through and the wrapper is just tender, about 15 minutes. Serve on a platter with chili oil, soy sauce, and vinegar, allowing diners to mix their dipping sauces to taste, or with one or more premade dipping sauces.

Makes about 40 dumplings.

Curing A Chinese Clay Pot

Made of earthenware, the lidded clay pot has an unglazed exterior and a dark glaze interior. It is flameproof, but must always have some liquid in it when it is over the heat, or it will break. Also, never put a hot clay pot on a cold surface. Instead, allow it to cool down on the turned-off burner. Before using a just-purchased clay pot or one that has not be used for a long time, wash carefully, fill with water, and let soak overnight.

Pot Stickers

Pork or Vegetable Stuffing for Pot
Stickers (recipes follow)

½ lb pot sticker wrappers

2½ tablespoons peanut oil

1 cup water

chili oil, soy sauce, and rice
vinegar for serving

One of the most popular appetizers in Chinese restaurants in America, these are a snap to make. The wrappers can be found in well-stocked supermarkets, usually in a refrigerator case in the produce section or elsewhere in the store.

Prepare the stuffing of choice. Place 1 heaping tsp stuffing in the middle of a wrapper. (Keep the remaining wrappers covered with a lightly dampened towel to prevent them from drying out.) Moisten the entire edge of the wrapper with water, lift both sides of the wrapper, and, using your thumb and index finger, pinch together at the center. Pleat the edge (that is, fold and twist the edge upon itself), starting from the center and working out to the ends, making sure you seal the edge tightly. Tap the bottom on the work surface or your palm to flatten slightly. Repeat until all the filling is used. Alternatively, you can use a pot sticker maker, following the instructions that come with the device. You should have about 24 pot stickers. Refrigerate the pot stickers for 1 hour before cooking, or to store them for future cooking, freeze them on the tray, then pack into a lock-top bag and freeze for up to 1 month.

To fry the pot stickers, select a heavy skillet (12 to 14 inches in diameter) with a lid. Place over high heat until hot, add the oil, and rotate the pan to coat the bottom evenly. Reduce the heat to medium-high and add the pot stickers, flat side down, arranging them in concentric circles. Cover the pan and let them sizzle, shaking the pan occasionally to prevent burning, for 2 minutes. They should be nicely browned on the bottom. Uncover, add the water, and re-cover. Steam-cook for another 3 to 4 minutes until slightly puffed and cooked through. Remove from the heat and transfer to a serving platter, browned side up. Discard any liquid in the pan. Serve with chili oil, soy sauce, and vinegar; allow diners to mix their dipping sauce to taste.

Makes 24 pot stickers.

Pork Stuffing for Pot Stickers

½ head napa cabbage, about ½ lb

1½ lb ground pork

½ tsp salt

4 green onions, cut into thirds

½-inch-piece fresh ginger, peeled

2 tsp soy sauce

2 tsp Shaoxing wine

1 tsp Asian sesame oil

2 eggs

1 tsp cornstarch

This recipe makes enough filling for about 50 potstickers, or about twice as many as the preceding pot sticker recipe yields. I like to make lots of pot stickers since they freeze well. Also, I frequently substitute ground chicken for the pork to accommodate the many people I know who avoid red meat.

In a food processor, finely shred the cabbage. Transfer to a bowl.

In another bowl, season the ground pork with the salt, then add it to the cabbage. Mix well and set aside.

In the food processor, process the green onions and ginger until finely chopped. Add the pork-cabbage mixture, soy sauce, and wine. Process to blend. Add all the remaining ingredients and process to a paste.

Vegetable Stuffing for Pot Stickers

1 package (14 oz) Chinese-style firm tofu

½ head napa cabbage, about ½ lb

2 cloves garlic

½-inch-piece fresh ginger, peeled

4 green onions, cut into thirds

3 fresh parsley sprigs

5 fresh cilantro sprigs

2 tsp soy sauce

2 tsp Shaoxing wine

1 tsp Asian sesame oil

1 carrot, shredded

2 fresh shiitake mushrooms, stems removed and caps very thinly sliced

This recipe makes enough filling for about 25 pot stickers.

Drain the tofu. Wrap it in paper towels and place on a plate. Put a second plate on top, and then rest a 1-lb weight (a can of food, for example) on the plate. Let stand for 30 minutes to press out excess moisture. Unwrap the tofu and squeeze by hand to remove any remaining moisture. Set aside.

In a food processor, finely shred the cabbage. Transfer to a bowl.

In the food processor, combine the garlic, ginger, green onions, parsley, and cilantro. Process until everything is finely chopped. Add the pressed tofu, soy sauce, Shaoxing wine, and sesame oil. Process to mix well. Add the carrot, process to mix, and transfer to the bowl with the cabbage. Add the mushrooms and stir to mix well.

Smoked Sea Bass

1 sea bass fillet, 1¼ to 1½ lb

Marinade:

2 cups ice water

5 tbs soy sauce

1 tsp oyster sauce

½-inch-piece fresh ginger, peeled and minced

¼ tsp Sichuan peppercorns

1 tbs brown sugar

1 tsp salt

½ tsp Asian sesame oil

Smoking mixture:

6 tbs Chinese black or oolong tea leaves

4 star anise

2 cinnamon sticks

18 cloves

½ tsp black peppercorns

6 cloves garlic, crushed

½ tsp Sichuan peppercorns

¼ cup white rice

¼ cup brown sugar

Preserved Cabbage (page 18) or other pickled vegetable relish

You'll need a sturdy wok and a well-ventilated kitchen to make this dish.

Place the sea bass in a nonreactive bowl. In a small bowl, combine all the ingredients for the marinade, mix well, and pour over the fish. Cover and marinate in the refrigerator for 4 hours.

Remove the sea bass from the marinade, pat dry, and set aside.

Combine all the ingredients for the smoking mixture in a wok or deep, heavy skillet and stir to mix well. Position a wire grill or a bamboo steamer 2 to 3 inches above the ingredients and place over medium heat. When smoke begins to rise, place the fish on the grill or in the steamer, cover the steamer or wok, and smoke the fish until it is cooked through and richly infused with the flavors of the smoking mixture, about 15 minutes.

Serve warm or cold, cut on the diagonal into ¼-inch-thick slices. Accompany with the cabbage or other relish.

Makes 6 to 8 servings.

Hot-and-Sour Soup

3 dried black mushrooms or black fungus

6 cups chicken broth

8 thin slices peeled fresh ginger

¼ lb cooked ham, cut into matchsticks

⅓ cup shredded green cabbage or bok choy

1 carrot, shredded

4 green onions, sliced

⅔ cup sliced bamboo shoots

4 fresh oyster mushrooms, sliced

1 package (14 oz) Chinese-style firm tofu, drained and cut into small cubes

1 tbs cornstarch

¼ cup rice vinegar, plus extra to taste

3 tbs soy sauce

white pepper to taste

3 eggs, lightly beaten

Asian sesame oil to taste

White pepper is what gives this soup its heat, so don't be timid about adding a fair amount, at least a tablespoon. Also, you may substitute chicken for the ham or omit the meat altogether, and you may omit the carrot and cabbage if you prefer a clearer broth.

In a bowl, combine the mushrooms or fungus with hot water to cover and let soak for 30 minutes. Drain and cut off the stems. Slice thinly and set aside.

In a saucepan, combine the chicken broth and ginger and bring to a boil over high heat. Reduce the heat to low and simmer for 5 minutes, then remove the ginger slices. Add the ham, cabbage, and carrot and let simmer for 5 minutes. Then add the green onions, bamboo shoots, black mushrooms or fungus, oyster mushrooms, and tofu cubes.

Meanwhile, dissolve the cornstarch in the ¼ cup vinegar. Add the mixture to the soup along with the soy sauce. Simmer for another 5 minutes. Season with pepper and slowly drizzle in the eggs while stirring continuously but gently. Simmer for another 2 minutes and add a few drops of sesame oil. Taste and adjust with more pepper, vinegar, and sesame oil until you achieve a balance you like between hot and sour. Serve immediately.

Makes 6 servings.

Winter Melon Soup

1 tbs Asian sesame oil

4 cloves garlic, minced

½-inch-piece fresh ginger, peeled and grated

½ tsp five-spice powder

¼ lb cooked ham or pork, cut into matchsticks

8 cups chicken broth

1 piece winter melon, 1 lb, seeded, if necessary, and peeled

4 green onions, finely chopped

8 fresh cilantro sprigs, finely chopped

In a large saucepan, heat the sesame oil over medium-high heat. When it is hot, add the garlic, ginger, and five-spice powder. Saute for 1 minute and add the ham or pork. Mix well, add the chicken broth, and bring to a boil.

Meanwhile, cut the melon into thin wedges or small cubes. Once the broth is boiling, add the melon. Reduce the heat to low and simmer for 2 minutes. Remove from the heat and add the green onions and cilantro. Serve immediately.

Makes 6 servings.

Hunan Homes' Hot and Sour Soup

1 package (14 oz) Chinese-style firm tofu, well drained

2 oz pork butt (optional)

⅓ cup bamboo shoot

2 tsp salt

2 tbs rice vinegar

½ tsp white pepper

1 tbs soy sauce

6 cups chicken broth

1 green onion, thinly sliced on the diagonal

1 tsp peeled and minced fresh ginger

2 tbs cornstarch

5 tbs water

1 egg, lightly beaten

1 tsp Asian sesame oil

Hunan Home's Restaurant in San Francisco's Chinatown serves a delicious version of this perennially popular soup. The flavors differ subtly from the recipe on page 25. You will have to do a bit of experimenting to match their delicate balance between hot and sour flavors.

Finely shred the tofu, pork butt, if using, and bamboo shoot.

In a small bowl, combine the salt, vinegar, white pepper, and soy sauce, mixing well.

In a saucepan, bring the chicken broth to a boil. Add the soy sauce mixture, tofu, pork if using, bamboo shoot, green onion, and ginger, stir well, and return to a boil.

Meanwhile, in a small bowl, dissolve the cornstarch in the water. Add to the boiling soup, stirring constantly. The broth will thicken slightly. Then slowly stir in the beaten egg; it will set in long strands. Remove from the heat and add the sesame oil. Ladle into bowls and serve immediately.

Makes 4 servings.

Cantonese Seafood and Vegetable with Noodles

24 jumbo shrimp, peeled and deveined

6 lobster tails

½ lb sea scallops, halved if large

1 tbs cornstarch

¼ cup warm water

2 tbs Shaoxing wine

1½ lb Chinese wheat noodles (mein)

2 tbs Asian sesame oil

florets from 1 broccoli stalk

2 carrots, sliced on the diagonal

1 small bok choy, coarsely chopped

1 cup snow peas, trimmed

¼ cup peanut oil, or as needed

½-inch-piece fresh ginger, peeled and minced

4 cloves garlic, minced

1 green bell pepper, cut into large squares

1 red bell pepper, cut into large squares

4 green onions, cut into 1-inch lengths

2 tbs oyster sauce

2 tbs soy sauce

½ cup chicken broth

8 fresh cilantro sprigs, chopped

This dish takes a bit of preparation, but the effort is well rewarded.

Bring a large saucepan of salted water to a boil. Add the shrimp and cook until they begin to turn pink, about 2 minutes. Using a slotted spoon, remove them from the boiling water and immediately plunge them into ice water to halt the cooking. Repeat with the lobster tails, adding them to the ice water as well (they will need to cook a few minutes longer). Let the seafood cool in the water bath for about 5 minutes. Drain and pat dry with paper towels. You may reserve the salted water for cooking the noodles.

In a large nonreactive bowl, combine the shrimp, lobster tails, and sea scallops. In a small bowl, dissolve the cornstarch in the warm water, then stir in the Shaoxing wine. Pour the mixture over the seafood and stir to coat the seafood evenly. Set aside while you prepare the rest of the dish.

Return the salted water to a boil (or bring a new batch to a boil if you have discarded the first one). Add the noodles and boil until just tender, about 6 minutes or according to package directions. Drain, rinse with cold water, and drain again. Place in a bowl, drizzle with the sesame oil, toss well, and set aside.

Bring another saucepan of salted water to a boil. Add the broccoli and carrots and blanch for 15 seconds. Then add the bok choy and blanch for 30 seconds. Finally, add the snow peas and blanch for 1 minute. Drain the vegetables and plunge them into ice water to halt the cooking. Leave for about 5 minutes, then drain and set aside.

In a wok or deep skillet, heat the peanut oil over medium-high heat. When it is hot, add the cooked noodles and fry, stirring as needed to prevent burning, until browned on the bottom, about 7 minutes. Flip over the noodles and brown them on the other side. Once both sides are browned, transfer the noodles to the center of a large warmed platter and keep warm.

Add more oil if necessary, then add the ginger and garlic. Stir-fry until they sizzle and are fragrant, about 15 seconds. Add the red and green peppers and stir-fry for 1 minute. Then add the blanched vegetables, green onions, oyster sauce, and soy sauce. Mix well and stir-fry for another 30 seconds. Pour in the broth and add the seafood. Stir-fry until the sauce thickens and the seafood is cooked, about 3 minutes. Remove from the heat.

Pour the contents of the wok over the noodles. Sprinkle with the cilantro and serve immediately.

Makes 6 servings.

Garlic-Tangerine Sizzling Sea Scallops

Marinade:

1 tsp sugar

1 tsp Shaoxing wine

2 tsp Asian sesame oil

2 cloves garlic, crushed and minced

½ tsp Sichuan peppercorns, lightly crushed

8 thin slivers dried tangerine peel (cut after it is soaked in warm water for 20 minutes to soften)

salt to taste

1½ lb sea scallops

Tangerine sauce:

2 tsp chili-garlic paste

1 tbs hoisin sauce

1 tbs soy sauce

1/4 cup tangerine juice

2 tsp rice vinegar

1 tsp light brown sugar

1 tsp Shaoxing wine

1 tsp cornstarch

¼ cup hot water

4 dried red chilies, soaked in hot water for 30 minutes to soften

3 tbs corn oil

½-inch-piece fresh ginger, peeled and minced

4 cloves garlic, minced

1 zucchini, cut into matchsticks

16 thin slivers dried tangerine peel (cut after it is soaked in warm water for 20 minutes to soften)

4 green onions, cut into 1-inch lengths

2 tsp Asian sesame oil

A splendid show-off piece, this dish will impress your guests when you deliver it sizzling on a hot iron griddle. It can also be made with shrimp or a combination of scallops and shrimp. You can also substitute the more readily available orange peel for the tangerine peel.

To make the marinade, in a bowl, combine all the ingredients for the marinade, mixing well. Add the scallops, stir to coat, cover, and let stand for 1 hour.

To make the sauce, combine all the ingredients, mixing well. Set aside. In a small bowl, dissolve the cornstarch in the hot water. Set aside. Drain the chilies and set aside. Place a cast-iron skillet over high heat about 10 minutes before serving.

In a wok or deep skillet, heat the corn oil over high heat. When it is hot, add the ginger and garlic. Stir-fry until they sizzle and are fragrant, about 15 seconds. Add the scallops and their marinade, the zucchini, and the chilies and stir-fry continuously for 30 seconds. Add the tangerine peel and the reserved cornstarch liquid and mix well. Then add the green onions and the tangerine sauce, mix well, and stir-fry until the sauces thickens, 1 to 2 minutes. Remove from heat and add the sesame oil.

To serve, pour the contents of the wok into the preheated skillet and serve immediately.

Makes 4 servings.

Shrimp with Black Bean Sauce

1 tbs cornstarch

⅓ cup warm water

3 tbs peanut or corn oil

2 cloves garlic, minced

2 tbs salted black beans, soaked in cold water to cover for 15 minutes and drained

1 lb shrimp, peeled and deveined

3 green onions, coarsely chopped

2 tbs Shaoxing wine

2 tbs soy sauce

6 fresh cilantro sprigs, chopped

You can create a variety of Cantonese dishes using these directions for black bean sauce. Beef, pork, chicken, scallops, squid, clams, or mussels can be substituted for the shrimp. Adjust the cooking times as needed: shrimp and scallops cook the fastest, while chicken, beef, and pork take a little longer. Nice additions include bell peppers, asparagus, and broccoli (just blanch them and add along with the shrimp or scallops or when the chicken, beef, or pork is almost cooked).

Dissolve the cornstarch in the warm water and set aside. In a wok or deep skillet, heat the oil over high heat. When it is hot, add the garlic and black beans and stir-fry until fragrant, about 30 seconds. Add the shrimp and green onions and stir-fry until the shrimp begin to turn pink, about 1 minute. Add the wine, soy sauce, and the cornstarch mixture. Stir continuously until the mixture thickens, 1 to 2 minutes. Sprinkle with the cilantro and serve.

Makes 4 servings.

Shrimp with Snow Peas

40 snow peas, ends trimmed

1 tbs soy sauce

1 tbs hoisin sauce

3 tbs peanut oil

1 lb shrimp, peeled and deveined

1 cup sliced water chestnuts

2 green onions, coarsely chopped

Although not traditional, for variety I sometimes mix green beans and snow peas instead of using only snow peas.

Bring a saucepan of salted water to a boil. Add the snow peas and blanch for 1 minute. Drain the snow peas and plunge into ice water to halt the cooking. In a small bowl, stir together the soy sauce and hoisin sauce.

In a wok or deep skillet, heat the peanut oil over high heat. When it is hot, add the shrimp and stir-fry for 30 seconds. Add the hoisin-soy mixture and the water chestnuts and stir-fry until the shrimp just begin to turn pink, about 1 minute longer. Drain the snow peas and add to the shrimp along with the green onions. Mix well, stir-fry for 1 minute, and serve at once.

Makes 4 servings.

Kung Pao Chicken

2 tbs Shaoxing wine

2 tbs soy sauce

2 tbs hot water

1 egg white

2 tsp cornstarch

2 lb boneless chicken breasts, cut into bite-sized pieces

½ cup chicken broth

¼ cup Asian sesame oil

¼ cup corn oil

⅓ cup dry-roasted peanuts

6 small dried red chilies

½-inch-piece fresh ginger, peeled and minced

3 cloves garlic, minced

3 Sichuan peppercorns, ground

4 green onions, cut into 1-inch lengths

½ red bell pepper, diced

½ green bell pepper, diced

Perhaps one of the most frequently ordered dishes in Chinese restaurants in America, kung pao chicken is quite simple to make and primarily uses readily available ingredients.

In a bowl, combine the wine, soy sauce, and hot water. Stir in the egg white until well blended, then dissolve 1 tsp of the cornstarch in the mixture. Add the chicken, stir to coat, cover, and let stand for 1 hour. In a small bowl, dissolve the remaining cornstarch in the chicken broth and set aside.

In a wok or deep skillet, heat the sesame and corn oils over high heat. When the oils are hot, add the peanuts and stir-fry until golden brown. Using a slotted spoon, transfer to paper towels to drain. Add the chilies, ginger, and garlic to the pan and stir-fry over high heat until fragrant, about 30 seconds. Then add the chicken and its marinade and stir-fry for 2 minutes. Add the Sichuan pepper, green onions, and bell peppers and stir to mix well. Pour in the cornstarch mixture and continue to cook and stir until the sauce begins to thicken, about 3 minutes.

Return the peanuts to the pan and cook, stirring until the sauce is nicely thickened and the chicken and vegetables are just tender, about 2 minutes longer. Serve immediately.

Makes 4 to 6 servings.

Sichuan Chicken Salad

2 boneless whole chicken breasts

Marinade:

2 tbs soy sauce

2 tbs Asian sesame oil

1 tsp chili oil

2 tbs rice vinegar

½ tsp ground ginger

½ tsp five-spice powder

pinch of sugar

2 tbs corn oil

2 oz bean thread noodles

2 green onions, chopped

3 celery stalks, thinly sliced on the diagonal

butter lettuce leaves

6 fresh cilantro sprigs, coarsely chopped

In a medium saucepan, pour in enough water to cover the chicken breasts. Bring to a boil, add the chicken breasts, remove from the heat, cover, and let stand for 30 minutes.

Meanwhile, make the marinade: In a medium bowl, combine all the ingredients, mixing well.

Remove the chicken from the pan, and cut into bite-sized cubes. Add the cubes to the marinade and stir to coat well. Set aside.

In a wok or deep skillet, heat the corn oil over high heat. When it is hot, add the bean thread noodles in small batches. They will puff up upon contact with the hot oil. Fry for 10 to 15 seconds, turn over, and fry on the second side for about 10 seconds. Using a slotted spoon, transfer to paper towels to drain and cool.

Add the green onions and celery to the chicken mixture. To assemble the salad, make a bed of the butter lettuce leaves on a platter. Put the bean threads around the edge and fill the center with the marinated chicken. Garnish with the cilantro.

Makes 4 servings.

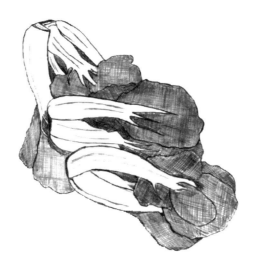

Barbecued Spareribs

6 lb pork spareribs, in racks

6 tbs hoisin sauce

2 tbs honey

4 cloves garlic, minced

1/2-inch-piece fresh ginger, peeled and minced

3 tbs soy sauce

2 tbs salted black beans, soaked in cold water to cover for 15 minutes and drained

1 tbs oyster sauce

1/2 tsp five-spice powder

2 tbs Asian sesame oil

Bring a large pot of water to a boil. Add the ribs and boil for 15 minutes. Remove from the heat and drain. Pat the ribs dry with a paper towel. Place in a large shallow bowl.

In a small bowl, combine all the remaining ingredients. Mix well and pour over the ribs. Turn to coat well. Cover and marinate in the refrigerator for at least 4 hours or preferably overnight. Turn the ribs occasionally.

Light a fire in a charcoal grill. When the coals are hot, remove the racks of ribs from the marinade and place, meat side down, over the fire. Grill for 10 minutes. Turn the racks over, baste with the marinade, and continue to cook until done, 5 to 7 minutes longer. Remove from the grill and serve.

Makes 6 servings.

Beef and Asparagus in Oyster Sauce

Marinade:

2 cloves garlic, minced

1/2-inch-piece fresh ginger, peeled and grated

1 tbs Shaoxing wine

3 tbs soy sauce

1 tsp Asian sesame oil

1 tsp oyster sauce

3/4 lb London broil or similar cut, thinly sliced into strips

2 tsp cornstarch

1/4 cup hot beef broth or water

2 tbs peanut oil

1 lb asparagus, trimmed, peeled if stalks are tough, and cut on the diagonal into 1-inch lengths

4 green onions, cut into 2-inch lengths

To make the marinade, in a small bowl, combine all the ingredients, mixing well. Place the beef in a bowl, pour the marinade over the top, and stir to coat evenly. Let stand at room temperature for 30 minutes.

Meanwhile, in a small bowl, dissolve the cornstarch in the hot broth or water. In a wok or deep skillet, heat the peanut oil over high heat. When it is hot, add the beef and its marinade and stir-fry for 2 minutes. Add the asparagus, green onions, and cornstarch mixture and continue to stir-fry until the beef and vegetables are tender and the sauce has thickened, about 3 minutes longer. Serve immediately.

Makes 4 servings.

Beef in Chili-Hoisin Sauce

Marinade:

2 tbs soy sauce

2 tbs hoisin sauce

1 tbs chili-garlic paste

1 tbs Asian sesame oil

½ tsp chili oil

1 tsp sugar

½ tsp salt

1½ lb London broil or similar cut, thinly sliced into strips

2 tbs corn oil

3 small dried red chilies, soaked in warm water to cover for 20 minutes and drained

4 green onions, cut into 1-inch lengths

chopped fresh cilantro for garnish

To make the marinade, in a small bowl, combine all the ingredients, mixing well. Let stand for 5 minutes.

Place the beef in a bowl, pour the marinade over it, stir to coat evenly, and let stand at room temperature for 10 minutes.

In a wok or deep skillet, heat the corn oil over high heat. When it is hot, add the chilies and stir-fry until they sizzle and are fragrant, about 10 seconds. Add the beef and its marinade and stir-fry for 1 minute. Add the green onions and continue to stir-fry until the beef is tender, 3 to 4 minutes longer. Garnish with the cilantro and serve immediately.

Makes 6 servings.

Dry-Fried Long Beans

Marinade:

2 tbs soy sauce

1 tbs rice vinegar

1 tbs water

½ tsp sugar

½ tsp Asian sesame oil

1 lb long beans, cut into 2-inch lengths

2 tsp corn oil

½-inch-piece fresh ginger, peeled and finely minced

2 cloves garlic, finely minced

1 tsp sesame seeds, toasted (page 227)

You can substitute standard green beans if no Chinese long beans are available at the market.

To make the marinade, in a small bowl, mix together all the ingredients. Set aside.

Bring a saucepan of water to a boil. Add the beans and blanch for 45 seconds. Drain the beans and plunge into ice water to halt the cooking. Let cool for 5 minutes, then drain and place in a bowl. Pour over the marinade, stir the beans to coat evenly, and let stand for 20 minutes.

In a wok or deep skillet, heat the corn oil over high heat. When it is hot, add the ginger and garlic and stir-fry until fragrant, about 30 seconds. Add the green beans and their marinade and continue to stir-fry until the liquid has almost fully evaporated, 1 to 2 minutes. Remove from the heat, sprinkle with the sesame seeds, and serve immediately.

Makes 4 servings.

Eggplant with Ginger and Garlic

4 tsp Asian sesame oil

½ tsp chili oil

4 cloves garlic, minced

½-inch-piece fresh ginger, peeled and minced

3 lb slender Chinese or Japanese eggplants, sliced on the diagonal ¼ inch thick

¼ cup soy sauce

2 tsp rice vinegar

2 tsp sugar

½ cup chicken broth or water

3 green onions, finely chopped

When this dish is served, the eggplant should be slightly crunchy rather than soft and mushy.

In a wok or deep skillet, heat the sesame and chili oils over high heat. When the oils are hot, add the garlic and ginger and stir-fry until fragrant, about 30 seconds. Add the eggplant and coat well with the oil. Stir-fry for 2 minutes. Add the soy sauce, rice vinegar, sugar, and chicken broth or water and cook over high heat, stirring continuously, until the liquid is reduced, about 3 minutes. Add the green onions and cook for 1 minute longer, then serve.

Makes 6 servings.

Bok Choy with Mushrooms

8 dried black mushrooms or black
  fungus

1 tsp cornstarch

2 tbs soy sauce

2 tbs warm water

2 tbs peanut oil

¼-inch-piece fresh ginger, peeled
  and minced

½ lb bok choy, coarsely chopped

In a bowl, combine the mushrooms or fungus with warm water to cover and let soak for 30 minutes. Drain and cut off the stems. Cut the mushrooms or fungus into ¼-inch-thick slices. In a small bowl, dissolve the cornstarch in the soy sauce and the 2 tbs hot water.

In a wok or deep skillet, heat the peanut oil over high heat. When it is hot, add the ginger and mushrooms or fungus and stir-fry for 1 minute. Add the bok choy and mix well. Stir in the cornstarch mixture and continue to stir-fry until the sauce thickens and the bok choy is tender, about 1 minute. Serve immediately.

Makes 4 servings.

Snow Peas with Fresh Shiitakes

1 lb snow peas, trimmed

1 tbs corn oil

¼-inch-piece fresh ginger, peeled
  and minced

6 fresh shiitake mushrooms, stems
  removed and caps thinly sliced

8 water chestnuts, sliced

1 tbs Asian sesame oil

3 tbs pine nuts, toasted (page 227)

Bring a saucepan of water to a boil. Add the snow peas and blanch for 20 seconds. Drain the snow peas, plunge immediately into ice water to halt the cooking, and let cool for 5 minutes. Drain again.

In a wok or deep skillet, heat the corn oil over high heat. When it is hot, add the ginger and stir-fry until fragrant, about 20 seconds. Add the mushrooms, snow peas, and water chestnuts and stir-fry until the snow peas and mushrooms are tender, about 2 minutes longer. Remove from the heat, add the sesame oil and pine nuts, and toss well. Serve immediately.

Makes 4 servings.

Broccoli in Black Bean Sauce

1 tbs salted black beans, soaked
  in cold water to cover for 15
  minutes and drained

2 tbs Shaoxing wine

3 broccoli stalks, cut into bite-
  sized florets

1 tbs corn oil

2 cloves garlic, minced

½-inch-piece fresh ginger, peeled
  and minced

Chop the drained black beans finely and place in a small bowl. Add the wine and let stand for 20 minutes.

Bring a saucepan of water to a boil. Add the broccoli and blanch for 30 seconds. Drain the broccoli and immediately plunge into ice water to halt the cooking. Set aside.

In a wok or deep skillet, heat the oil over high heat. When it is hot, add the garlic and ginger and stir-fry until fragrant, about 30 seconds. Drain the broccoli and add to the pan. Stir-fry until heated through, 1 to 2 minutes. Add the black beans and wine and mix well. Serve immediately.

Makes 4 servings.

Stir-fried Vegetables with Almonds

1 broccoli stalk, cut into bite-sized florets

2 carrots, thinly sliced on the diagonal

1 tsp cornstarch

¼ cup hot chicken broth or water

3 tbs corn oil

½ onion, coarsely chopped

1 clove garlic, finely minced

¼-inch-piece fresh ginger, peeled and minced

1 red bell pepper, diced

3 celery stalks, thinly sliced on the diagonal

2 tbs soy sauce

4 green onions, cut into 1-inch lengths

¼ cup blanched almonds

12 ears baby corn

6 water chestnuts, sliced

¼ cup sliced bamboo shoots

Bring a saucepan of water to a boil. Add the broccoli and carrot and blanch for 40 seconds. Drain the vegetables and plunge into ice water to halt the cooking. Drain again. In a small bowl, dissolve the cornstarch in the chicken broth or water. Set aside.

In a wok or deep skillet, heat the corn oil over high heat. When it is hot, add the onion, garlic, and ginger and stir-fry until the onion begins to soften, about 2 minutes. Add the bell pepper and celery and stir-fry for 1 minute longer. Add the blanched vegetables, mix well, and then add the soy sauce, green onions, almonds, baby corn, water chestnuts, bamboo shoots, and reserved cornstarch mixture. Continue to stir-fry until the sauce thickens, 1 to 2 minutes. Serve immediately.

Makes 6 servings.

Yakisoba with Meat and Vegetables

....
Mixed Chow Mein

1 package (14 oz) yakisoba noodles

1 cup hot water

1 tbs corn oil

1 tbs Asian sesame oil

½ small onion, finely chopped

¾-inch-piece fresh ginger, peeled and minced

½ tsp five-spice powder

1 carrot, thinly sliced on the diagonal

2 celery stalks, sliced on the diagonal into ¼-inch-thick slices

2 cups shredded cabbage or bok choy

florets from 1 broccoli stalk

about 1 cup diced cooked pork loin, chicken, or beef

2 tbs soy sauce

⅓ cup chicken broth or water

Although they are a Japanese version of a Chinese noodle, I like yakisoba noodles because they come precooked, allowing you to stir-fry them quickly with meats and vegetables for an easy meal. You can substitute nearly any vegetable and/or meat for those listed here, and you can use fresh or dried Chinese noodles (mein) in place of the yakisoba. If you decide to use the latter, boil them until tender (most packages suggest cooking times), drain, and then stir-fry them in the wok. Also, a flavor packet generally comes with the yakisoba; you may use it in place of the five-spice powder, although it probably includes msg.

In a bowl, combine the yakisoba with hot water to cover and let stand until the noodles loosen easily, about 5 minutes. Drain.

In a wok or deep saucepan, heat the corn and sesame oils over high heat. When the oils are hot, add the onion, ginger, and five-spice powder and stir-fry until fragrant, about 45 seconds. Add the carrots, celery, and cabbage or bok choy and stir-fry until they begin to soften, about 2 minutes. Add the drained noodles and stir-fry for 1 minute. Add the broccoli florets, diced meat or poultry, soy sauce, and chicken broth or water and stir-fry until all the ingredients are heated through, about 2 minutes longer. Remove from the heat and serve immediately.

Makes 2 servings.

Sesame Noodles

2 lb Chinese egg noodles

½ cup Asian sesame oil

½ cup soy sauce

salt to taste

chopped fresh cilantro to taste
(optional)

3 tbs Shaoxing wine

2 tsp sugar

1 tsp chili oil

6 green onions, chopped

This is my version of a favorite noodle dish served at Jing-Jing restaurant in Palo Alto, California.

Bring a large saucepan of salted water to a boil. Add the noodles and cook until just tender, about 6 minutes or according to package directions. Drain well and place in a bowl.

While the noodles are cooking, in a small bowl, combine all the remaining ingredients, mixing well. Then add to the drained noodles and toss well. Serve warm or cold.

Makes 4 to 6 servings.

Cinnamon Noodles

2 tbs peanut oil

½ onion, finely chopped

½-inch-piece fresh ginger, grated

2 cloves garlic, minced

1 tsp ground cinnamon or cassia

½ lb beef shoulder meat, cut into
small cubes

1 tbs soy sauce

1 carrot, thinly sliced on the
diagonal

3 celery stalks, thinly sliced on the
diagonal

3 cinnamon sticks

6 cups beef broth

salt to taste

1 lb flat Chinese egg noodles

6 fresh cilantro sprigs, chopped

Great in the winter, this noodle soup is fragrant and hearty. Any type of noodle can be used, but flat egg noodles or Japanese udon noodles are my favorites.

In a large saucepan, heat the oil over high heat. When it is hot, add the onion, ginger, and garlic. Saute until the onion begins to soften, about 1 minute, then add the ground cinnamon and beef. Mix well and allow the beef to brown completely on all sides. Add the soy sauce, carrot, and celery. Mix well and cook, stirring, for 2 minutes. Add the cinnamon sticks, beef broth, and salt. Bring to a boil, reduce the heat to low, and simmer, uncovered, until the beef is tender, about 50 minutes.

In another large saucepan, bring salted water to a boil. Add the noodles and cook until just tender, about 6 minutes or according to package directions. Drain and rinse under warm water.

Add the noodles to the soup, stir well, and remove from the heat. Cover and let stand for 15 minutes. Just before serving, garnish with the cilantro.

Makes 4 servings.

India

The vast Indian subcontinent has a documented history dating back almost four thousand years. It is a land of great rivers, fertile plains, steamy jungles, high and jagged peaks, parched deserts, and a multitude of cultures and languages. Indian cuisine reflects this long timeline and great diversity. In fact, of the world's great cuisines, I find no other table more difficult to describe succinctly. Perhaps the best way to discover India's culinary heritage is by simply cooking it.

Noted Indian cook Madhur Jaffrey writes that cooking Indian food is like painting with spices. Indeed, Indian cuisine draws upon a bounty of wonderful spices, and many that we in the West now take for granted came from India or came to the West via India. Native to India are pepper, cardamom, mustard, fenugreek, tamarind, and cumin. Spices that are probably not subcontinent originals but that Indian cooks regard as essential are mace, nutmeg, ginger, cloves, and chilies. Of these, only chilies came from the West, brought by the Portuguese after the discovery of the Americas (fresh chilies might include green Thais or jalapeños as well as Fresnos; dried chilies could be either arbol or cayenne). The other spices were transported to India via trade with Southeast Asia. The Western cook's debt to India is deep. This bounty of spices makes for long ingredient lists in recipes; don't be intimidated, however, for most of the spices are simply measured into the dish and blended together. Very simple.

But there is much to learn from the Indian kitchen beyond its contributions to the spice shelf. One important piece of knowledge is use of the *tarka,* an infusion of flavor created by immersing spices or other agents (such as onions) in hot oil. While this technique is not unique to the subcontinent, it reaches its zenith there. Indian cooks also know how to use the same spice in different ways and in different blends to achieve a totally different taste.

A second area of knowledge are the dietary beliefs. Many Indians rely on a varied, high-fiber vegetarian diet. Protein primarily comes from legumes, including lentils. Indians use three main kinds of lentils: masoor dal—the red or orange lentil, mung dal—yellow lentils, and regular brown lentils; split green peas and dried chickpeas are also popular. The use of various grains such as rice, wheat, and millet, as well as a multitude of vegetables and fruits, ensures a balanced, nutritious diet. Contrary to popular belief, however, most Indians are not vegetarians. Muslims eat beef, lamb, and chicken. Christians in Goa consume pork. Some Hindus enjoy lamb and fish. But all consume these foods in moderation, enjoying them as a small part of a larger meal.

Indian meals should be accompanied with any of various Indian breads—nan, *kulcha,* roti, chapati—all of them yet another source of fiber. I generally do not bake my own breads, preferring to purchase them instead, usually by advance order from an Indian restaurant. Many Bay Area Indian markets sell bread, although it usually is frozen. You can also make Indian breads at home, if you like.

Suggested Menus

A Quick Taste of India for Four

This menu is an easy one to make when you get home from work. The chicken requires 30 minutes of marinating but cooks quickly. The okra should be doused with vinegar to remove its viscid quality, and some tamarind water must also be prepared, but while this is going on, you can parboil your new potatoes and prepare the spice paste for the eggplant. Total time is about 1¼ hours.

Chicken in a Turmeric Yogurt Sauce
Basmati Rice
Okra and New Potatoes in an Ajowan Cream Sauce
Tamarind Eggplant
Fresh Fruit with Cardamom
Mango Lassi

A Spicy Dinner for Four

Some advance work is necessary to prepare this hot-and-spicy dinner. The lamb should be left to marinate overnight, while the dal must be soaked for at least 5 hours. Just leave the latter soaking in the morning before you head out of the house, and they'll be ready to go in the evening. Everything else can be prepared quickly.

Curried Lamb with Almonds and Cashews

Spicy Eggplant with Tomatoes

Basmati Rice

Dal

Raita

Fresh Fruit with Cardamom

Mango Lassi

A Vegetarian Sampler for Six

This last menu features vegetarian dishes from various regions of India. The pilaf requires some soaking, but you can just leave the items to soak before you go out in the morning. The chutney should be allowed to sit for 72 hours before finishing, and can be prepared in advance. The rest of the dishes cook quickly.

Cashew Rice Pilaf with Apricots and Mission Figs

Tamarind Eggplant or Spicy Eggplant with Tomatoes

Spinach with Paneer Cheese

Curried Cauliflower and Potatoes

Tamarind Banana Chutney

Almond Rice Pudding

Mango Lassi

Curried Lamb with Almonds and Cashews

....

Marinade:

2 yellow onions, coarsely chopped

4 cloves garlic

2 green serrano chilies, seeded

1-inch-piece fresh ginger, peeled and cut into 3 or 4 pieces

1 tbs cumin seeds

1 tsp ground turmeric

1 tbs coriander seeds

1 tsp fenugreek seeds

½ tsp cayenne pepper

5 tbs tamarind water (page 227)

2 green onions, coarsely chopped

1 shallot, coarsely chopped

3 lb boneless lamb, cut into 1-inch cubes

4 tbs ghee

1 tsp peanut oil

1 onion, coarsely chopped

1 tbs fennel seeds

½ cup coconut milk

½ cup water

¼ cup cashews

¼ cup blanched almonds

salt to taste

white pepper to taste

This dish requires overnight marinating but is otherwise quite simple. It helps if you have some tamarind water already prepared; if not, you will have to soak a small piece of tamarind in warm water for 15 minutes before you begin.

To make the marinade, in a food processor or blender, place the yellow onions, garlic, chilies, and ginger. Grind coarsely, then add the cumin seeds, turmeric, coriander seeds, and fenugreek seeds. Continue to grind until the seeds have broken down. Transfer to a large glass bowl and stir in the cayenne and tamarind water. Then add the green onions and shallot, mixing well to form a paste. Add the lamb, and rub the paste over all the surfaces. Cover and refrigerate overnight.

The next day, heat the ghee and the peanut oil in a large saucepan over medium-high heat. When hot, add the onion and cook, stirring, until soft and golden, 5 to 8 minutes. Add the lamb along with all its marinade and the fennel seeds. Brown the meat well, stirring often to prevent sticking. As soon as the meat is browned on all sides, add the coconut milk and the water, reduce the heat to low, cover, and cook until the lamb is tender, about 45 minutes.

Uncover the pot and add the cashews and almonds along with the salt and white pepper. Stir well and continue to cook until the liquid has evaporated, 10 to 15 minutes, then serve.

Makes 6 servings.

Pork Vindaloo

2 yellow onions, quartered

8 cloves garlic

3 tomatoes, peeled

4 Fresno chilies, seeded

1-inch-piece fresh ginger, peeled
   and minced

1 tbs coriander seeds

1 tsp cumin seeds

½ tsp dry mustard

1 tsp ground turmeric

juice of 1 lemon

5 tbs ghee or peanut oil

1 shallot, minced

2 tbs distilled white vinegar

2½ lb pork stew meat, cut into
   cubes

3½ cups beef broth or water

1 tsp salt

¼ tsp black pepper

1 tsp arrowroot

4 green onions, coarsely diced

8 fresh cilantro sprigs, coarsely
   chopped

This dish comes from the former Portuguese colony of Goa in western India. You can substitute beef, if you prefer. Serve with basmati rice.

In a food processor, combine the yellow onions, garlic, tomatoes, chilies, and ginger. Grind to a fine paste. Set aside.

In a small dry skillet, toast the coriander and cumin seeds over medium heat for 1 minute. Transfer to a mortar and grind well. Add the mustard and turmeric and mix well. Add to the onion paste along with lemon juice; blend well.

In a large saucepan, heat the ghee or oil over medium-high heat. When it is hot, add the paste. Stir constantly for 2 minutes and add the shallot. Mix well again and add the vinegar and pork. Brown the pork well on all sides, stirring often. Pour in the beef broth or water and add the salt and pepper. Bring to a boil, reduce the heat to low, and simmer until the meat is tender, about 45 minutes.

During the last few minutes of cooking, ladle out about ¼ cup of the liquid and stir the arrowroot into it until dissolved. Return the mixture to the pot and cook, stirring, until the liquid thickens slightly, about 1 minute. Garnish with the green onions and cilantro just before serving.

Makes 6 servings.

Preparing Tamarind Water

Place a 1-inch lump of tamarind paste in about ¼ cup hot water and leave to soak for 10 to 15 minutes. Then, using your fingers, work the lump to release its essence fully into the water. Pour the liquid through a fine-mesh sieve to remove any fibers and seeds. The water can now be used, or it can be stored in the refrigerator in a tightly covered jar for up to 2 weeks.

Spicy Lime Chicken

2 yellow onions, quartered

1-inch-piece fresh ginger, peeled

12 cloves garlic

2 green onions, cut into 1-inch
   lengths

½ tsp grated lime zest

2 cups plain yogurt

salt to taste

2 tsp garam masala

2 tsp ground cumin

2 tbs ground coriander

2 tsp ajowan

1 tsp black cumin seeds

2 lb boneless chicken breasts, cut
   into narrow strips

4 tbs ghee

1 tsp mustard seeds

6 green serrano chilies, seeded
   and finely minced

½ cup lime juice

½ cup cashews or macadamia nuts

1 tomato, diced

¼ cup fresh cilantro leaves,
   coarsely chopped

¼ cup fresh mint leaves, coarsely
   chopped

½ tsp white pepper

dash of ground nutmeg

hot cooked basmati rice for
   serving (page 49)

2 limes, cut into wedges

Nimbu (sometimes spelled nimboo) means lime, hence the name. Serve with basmati rice.

In a food processor or blender, combine the yellow onions, ginger, garlic, and green onions and process until finely ground to a smooth paste. Add the lime zest, yogurt, salt, 1 tsp of the garam masala, 1 tsp of the ground cumin, 1 tbs of the ground coriander, 1 tsp of the ajowan, and ½ tsp of the black cumin seeds. Whirl for a couple of seconds. Pour the mixture into a glass bowl and add the chicken strips. Mix well, cover, and refrigerate for 4 to 6 hours.

In a small dry skillet, toast the remaining garam masala, ground cumin, ground coriander, ajowan, and black cumin over medium heat for 3 to 4 minutes. Set aside.

In a large skillet, heat 1 tbs of the ghee. When it is hot, add the chicken and its marinade. Cover and cook over low heat for 10 minutes. Meanwhile, in another large skillet, heat the remaining 3 tbs ghee over medium-high heat. When it is hot, add the mustard seeds. When the mustard seeds begin to pop, add the chilies and the dry-roasted spices. Mix well and saute for 30 seconds, then add the chicken, mixing well. Cover and cook over medium heat for 15 minutes.

Add the lime juice, mix well, and cook for another 3 minutes. Meanwhile, in a bowl, stir together the nuts, tomato, cilantro, mint, white pepper, and nutmeg. Spoon the basmati rice onto a platter and top with the chicken. Pour the tomato mixture over the chicken. Serve with the lime wedges.

Makes 4 servings.

North India's Spicy Chicken Curry

Murgh Masala

Dry masala:

1 large onion, coarsely chopped

3 cloves garlic, crushed

1-inch-piece fresh ginger, peeled and minced

2 tbs ground coriander

2 tsp cumin seeds

2 tsp ground turmeric

¼ tsp ground red chili or cayenne pepper

6 whole cloves

seeds from 3 cardamom pods

2 cinnamon sticks

1 chicken, 3 lb, skinned and cut into 8 serving pieces

4 tbs butter

4 large ripe tomatoes, coarsely chopped

salt to taste

North India restaurant, in San Francisco's Cow Hollow, is best known for its tandoori. This dish, however, one of their delicious spicy curries, goes together on the stove top, which is more suitable for home cooks. If you don't like using butter, you can substitute canola or safflower oil. Also, if you prefer, you can use boneless chicken, or even just white meat.

To make the masala, in a food processor or blender, combine all the ingredients and grind until pulverized. Rub the mixture well into the chicken pieces, coating them evenly.

In a wok or heavy skillet, heat the butter or oil over medium-high heat. Add the chicken pieces and brown well on all sides, about 10 minutes. Add the tomatoes, cover, reduce the heat to low, and simmer until the chicken is cooked through and the sauce has thickened, about 10 minutes. If the sauce threatens to scorch, add a little water to the pan. Season lightly with salt, transfer to a serving dish, and serve at once.

Makes 4 servings.

Chicken in a Turmeric Yogurt Sauce

2 tsp ground turmeric

1 cup low-fat plain yogurt

4 boneless, skinless chicken breast halves, cut into bite-sized strips

½ tsp cumin seeds

1 tsp fenugreek seeds

2 tbs ghee or 1 tsp olive oil

½ cup finely chopped onion

Although this dish requires 30 minutes of marinating, it cooks quickly in a stir-fry manner. In fact, it is ideally prepared in a wok. The chicken takes on the tart flavor of the yogurt, so this dish will be appreciated by those who like tangy sauces.

In a bowl, using a spoon or small whisk, stir the turmeric into ⅔ cup of the yogurt, mixing well. Add the chicken and turn to coat well. Cover and marinate for 30 minutes. Meanwhile, in a mortar grind together the cumin and fenugreek to a fine powder.

Preheat a wok or deep skillet over medium-high heat, then add the ghee or oil. When it is hot, add the cumin-fenugreek mixture and allow to sizzle briefly before adding the chopped onion. Stir-fry the onion until it softens, about 3 minutes, then add the chicken with its marinade. Stir-fry the chicken for a minute and then reduce the heat to medium. Cook until the chicken is done, 5 to 7 minutes. Remove from the heat and mix in the remaining ⅓ cup yogurt. Serve immediately.

Makes 4 servings.

Mango Lassi

2½ lb mangoes, peeled, pitted, and chopped, about 1¼ cups

1 cup orange juice

¼ cup extra-fine sugar

1 tbs rose water

4 cups plain yogurt, well chilled

I generally use mangoes for lassi, but I have substituted peaches on occasion.

In a food processor or blender, combine the mango flesh, orange juice, sugar, and rose water. Puree until smooth. Add the yogurt and process until blended. Refrigerate for at least 15 minutes before serving.

Makes 8 servings.

Biryani

1 tbs saffron threads

¼ cup milk, heated

2 yellow onions, quartered

2 shallots

2 green onions, cut into 1-inch lengths

1-inch-piece fresh ginger, peeled
  and cut into 4 pieces

4 Fresno chilies, seeded and
  coarsely chopped

12 cloves garlic, cut up

1 cup fresh cilantro leaves

½ cup fresh mint leaves

seeds from 6 cardamom pods

6 whole cloves

1 tsp coriander seeds

1 tsp black cumin seeds

½ tsp kalonji (nigella)

½ tsp ground cinnamon

¼ tsp ground nutmeg

¼ tsp ground mace

½ tsp black pepper

kosher salt, if needed

juice of 3 lemons

juice of 1 lime

2 cups plain yogurt

4 lb boneless chicken breasts, cut
  into narrow strips

3 tbs ghee or peanut oil

pinch of asafetida

pinch of amchur

1 yellow onion, finely chopped

2 cloves garlic, finely minced

½-inch-piece fresh ginger, peeled
  and finely minced

2 cups chicken broth

10 tomatoes, coarsely chopped

2½ cups basmati rice

salt to taste

⅓ cup dried figs

⅓ cup cashews

⅓ cup raisins

½ cup fresh cilantro leaves,
  coarsely chopped

One of northern India's classic dishes, biryani can be made with a variety of meats and vegetables. It is essentially an Indian pot-au-feu.

Soak the saffron in the warm milk for 10 minutes. In a food processor, combine the yellow onions, shallots, green onions, ginger, chilies, and garlic. Process for a few seconds until coarsely chopped. Add the saffron and milk and cilantro and mint leaves. Process until a smooth paste forms. Set aside.

In a mortar, combine the cardamom, cloves, coriander seeds, black cumin seeds, kalonji, cinnamon, nutmeg, mace, and black pepper. If needed to facilitate grinding, add a little kosher salt. Grind the mixture to a powder. Add to the paste, mix well, and place in a large glass bowl. Stir in the lemon and lime juices, and then mix in the yogurt, blending well. Add the chicken strips, cover, and marinate for 4 to 6 hours in the refrigerator.

In a stockpot, heat the ghee or peanut oil over medium-high heat. When it is hot, add the asafetida and allow it to sizzle. Then add the amchur and again allow it to sizzle. Add the onion, garlic, and ginger and saute, stirring constantly, until the onion is soft and golden, 5 to 8 minutes. Add the chicken with its marinade. Cook the chicken for about 10 minutes, stirring often to prevent sticking. Add the chicken broth and tomatoes, bring to a boil, and add the rice and salt, mixing well. Bring to a boil again, reduce to a simmer, and mix well again. Cook until the liquid has been mostly absorbed, 10 to 12 minutes. Add the figs, cashews, and raisins and cook for another 3 minutes.

Remove from the heat and serve on a large platter. Garnish with the cilantro and serve.

Makes 6 to 8 servings.

Bengali-Style Grilled Swordfish

1 tbs ground turmeric

1-inch-piece fresh ginger, peeled
   and minced

½ tsp cayenne pepper

½ tsp white pepper

1 tsp ground cumin

1 tsp ground coriander

2 cloves garlic, crushed

2 tsp dry mustard

1 tsp kosher salt

4 green serrano chilies, seeded
   and finely chopped

1 cup peanut or almond oil

6 swordfish steaks, each about 1
   inch thick

6 pieces banana leaf, each about
   3 times the width of a fish steak

12 fresh cilantro sprigs

chutney for serving

This dish also works well with tuna, sea bass, or salmon.

In a mortar or small food processor, combine the turmeric, ginger, cayenne pepper, white pepper, cumin, coriander, garlic, mustard, and kosher salt. Grind for a minute, crushing the ginger and garlic well. Add the chilies and grind for another minute, blending into a paste. Transfer the paste to a large bowl. Add the ¼ cup of the oil and mix well. Add the fish, coating it well with the marinade. Marinate for 20 to 30 minutes at room temperature.

Meanwhile, light a fire in a charcoal grill. To make the banana leaves pliable, grill them for a few seconds on each side over the hot coals. Alternatively, immerse them in hot water for about 1 minute until they are soft and pliable enough to fold, then wipe dry. Brush both sides of the leaves with the remaining ¾ cup oil. Place a swordfish steak on a leaf, rub with a bit of the marinade, and place 2 sprigs of cilantro on top. Carefully wrap the fish in the leaf, then tie with kitchen string to secure the leaf in place.

Place the leaf packets over medium-hot coals and grill the swordfish steaks for 6 to 7 minutes on each side; the cooking time will depend on the thickness of the steaks. Serve with chutney.

Makes 6 servings.

Basmati Rice

• •

3 cups water

½ tsp lemon juice

1 tsp ghee or olive oil

2 green onions

1-inch-piece fresh ginger, peeled

2 curry leaves (optional)

1½ cups basmati rice, rinsed

Rice is rarely simpler or more delicious.

In a medium-sized saucepan, combine the water, lemon juice, ghee or oil, green onions, ginger, and curry leaves and bring to a boil. Add the basmati rice and return to a boil. Reduce the heat to low, cover, and cook until the rice is tender, about 20 minutes. The rice is ready when the kernels are soft, loose, and separate. If it is underdone, cook for another 5 minutes or so. Discard the green onions, ginger, and curry leaves. Fluff the rice and serve.

Makes 4 to 6 servings.

Dal

• •

Lentils with Bengali spices

1 cup masoor dal

3 cups water

½ tsp cumin seeds

½ tsp fennel seeds

½ tsp fenugreek seeds

½ tsp yellow mustard seeds

½ tsp kalonji (nigella)

1 tbs ghee or mustard oil

pinch of asafetida

3 cloves garlic, minced

2 cups water or broth

salt to taste

This version of dal is made with panch phoran, a Bengali mixture of whole seeds that includes cumin, fennel, fenugreek, mustard seed, and kalonji, combined in equal proportions. Many Indian markets sell a premixed version.

Place the masoor dal in a bowl, add the 3 cups water, and let soak for at least 5 hours.

In a small dry skillet, toast the cumin, fennel, fenugreek, mustard seeds, and kalonji over medium heat for 3 to 4 minutes. Set aside.

In a medium-sized saucepan, heat the ghee or mustard oil over medium-high heat. When it is hot, add the asafetida and allow to sizzle for a moment. Add the dry-roasted spices and cook for 2 minutes. Add the garlic and continue to cook, stirring, for another 2 minutes.

Meanwhile, drain the dal and rinse them briefly in a colander. Add the dal to the pan and stir gently but thoroughly. Add the 2 cups water or broth and salt, bring to a boil, and then reduce the heat to low. Cook, uncovered, until the dal becomes a thick puree, about 35 minutes, then serve.

Makes 6 servings.

Cashew Rice Pilaf with Apricots and Mission Figs

3 tbs masoor dal

3 tbs brown lentils

3 tbs split green peas

4½ cups cold water

12 dried apricots

12 dried Mission figs

½ cup hot water

3 tbs ghee or 2 tbs olive oil

1 tsp anardana (dried pomegranate
seeds), ground to a powder

pinch of asafetida

pinch of amchur

2 tsp garam masala

1 onion, finely chopped

1½ cups basmati rice

½ cup tamarind water (page 43)

3 cups water

½ tsp ground turmeric

salt to taste

1 tsp peanut oil

1 tsp cumin seeds

¼ tsp cayenne pepper

½ cup cashews (whole or pieces)

8 fresh cilantro sprigs, coarsely
chopped

¼ cup shredded dried coconut

One of my favorite ways to use dried fruits is in pilafs. In this version, dried apricots and Mission figs give the dish a nice sweet touch to balance the exotic blend of Indian spices. This dish takes some lead time for preparation, especially for soaking the dal and fruits.

In a bowl, combine the masoor dal, brown lentils, and split green peas and pour in 1½ cups of the cold water. Let soak for at least 5 hours. Transfer to a saucepan, bring to a boil, and boil for 15 minutes. Drain and reserve.

Meanwhile, in a shallow bowl, combine the dried apricots and Mission figs and pour in the hot water. Let stand for 1 hour. Remove the fruit from the water and coarsely chop. Reserve the fruit and the water.

In a 2-quart saucepan, heat the ghee or olive oil over medium-high heat. When it is hot, add the anardana and let sizzle for a moment, then add the pinch of asafetida. Again let sizzle for a moment, then add the amchur. Let sizzle once again and add 1 tsp of the garam masala and the onion. Stir the onion well, coating it with the ghee or oil. Add the parboiled legumes and mix well. As soon as the onion is soft, add the basmati rice and mix well. Pour in the tamarind water and reserved fruit water and allow the rice to absorb the liquid before adding the remaining 3 cups water. Bring to a boil, add the turmeric and salt, reduce the heat to low, and add the reserved chopped fruits and the remaining 1 tsp garam masala. Cook until the rice and the legumes are done, 25 to 30 minutes.

While the rice is cooking, in a skillet, heat the peanut oil over medium-high heat. When it is hot, add the cumin seeds and cayenne pepper. Allow to sizzle for a moment and then add the cashews. Stir-fry the cashews until they start to turn a golden brown, about 1 minute. Remove from the heat.

When the pilaf is ready, stir in the cashews and cilantro. Turn out onto a warmed platter, top with the coconut, and serve.

Makes 6 servings.

Okra and New Potatoes in an Ajowan Cream Sauce

½ lb okra pods

½ cup distilled white vinegar

12 uniformly sized small new potatoes

2 tbs ghee or 1 tsp olive oil

pinch of asafetida

pinch of amchur

2 tsp ajowan

3 cloves garlic, minced

½ cup lemon juice

¼ cup water

salt to taste

white pepper to taste

1 cup sour cream

½ cup plain low-fat yogurt

1 tsp paprika

½ tsp cayenne pepper

At first, I didn't understand the aversion that many Americans have to okra, especially given that in Louisiana it is prepared in many fine ways. Then I discovered that they think okra has to be slimy. Well, it is true that okra has a tendency to become viscous if it is not properly treated, but this unpleasant quality can be removed by dousing the okra with vinegar, as in this recipe. In India, lemon juice and tamarind water are used in place of the vinegar with the same results. For this recipe, which calls for lemon juice, I still treat the okra with vinegar beforehand.

Place the okra pods in a bowl and douse with the white vinegar, tossing gently to coat evenly. Set aside for 30 minutes.

Meanwhile, cook the potatoes in boiling salted water until they are soft, 20 to 25 minutes. Drain the potatoes well, then quarter them. Set aside.

Drain and rinse the okra pods. Cut off the tops. In a 1-quart saucepan or large skillet, heat the ghee or oil. As soon as it is hot, add the asafetida and let it sizzle a moment before adding the amchur. Again let sizzle for a moment and add the ajowan. Cook for 1 minute and add the garlic and the okra. Cook for 3 minutes, stirring constantly. Add the reserved quartered potatoes and cook for another 2 minutes, stirring constantly. Add the lemon juice, water, salt, and white pepper and bring to a boil. Reduce the heat to medium-low and simmer until the okra is tender, about 15 minutes; the potatoes will dissolve into the sauce a bit.

Meanwhile, in a bowl, mix together the sour cream, yogurt, paprika, and cayenne. When the okra is cooked, add the sour cream mixture, mix well, and serve.

Makes 4 to 6 servings.

Curried Cauliflower and Potatoes

Aloo Gobhi

4 potatoes, peeled

1 cauliflower, cut into florets

4 tbs ghee or 2 tbs peanut oil

2 green serrano chilies, seeded and diced

½-inch-piece fresh ginger, peeled and minced

½ tsp ground cumin

½ tsp cumin seeds

½ tsp mustard seeds

1 shallot, diced

3 cloves garlic, minced

1 tsp ground turmeric

1 tsp ground coriander

1 tsp garam masala

2 tsp jaggery or 3 tsp brown sugar

salt to taste

6 fresh cilantro sprigs, coarsely chopped

Parboil the potatoes in boiling salted water for 10 minutes. Drain and cut into cubes. Blanch the cauliflower florets in boiling salted water for 2 minutes. Drain and plunge into an ice water bath.

In a large skillet, heat the ghee or oil over medium-high heat. When it is hot, add the chilies, ginger, ground cumin, and cumin and mustard seeds and saute until the mustard seeds begin to pop. Then add the shallot, garlic, turmeric, coriander, and garam masala. Stir well and cook over medium-high heat until the shallot begins to soften, about 3 minutes. Add the jaggery or brown sugar, mix well, and reduce the heat to medium. Add the potatoes and cauliflower. Mix well and season with salt. Cook until the potatoes are browned and all the vegetables are tender, about 15 minutes. (You may add about ¼ cup water or chicken broth to prevent the potatoes from sticking.) Stir the mixture gently as you do not want to mash the potatoes. Remove from the heat, sprinkle with the cilantro, and serve.

Makes 6 to 8 servings.

Yogurt Potatoes

18 new potatoes

1 tsp cumin seeds

1 tsp mustard seeds

½ tsp coriander seeds

2 cups plain yogurt

1 tsp mustard oil

3 green onions, thinly sliced

12 fresh cilantro sprigs, chopped

A simple yet flavorful way to serve potatoes.

Cook the potatoes in boiling salted water until they are tender, 20 to 25 minutes; the timing will depend on their size.

Meanwhile, in a small dry skillet, toast the cumin and mustard seeds over medium heat for about 4 minutes. In a mortar, crush the dry-roasted seeds along with the coriander seeds. Combine the crushed seeds with the yogurt and mustard oil. Mix well and set aside.

When the potatoes are done, drain and allow to cool for 5 minutes. If desired, cut the potatoes in half. Pour the yogurt mixture over the potatoes and add the green onions and cilantro. Mix thoroughly, then serve.

Makes 6 servings.

Bitter Gourd with Panch Phoran

2 tbs ghee or mustard oil

½ tsp cumin seeds

½ tsp fennel seeds

½ tsp fenugreek

½ tsp mustard seeds

½ tsp kalonji (nigella)

pinch of asafetida

3 cloves garlic, minced

½-inch-piece fresh ginger, peeled and minced

½ onion, finely chopped

2 bitter gourds, thinly sliced

2 carrots, thinly sliced

salt to taste

black pepper to taste

1 cup water

8 fresh cilantro sprigs, chopped

Bitter gourd, also known as bitter melon, is used extensively in southern Chinese cooking, but is also common in Indian cuisine. It is available in Asian markets, especially in the summer months. Many people consider its bitter flavor an acquired taste, and some insist that scotch drinkers generally like it. Panch phoran is the Bengali spice mixture of cumin, fennel, fenugreek, mustard seeds, and kalonji.

In a medium-sized saucepan, heat the ghee or oil over medium-high heat. When it is hot, add the cumin, fennel, fenugreek, mustard seeds, and kalonji. When the mustard seeds begin to pop, add the asafetida, garlic, and ginger. Reduce the heat to medium-low and cook for 2 minutes, stirring occasionally. Add the onion and continue to cook, stirring, for another 3 minutes. Add the bitter gourds and carrots along with the salt and pepper. Continue to cook over medium-low heat for another 5 minutes, stirring occasionally. Add the water, raise the heat, and bring to a boil. Reduce the heat to low and cook until the gourds and carrots are tender, another 10 minutes. Garnish with the cilantro just before serving.

Makes 4 servings.

Spinach with Paneer Cheese

Sag Paneer

½-inch-piece ginger, peeled and cut up

2 green onions, cut into thirds

2 cloves garlic

1 shallot

½ tsp ground cumin

1 tsp ground turmeric

2 tbs ghee or mustard oil

½ lb paneer cheese, cut into small cubes

1 tsp garam masala

2 lb spinach, well rinsed and finely chopped

2 tbs water

salt to taste

In a small food processor or blender, combine the ginger, green onions, garlic, and shallot and process to a paste. Add the cumin and turmeric and mix well. Set aside.

In a large saucepan or saute pan, heat the ghee or oil over medium heat. When it is hot, add the spice paste and stir well. Add the paneer cheese and fry until golden brown on all sides, about 5 minutes. Using a slotted spoon, remove from the pan and set aside.

Add ½ tsp of the garam masala to the remaining hot oil, stirring well to incorporate it into the oil. Add the spinach, water, and salt. Reduce the heat to low and cook for 10 minutes, stirring occasionally. Return the paneer cheese to the pan along with the remaining ½ tsp garam masala. Cook for another 7 minutes to blend the flavors, then serve.

Makes 6 servings.

Spicy Eggplant

2 eggplants, halved lengthwise

6 cloves garlic

salt to taste

1 tsp fennel seeds

1 tsp cumin seeds

1 tsp coriander seeds

2-inch-piece fresh ginger, peeled and cut up

1 tsp amchur

seeds from 8 cardamom pods

3 green serrano chilies, seeded

⅓ cup plain yogurt

2 tbs ghee or olive oil

1 onion, finely chopped

1 shallot, finely chopped

5 large tomatoes, peeled and coarsely chopped

juice of ½ lemon

8 fresh cilantro sprigs, coarsely chopped

For this dish I use the common ovoid purple eggplant.

Preheat an oven to 400 degrees F. Place the halved eggplants cut side up in a baking dish and cut deep slits into the flesh.

In a small food processor, blender, or mortar, combine the garlic, salt, fennel, cumin, coriander, and ginger and grind to a coarse paste. Add the amchur, cardamom, and chilies and grind to a smooth paste.

Spread half of the paste over the cut surface of each eggplant half. Bake until tender, about 20 minutes. Remove from the oven and, when cool enough to handle, peel away the skin. Place the flesh in a food processor or blender and add the yogurt. Puree to a paste.

In a large skillet, heat the ghee or oil over medium-high heat. Once it is hot, add the other half of the spice paste and stir well. Add the onion and shallot and saute until they begin to soften, about 3 minutes. Then add the tomatoes and cook, stirring occasionally, for 3 minutes. Add the eggplant puree, mix well, and cook until the eggplant is warmed through, about 3 minutes longer. Add the lemon juice and cilantro, mix well, and serve.

Makes 6 servings.

Tamarind Eggplant

3 Japanese eggplants, thinly sliced

1 cup tamarind water (page 43)

3 cloves garlic

¼ tsp salt

seeds from 6 cardamom pods

1 tsp cumin seeds

½ tsp black peppercorns

1 tsp coriander seeds

2 tbs peeled and grated fresh
   ginger

4 cloves

½ tsp freshly grated nutmeg

½ tsp ground cinnamon

1 tbs peanut or olive oil

pinch of asafetida

pinch of amchur

½ onion, finely chopped

1 tsp palm sugar or 2 tsp brown
   sugar

juice of 1 lime

In this dish, the eggplant is briefly marinated in tamarind water and then panfried in a paste of aromatic spices. As the eggplant softens, more tamarind water and the juice of a lime are added and allowed to cook down. The result is a sour and tangy picklelike dish. Although Indian cooks would more likely use an ovoid eggplant, I prefer slender Japanese (or Chinese) eggplants for this dish.

Slice the eggplants and place the slices in a shallow bowl. Pour the tamarind water over them. Let stand for 10 to 15 minutes.

Meanwhile, in a spice mill or mortar, grind the garlic with the salt. As it begins to break down, add the cardamom, cumin, peppercorns, coriander, ginger, and cloves. Grind into a paste and add the nutmeg and cinnamon. Mix well and set aside.

Drain the eggplant slices, reserving the tamarind water. In a large skillet or saute pan, heat the oil over medium-high heat. When it is hot, add the asafetida and let it sizzle a moment before adding the amchur. Again let sizzle for a moment, then add the spice paste. Cook for 1 minute and add the onion and the eggplant. Let the onion and eggplant brown and soften for several minutes, turning it occasionally. Dissolve the sugar in the lime juice. As the eggplant softens, add the lime juice mixture and a ¼ cup of the reserved tamarind water. Once the liquid is absorbed, add another ¼ cup of the tamarind water. Repeat this until you use up all the tamarind water. By this time (after 10 to 12 minutes), the eggplant should be completely soft and cooked. Serve hot.

Makes 4 to 6 servings.

Raita

Indian Cucumber-Yogurt Sauce

There are many versions of raita, but I like the simple ones. Here are two of my favorites.

Raita I

2 cups plain yogurt

1 tsp cumin seeds

1 tsp fennel seeds

1 cucumber, peeled, seeded, and
   finely diced

½ tsp cayenne pepper

Place the yogurt in a fine-mesh sieve and allow to drain for 30 minutes.

Meanwhile, in a small dry skillet, toast the cumin and fennel seeds over medium heat for about 4 minutes. Set aside.

Transfer the drained yogurt in the sieve to a bowl. With a whisk, beat until smooth. Add the dry-roasted spices, the cucumber, and the cayenne, mixing well.

Makes about 1½ cups.

Raita II

2 cups plain yogurt

1 cucumber, peeled, seeded, and
   finely diced

½ cup fresh mint leaves, coarsely
   chopped

½ tsp cayenne pepper

Place the yogurt in a fine-mesh sieve and allow to drain for 30 minutes. Transfer the drained yogurt in the sieve to a bowl. With a whisk, beat until smooth. Add the cucumber and mint leaves. Mix well and dust the top with the cayenne.

Makes about 1½ cups.

Tamarind Banana Chutney

3 cups warm tamarind water
   (page 43)

1 tsp cayenne pepper

1 tbs peeled and grated fresh
   ginger

2 tsp amchur

salt to taste

⅓ cup jaggery or ½ cup dark brown
   sugar

½ cup raisins

3 bananas

While mango chutney is available in stores under several different labels, tamarind chutney is nowhere to be found. This dish goes well with roasted or grilled meats and chicken. It is a simple recipe, although it does need to sit for 72 hours before finishing.

In a bowl, combine all the ingredients except the raisins and bananas. Mix well to dissolve the sugar. Add the raisins and let soak for 72 hours.

Transfer the mixture to a saucepan and bring to a boil. Peel the bananas, break them into small pieces, and add to the liquid. Boil for 1 minute, then remove from the heat. Let cool and serve.

Makes about 2½ cups.

Fresh Fruit with Cardamom

6 cups mixed fruits (try apple
 slices, raspberries, and Mission
 figs; carambola, cucumber, and
 tangelos; or Asian pear slices,
 strawberries, and mangoes)

Chat Masala:

2 tbs amchur

1 tbs black salt

½ tsp cayenne pepper

1 tbs cumin seeds

1 tsp fennel seeds

1 tbs garam masala

½ tsp ground ginger

Yogurt-Cardamom Dressing:

2 cups plain yogurt

seeds from 10 cardamom pods,
 ground to a powder

½ tsp amchur

3 tbs honey

Depending on what is in season, try any of the suggested fruit combinations sprinkled with a spice blend called chat masala and topped with a yogurt-cardamom dressing.

Place the fruits in a large bowl. To make the chat masala, in a small bowl, stir together all the ingredients. To make the dressing, in yet another bowl, stir together all the ingredients.

Sprinkle the chat masala on the fruits to taste. You probably won't want to use it all; reserve the remainder for future use. Pour the dressing over fruits, mix gently, and serve.

Makes 6 servings.

Almond Rice Pudding

1 cup basmati rice, rinsed

4 cups water

1 tsp grated lemon zest

1 tsp grated orange zest

½ tsp salt

6 cups milk

2 cinnamon sticks

8 whole cloves

seeds from 10 cardamom pods, ground to a powder

2 cups sugar

½ cup slivered blanched almonds, toasted (page 227)

1 tsp ground cinnamon

Place the basmati rice in a bowl with water to cover and let stand for 1 hour. In a large saucepan, bring the water to a boil. Drain and rinse the rice and add it to the boiling water along with the lemon and orange zests and the salt. Cook over medium heat for 20 minutes. Add the milk, cinnamon sticks, cloves, cardamom, and sugar. Bring to a boil again and then reduce the heat to low. Simmer, stirring occasionally to prevent the rice from sticking, for 1 hour. It should be thick and creamy at this point; do not allow it to boil at any time during the cooking.

When the pudding is ready, remove from the heat and stir in the toasted almonds. Mix thoroughly and turn into a bowl. Top with the ground cinnamon. It can be served warm immediately, or later at room temperature or chilled.

Makes 6 servings.

Italy

In her respected *The Classic Italian Cookbook,* celebrated cook and culinary authority Marcella Hazan notes that Italian cooking doesn't really exist. There is no true national dish and the cuisine is incredibly varied from one end of the Boot to the other. Put simply, Italian food is defined by region, and the food found in Tuscany is quite distinct from that found in Lombardy, Emilia-Romagna, or Sicily.

This chapter is equally eclectic. It is a collection of recipes that I have encountered during my travels in Italy and in visits to the homes of Italian-American friends and acquaintances. Pasta and pizza are ubiquitous these days, so I have pretty much neglected them except to include a wonderful wild-mushroom cream sauce that I first had near Lake Como, a basic fresh tomato sauce, a pesto sauce, and an *al forno* pasta dish that I enjoyed at the home of a New York friend.

The recipes are mainly Italian wintertime dishes, hearty fare such as polenta, risotto, and baked pasta that deliver warm comfort on cold days. The reason for this is twofold: my travels in Italy have primarily been in the fall and winter months, and despite the fact that Italian cooking is highly seasonal, most cookbooks ignore these cool-weather dishes. Lastly, I have included a smattering of Italian desserts that are quite good and go well with almost any cuisine.

Suggested Menus

San Francisco Italian Dinner for Six

Much of the work for this menu can be done in advance. The polenta can be cooked early in the day, left to set, and then cut into pieces and broiled with the Gorgonzola just before serving. The cioppino can be cooked up to the point where the snapper and shrimp are added and then finished at dinnertime. Finally, the dessert must sit in the refrigerator for at least 6 hours before it can be unmolded, decorated, and served.

Grilled Polenta with Gorgonzola
Cioppino
Green Salad
Sourdough Bread
Tiramisù

Formal Winter Dinner for Four

The classic Italian meal has six courses, as does this menu. Some of the courses here must be made in advance, while others offer the cook an opportunity to assemble some portion of a dish earlier in the day, with just some last-minute cooking at the end. The mussels must be readied in advance, while the risotto must all be done just before serving. The pork tenderloin can be prepared up to the point where the cream is added and then finished in just about 8 minutes at dinnertime. The zucchini can be fully assembled earlier in the day and then be put in to bake when the risotto is served. From this point on, the meal is very easy to do, with just a salad, a cheese course, and a dessert. The salad, which is always very simple, is eaten after the main course and signifies the approaching end of the meal. The cheese course offers a nice transition—a chance to linger and rest for a bit. The dessert can be prepared in the morning and served at room temperature or reheated for 10 minutes in an oven preheated to 250 degrees F.

Marinated Mussels with Artichokes and Red Peppers

Mushroom Risotto

Pork Tenderloin with Capers and Prosciutto

Zucchini Gratin

Green Salad

Gorgonzola, Fontina, and Smoked Mozzarella with Crackers and Pear Slices

Baked Apples with Amaretti

Marinated Mussels with Artichokes and Red Peppers

3 lb mussels, well scrubbed and debearded

½ cup water or fish stock

4 red bell peppers, roasted (page 227)

1 can (13½ oz) artichoke hearts, drained

4 cloves garlic

¾ cup olive oil

juice of 4 lemons

1 tbs fresh oregano leaves

1 tbs fresh marjoram leaves

6 fresh basil leaves, chopped

salt to taste

black pepper to taste

Discard any mussels that fail to close to the touch. In a large saucepan, combine the mussels and water or fish stock and place over high heat. Cover, bring to a boil, and cook, stirring and shaking the pan occasionally, until the mussels open, about 5 minutes. Remove from the heat and discard any mussels that failed to open. Let cool.

Meanwhile, in a food processor, combine the roasted peppers, artichokes hearts, and garlic. Process until coarsely ground. When the mussels are cool enough to handle, remove them from their shells and place in a large bowl. Pour the olive oil over them and stir in the artichoke mixture. Mix well. Add the lemon juice and stir in the herbs, salt, and pepper. Cover and marinate in the refrigerator for 4 to 6 hours. Serve at room temperature.

Makes 6 servings.

Grilled Shrimp with Oil and Lemon

Gamberi al Ferri con Olio e Limone

2 lb shrimp in their shells

1 cup dried bread crumbs

1 tsp salt

½ cup olive oil

juice of 2 lemons, plus extra juice for serving

1 tbs black pepper

Soak a batch of round wooden toothpicks in water to cover for 5 minutes. Meanwhile, rinse the shrimp and remove the straggly feet but leave the shells intact. Pat dry with paper towels.

Drain the toothpicks. Run a toothpick through the entire length of each shrimp. This will prevent the shrimp from curling during grilling. In a large bowl, combine all the remaining ingredients, mixing well. Add the shrimp and mix well again with your hands to coat the shrimp completely. Cover and marinate for 1 hour at room temperature.

Meanwhile, light a fire in a charcoal grill. When the coals are medium-hot, remove the shrimp from the marinade and place over the coals. Grill for about 90 seconds per side. Serve with additional lemon juice for dipping.

Makes 6 servings.

Piedmontese Anchovy and Olive Oil Dip

Bagna Cauda

1 cup extra-virgin olive oil

4 tbs butter

4 cloves garlic, minced

12 anchovy fillets in olive oil, drained and minced

blanched vegetables

crusty Italian bread, cut into slices

Although the Piedmontese generally serve this with raw and blanched vegetables, I prefer just the blanched ones. I like to serve broccoli, cauliflower, carrots, and artichoke hearts, but feel free to mix vegetables to your taste and to match what is seasonally available. Although traditionally made and served in an earthenware pot, a fondue pot can be used for serving.

In a medium saucepan, heat the olive oil and butter over medium-high heat until the butter begins to foam, about 1½ minutes. Add the garlic and reduce the heat to low. Let the garlic sizzle for several seconds, but do not let it brown. Add the anchovies and cook, stirring frequently, until they dissolve, 2 to 3 minutes.

Transfer to a fondue pot and place over a tabletop alcohol or canned heat burner. Serve with the vegetables and bread for dipping.

Makes 8 servings.

Quick Minestrone

⅓ cup olive oil

2 onions, coarsely chopped

2 carrots, sliced on the diagonal

4 celery stalks, sliced on the diagonal

1 large zucchini, diced

1 cup shredded red cabbage

1 cup drained cooked small white (navy) beans

1 cup canned plum tomatoes, cut up, with their juices

2 cups chicken broth

½ cup orzo or other small pasta

salt to taste

½ tsp black pepper

A wonderful winter soup. I often add diced meats, especially ham or chicken, but it's great without them as well. Since this recipe calls for cooked beans (which often means canned), it prepares quickly.

In a large saucepan, heat the olive oil over medium-high heat. When it is hot, add the onions and saute until soft and golden, about 8 minutes. Add the carrots and celery and saute for another 2 minutes. Add the zucchini, cabbage, white beans, tomatoes with their juices, and the broth. Bring to a boil, add the orzo, and reduce the heat to low. Simmer, uncovered, until the vegetables and orzo are tender and the flavors are blended, about 20 minutes. Season with salt and pepper before serving.

Makes 4 servings.

Spinach-Anchovy Loaf with Roasted Red Pepper Puree

1½ lb spinach, stems trimmed and carefully rinsed

1 can (3½ oz) albacore tuna packed in water, drained and finely flaked

6 anchovy fillets in olive oil, drained and finely chopped

3 slices white bread, crusts removed

½ cup milk

2 eggs

½ cup grated Parmesan cheese

¼ cup dried bread crumbs

1 tbs fresh oregano leaves

2 tbs grated romano cheese

1 tsp ground nutmeg

juice of 1 lemon

¼ cup olive oil

Roasted Red Pepper Puree (page 210)

lemon wedges

I have been making this loaf for years and it has always been popular. You will need some cheesecloth to wrap it for cooking. The dish can be served warm or cold, and it makes a wonderful brunch or lunch dish as well, in which case it makes 6 servings. I serve it with a Spanish roasted red pepper sauce.

Bring a large pot of salted water to a boil, add the spinach, and cook, stirring as necessary, until tender, 3 to 5 minutes. Drain well and let cool. Once the spinach is cool enough to handle, squeeze out all the excess moisture. It is best to do this a handful at a time. Chop the spinach finely and place in a large mixing bowl.

Add the tuna and anchovies to the spinach and stir to combine. In a smaller bowl, soak the bread in the milk for 5 minutes. Break the eggs over the spinach and mix in with your hands. Wring the milk from the bread and break up the bread into smaller pieces. Discard the milk and mix the bread in with the spinach. Add the Parmesan, bread crumbs, oregano, romano cheese, and nutmeg. Mix thoroughly. Add the lemon juice and olive oil. Mix thoroughly. Lay a double thickness of cheesecloth about 2 feet long and 1½ feet wide on a countertop. Spread the spinach mixture over the middle of the cheesecloth, molding it into a loaf about 2 inches high and 5 inches wide. The loaf will be 10 to 12 inches long. Wrap it carefully in the cheesecloth. Tie the ends securely with additional narrow strips of cheesecloth. Set in a large saute pan and add water to cover.

Place over medium heat, bring to a slow, steady boil, and cook until the loaf is set, 35 to 40 minutes. Carefully remove the loaf from the pan and place on a wooden board. Let cool for 5 minutes and remove the cheesecloth. Serve sliced warm or cold with the pepper puree and lemon wedges.

Makes 10 to 12 servings.

Frittatas

Frittatas are open-faced Italian omelets that are wonderful fare for breakfast, brunch, lunch, or even dinner. I brown mine under the broiler, although many Italians slide them out of the skillet, flip them over, and brown the second side on the stove top. A good-quality nonstick heavy-bottomed skillet or an anodized aluminum pan works best. I vary the ingredients constantly, but here are two of my favorites.

Cheese Frittata

6 eggs

¼ tsp salt

½ tsp white pepper

⅓ cup milk

3 tbs butter

1 cup grated Parmesan cheese

¼ cup crumbled Gorgonzola cheese

2 tbs grated romano cheese

Preheat a broiler. In a bowl, beat the eggs until blended. Add the salt, pepper, and milk and mix well.

In a flameproof heavy-bottomed nonstick skillet, melt the butter over medium heat. As soon as it begins to foam, add the eggs. Tilt the pan gently to spread the eggs evenly over the bottom of the pan. Reduce the heat to low and cook for about 10 minutes until the eggs are beginning to set. Add the cheeses, mix them in gently with a fork, and cook until the bottom is nicely golden and the eggs are set, about 5 minutes longer.

Transfer the skillet to the broiler to brown the top of the frittata lightly, 1 to 2 minutes. Invert onto a plate and serve.

Makes 4 servings.

Mushroom and Spinach Frittata

½ lb spinach, stems trimmed and carefully rinsed

6 eggs

¼ tsp salt

½ tsp white pepper

⅓ cup milk

2 tbs olive oil

2 tbs butter

½ lb button mushrooms, thinly sliced

1 shallot, chopped

2 tsp Dijon mustard

1 tsp dried oregano

1 cup grated Parmesan cheese

2 tbs grated romano cheese

Preheat a broiler. Bring a saucepan of salted water to a boil, add the spinach, and cook, stirring as necessary, until tender, 3 to 5 minutes. Drain well and, when cool enough to handle, squeeze out excess water. Coarsely chop and set aside.

In a bowl, beat the eggs until blended. Add the salt, pepper, and milk and mix well.

In a flameproof heavy-bottomed nonstick skillet, heat the oil and butter over medium heat. When the butter foams, add the mushrooms and shallot and saute for 1 minute. Add the mustard, oregano, and spinach, mix well, and pour in the eggs. Tilt the pan gently to spread the eggs evenly over the bottom of the pan. Reduce the heat to low and cook for about 10 minutes until the eggs are beginning to set. Add the cheeses, mix them in gently with a fork, and cook until the bottom is nicely golden and the eggs are set, about 5 minutes longer.

Transfer the skillet to the broiler to brown the top of the frittata lightly, 1 to 2 minutes. Invert onto a plate and serve.

Makes 4 servings.

Cioppino

··

San Francisco Seafood Stew

3 cups fish stock or water

24 littleneck clams, well scrubbed

24 mussels, well scrubbed and debearded

2 lb squid, cleaned and cut into rings (page 227)

½ cup olive oil

2 onions, coarsely chopped

8 cloves garlic, minced

1 tbs fresh oregano leaves

1 tbs fresh marjoram leaves

2 tsp fresh thyme leaves

1 cup dry white wine

2 cups canned plum tomatoes, cut up, with their juices

1 lb red snapper fillet, with skin intact, cut into small pieces

1 lb shrimp, peeled and deveined

1 tsp salt

2 tsp black pepper

¼ tsp cayenne pepper

10 fresh parsley sprigs, chopped

San Francisco's early Italian immigrants, many of them fishermen, created this seafood stew in their new home. It is traditionally served with sourdough bread. Cleaning squid is quite a bit of work, so you can save time if you buy it already cleaned (it costs a bit more); you'll need about 1½ lb.

In a saucepan, bring the stock or water to a boil. Discard any clams or mussels that do not close to the touch and add to the pan along with the squid. Cook for 5 minutes until the clams and mussels open. Remove from the heat. Using a slotted spoon, remove all the shellfish from the pan. Discard any unopened clams or mussels. Select 6 clams and 6 mussels to leave in their shells for presentation. Shell the rest. Reserve the cooking liquid and set it aside with all the shellfish.

In a stockpot, heat the olive oil over medium-high heat. When it is hot, add the onions and saute until soft and golden, 6 to 7 minutes. Add the garlic and the herbs and saute for 1 minute. Add the white wine and let reduce for 30 seconds. Add the tomatoes with their juices, reduce the heat to low, and cook for 15 minutes. Add the squid and the shellfish cooking liquid—but not the other shellfish—to the pot and simmer for another 15 minutes.

Add the snapper and shrimp and simmer for 3 minutes. Add the reserved shelled and unshelled mussels and clams and mix well. Then add the salt, black pepper, cayenne pepper, and parsley, mixing well. Simmer for 2 minutes to blend the flavors, then serve at once.

Makes 6 servings.

Baked Penne

Penne al Forno

1 lb penne

1 tsp salt

3 cups Quick Tomato Sauce (page 73)

1 lb mozzarella cheese, shredded

1 cup grated Parmesan cheese

3 tbs grated romano cheese

Preheat an oven 400 degrees F.

Bring a large pot of salted water to a boil. Add the penne and cook until al dente, about 10 minutes. Drain, rinse under cold running water, and place in a large baking dish. Pour the sauce over the top and mix well. Stir in the mozzarella and half of the Parmesan and romano cheeses. Sprinkle the remaining cheeses over the top.

Bake until the cheese melts and the surface is browned, 25 to 30 minutes. Let cool for a few minutes before serving.

Makes 6 to 8 servings.

Pork Tenderloin with Capers and Prosciutto

3 tbs Dijon mustard

1 pork tenderloin, about 1¼ lb

¼ cup Worcestershire sauce

½ tsp salt

½ tsp white pepper

2 tbs olive oil

2 tbs butter

2 shallots, chopped

½ cup chicken broth

½ cup heavy cream

¼ cup capers

8 slices prosciutto, diced

In a large bowl, rub the mustard over the pork tenderloin. Be sure that you are spreading it evenly. Douse the tenderloin with the Worcestershire sauce. Cover tightly and marinate in the refrigerator for 1 hour.

Transfer the tenderloin to a cutting board. Cut into 8 equal slices. Season with salt and pepper. In a large skillet or saute pan, heat the olive oil and butter over medium heat. As soon as the butter foams, add the shallots and the pork tenderloin slices. Cook, turning once, until the meat is just soft to the touch, about 12 minutes total. Transfer to a plate.

With the pan still over medium heat, pour in the chicken broth and deglaze, stirring with a wooden spoon to dislodge any pork drippings. Cook for about 10 minutes, stirring often. The sauce will thicken. Add the cream, bring to a boil, and reduce the heat to low. Return the pork slices and any juices that have collected on the plate to the pan. Add the capers and prosciutto and cook over low heat until the pork is heated through, about 3 minutes. Serve the pork slices immediately with the sauce spooned over the top.

Makes 4 servings.

Italy • 67

Risotto Milanese

2 tbs olive oil

5 tbs butter

2 shallots, chopped

10 to 12 saffron threads

½ cup dry white wine

2 cups Arborio rice

5 cups chicken broth, at a gentle simmer

1 tsp white pepper

⅓ cup grated Parmesan cheese

4 fresh parsley sprigs, finely chopped

In a large saucepan, heat the olive oil and butter over medium-high heat. When the butter foams, add the shallots and saute for 1 minute. Add half of the saffron and 1 tbs of the white wine. Saute until the saffron diffuses its color and flavor, about 2 minutes. Add the rice and stir well to coat with the oil and butter, about 2 minutes.

Add the remaining wine, mix well, and reduce the heat to medium. Stirring often, allow the rice to absorb the liquid. Now add ½ cup of the simmering broth and cook, stirring often, until the liquid is absorbed. Add another ½ cup broth and again allow the rice to absorb it. Repeat in this manner until the rice is al dente, with each kernel slightly firm at the center. If you have used up all the broth and the rice is still not done, add hot water as needed. Midway through the process, add the remaining saffron along with the white pepper. When the rice is ready, gently mix in the cheese and let stand for a minute or two, then sprinkle with parsley and serve in a deep dish.

Makes 6 servings.

Mushroom Risotto

∙∙

Risotto al Funghi

1 oz dried porcini mushrooms, soaked in ½ cup warm water for 30 minutes

2 tbs olive oil

6 tbs butter

2 shallots, chopped

½ lb fresh Italian brown (cremini) mushrooms, sliced

10 to 12 saffron threads

2 cups Arborio rice

½ cup dry white wine

about 4 cups chicken broth, at a gentle simmer

½ cup heavy cream

1 tsp freshly ground white pepper

2 tbs grated romano cheese

⅓ cup grated Parmesan cheese

4 fresh parsley sprigs, finely chopped

Drain the porcini, reserving the water, and thinly slice them.

In a stockpot, heat the olive oil and butter over medium-high heat. When the butter foams, add the shallots and both kinds of mushrooms and saute for 1 minute. Add half of the saffron and 1 tablespoon of the white wine and saute until the saffron diffuses its color and flavor, about 2 minutes. Add the rice and stir well to coat with the oil, about 1 minute.

Add the remaining wine and the mushroom soaking water, mix well, and reduce the heat to medium. Stirring often, allow the rice to absorb the liquid. Now add ½ cup of the simmering broth and cook, stirring often, until the liquid is absorbed. Add another ½ cup broth and again allow the rice to absorb it. Repeat in this manner until the rice is almost al dente, with each kernel slightly firm at the center, then add the cream and cook until absorbed. If you have used up all the broth and the rice is still not done, add hot water as needed. Midway through the process, add the remaining saffron along with the white pepper. When the rice is cooked, gently mix in the cheeses and let stand for a minute or two, then sprinkle with parsley and serve in a deep dish.

Makes 6 servings.

Veal Scaloppini with Anchovies, Capers, and Pancetta

Scaloppine Piccanti

½ cup (¼ lb) butter

¼ lb pancetta, diced

8 anchovy fillets in olive oil, drained and coarsely chopped

¼ cup capers

1 cup all-purpose flour

½ tsp white pepper

½ tsp salt

½ tsp paprika

2 lb veal scallops, pounded flat

3 tbs olive oil

¼ cup dry vermouth

⅔ cup heavy cream

In a small skillet, melt the butter over medium heat. When it foams, add the pancetta, anchovies, and capers and saute for 2 minutes, mashing the anchovies with a wooden spoon. Remove from the heat and set aside.

In a paper bag, combine the flour, white pepper, salt, and paprika. A few at a time, add the veal scallops to the bag and shake vigorously for a few seconds to coat the veal. Tapping off any excess flour, transfer the coated scallops to a plate. Repeat until all the veal is coated. (Alternatively, mix together the flour and other ingredients on a plate and dredge the scallops in the mixture, again tapping off any excess.)

In a large skillet or saute pan, heat the olive oil over high heat. When it is hot, gently slip the veal into the oil, working in batches if necessary. Brown it nicely on both sides, about 1 minute on each side. Transfer the meat to a warmed platter; keep warm.

Reduce the heat to medium-low, add the vermouth, and deglaze the pan, stirring with a wooden spoon to dislodge any browned bits and incorporate all the juices. Add the pancetta mixture and raise the heat to medium. Add the cream and stir to combine. Let the sauce thicken slightly, 1 to 2 minutes. Remove from the heat and pour over the veal.

Makes 6 servings.

Pasta Sauces

Pasta is certainly ubiquitous in San Francisco, appearing seemingly on every menu of every restaurant. Here I've included just a few of my favorite sauces, all of them quite easy. The mushrooms in a marsala cream sauce is something I picked up when visiting Italy's beautiful Lake Como, and it's wonderfully aromatic. The classic fresh tomato sauce is delightfully smooth and different than typically heavy, long-cooked tomato sauces; don't skimp on the olive oil. The quick tomato sauce is a perfect companion to a hectic lifestyle, which is all too common these days. Pesto is a perennial favorite, and so easy to make it doesn't even require cooking, although you must use fresh ingredients. I have included only the sauce recipes, leaving the choice of pasta up to you. Most people have their own favorite pasta shapes, especially with certain sauces; and by varying the pasta you can create a new meal from an old sauce. I love fresh pasta, and the Bay Area has no shortage of places to buy it. But dried pasta, more often than not, is my reliable standby; it's always there when I need it, and the variety of shapes is unbeatable.

Mushrooms in a Marsala Cream Sauce

Funghi al Como

1 oz dried porcini mushrooms, soaked in ½ cup warm water or beef or chicken broth for 30 minutes

¼ cup olive oil

4 tbs butter

1 onion, finely chopped

1 shallot, finely chopped

4 cloves garlic, minced

1 lb fresh Italian brown (cremini) mushrooms, thinly sliced

2 tbs fresh marjoram leaves

1 tbs fresh thyme leaves

1 tsp fresh chopped rosemary

½ cup Marsala wine

1 cup heavy cream

1 tsp salt

white or black pepper to taste

1 tsp arrowroot (optional)

chopped fresh parsley (optional)

This sauce is rich and thick, with a wonderful aroma. It is suitable for any pasta, but try spooning it over ravioli, polenta, or gnocchi for a special meal.

Drain the porcini, reserving the water or broth, and thinly slice them. Set aside.

In a saucepan, heat the olive oil and butter over medium-high heat. When the butter foams, add the onion and shallot and saute for 1 minute. Add the garlic, mix well, and cook until the onion is soft and golden, about 5 minutes longer. Add both kinds of mushrooms, the fresh herbs, and the porcini soaking water. Stir well to coat the mushrooms with the oil and butter. Cook for 5 minutes, stirring often. Add the Marsala, cook for 1 minute, again stirring often. Reduce the heat to low and cook until the mushrooms are tender, about 3 minutes longer.

Pour in the cream and season with salt and pepper. Leave over low heat until the cream is heated through. If the sauce is too thin for your taste, remove ¼ cup of the liquid, dissolve the arrowroot in it, and stir the mixture into the sauce until it thickens slightly. Garnish with parsley, if desired.

Makes about 2 cups, enough for 4 servings.

Italian Tomato Sauces

The tomato was introduced to Italy in the sixteenth century by the Spanish, who at the time ruled most of southern Italy. It was not an instantaneous hit, and indeed it took well over two centuries to work its way into the daily repertoire of the Italian cook. Today, of course, Italy's "golden apple" is a popular base for all kinds of Italian sauces. Perhaps the most common tomato sauce in Italy combines olive oil, garlic, tomatoes, carrots, and celery. In contrast, the American palate seems to prefer heavy, long-cooked sauces, either a ragu (meat sauce) or a marinara sauce (highly seasoned meatless sauce).

Here are two recipes for simple basic tomato sauces. One is a fresh tomato sauce typical of Emilia-Romagna. The second is a quick sauce that calls for canned tomatoes, canned tomato sauce, and tomato paste, useful when relying on what you have in your cupboard.

Classic Fresh Tomato Sauce

2 lb ripe plum tomatoes, halved lengthwise

¼ cup water

1 carrot

2 celery stalks

2 tbs plus ½ cup olive oil

3 cloves garlic

1 onion, finely chopped

½ tsp salt

½ tsp sugar

½ tsp black pepper

6 fresh parsley sprigs

In a large saucepan, combine the tomatoes and water and place over medium heat. Bring to a steady simmer and cook, uncovered, for 10 minutes.

Meanwhile, cut the carrot in half crosswise, then split each half lengthwise into 4 sticks, dice, and set aside. Trim the celery, removing the bottom white part and any leaves. Reserve the leaves. Cut each stalk in half lengthwise, then dice. Combine the diced carrots and celery and set aside.

In a small skillet, heat the 2 tbs olive oil over medium-high heat. When it is hot, add the garlic and onion and saute for 1 minute. Add the diced vegetables and saute until they begin to soften, about 2 minutes. Remove from the heat and add to the cooked tomatoes.

Mix the salt, sugar, and pepper into the tomato mixture, stirring well. Then add the reserved celery leaves and the parsley sprigs and reduce the heat to low. Continue to cook, uncovered, until all the vegetables are very tender, about 20 minutes. Remove from the heat and remove and discard the celery leaves and parsley sprigs.

Pass the tomato mixture through a food mill placed over a clean saucepan. (Alternatively, puree in a blender or food processor and pass through a sieve or colander lined with cheesecloth; in this case, it's preferable to seed the tomatoes before cooking.) Add the ½ cup olive oil and place over low heat. Bring to a gentle simmer and cook for 15 minutes to blend the flavors. Taste and adjust the seasonings.

Makes about 3 cups.

Quick Tomato Sauce

2 tbs olive oil

1 onion, chopped

3 cloves garlic, minced

1 tsp dried oregano

½ tsp dried marjoram

1 can (15 oz) tomato sauce

1 can (14½ oz) stewed tomatoes,
  diced, with juices

½ tsp salt

1 can (6 oz) tomato paste

¼ cup milk

¼ tsp white pepper

In a saucepan, heat the olive oil over medium-high heat. When it is hot, add the onion and saute for 1 minute. Add the garlic, oregano, and marjoram and saute until the onion is soft and golden, about 5 minutes longer. Add the tomato sauce, stewed tomatoes and juices, and salt and bring to a boil. Stir in the tomato paste, mixing well to incorporate it fully. Cook for 5 minutes. Add the milk and white pepper, mixing well. Cook for 1 minute longer and serve.

Makes about 3 cups.

Variations: Add 6 Italian sausages, left whole or coarsely chopped, when you add the garlic and herbs. Cook until the sausage is browned completely before adding the tomato sauce. Or add 1 lb fresh button mushrooms with the garlic and cook for 3 minutes before adding the tomato sauce. Or soak ¼ cup sun-dried tomatoes in water to cover for 5 minutes, drain, thinly slice, and add with the onion, then proceed as directed.

Pesto

Genoese Basil, Pine Nut, and Olive Oil Sauce

4 cups firmly packed fresh basil
  leaves

1 cup extra-virgin olive oil

⅓ cup pine nuts, toasted (page 227)

4 cloves garlic, crushed

2 tsp salt

1 cup grated Parmesan cheese

3 tbs grated romano cheese

True pesto can only be made in northwestern Italy where a short-leaf variety of basil flourishes. Although traditionally made in a marble mortar, a blender works just fine and is quicker. Pesto is wonderful over all types of pasta, both hot and cold. This recipe makes enough for 12 servings of pasta and will keep well in the refrigerator for about 1 month. Just be sure to cover the surface with a thin film of olive oil so that it will not darken. Pesto also freezes well, but you should not add the cheese until you are ready to use it.

In a blender or small food processor, combine the basil, half of the olive oil, pine nuts, garlic, and salt. Process on low speed to chop coarsely. Remove the blender lid, increase the speed to the puree setting, and slowly drizzle in the remaining olive oil. Cover the blender and increase the speed to liquefy for a few seconds, then turn it off. Using a rubber spatula, scrape down the sides of the container, mixing together all of the contents. Re-cover and run at high speed for a few seconds. Turn off again and again scrape down the sides with the rubber spatula, mixing well. Pour into a bowl and stir in the grated cheeses just before serving.

Makes about 3 cups

Rose Pistola's Gnocchi with Calamari Bolognese

1 lb fresh potato gnocchi

6 oz cleaned squid

¼ cup extra-virgin olive oil, plus extra for drizzling

2 cloves garlic, lightly crushed

¼ cup chopped onion

2 tbs chopped fresh parsley

2 tsp anchovy paste

1 tsp harissa, homemade (page 161) or purchased

1 cup tomato sauce

¼ cup dry white wine

salt to taste

black pepper to taste

In San Francisco's North Beach, chef Reed Hearon's always-busy Rose Pistola restaurant serves light, fluffy potato gnocchi with this slightly spicy sauce. The North African chili-based seasoning known as harissa is what delivers the heat. Look for freshly made potato gnocchi at a reliable Italian delicatessen or make your own from a favorite recipe.

Bring a large saucepan of salted water to a boil. Add the gnocchi and boil gently until tender. They will float when they are ready.

Meanwhile, pass the squid through a meat grinder fitted with a coarse plate. (Alternatively, grind coarsely in a food processor.) In a saucepan, heat the olive oil over medium-high heat. Add the garlic, onion, parsley, anchovy paste, harissa, and ground squid and cook, stirring, until the squid has rendered its liquid, a few minutes. Add the tomato sauce and white wine and cook, stirring, until the mixture is reduced by one-third.

When the gnocchi are ready, drain and add to the squid mixture. Continue to cook, stirring, until the gnocchi have absorbed the remaining liquid, about 1 minute. Season with salt and pepper, remove from the heat, and drizzle on a little more olive oil. Serve immediately.

Makes 4 to 6 servings as an appetizer.

Fennel with Parmesan

Finocchio

3 large or 4 medium fennel bulbs

6 tbs butter

1 shallot, chopped

2 cloves garlic, minced

1 tsp dried thyme

½ tsp salt

3 tbs grated Parmesan cheese

Fennel, called finocchio in Italian, has a broad bulbous base, long stalks, and feathery foliage. It may be eaten raw or cooked and has a sweet, aniselike flavor.

Trim away the stalks and leaves (reserve the leaves for flavoring another dish, such as Sicilian Artichokes and Zucchini in Garlic Sauce on page 76) and the base of the core from each fennel bulb. Then cut the bulbs lengthwise into ½-inch-thick slices.

In a large skillet or saute pan, melt the butter over medium heat. When it foams, add the shallot and garlic and saute for 1 minute. Add the thyme and the fennel slices, mixing well to coat the slices with the butter. Add the salt along with water just to cover. Cover the pan and cook for 30 minutes. Every 5 minutes, uncover the pan and give the contents a good stir. After 30 minutes, uncover and cook for 5 minutes to evaporate some of the liquid. Remove from the heat and transfer to a warmed platter. Sprinkle with the cheese.

Makes 4 servings.

Green Beans with Pancetta and Pine Nuts

Fagiolini Verde con Pancetta e Pinoli

2 tbs butter

1 tbs olive oil

1 onion, finely chopped

salt to taste

2 tbs fresh marjoram leaves or
   1 tsp dried marjoram

¼ lb pancetta, diced

½ lb green beans, ends trimmed

½ cup pine nuts, toasted (page 227)

3 tbs balsamic vinegar

In a large skillet or saute pan, melt the butter with the olive oil over medium-high heat. When the butter foams, add the onion, salt, marjoram, and pancetta. Mix well and cook for 1 minute, stirring often. Reduce the heat to medium, add the green beans, and continue to cook, stirring often, until the vegetables are cooked but still crunchy, 3 to 5 minutes.

Remove from the heat and add the pine nuts, then douse with the vinegar. Mix well, transfer to a platter, and serve warm.

Makes 4 servings.

Sicilian Artichokes and Zucchini in Garlic Sauce

Frittedda

2 cans (15 oz each) artichoke hearts, drained

1 tbs lemon juice

½ cup olive oil

8 cloves garlic, minced

1 red onion, chopped

2 tbs fresh oregano leaves

2 zucchini, thinly sliced

1 lb peas, shelled

2 cups cooked shelled fava beans

1 cup fresh fennel leaves, chopped

½ cup dried bread crumbs

¼ cup grated Parmesan cheese

½ tsp paprika

Preheat an oven to 350 degrees F.

In a bowl, place the artichoke hearts and douse them with the lemon juice. Stir to coat and set aside.

In a large skillet or saute pan, heat the olive oil over medium-high heat. When it is hot, add the garlic, onion, and oregano and saute for 1 minute. Add the zucchini, mix well, and cook for 2 minutes, stirring often. Add the peas, cooked fava beans, and fennel leaves and stir well. Reduce the heat to low and cook for 3 minutes. Remove from the heat and transfer to a baking dish. Mix in the artichoke hearts.

In a small bowl, stir together the bread crumbs, cheese, and paprika. Sprinkle evenly over the top. Bake until the top is browned and the vegetables are tender, about 20 minutes. Serve at once.

Makes 6 to 8 servings.

Baked Zucchini

Zucchini Gratin

2 large zucchini, thinly sliced

3 tbs butter, cut into 6 pieces

2 tbs olive oil

½ onion, chopped

2 tomatoes, peeled and chopped

1 tbs fresh oregano leaves or ½ tsp dried oregano

⅓ cup grated Parmesan cheese

1 tablespoon grated romano cheese (optional)

Preheat an oven to 400 degrees F. Lightly oil the bottom and sides of a medium baking dish.

Bring a saucepan of salted water to a boil, add the zucchini, and boil for 2 minutes. Drain and transfer to the prepared baking dish. Stir the butter pieces into the zucchini, mixing well to melt them.

In a skillet, heat the olive oil over medium-high heat. When it is hot, add the onion and tomatoes and saute for 1 minute. Add the oregano and cook until the onion is soft, about 4 minutes longer. Pour over the zucchini and then stir in to mix well. Sprinkle the top evenly with the Parmesan cheese and the romano cheese, if using.

Bake until the cheese is browned and the contents are bubbling, 12 to 15 minutes. Serve at once.

Makes 4 servings.

Basic Polenta

7 cups water or chicken broth

1 tbs salt

2 tbs butter

2 cups polenta

Polenta is another recent arrival in Italy, again having traveled there from the New World. It is mostly eaten in northern Italy, especially in Lombardy, Piedmont, and the Veneto. There are two basic types: fine grain and coarse grain. Both are available in markets, although coarse grain is generally more readily available. I have recently been experimenting with a quick cooking, fine-grained polenta that takes only about 7 minutes to cook; it's an incredible time saver if you can find some. In order to cook polenta correctly, you must stir the pot continuously. Once cooked, it can be eaten in two ways: it can be consumed as is, perhaps with some cheese stirred in or a sauce ladled over the top, or it can be poured into a baking pan, allowed to cool and set, cut into pieces as desired, and then fried or grilled.

In a heavy saucepan, bring the water or broth to a boil. Add the salt and butter and reduce the heat to medium-low. Add the polenta in a slow, steady stream while stirring constantly with a sturdy wooden spoon. Continue to cook at a steady simmer, stirring continuously, for 20 minutes. You may need to adjust the heat every now and again to maintain the simmer. The polenta is done when it pulls away from the sides of the pan as you stir, and it no longer has a grainy taste. To serve, see the head note for suggestions.

Makes 6 to 8 servings.

Polenta with Gorgonzola

1 recipe basic polenta (see above)

olive oil

3 oz Gorgonzola cheese, at room temperature

Prepare the polenta as directed in the previous recipe and pour into a shallow baking pan or dish. Spread to create an even layer. It should be about ½ inch thick. Let cool completely until firm.

Preheat a broiler. Cut the polenta into 2-by-4-inch pieces. Lightly brush both sides of each piece with olive oil. Spread one side of each piece with a little Gorgonzola cheese and place cheese side up on a greased baking sheet. Broil until the cheese is lightly browned and the polenta is heated through, 2 to 3 minutes. Serve hot.

Makes 6 to 8 servings, 10 to 12 as an appetizer.

Tiramisù

2 cups brewed espresso, cooled

½ cup superfine sugar

¼ cup coffee liqueur (Kahlúa or similar)

¼ cup Marsala wine

1 package (7 oz) lady fingers

2 egg yolks

1 lb mascarpone cheese

4 oz semisweet chocolate, shaved

Topping:

1 cup heavy cream

¼ teaspoon pure vanilla extract

2 tbs confectioners' sugar

2 oz semisweet chocolate, shaved

This dessert, which translates from the Italian as "pick-me-up," has become ubiquitous in San Francisco's Italian restaurants. It is rather expensive to make because of the high cost of mascarpone cheese, and some restaurants cut corners by mixing in some ricotta cheese with its more pricy kin. This recipe calls for unmolding the cake onto a serving platter before adding the topping, but for an informal presentation you can add the topping while the tiramisù is still in the pan—which you don't have to line—and then scoop out servings.

Line a 9-by-5-inch loaf pan with waxed paper. Be sure to crease the bottom perfectly. If you have an identical pan, slip it inside the first pan and press down gently to create a perfect fit. Lightly butter the waxed paper. Place the pan in the refrigerator until needed.

In a large shallow bowl, stir together the espresso, superfine sugar, liqueur, and Marsala until the sugar dissolves. Scoop out ⅓ cup of this mixture and set aside.

Remove the prepared pan from the refrigerator. One at a time, dip the lady fingers into the espresso mixture remaining in the bowl (do not oversoak them; just a quick dip will do), and arrange them in a single layer in the bottom of the pan, cutting them to fit where necessary.

When the layer is finished, in a bowl, combine the reserved ⅓ cup espresso mixture and the egg yolks. Whisk to blend. Add the mascarpone and fold in gently just until blended. Do not overmix or you will break the consistency of the cheese. Spoon half of this mixture over the layer of lady fingers in the pan. Sprinkle with half of the shaved chocolate. Now dip the remaining lady fingers in the espresso mixture remaining in the bowl and arrange on top of the chocolate layer, again cutting as necessary to fit. Spoon the remaining cheese mixture over the top, and then scatter on the remaining chocolate. Cover and refrigerate for 6 to 8 hours.

Just before serving, uncover the loaf pan and carefully invert onto a serving plate. Lift off the pan and gently peel off the waxed paper.

To make the topping, in a bowl, whip the cream with the vanilla and confectioners' sugar until soft peaks form. Decorate the cake with the whipped cream and sprinkle with the chocolate.

Makes 8 servings.

Apple Fritters

5 pippin or Granny Smith apples

½ cup superfine sugar

3 tbs dark rum

1 tbs amaretto or Frangelico (hazelnut liqueur)

1 tsp grated lemon zest

1 cup all-purpose flour

½ tsp salt

1⅓ cups water

corn oil for frying

confectioners' sugar

Peel and core the apples, then cut into slices ⅓ inch thick. In a bowl, stir together the superfine sugar, rum, liqueur, and lemon zest. Add the apple slices and stir to coat evenly. Set aside for 1 hour.

In another bowl, sift together the flour and salt. Add the water and whisk well to form a batter.

In a skillet, pour in oil to a depth of ½ inch and place over medium-high heat. When the oil is hot, working quickly in batches, pat the apples slices dry with paper towels and then slip them into the batter. Remove with a slotted spoon, allowing excess batter to drip back into the bowl, and then slip the slices into the hot oil. Fry until golden brown on both sides, 2 to 3 minutes on each side. Using the slotted spoon, transfer to paper towels to drain. Sift confectioners' sugar over the top and serve warm.

Makes 6 servings.

Baked Apples with Amaretti

8 pippin or Granny Smith Apples

10 packages amaretti (see head note)

½ cup (¼ lb) butter, at room temperature

½ cup superfine sugar

2 tsp ground cinnamon

1 cup dry vermouth

1 cup water

vanilla ice cream (optional)

Amaretti are Italian macaroons with an almond flavor. They are often sold wrapped two to a package, under the label Lazzoroni.

Preheat an oven to 400 degrees F.

Using an apple corer or a vegetable peeler and starting from the stem end, core each apple to within about ⅓ inch of the base, forming a cavity about ½ inch in diameter. Then peel a ribbon of skin off the top ½ inch of each apple.

Open 6 packages of the cookies, and crush the 12 amaretti cookies into coarse pieces. Place in a bowl and add the butter and sugar. Using your hands, mix them together to distribute the ingredients evenly. Divide the mixture into 8 equal portions and stuff a portion into the cavity of each apple. Sprinkle the cinnamon on the tops of the apples, dividing it evenly.

Stand the apples upright in a baking pan or dish. Pour the vermouth and water into the bottom of the pan. Bake until the apples are tender when pierced, about 50 minutes. Remove from the oven and transfer the apples to individual serving plates.

Pour the liquid that remains in the baking pan or dish into a small saucepan and reduce over high heat until a syrup forms. Pour it over the apples, dividing it evenly. Serve the apples warm or at room temperature, each with a package of amaretti. They also go extremely well with a scoop of vanilla ice cream.

Makes 8 servings.

Caramel Pears

6 Bosc or Anjou pears

1 tbs lemon juice, if needed

2 lb chocolate caramels

¼ cup rum

2 tbs sambuca

⅔ cup blanched almonds, finely chopped

½ cup semisweet chocolate chips

fresh mint leaves

The pears may be peeled or left unpeeled. In either case, cut a thin slice off the bottom of each one so it will stand upright on a plate. If you do peel them, place them in a bowl with water to cover, adding the lemon juice to prevent discoloration. Set aside.

In the top pan of a double boiler placed over rapidly boiling water in the lower pan, combine the caramels, rum, and sambuca. As soon as the caramels begin to melt, reduce the heat to low. As they melt, stir occasionally with a wooden spoon. Once they are fully melted, remove from the heat but keep the top pan over the bottom pan so that the caramel will stay soft and pliable.

Line a baking sheet and a platter with waxed paper. Mix together the almonds and chocolate chips on the prepared baking sheet. One at a time, roll the pears in the caramel sauce, coating completely and using a spoon to help maneuver the fruit. Then transfer them, bottom down, to the almond-chocolate mixture. Sprinkle a bit of the mixture around the top of each pear. As each pear is done, transfer it to the lined platter. Let stand for 1 hour until the caramel has set.

To serve, transfer to individual plates and garnish with mint leaves.

Makes 6 servings.

Amaretto Souffle

4 eggs, separated, plus 1 egg white

⅔ cup sugar

1 tbs Cointreau or Grand Marnier

5 tbs amaretto

½ tsp cream of tartar

Preheat an oven to 400 degrees F. Butter and sugar a 1½-quart souffle dish. Set aside in a cool spot.

In a bowl, combine the egg yolks and sugar. Whisk together until the yolks are a pale yellow. Add both liqueurs and mix well.

In another bowl, using an electric mixer or a clean whisk, beat the 5 egg whites with the cream of tartar until the whites hold stiff peaks. Using a rubber spatula, stir about one-fourth of the egg whites into the yolk mixture to lighten it, then gently fold in the remaining whites just until no white streaks remain. Pour into the prepared dish.

Bake until a toothpick inserted into the center of the souffle comes out clean and the top has risen nicely, 20 to 25 minutes. Serve at once.

Makes 4 servings.

Japan

Perhaps nowhere else is food as revered an art form as it is in Japan. From the techniques of preparation to the presentation to the consumption, Japanese cuisine transcends the commonplace. It is actually a very simple, almost austere cuisine, born of the isolation and agricultural poverty of the Japanese islands. It has but three main components: dashi, a stock made from dried bonito and kelp; shoyu, a light soy sauce; and *gohan,* the gift of the gods, the ubiquitous rice. From these modest beginnings, the Japanese elevate their cooking to dazzling heights.

Sushi is an excellent example of the soaring nature of the cuisine. It is nothing more than vinegared rice shaped into a bite-sized piece, flavored with a touch of wasabi (green Japanese horseradish), topped with a slice of fresh fish, and sometimes wrapped with a bit of nori (dried seaweed). You dip it in soy sauce that is perhaps spiced with a bit more wasabi. It is indeed simple, but anyone who has seen a platter of sushi knows how hauntingly beautiful an array of several different kinds can be.

Yes, it is food practiced as art, but the key to its success is freshness. The availability of fresh fish makes or breaks sushi. It should almost never be attempted with frozen fish, the few exceptions to the rule including saba (pickled mackerel) and unagi (broiled freshwater eel), both of which are usually sold frozen in Japanese markets.

Or consider the Japanese reverence for noodles *(menrui).* The noodle broth must be perfectly clear and not overseasoned. It must also be piping hot, but it must not have come to a boil. Just a nice slow simmer. If fresh noodles are used, they should be made that very day.

Given this simplicity, I find it remarkable that people will readily go out for a Japanese meal but hesitate to make one at home. I suspect they fear the inability to replicate the beauty of Japanese food. Actually, the only trick to Japanese cuisine is familiarizing yourself with Japanese ingredients. Granted, the Japanese place great importance on the presentation and you should, too. Be creative, though, even if it means not following tradition. You might also consider investing in Japanese serving bowls and platters. That alone will enhance your presentation.

The recipes in this section focus on the two aspects of Japanese cooking that are the most suitable for re-creating in the Western kitchen. The first looks at the basics of the cuisine: the soups, noodle dishes, and pickles. The second is a detailed account on how to make a sushi dinner at home.

Suggested Menus

A Formal Japanese Dinner for Four

A formal Japanese dinner consists of an appetizer, a clear soup, and raw fish at the start of the meal; a main course of something grilled, something simmered, something fried, and a dressed salad; and then boiled rice, miso soup, some pickles, tea, and fruit. Of course, just small amounts of each dish are prepared. Nevertheless, such an extensive menu can be overwhelming. For my version of a formal Japanese dinner I have eliminated the fried food and the miso soup. The appetizer is a light and flavorful marinated tofu that my good friend Jeff Samberg introduced me to at a local restaurant. It must be drained carefully to remove excess moisture and marinated overnight, but in truth it is a simple dish to prepare. The soup is also light, and the amount served is barely a cupful. The sashimi course is one that can be omitted if you wish, but I find any sashimi a delight. The main course consists of steamed fish with buckwheat noodles, a burdock root salad, grilled Japanese eggplant, plain white rice, and some pickles. The pickles need to be made in advance or, failing that, you can purchase them. For dessert, fresh fruit is the ideal choice.

Marinated Tofu

Clear Soup with Shrimp

Sea Bream Sashimi

Wasabi, Pickled Ginger, Miso Sauce

Sea Bass Steamed with Cha-Soba Noodles

Gobo with Sesame Seed Dressing

Grilled Eggplant

White Rice

Pickles

Fresh Peaches or Pears

Tea

Sushi Party for 12

See page 95 for the menu and the directions for preparing this sushi feast.

Marinated Tofu

1½ lb Japanese-style soft tofu

½ cup soy sauce

¼ cup honey

1-inch-piece fresh ginger, peeled and grated

1 tbs mirin

¼ cup sesame seeds, toasted (page 227)

½ cup all-purpose flour

2 tbs corn oil

1 tsp dried bonito flakes

3 green onions, thinly sliced

This dish is similar to one served at Gombei Japanese restaurant in Menlo Park, California.

Drain the tofu and cut into ½-inch-thick slices. Place the tofu on a platter or shallow dish and place a paper towel over it to absorb any excess moisture. Leave the towel on for 1 hour, then turn the tofu over and place another paper towel over it. Again leave for 1 hour.

Meanwhile, in a small bowl, mix together the soy sauce and honey. Press all the juice out of the grated ginger and add to the soy mixture. Then add the mirin and mix well. Pour the soy mixture over the tofu, cover, and refrigerate overnight. Spoon the marinade over the tofu occasionally as it marinates.

In a suribachi or other mortar, grind the toasted sesame seeds just enough to break them down (but not into a paste). Mix with the flour. Remove the tofu slices from the marinade, reserving the marinade, and dust them in the flour-sesame mixture.

In a skillet, heat the corn oil over medium-high heat. When it is hot, add the tofu slices and fry, turning once, until golden brown on both sides, about 2 minutes on each side. Place in a warm oven. Pour the reserved marinade into a small pan and boil for 5 minutes to reduce slightly. Serve the tofu on a small plate drizzled with the marinade and topped with bonito flakes and green onions.

Makes 4 servings.

Grilled Shiitakes

12 fresh shiitake mushrooms, stems removed

7 tbs soy sauce

5 tbs lemon juice

2 tbs rice vinegar

1 tsp mirin

3 green onions, sliced

If the recipe for Marinated Tofu seems too time-consuming, serve this quick appetizer.

Light a fire in a charcoal grill.

In a bowl, marinate the shiitakes in 2 tbs of the soy sauce for 10 minutes. Remove from the marinade and place bottom side down over hot coals. Grill for 2 minutes, then turn and grill for 2 minutes on the second side.

Meanwhile, in a small bowl, mix together the remaining 5 tbs soy sauce, lemon juice, rice vinegar, and mirin to form the sauce. Allow 3 mushrooms per person and pour one-fourth of the sauce over each serving. Sprinkle the green onions over the mushrooms and serve.

Makes 4 servings.

Basic Dashi

6 cups water

2-inch-square konbu

3 tbs dried bonito flakes

Dashi is a central flavoring agent of Japanese cooking. You can buy dashi-no-moto, a tea-bag stock infusion, as well as hon-dashi, granules that you dissolve in hot water, but most brands contain monosodium glutamate (msg). For those who care to make their own stock without msg, here's the recipe. Keep your kitchen well ventilated; the fish smell is strong.

In a medium saucepan, bring the water to a boil. Add the konbu and the bonito flakes and reduce the heat to low. Simmer, uncovered, for 30 minutes. Strain before using.

Makes about 5 cups.

Miso Soup

4 cups Basic Dashi (preceding)

¼ cup red miso

3 fresh shiitake mushrooms, stems removed and caps cut into narrow strips

4 fresh trefoil (mitsuba) sprigs, coarsely chopped

2 green onions, thinly sliced

¼ cake (3 to 4 oz) Japanese-style soft tofu, cut into small cubes

½ tsp shichimi

Miso is made from crushed soybeans combined with wheat, rice, or barley along with a yeast mold that ferments the miso. Several different varieties are available. This recipe calls for red miso, one of the more common varieties, but you can use any kind you wish.

In a medium saucepan, slowly bring the dashi to a simmer. It should not boil. Once it is simmering, remove ¼ cup and dissolve the red miso in it. Stir well, perhaps with a fork or a whisk to blend completely. Set aside.

Add the mushrooms, trefoil, green onions, and tofu to the simmering dashi. Add the reserved miso to the soup and stir well. Simmer briefly, no more than 3 minutes. Sprinkle the shichimi over the top and serve.

Makes 4 servings.

Clear Soup with Shrimp

8 medium shrimp, peeled and
    deveined

1 tsp arrowroot

2 cups water

1 green onion

1 small piece wakame seaweed,
    soaked in warm water to cover
    for 20 minutes and drained

2 tbs coarsely chopped watercress

4 cups Basic Dashi (page 85)

1 tbs light soy sauce

sansho or shichimi (optional)

Dredge the shrimp in the arrowroot. In a saucepan, bring the water and green onion to a boil. Add the shrimp and boil until they just turn pink and curl, about 3 minutes. Drain and reserve the shrimp. Cut the wakame seaweed into small, thin strips and toss gently with the shrimp. Add the watercress and mix gently. Set aside.

In a medium saucepan, bring the dashi to a gentle simmer. Add the soy sauce and simmer for 3 minutes. Place 2 shrimp in each bowl along with some of the wakame and watercress. Carefully pour 1 cup of the dashi over the shrimp. Sprinkle with sansho or shichimi, if desired.

Makes 4 servings.

Udon or Soba Noodles in Broth

1 recipe Basic Dashi (page 85)

2 tbs sugar

3 tbs light soy sauce

2 tbs soy sauce

2 tbs mirin

cooked udon or soba noodles for 6
    (see head note)

4 green onions, chopped

This recipe can be used for both soba and udon noodles. Udon are white wheat-flour noodles; soba are thinner and made primarily from buckwheat flour. Udon are often sold precooked in vacuum packs, while soba are almost exclusively sold dried. Whichever you use, follow the directions on the package for cooking them before adding them to the soup; the package should also tell you how much to use per person. They should be fully cooked but still rather firm.

The cooked noodles, along with some broth, are served most commonly with thin slices of cooked pork, finely chopped green onion, and perhaps a tsukemono (a Japanese pickle). There are many other possible additions: an egg, either hard-boiled and sliced or added raw to the broth; chicken; tempura; or a slice or two of fish cake. Simple but quite stunning when assembled.

In a large saucepan, heat the dashi almost to a boil. Add the sugar, soy sauces, and mirin. Reduce the heat to low. Add the cooked soba or udon noodles. Continue to simmer until the noodles are heated through, about 2 minutes. Serve garnished with the green onions.

Makes 6 servings.

Sashimi

When you serve sashimi, three elements must be emphasized. First, the fish must be fresh. It should have been bought that day and must never have been frozen. Second, the garnishes are an integral part of the dish and great care should be employed in their preparation and presentation. Third, the condiments that accompany the sashimi should be varied and nicely presented.

Many kinds of fish are suitable for sashimi, but the most readily available are red tuna (maguro), sea bream (tai), flounder (hirame), yellowtail tuna (hamachi), and sea bass (suzuki). Of these, sea bream and flounder are the least expensive. A serving size is 4 to 6 pieces. Each piece is fairly thin, no more than ⅜ inch thick, and about 1 inch long. There are four ways to slice sashimi, although the most common are the flat cut and the diagonal cut, which are just what they sound like: the flat cut is mostly for softer flesh fish such as sea bream, while the diagonal cut allows thin slicing of firmer fish such as tuna.

Sashimi should be served on a small plate along with a few garnishes. The most common garnishes are wasabi (Japanese green horseradish), shredded daikon radish, and shredded carrot. Technically, the wasabi is a condiment, but it may be placed on the plate with the sashimi. You can also arrange the wasabi in a small bowl for all to share. Other condiments are pickled ginger, which is typically store bought, and tosa soy sauce, ponzu sauce, and a miso sauce, for which recipes follow.

Sea Bream Sashimi

1¼ lb sea bream

¼ cup shredded daikon

1 carrot, shredded

4 fresh trefoil (mitsuba) or watercress sprigs

wasabi and pickled ginger for serving

Slice the sea bream thinly across the grain in pieces than are no more than 1 inch long and ¾ inch wide. Each slice should be about ⅜ inch thick. Arrange on small plates and decorate with the shredded daikon, shredded carrot, and the trefoil or watercress sprigs. Serve with wasabi, shoga, and at least one of the following sauces.

Makes 4 servings.

Tosa Soy Sauce

¼ cup sake

¼ cup mirin

2-inch-square konbu

2 cups soy sauce

½ cup tamari

¼ cup dried bonito flakes

Although this sauce can be used immediately, it tastes best if allowed to age for at least 1 month before eating—store it in a cool, dark place—and it keeps for about a year.

In a small saucepan, mix together the sake and mirin. Bring to a boil. Add the konbu and reduce the heat to low. Add the soy sauce and the tamari, stir well, and add the bonito flakes. Simmer for 2 minutes.

Remove from the heat, let cool, and then let stand for 24 hours. Strain the liquid before using.

Makes about 3 cups.

Ponzu Sauce

1 cup lemon juice

⅓ cup rice vinegar

1 cup soy sauce

¼ cup mirin

2-inch-square konbu

4 tbs dried bonito flakes

Like the Tosa Soy Sauce, this sauce is ideally aged for at least a month, but this is an overnight version.

In a saucepan, combine all the ingredients and bring to a boil. Reduce the heat to low and simmer for 2 minutes.

Remove from the heat, let cool, and then let stand for 24 hours. Strain and use immediately, if desired, or allow to age (see head note) in a cool, dark place.

Makes about 2 ½ cups.

Miso Sauce

3 egg yolks

1 cup white miso

3 tbs sake

1 tsp mirin

1 tsp sugar

⅔ cup water

3 tbs rice vinegar

In a bowl, lightly beat the egg yolks, then mix in the miso. Add the sake, mirin, and sugar. Blend well and add the water and the vinegar.

In the bottom pan of a double boiler, bring water to a boil. When the water is boiling, transfer the miso mixture to the top pan and stir until it thickens, 2 to 3 minutes. Remove from heat and let cool completely.

Makes about 1 cup.

Chicken Teriyaki

Teriyaki sauce:

½ cup sake

½ cup soy sauce

½ cup mirin

1 tbs sugar

2 lb skinless, boneless chicken leg and thigh meat

2 cloves garlic, finely minced

¼-inch-piece fresh ginger, peeled and finely minced

½ cup teriyaki sauce

1 tbs corn oil

1 tsp ground sansho pepper

1 tsp sesame seeds

You can use bottled teriyaki sauce, but I prefer to make my own.

To make the sauce, in a medium saucepan, combine all the ingredients. Bring to a boil, stirring to dissolve the sugar. Reduce the heat to low and simmer for 1 minute. Remove from the heat. It is ready to use immediately, but it will keep in the refrigerator indefinitely. Makes about 1½ cups.

Cut the chicken meat into long strips, and pierce with a fork on both sides. In a bowl, combine the chicken, garlic, ginger, and 2 tbs of the teriyaki sauce. Mix well and let stand for 15 minutes.

In a large skillet, heat the corn oil over medium-high heat. When it is hot, add the chicken strips and brown evenly on all sides, 8 to 10 minutes; stir with a wooden spoon to prevent it from sticking or burning. Transfer the chicken to a plate, but leave the juices in the skillet. Add the remaining 6 tbs teriyaki sauce to the skillet and bring to a boil. Stir well and reduce the heat to low. Allow to reduce and thicken slightly for about 1 minute. Return the chicken to the skillet and heat until cooked through, about 5 minutes, stirring often to completely coat the chicken with the sauce. Remove from the heat. Serve garnished with the sansho and sesame seeds.

Makes 4 servings.

Sea Bass Steamed with Cha-Soba Noodles

···

*1⅓ lb sea bass fillet, cut into 4
equal pieces*

salt to taste

½ tsp ground sansho pepper

½ lb dried cha-soba noodles

¼ cup sake

2 cups Basic Dashi (page 85)

¼ cup mirin

¼ cup soy sauce

1 cup dried bonito flakes

*1 sheet nori, toasted briefly over a
gas flame or electric burner and
shredded*

2 green onions, finely chopped

*4 fresh trefoil (mitsuba) or
watercress sprigs*

For this dish you will need 4 large heatproof Japanese rice bowls with covers. The dishes are set in a pan of simmering hot water, and the fish steams for about 10 minutes. Alternatively, you could use souffle dishes. Don't worry too much about the covers; you will use plastic wrap to seal the bowls anyway. The covers are for table presentation. Finally, the dish is served with a warm dashi-based sauce and garnished with shredded toasted nori, green onions, and trefoil.

Season the fish with salt and sansho. Set aside. Boil the cha-soba noodles according to package directions. Drain and rinse the noodles.

Place a piece of fish in each bowl. Arrange an equal amount of noodles in a mound around each piece of fish. Add 1 tablespoon sake to each bowl. Cover tightly with plastic wrap.

In a large baking pan, pour in water to a depth of about 2 inches. Bring to a simmer on the stove top. Place the bowls in the water and steam for 10 minutes.

While the fish is steaming, make the sauce: In a saucepan, combine the dashi, mirin, and soy sauce. Bring to a boil and add the bonito flakes. Reduce the heat to low and simmer for 1 minute. Strain the liquid.

When the fish is ready, remove the plastic wrap and add about ½ cup of the sauce to each bowl. Sprinkle some shredded nori and green onion over the top. Garnish each dish with a trefoil or watercress sprig. Top with the lids and serve.

Makes 4 servings.

Grilled Eggplant

4 Japanese eggplants

¼ cup Asian sesame oil

4 tsp peeled and grated fresh ginger

2 lemons, cut into quarters

soy sauce

Light a fire in a charcoal grill. Oil the grill rack.

Rub the whole eggplants with the sesame oil, covering them completely. Place on the grill rack over hot coals and grill, turning as needed, until the skin is evenly charred, about 15 minutes. Remove from the grill and plunge into cold water. Peel off the charred skin, and make 4 long cuts in each eggplant, turning them into fans. Serve with the ginger, lemons, and soy sauce for sprinkling over the top.

Makes 4 servings.

Spinach Salad

4 quarts water

salt to taste

1 tbs rice vinegar

3 large bunches spinach, stems trimmed and carefully rinsed

6 cups Basic Dashi (page 85)

⅓ cup mirin

½ cup light soy sauce

1 cup dried bonito flakes

In a large saucepan, bring the water, salt, and vinegar to a rapid boil. Drop in the spinach and boil for 2 minutes. Drain and rinse with cold water. Let cool.

Meanwhile, in a medium saucepan, combine the dashi, mirin, and soy sauce. Bring to a boil and reduce the heat to low. Simmer for 5 minutes and remove from the heat. Let cool.

Pour the cooled dashi mixture over the cooled spinach. Cover and refrigerate overnight. Just before serving, add the dried bonito flakes.

Makes 6 servings (12 servings as a light appetizer).

Gobo with Sesame Seed Dressing

....

6 cups water

4 tbs rice vinegar

1 tsp lemon juice

4 burdock roots

1½ cups plus 2 tbs Basic Dashi (page 85)

2 tbs mirin

3 tbs light soy sauce

1 tsp tamari

5 tbs sesame seeds, toasted (page 227)

1 tbs sugar

Gobo, also known as burdock root, looks like a long brown twig or stick and is quite delicious, albeit a fair bit of work to prepare. A word of caution, however: gobo discolors quickly, so have ready the bowl of water with vinegar and lemon juice mixed in before you start working with the gobo.

In a bowl, combine 4 cups of the water, 1 tbs of the vinegar, and the lemon juice. Scrub the burdock roots, but do not peel. Pound them with a mallet so that they flatten out. Cut each root into 2-inch-long pieces and drop the pieces into the water mixture. Let stand for 1 hour.

Drain the roots and rinse under cold running water. Place in a medium saucepan with the remaining 2 cups water and bring to a boil. Reduce the heat to low and simmer for 5 minutes. Drain and place in a bowl with cold water to cover. Set aside.

In a medium saucepan, combine the 1½ cups dashi, the mirin, light soy sauce, and tamari. Bring to a gentle simmer. Drain the burdock and add it to the simmering mixture. Simmer for 5 minutes. Remove from the heat and let cool.

Meanwhile, in a suribachi or mortar, grind the toasted sesame seeds (in a suribachi, you should be able to make a paste; in a mortar, just break down the seeds). Add the sugar, the remaining 3 tablespoons rice vinegar, and the remaining 2 tbs dashi. Drain the burdock roots, discarding the liquid, add it to the suribachi or mortar, and pound with the pestle to ensure the dressing penetrates the root. Transfer the mixture to a bowl, cover with plastic wrap, and refrigerate overnight. Serve in small amounts.

Makes about 6 servings.

Boiled White Rice

∙∙

Gohan

1½ cups short-grain white rice

2½ cups water

1 tsp salt, or to taste

The Japanese are arguably the world's fussiest people when it comes to rice, with regard both to the quality of the rice itself and the rules for preparing it. Today, of course, most Japanese simply use a rice cooker.

About 1 hour before cooking, rinse the rice in cold water several times until the water is clear rather than milky white. Let drain in a colander for 1 hour.

Place the drained rice, water, and salt in a saucepan that has a tight-fitting lid. Bring to a boil over medium-high heat. Once it starts to boil, turn up the heat to high. The lid will start to clank, but do not uncover. Reduce the heat to low and cook until all of the water has been absorbed and the rice is tender, 15 to 20 minutes. Remove from the heat and do not uncover for another 20 minutes.

Makes 4 servings.

Sushi Rice

∙∙

10 cups short-grain rice

12 cups water

2 tbs salt

1½ cups rice vinegar

2½ cups sugar

Wash the rice carefully in running water and drain. Place it in a large stockpot with the water and salt. Bring to a boil, cover, and reduce the heat to medium-low. Cook until the rice is tender and the water is absorbed, about 30 minutes. Let cool slightly.

In a pitcher, stir together the vinegar and sugar until the sugar dissolves. Turn the rice out onto a large tray or wooden bowl. While gently turning the rice with a wooden paddle, slowly pour the vinegar mixture over the surface. Ideally, you will have someone fanning the rice as well, so that it cools more quickly and absorbs the vinegar mixture better. Be careful not to crush the kernels as you turn the rice. Let cool completely before using. Store at room temperature covered with a moist towel to keep the rice grains from hardening.

Makes about 20 cups rice.

Mixed Pickles

2 cucumbers, peeled and cut into
  eighths

1 onion, cut into quarters and
  layers separated

1 small cauliflower, cut into bite-
  sized florets

1 small daikon, sliced

2 cups sugar

⅔ cup rice vinegar

¼ cup kosher salt

2 cups boiling water

This recipe needs to be prepared a day in advance of serving.

Place all the vegetables in a large bowl. Mix the sugar, vinegar, and salt in a metal bowl or heatproof glass bowl. Pour the boiling water into the vinegar mixture and stir to dissolve the sugar and salt. Pour the liquid over the vegetables. Let cool, then transfer to a glass jar, cover, and refrigerate overnight before serving.

Makes about 6 cups.

Pickled Cabbage

¼ head white cabbage

5 cups rice vinegar

2 tbs kosher salt

5 tbs sugar

2 cups water

While Koreans are the kings of the pickled cabbage realm, the Japanese do have a number of similar dishes. This is a simple one.

Break apart the cabbage into chunks. Place inside a 6-cup glass jar (a sterilized mason jar would be ideal). Combine all the remaining ingredients in a saucepan and bring to a boil, stirring to dissolve the salt and sugar. Remove from the heat and let cool.

Pour the cooled liquid over the cabbage in the jar. Cover tightly and store in a cool, dark place for 72 hours before serving. Refrigerate to store longer than 72 hours.

Makes about 4 cups.

A Sushi Party for Twelve

One my favorite dinner parties is to invite a dozen or so people, have them bring some fish for sushi, and then have everyone make their own nigiri sushi and makisushi. From experience I have found it useful to tell each guest how much and what kind of fish to bring. Otherwise you might end up with a boatload of tuna. I generally make the sushi rice the night before, and then the day of the party I prepare the soup and a dessert. For this menu, I have chosen a spinach salad, which needs to be prepared the night before, but you could serve Grilled Eggplant (page 91) instead. The dessert of oranges infused with Cointreau can be found in the Moroccan chapter (page 170). These parties have always been rather amusing, for I find people enjoy eating their own creations.

Miso Soup
Spinach Salad

Nigiri Sushi:
Maguro, Saba, Unagi, Ebi, Tako, Sake,
Hamachi, Tobiko, Ikura, Hirame

Makisushi:
California Rolls, Cucumber Rolls, Shiitake Rolls

Wasabi
Pickled Ginger

Macerated Oranges

Sake
Japanese Beer
Green Tea

Preparation Schedule for Sushi Party

Sushi equipment:

3 wood or marble boards

3 pairs of scissors

3 damp towels

3 bowls of water

3 to 6 rice paddles

3 to 6 sushi rolling mats

3 to 6 sharp knives

12 soy dipping bowls

12 small plates

toothpicks or small skewers

Sushi condiments:

wasabi

pickled ginger

soy sauce

Sushi foodstuffs:

1 recipe sushi rice

36 medium shrimp

½ lb pickled mackerel (saba)

½ lb broiled eel (unagi)

4 dried shiitake mushrooms

1 can (6 oz) crabmeat

1 Japanese cucumber

2 ripe avocados

3 packages (¾ oz each) nori sheets

2 packages (½ oz each) conical nori

1 lb red tuna (maguro)

¾ lb yellowtail (hamachi)

¼ lb boiled octopus (tako)

½ lb cured salmon (sake)

5 oz flounder (hirame)

2 ounces flying fish roe (tobiko)

2 ounces salmon roe (ikura)

Note that you will have to adjust the portions of some of the listed recipes to feed a party of 12: Plan on tripling the Miso Soup recipe (page 85), doubling the Spinach Salad recipe (page 91), and doubling the Macerated Oranges recipe (page 170). The following lists outline what you will need for the sushi part of the meal; these items are over and above what's called for in the menu's other recipes.

The Day Before the Party

Prepare the sushi rice (page 93). Store at room temperature under a moist towel.

Prepare the dashi (page 85). For the miso soup and the spinach salad, a total of 18 cups of dashi will be needed, 12 cups for the miso soup and 6 cups for the spinach salad.

Once the dashi is prepared, the spinach salad (page 91) should be started, as it needs to sit overnight.

Chill the pickled ginger.

Prepare the shrimp. The shrimp must be skewered or toothpicked before cooking so that they will not curl when they are boiled. Simply run the skewer or toothpick down the middle of the shrimp from the head to the tail. Boil the shrimp for 3 minutes in lightly salted water. Drain and immerse in a bowl of cold water. Do not remove the skewers or the toothpicks until you are ready to butterfly them. Leave the shrimp in the cold water for 2 minutes, then drain. Chill in the refrigerator.

If using frozen saba and unagi, transfer to the refrigerator to thaw.

The Day of the Party

About 3 hours before your party, gently mix the sushi rice and discard any hardened kernels.

Butterfly the shrimp: Remove the skewer or the toothpick. Remove the shells but leave the final tail segment in place. Run a sharp knife along the bottom side of the shrimp beginning at the tail and working your way to the head. Gently separate the halves so that the shrimp flattens out. Clean out the veins. Refrigerate until ready to use.

About 2 hours before the party, remove the saba and the unagi from their packaging. Allow to come to room temperature.

Set and decorate your table. You will need at least three sushi making stations. Each station should have a wooden or marble board, a pair of scissors (to cut the nori to desired sizes), a sharp knife, a rice paddle, a sushi mat, a damp towel (to clean the knife and the board), and a small bowl of water.

About an hour before your party, marinate the shiitakes in soy sauce to cover for 1 hour. If you want the mushrooms less salty, dilute the soy sauce with 2 tbs of water.

Shaping Sushi

Nigiri sushi is easy to make: In the palm of your hand, form a clump of sushi rice into an appropriately sized and shaped "pad." Don't worry, as there is no right or wrong way or size. At the same time, be careful not to pack the rice too firmly. Smear the top of the pad with a bit of wasabi, and lay a slice of fish on it.

Making makisushi (rolls) requires a bit more technique. The following pointers should help.

Use a half sheet of nori (cut crosswise) to make 1 roll.

Place the nori shiny side down on the sushi rolling mat with the longer sides facing you.

Spread a thin layer of rice over the nori, extending it to the edges on three sides but leaving 1½ to 2 inches nori uncovered on the end farthest from you (the top). You will be rolling toward this uncovered edge.

Place your filling(s) across the rice parallel to the top edge. The filling(s) should be placed 1 inch in from the edge closest to you.

Lift the bottom edge of the mat, making sure that the bottom section wraps around the filling(s) before it is tucked under.

Use one hand to pull the bottom edge of the mat toward the top of the nori sheet and the other hand as a guide to keep it rolling directly onto itself.

Remove the mat. Slice the roll crosswise into 4 equal pieces. The rice should be evenly distributed around the core.

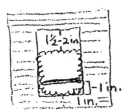   

The Day of the Party (continued)

Remove the spinach salad from the refrigerator and divide into individual portions. Set out on the table.

Open the canned crab. Drain and place in bowls. Peel the cucumber, halve, seed, and cut into thin spears. Set out on the table. Also set the avocados out with the crab, but do not cut them. You can peel and cut them as needed during the party.

About 30 minutes before the party, start to simmer the dashi for the miso soup (page 85).

If you are mixing wasabi from a powder, prepare it according to package directions. Place a bowl of pickled ginger at each sushi station. Set out the soy sauce, the sushi rice, and the nori.

About 15 minutes before the party, set out the fish. Divide among the various sushi stations and leave some room for the fish brought by your guests.

Reheat the unagi: follow package directions or place under broiler or in a hot oven for 3 to 5 minutes.

Continue with the preparation of the miso soup.

Drain the shiitake mushrooms. Remove and discard the stems. Cut the caps into narrow strips. Place at sushi prep stations.

When your first guests arrive, show them how to cut the fish, make individual sushi pieces, and make rolls. They can then teach others.

Serve the miso soup first. Sit back and enjoy your party.

Latin America

Latin America is arguably the world's greatest melting pot. The locals provided avocados, beans, maize (corn), chilies, tomatoes, tomatillos, yuca root (cassava or manioc, not the desert cactus), potatoes and other tubers, quinoa, and peanuts. The European conquerors brought beef, rice, citrus fruits, olive oil, and saffron. Africans came with bananas and plantains. Asia provided, first in trade, seasonings such as cilantro, cinnamon, cloves, cumin, mace, nutmeg, sugarcane, and turmeric. Later, with the limited Chinese and Japanese migration of the mid-nineteenth century, came ginger and soybeans. The result is quite a stew.

You will find Latin American food as varied as any in the world. While beans, corn, plantains, potatoes, rice, and yuca form the mainstay of local diets, the combination of these with chilies, cheese, cilantro, salsas, or coconut milk makes for a sumptuous feast. Beyond the wonderful flavors of the region's cuisines, what appeals to me most are the colors. Consider the bright yellow of Peru's *papa a la Huancaina,* the deep brown of Mexico's *pollo en mole poblano,* the vivid green of Guatemala's *pollo en pipián de almendra verde,* or the rich red of Chile's *congrio en fuente de barro.*

This chapter includes dishes from various countries in Latin America, with a particular concentration on the foods of Mexico, Colombia, and Peru. Mexican cuisine perhaps doesn't need much of an introduction, given its popularity in the United States. But it does go beyond the offerings of taquerias. Try making mole poblano—it is not that hard and you'll be amazed how good chocolate tastes in savory food.

Colombian food is a mixture of European, African, and native Indian. But it is also a mixture of tropical products such as yuca or plantains and Andean products such as potatoes or the tubers known as ullucos. While snacks are often fried, the more prominent dishes of Colombian cuisine are soups and stews. Colombians also eat plain white rice daily, although perhaps not to the extent that Asians do. Still, there is a rice porridge that Antioqueños often have for breakfast. Usually, though, rice is an accompaniment to a soup or stew.

Peruvian culinary tradition is heavily native Andean. Quinoa, potatoes, corn, and chilies are main components of the daily fare. A common spice in Peru is palillo, which is increasingly available in Bay Area Latin markets. It turns everything yellow, and Peruvians use it liberally. Turmeric, which doesn't have the same flavor but nevertheless imparts a yellow color, is an acceptable substitute.

Chili peppers are native to the Americas and play an important role in Latin American cooking. The more important ones are fresh Anaheims, Fresnos, habaneros, jalapeños, pasillas, poblanos, and serranos. While Bay Area markets offer more chili peppers than most markets elsewhere in the United States, I still find I have to adjust what I cook to which are seasonally available. Study the section on chilies (page 242) so you can substitute appropriately depending on what is in the market. Dried chilies are also frequently used. Among the most comon are anchos, cayennes, and New Mexicos.

One feature common to all Latin America is a love of rich, sugary desserts. *Flán de leche,* part of the Spanish inheritance, is perhaps the most common and best known sweet. Another beloved classic is *manjarblanco* or *dulce de leche,* a luscious, caramel-like paste. Requiring a copious amount of milk and a large copper vat, it is beyond the abilities of home cooks. You can find prepared versions in some Latin American markets, however. *Jalea de guayaba,* or guava paste, is another dessert item generally found in Latin markets. Serve it with slices of cotija cheese.

Suggested Menus

A Regional Mexican Meal for Four

Guacamole must be made at the last minute, but the tomatillo salsa can be made in advance. Both the soup and the chicken mole require a large amount of chicken broth, so prepare your chicken the day before according to the Stewed Chicken recipe on page 112. In order to have enough broth for both dishes you will have to prepare three chickens, or you can purchase broth. The mole sauce can also be prepared ahead of time, although you will need to have the broth on hand. The flán should be made in advance. The amaranth is a last-minute item but requires little effort. Although no recipe is given, a Caesar salad goes well with the main course. Do not forget that Caesar salad is actually a Mexican dish, created by a chef in Tijuana named Cesar.

Guacamole

Tomatillo Salsa

Tortilla Chips

Tortilla Soup

Oaxacan Chicken Mole

Amaranth with Corn and Beans

Flán de Leche

A Tropical Sampler for Four

This is an easy-to-do menu. The Shredded Flank Steak is the most time-consuming dish, but if you boil the flank steak the night before, the rest of the work should not take you more than 1¼ hours.

Venezuelan Avocado Soup

Shredded Flank Steak (Ropa Vieja)

Coconut Rice

Cuban Yuca in Lemon-Garlic Sauce

Swiss Chard with Onion and Tomato

Hearts of Palm Salad

Guava Paste and Cotija Cheese

An Andean Sampler for Six

The chicken on this menu is not a dish for the faint of heart. It is one of the spiciest concoctions I know. If you prefer a milder dish, make the Chilean sea bass instead. The ceviche requires at least 2 hours marinating time, but it can be made the night before. The peanut soup is relatively easy, although it does require chicken broth. The potato cakes are a last-minute item requiring frying. The flán is best made the night before serving.

Peruvian Ceviche
Ecuadorean Peanut-Potato Soup
Peruvian Spicy Chicken
Quinoa with Walnut Sauce
Ecuadorean Potato Cakes
Flán de Leche

A Bogotá Sunday Dinner for Eight

Ajiaco de pollo, Bogotá's celebrated chicken and potato stew, is not an easy dish to make. It requires advance preparation, including the laborious task of peeling a large number of potatoes. Two essential ingredients are hard to find. The herb known as guascas is available only freeze-dried and rarely encountered. The papa criolla is a marble-sized potato that is often available in Latin markets, either frozen or in cans. I prefer it frozen. Despite these difficulties, this is a most elegant dish and your guests will love the various accompaniments that go into it. Both the hot sauce and the avocado sauce can be prepared right before serving, especially if you have all the ingredients prepped. The chicken broth and the dessert should be made the day before. From that point, the meal will take another couple of hours, but most of that time is taken up by the unsupervised cooking of the soup. In Colombia, this meal would be served with curuba juice, but fresh curubas are not exported from Latin America due to their delicate flesh. Frozen curuba pulp is almost impossible to find outside of Miami and Jackson Heights, Queens. Do not be put off by the elaborate preparations. I grew up eating Sunday meals just like this and the result is worth your labor.

Bogotá's Potato-Chicken Stew
Colombian Hot Sauce
Colombian Avocado Sauce
Capers and Cream
Sweet Mamey

Fresh Salsa

· ·

Salsa Fresca

12 plum tomatoes, coarsely chopped

2 red serrano chilies, finely diced

2 green jalapeño chilies, finely diced

2 green onions, thinly sliced

½ yellow or red onion, finely diced

8 fresh cilantro sprigs, finely chopped

4 fresh parsley sprigs, finely chopped

¼ cup red wine vinegar

salt to taste

black pepper to taste

In a bowl, combine the tomatoes, chilies, green onions, and yellow or red onion. Stir well. Add the cilantro, parsley, vinegar, salt, and pepper and mix gently.

Makes about 3 cups.

Tomatillo Salsa

· ·

Salsa de Tomatillos

1 dried chili such as ancho or New Mexico

2 tbs olive or corn oil

2 lb tomatillos, husked

1 pasilla or poblano chili

2 jalapeño chilies

6 cloves garlic

1 onion, quartered

8 fresh cilantro sprigs, chopped

¼ cup water

salt to taste

black pepper to taste

First roast the dried chili. If you have a gas stove, just hold the chili in the flame for a couple of minutes, turning to roast all sides. Otherwise, roast in your oven at 450 degrees F for 10 minutes. Let cool, then break into pieces. You can roast the fresh chilies if you like (page 227), but for this salsa I generally don't.

In a large skillet, heat the oil over medium heat. When it is hot, add the tomatillos, fresh chilies, garlic, and onion. Cook until the tomatillos are soft and pale green, about 20 minutes. Add the dried chili, cilantro, and water. Season with salt and pepper. Simmer for about 5 minutes longer. Remove from the heat and puree in a food processor or blender.

Makes about 2 cups.

Mango-Chili Sauce

Salsa de Mango

3 mangoes

¼ cup water

1 tsp sugar

1 Fresno chili, seeded and diced

1 habanero chili, seeded and diced

2 green onions, thinly sliced

½ red onion, diced

½ cup distilled white vinegar

3 fresh cilantro sprigs, chopped

Serve with grilled fish or meats.

Peel, pit, and coarsely chop 2 of the mangoes. Peel, pit, and slice the remaining mango. Place the sliced mango in the blender with the water and sugar. Liquefy, then pour into a bowl and add the chopped mangoes. Add the chilies, green onions, and red onion and mix well. Stir in the vinegar. Add the cilantro just before serving.

Makes about 1 cup.

Colombian Hot Sauce

Ají Pique

1 plum tomato, finely diced

3 serrano chilies, seeded and finely diced

1 Fresno chili, seeded and finely diced

3 fresh cilantro sprigs, chopped

3 fresh parsley sprigs, chopped

3 green onions, thinly sliced

¼ cup water

½ cup distilled white vinegar

1 tsp sugar

1 habanero chili, seeded and finely diced (optional)

2 or 3 dashes of Tabasco sauce (optional)

This hot sauce must be made right before serving.

In a bowl, combine the tomato, chilies, cilantro, parsley, and green onions. Mix well. Add the water and the vinegar and then stir in the sugar. If you would like a hotter sauce, add the habanero or Tabasco.

Makes about 1 cup.

Colombian Avocado Sauce

Ají de Aguacate

3 large ripe avocados, pitted and peeled

2 Fresno or serrano chilies, seeded, if desired, and finely diced

5 fresh cilantro sprigs, finely chopped

2 green onions, finely chopped

juice of ½ lemon or 1 lime

salt to taste

This sauce is the classic accompaniment to Bogotá's Potato-Chicken Stew (page 109).

In a bowl, mash 2 of the avocados to a thick paste. Cube the remaining avocado and combine with the mashed ones. Add the chilies, cilantro, green onions, lemon or lime juice, and salt and mix well.

Makes about 2 cups.

Andean Spicy Peanut Sauce

Pipián de Maní

6 fresh cilantro sprigs

4 fresh parsley sprigs

4 green onions, cut up

2 Fresno chilies, seeded

1 habanero chili, seeded

3 tbs brown sugar

¼ cup lemon juice, or as needed

1 tbs peanut oil

½ cup soy sauce, or more as needed

Tabasco sauce to taste (optional)

2 cups crunchy peanut butter

While the peanut is now popular throughout the world, it is indigenous to South America. In Ecuador and southern Colombia, it is commonly used in a sauce for barbecued cuí, the Andean guinea pig. Other than in pet stores, guinea pig is not readily available in the Bay Area, but chicken and rabbit go quite well in this sauce. Marinate chicken, rabbit, or even pork for at least 15 minutes or, preferably, up to overnight before grilling. Skewer right before grilling. Reserve some of the sauce to serve as an accompaniment with dinner.

In a food processor, combine the cilantro, parsley, green onions, and chilies and process until coarsely chopped. Add the brown sugar, lemon juice, peanut oil, and soy sauce. Add the Tabasco sauce if you want an extra kick and process for a few seconds. Add the peanut butter in two batches, processing each time until it is incorporated. Add additional lemon juice and soy sauce if the sauce is too thick.

Makes about 2 cups.

Guacamole

....

Mexican Avocado Sauce

4 large avocados, pitted and peeled

2 tomatoes, finely diced

1 shallot, finely diced

2 serrano chilies, seeded and finely diced

6 fresh cilantro sprigs, finely chopped

juice of ½ lemon

salt to taste

Tabasco sauce to taste

Mole *is the Nahuatl word for "sauce" or "mixture."* Guaca *is derived from the Nahuatl word* ahuacatl, *which means "testicle."*

In a bowl, mash the avocados to desired consistency. (I like chunks in my guacamole, but others prefer a puree.) Add the tomatoes, shallot, and chilies. (You can add red onion or even a yellow onion, but you only need about 1 tbs finely diced onion. You can substitute jalapeños for a milder guacamole or habaneros for a hotter one.) Mix well. Add the cilantro, mix again, and stir in the lemon juice. Season with salt and Tabasco to taste. If you are not serving immediately, leave 2 avocado pits in the mixture and add an extra 2 tsp lemon juice.

Makes about 3 cups.

Appetizers and Salads

Chicken in Spicy Peanut Sauce

Pollo en Maní

1 recipe Andean Spicy Peanut Sauce (facing page)

3 lb boneless chicken

salt to taste

black pepper to taste

1 dried New Mexico chili

½ cup tamarind water (page 227), heated

2 tbs peanut oil

½ onion, diced

3 cloves garlic, thinly sliced

2 serrano chilies, seeded and diced

2 tsp ground cumin

juice of 2 limes

Light a fire in a charcoal grill, or preheat an oven to 400 degree F.

Have the peanut sauce ready. Season the chicken meat with salt and pepper. Cut into long strips about ½ inch wide and 2½ inches long; set aside. Soak the chili in the warm tamarind water for 10 minutes to soften, then drain, reserving the water.

In a small skillet, heat the peanut oil over medium heat. When it is hot, add the onion, garlic, serrano chilies, the softened chili, and cumin and saute until the onion is soft and golden, about 8 minutes. Remove from the heat and transfer to a food processor or blender. Process to blend, then add the reserved tamarind water, the lime juice, and the peanut sauce. Whirl to mix. Pour over the chicken, cover, and marinate overnight in the refrigerator.

Thread the chicken onto skewers. Grill over a hot charcoal fire for about 3 to 4 minutes on each side, or bake in the oven for 15 minutes.

Makes 6 to 8 servings.

Empanadas

....

Pastry dough:

4 cups all-purpose flour

2 tsp baking powder

1 tsp salt

2 cups (1 lb) butter, cut into 1-inch squares

⅔ cup ice water

Filling:

½ cup raisins

1/4 cup dry white wine

3 cloves garlic

2 tsp capers

8 pimiento-stuffed green olives, minced

1 tsp ground cumin

2 tbs olive oil

2 onions, finely chopped

1 lb ground beef

salt to taste

white pepper to taste

1 tbs fresh oregano leaves or 1 tsp dried oregano

Worcestershire sauce to taste (optional)

3 white potatoes, cooked, peeled, and cubed

16 black olives, pitted

2 eggs

1 tsp water

Empanadas are originally from Galicia in northwestern Spain, but they are now common throughout Latin America. There are, however, many variations among Latin American empanadas. Some are made with wheat flour, others with corn flour. In Argentina and Chile, they are large and baked, with one or two serving as a main dish. In Colombia, they are smaller and fried. They fall into the category of street food or appetizers. In Venezuela, empanadas are similar to Colombian ones only they are baked. This recipe is from Chile. If you are short of time, buy premade empanada wrappers in a Latin American market (they are usually in the freezer section).

To make the pastry dough, in a large bowl, sift together the flour, baking powder, and salt. Add the butter squares and work them into the flour mixture with a pastry blender or 2 knives. Slowly add the ice water, working it in to form a dough. Knead well by hand or by using the dough hook on a stand mixer. Transfer to a flour-dusted board and knead until smooth. Wrap in plastic wrap and refrigerater for 1 hour before using.

To make the filling, in a small bowl, soak the raisins in the white wine. In another small bowl, mash together the garlic, capers, and green olives. Mix in the cumin.

In a large skillet, heat the olive oil over medium heat. When it is hot, add the onions and the mashed garlic mixture and saute until the onion is soft, about 5 minutes. Add the ground beef, season with salt and white pepper, and add the oregano. Stir well. Season with Worcestershire sauce, if desired. Stirring constantly to prevent sticking, cook until the meat is almost browned, about 5 minutes or so. Add the potatoes, raisins, and wine. Mix well and continue to cook for another 5 minutes. Remove from the heat and let cool for 20 minutes.

Preheat an oven to 350 degrees F.

Place the dough on a floured board and divide into 16 equal balls. Roll out each ball into a 6-inch round. Place a few tbs of the beef mixture in the center of each round, leaving a 2-inch border around the edges, and top the filling with a black olive. Fold in half to form a half moon. The mixture inside will spread out a bit. Then lift the edge of the dough and fold the edge back over itself along the edge. With your fingers or a fork, press down along the edges to seal. Place on a lightly greased baking sheet or pan. Repeat until all the empanadas are formed.

In a small bowl, beat the eggs with the water. Brush this mixture over the tops of the empanadas. Bake until golden brown, about 20 minutes. Serve hot from the oven.

Makes 16 empanadas; 8 servings.

Ecuadorean-Style Ceviche

Ceviche Ecuatoriano

1½ lb red snapper fillet

10 oz bay scallops

juice of 6 limes

juice of 4 lemons

1-inch-piece fresh ginger, peeled and finely grated

salt to taste

32 large shrimp, peeled and deveined

½ tsp prepared horseradish

3 dashes of Tabasco sauce

¼ cup ketchup

½ red onion, finely diced

2 jalapeños, seeded and finely diced

2 green onions, finely chopped

4 plum tomatoes, finely diced

7 fresh cilantro sprigs, finely chopped

7 fresh parsley sprigs, finely chopped

¼ cup olive oil

2 cups popped popcorn

Ecuadorean ceviche includes tomatoes, which sets it apart from its Peruvian kin, plus it is served with popcorn. This dish is one I enjoyed with friend Jeff Samberg in Quino's Restaurant in Otavalo.

Cut the red snapper into small pieces about 1 inch long and ½ inch wide. Combine with the bay scallops in a nonreactive bowl. Pour the citrus juices over the fish and scallops. Add the ginger and season with salt.

Cook the shrimp in boiling water for 3 minutes. Drain, rinse with cold water, and add to the fish and scallops. Cover and refrigerate for at least 2 hours or preferably overnight.

Just before serving, in a small bowl, mix together the horseradish, Tabasco sauce, and ketchup. Stir well and add to the ceviche. Add the red onion, chilies, green onions, and tomatoes and mix well. Mix in the cilantro and parsley and stir in the olive oil. Serve cold with the popcorn.

Makes 8 servings.

Peruvian-Style Ceviche

Ceviche Limeño

1 lb red snapper fillet

½ lb bay scallops

juice of 10 limes

1-inch-piece fresh ginger, peeled
and finely diced

salt to taste

24 large shrimp, peeled and
deveined

2 jalapeño chilies, seeded and
finely diced

2 green onions, thinly sliced

5 fresh cilantro sprigs, finely
chopped

5 fresh parsley sprigs, finely
chopped

3 tbs olive oil

saltine crackers

In Peru, ceviche is marinated in pure lime juice and then the various other ingredients are added. It is the acid in the lime juice that "cooks" the fish by altering its texture.

Cut the red snapper into small pieces about 1 inch long and ½ inch wide. Combine with the bay scallops in a nonreactive bowl. Pour the lime juice over the fish and scallops. Add the ginger and season with salt.

Cook the shrimp in boiling water for 3 minutes. Drain, rinse with cold water, and add to the fish and scallops. Marinate for at least 2 hours or preferably overnight.

Just before serving, add the jalapeños, green onions, cilantro, and parsley and stir well. Mix in the olive oil. Serve cold with saltine crackers.

Makes 6 servings.

Hearts of Palm Salad

1 head butter lettuce, leaves
separated

1 can (14 oz) hearts of palm,
drained and rinsed

1 roasted red pepper, cut into
long, narrow strips (page 227)

½ cup olive oil

3 tbs distilled white vinegar

½ tsp Dijon mustard

juice of 1 lime

½ tsp dried chervil

¼ tsp dried oregano

¼ tsp dried basil

1 green onion, thinly sliced

4 fresh parsley sprigs, chopped

Hearts of palm are today being touted as a crop substitute for coca in the Amazon Basin. So buying hearts of palm may just help combat the drug trade and preserve precious tropical habitat.

Arrange a bed of lettuce on a large platter. Top with the hearts of palm. Decorate with the pepper strips.

In a small bowl, stir together the olive oil, vinegar, mustard, lime juice, chervil, oregano, and basil to make a vinaigrette. Drizzle the vinaigrette over the salad and sprinkle the green onion and parsley over the top.

Makes 4 servings.

Bogotá's Potato-Chicken Stew

Ajiaco de Pollo Santa Ferreño

2 chickens, about 3½ lb each, cut into serving pieces

3 quarts water

2 carrots

1 celery stalk with leaves

1 onion

2 fresh cilantro sprigs

3 fresh parsley sprigs

2 fresh thyme sprigs

7 cloves garlic

2 bay leaves

½ tsp white peppercorns

4 tbs olive oil

2 shallots, chopped

4 tsp guascas or thyme

2 lb white potatoes, peeled and sliced

1 lb russet potatoes, peeled and sliced

1 lb red new potatoes, diced

2 lb papas criollas

6 ears of corn, cut into thirds

1 jar (8 oz) capers

2 cups (1 pint) heavy cream

Colombian Hot Sauce (page 103)

Colombian Avocado Sauce (page 104)

This stewlike soup is served as the Sunday meal in Bogotá. It calls for guascas, an herb native to the high Andes of Colombia that is very hard to find, even in the Bay Area. There is no substitute, but try thyme mixed with a bit of oregano.

In a stockpot, combine the chicken, water, carrots, celery, and onion. Gather together the cilantro, parsley, and thyme sprigs, 4 of the garlic cloves, the bay leaves, and peppercorns, and tie together in a small cheesecloth bag to make a bouquet garni. Drop into the stockpot and bring to a boil. As soon as it reaches a boil, cover tightly and remove from the heat. Let stand, covered for 30 minutes. Then, promptly remove the chicken to prevent overcooking. When the chicken is cool enough to handle, remove and discard the bones and set the meat aside. Strain the broth, refrigerate until the fat congeals on top, then lift off and discard the fat. Set the broth aside.

Mince the remaining 3 garlic cloves. Rinse the stockpot, add the olive oil, and heat over medium heat. When it is hot, add the minced garlic and shallots and saute until soft, about 3 minutes. Add 1 tsp guascas or thyme and the sliced white and russet potatoes. Stir well. Cook for 3 minutes, stirring often. Add the diced new potatoes and cook for another 3 minutes, stirring often. Add 2½ quarts of the chicken broth and bring to a boil. Reduce the heat to low and add the papas criollas (whole). Cook, stirring often to prevent the potatoes from sticking, for 50 minutes.

Add the cut ears of corn and the remaining 3 tsp guascas or thyme. Bring to a boil, reduce the heat to low, and simmer for another 10 minutes. By this point, the potatoes will have broken down considerably although probably not completely. Remove some of the larger pieces of potatoes along with some of the broth and puree in a blender or food processor. Return the pureed mixture to the pot, add the chicken meat, and bring to a boil to heat through. Serve with capers, cream, the hot sauce, and the avocado sauce for diners to add to taste.

Makes 8 to 10 servings.

Mexican Tortilla Soup

12 stale corn or flour tortillas

¼ cup corn oil

2 tbs olive oil

½ onion, diced

3 cloves garlic, minced

½ tsp dried oregano

½ tsp dried thyme

1 tsp dried marjoram

2 chayotes, peeled and diced

1 carrot, sliced

4 plum tomatoes, peeled and diced

8 cups chicken broth

salt to taste

2 tbs achiote paste

4 eggs

chopped fresh cilantro

½ lb Monterey jack cheese, cut into thin strips

An excellent way to use up stale tortillas.

Cut the tortillas into long, narrow strips. Let them air dry on a plate for 30 minutes. In a skillet, heat the corn oil over medium-high heat. Working in batches, fry the tortilla strips for about 1 minute. Using a slotted spoon, transfer to paper towels to drain.

Meanwhile, in a stockpot, heat the olive oil over medium heat. When it is hot, add the onion, garlic, oregano, thyme, and marjoram and saute until the onion is soft and golden, about 8 minutes. Add the chayotes, carrot, and tomatoes and cook, stirring, for 2 minutes. Add the broth, bring to a boil, and reduce the heat to low. Season with salt. Remove some the hot broth and dissolve the achiote paste in it. Return to the soup and stir well. Cook for 20 minutes to blend the flavors and cook the vegetables.

One at a time, add the eggs: break each one over the soup and give it a swirl before adding the next egg. Cook for 5 minutes longer.

Line the soup bowls with the fried tortillas. Ladle the soup into the bowls. Garnish with cilantro and jack cheese.

Makes 4 to 6 servings.

Ecuadorean Peanut-Potato Soup

Sopa de Maní

2 lb white potatoes, peeled

2 tbs olive or peanut oil

1 onion, chopped

2 cloves garlic, minced

1 shallot, chopped

1 cup dry roasted peanuts, coarsely ground

6 cups chicken broth

2 cups crunchy peanut butter

salt to taste

white pepper to taste

1 cup half-and-half

One of my favorite soups.

Boil the potatoes in salted water until tender, about 25 minutes. Drain and, when cool enough to handle, slice the potatoes.

In a saucepan, heat the oil over medium heat. When it is hot, add the onion, garlic, and shallot and saute until soft, about 5 minutes. Add the peanuts and potatoes, stir well, and pour in the broth. Bring to a boil and add the peanut butter, stirring well to mix. Season with salt and pepper. Simmer for 15 minutes to blend the flavors.

Remove the potatoes from the pan along with some of the broth, and place in a food processor or blender. Puree until smooth, return to the pan, and add the half-and-half. Bring to a simmer and cook until heated through, 3 to 5 minutes longer. Serve hot.

Makes 6 to 8 servings.

Venezuelan Avocado Soup

Sopa de Aguacate

2 large avocados, pitted, peeled, and cut up, plus 4 thin slices for garnish

1½ cups chicken broth

2 fresh cilantro sprigs, plus finely chopped cilantro for garnish

salt to taste

white pepper to taste

1 cup heavy cream or half-and-half

2 jarred pimientos, sliced

Roberta Fleischman, born in Caracas of Italian parents and married to an American of Eastern European Jewish heritage, taught me this soup. It is wonderful on warm summer nights.

In a blender, combine the cut up avocados, broth, cilantro sprigs, salt, and pepper. Puree to a semiliquid consistency. Pour into a glass bowl and add the cream or half-and-half. Cover and chill well.

Serve cold garnished with finely chopped cilantro, an avocado slice, and pimiento slices.

Makes 4 servings.

Puerto Rican Shrimp and Rice Soup

Asopao de Camarones

2 tbs olive oil

1 onion, diced

5 cloves garlic, minced

2 tsp ground cumin

½ tsp ground turmeric

½ tsp saffron soaked in 1 tbs hot water for 5 minutes

2 tbs capers

16 pitted green olives, sliced

1 cup cooked white rice

4 cups chicken or fish broth

2 cups bottled clam juice or additional broth

salt to taste

white pepper to taste

6 langoustines or crayfish

48 shrimp, peeled and deveined

chopped fresh parsley and cilantro

3 lemons, cut into wedges

In a stockpot, heat the olive oil over medium heat. When it is hot, add the onion, garlic, cumin, and turmeric and saute until the onion is soft, about 5 minutes. Add the saffron and its water, the capers, and the olives. Stir well to spread the color of the saffron. Add the rice and stir well. Add the broth and clam juice and season with salt and white pepper. Bring to a boil and add the langoustines. Cook for 2 minutes and then add the shrimp. Reduce the heat to low and simmer until the shellfish is done, about 3 minutes. Garnish with parsley and cilantro. Serve with the lemon wedges.

Makes 6 servings.

Oaxacan Chicken Mole

....

Pollo en Mole de Olla Poblano

Traditionally, this dish is made with turkey, but in most Bay Area Mexican restaurants chicken is substituted. You can buy mole poblano sauce in jars in the Mexican section of supermarkets or in Latin American markets. Doña Maria is a good brand. But you can make your own, too. Here are both ways.

How to use mole poblano from a jar

1 cup chicken broth

⅔ cup mole sauce

1 chicken, about 3½ lb, cut into serving pieces

sesame seeds

Prepare the chicken according to the directions for Stewed Chicken, following.

In large skillet, bring the chicken broth to a boil and add the mole sauce. Stir well to dissolve. Reduce the heat to low and add the chicken pieces. Mix the chicken with the sauce, coating it completely. Heat through. Sprinkle with sesame seeds before serving.

Makes 4 servings.

Stewed Chicken

....

Pollo Guisado

2 tbs olive oil

1 onion, cut into eighths

5 cloves garlic

2 shallots, coarsely chopped

3 tomatoes, quartered

1 tsp ground cumin

2 tsp dried oregano or 1 tbs fresh oregano leaves

2 tsp dried thyme or 1 tbs fresh thyme leaves

1 or 2 chickens, about 3½ lb each, cut into serving pieces

salt to taste

2 celery stalks

1 onion studded with 12 whole cloves

4 fresh parsley sprigs

4 fresh cilantro sprigs

3 bay leaves

For most chicken dishes, Latin Americans stew a chicken and then use the broth to create the sauces. The advantage of this process is not only a very tender chicken and a rich, nutritious sauce, but also the ability to stew a week's worth of chicken and to make a different sauce every night. In recipes which call for stewed chicken, you can substitute poached, boneless, skinless chicken and packaged chicken broth.

In a stockpot, heat the olive oil over medium-high heat. Add the onion cut into eighths, the garlic, shallots, tomatoes, cumin, oregano, and thyme. When the onion is soft and golden, add the chicken pieces and mix well. Add water to cover plus 2 additional cups. Season with salt to taste. Add the celery, the whole onion studded with cloves, parsley, cilantro, and bay leaves. Bring to a boil, reduce the heat to low, and simmer for 15 minutes. Remove from the heat, cover tightly, and let stand for 30 minutes. Then remove the chicken pieces promptly so they do not overcook.

Strain the broth and let cool. Once the broth has cooled, you can store the chicken pieces in it, or you can store them separately. Cover the broth and store in the refrigerator for up to 1 week or in the freezer for up to a 3 months. Discard any fat that congeals on the surface before using.

Makes 8 to 10 cups broth.

How to make your own mole poblano

2 chickens, about 3½ lb each, cut into serving pieces

1 dried negro or New Mexico chili

3 dried ancho chilies

2 pasilla chilies

2 poblano chilies

4 jalapeño chilies

2 serrano chilies

4 tbs lard or olive oil

5 cups chicken broth

2 onions, chopped

3 shallots, chopped

6 cloves garlic

3 tomatoes, peeled and chopped

2 day-old tortillas, cut into strips

½ cup blanched almonds, toasted (page 227)

¼ cup pine nuts, toasted (page 227)

½ cup peanuts, toasted (page 227)

¼ cup sesame seeds, toasted (page 227), plus extra for garnish

½ tsp aniseeds

¼ cup raisins

1 tsp coriander seeds

seeds from 5 cardamom pods

3 whole cloves

½ tsp cumin seeds

3 cinnamon sticks, broken into pieces

¼ cup almond or peanut oil

4 ounces unsweetened chocolate

Prepare the chickens according to the directions for Stewed Chicken (preceding page). Set aside.

Soak the dried negro or New Mexico chili and anchos in water to cover for 20 minutes. Drain, reserving the water, and remove their seeds and membranes. Remove the seeds and membranes from all the fresh chilies and cut into large pieces. In a skillet, heat 3 tbs of the lard or oil over medium heat and add the fresh chilies. Fry for about 1 minute, then add the dried chilies and their soaking water. Cook for 3 minutes longer. Transfer to a bowl and add 1 cup of the broth. Let stand for 30 minutes, stirring every 10 minutes.

Meanwhile, in the same skillet, heat the remaining 1 tbs lard or oil over medium heat. When it is hot, add the onions, shallots, garlic, tomatoes, and tortillas and saute until the onions are soft, 5 to 7 minutes. Transfer the onion mixture to a blender or food processor and grind to a paste. Remove the chilies from the broth and add to the onion paste. Grind again, adding the broth left over from soaking in a steady stream. Transfer the paste to a large bowl. In the blender or food processor, combine the almonds, pine nuts, peanuts, sesame seeds, aniseeds, raisins, coriander seeds, cardamom seeds, cloves, cumin seeds, and cinnamon sticks. Grind to a paste, adding another 1 cup of chicken broth to facilitate the grinding. (In a blender you might have to do the grinding in stages so as to not overwhelm the motor.) Add to the chili-onion mixture. Mix well.

In a large skillet or a saucepan, heat the almond or peanut oil over medium heat. When it is hot, add the contents of the bowl and saute, stirring constantly, for about 5 minutes. Add the remaining 3 cups broth and the chocolate pieces and continue stirring constantly until the chocolate is dissolved. Add more chicken broth if needed to help dissolve the chocolate. Let the sauce cook and thicken, but stir it often.

To assemble the dish, add the cooked chicken to the pan and heat through. Sprinkle with additional sesame seeds and serve.

Makes 8 servings.

Peruvian Spicy Chicken

Ají de Gallina

2 chickens, about 3½ lb each, cut into serving pieces

1 loaf white bread, 1 lb

3 cups milk

1 habanero chili, seeded

6 Fresno or serrano chilies, seeded

2 ajís amarillos (see head note)

½ cup olive oil

3 onions, chopped

3 shallots, chopped

6 cloves garlic, minced

1-inch-piece fresh ginger, peeled and grated

½ tsp ground cloves

1 tsp dried oregano

½ tsp dried marjoram

1 tsp dried thyme

2 tsp ground palillo or turmeric

juice of 1 lime

juice of 2 oranges

2 cups walnuts

salt to taste

white pepper to taste

2 cups chicken broth

Arguably, this is the national dish of Peru. Spicy as all hell, it is a preparation for those who love heat. It is difficult to find fresh yellow chili peppers (ajís amarillos), but you can use dried ones. Soak them in water for 20 minutes. Pickled ones are fairly common and can be used as well. You might even find them frozen. Also, a ground paste is available; use about 2 tsp, adding it when you add the oregano.

Prepare the chicken according to the directions for Stewed Chicken (page 112).

Trim off the crusts from the bread loaf and coarsely rip apart the bread. In a large bowl, combine the bread and milk and let stand until the bread absorbs the liquid.

In a large skillet or saute pan, heat the olive oil over medium heat. When it is hot, add the onions, shallots, garlic, chilies, ginger, and cloves and saute until the onion is soft, about 5 to 7 minutes. Add the oregano, marjoram, thyme, and palillo or turmeric. Cook for 3 minutes, then add the lime and orange juices. Cook for another 2 minutes and remove from the heat.

Pour the onion mixture into the bread mixture. Add the walnuts and season with salt and pepper. Working in batches if necessary, process in a blender or food processor. Set aside.

Remove the chicken meat from the bones and discard the bones. Heat the chicken broth in a large saucepan and add the pureed sauce. Bring to a boil. Add the chicken meat and heat through.

Makes 6 to 8 servings.

Guatemalan Chicken in Spicy Green Almond Sauce

Pollo en Pipián de Almendra Verde

2 chickens, about 3½ lb each

2 tbs olive oil

2 green jalapeño chilies, seeded and diced

1 green poblano chili, seeded and diced

1 yellow onion, quartered

½ tsp dried oregano

½ tsp dried thyme

½ tsp dried marjoram

1 tsp ground cumin

1 cup blanched almonds, toasted (page 227)

10 fresh cilantro sprigs

5 fresh parsley sprigs

4 green onions, cut into thirds

salt to taste

black pepper to taste

1 cup chicken broth

Add a habanero chili for an extra-spicy sauce.

Prepare the chickens according to the directions for Stewed Chicken on page 112.

In a large skillet, heat the olive oil over medium heat. When it is hot, add the chilies and yellow onion and saute until soft, about 5 minutes. Add the oregano, thyme, marjoram, and cumin. Mix well and cook for 3 more minutes. Remove from the heat.

In a food processor, coarsely grind the almonds with the cilantro, parsley, and green onions. Then add the onion-chili mixture, salt, and pepper. Grind to a thick sauce consistency.

To assemble the dish, in a large skillet, heat the chicken broth. Add the pureed sauce and bring to a boil. Let thicken slightly, then add the chicken pieces. Reduce the heat to low and cook until the chicken is heated through, then serve.

Makes 8 servings.

Note: You can also roast uncooked chicken using the sauce. Just add 1 cup chicken broth to the sauce and pour it over it the chicken, whole or cut into serving pieces. Roast the cut-up chicken in an oven preheated to 350 degrees F until tender, about 45 minutes. A whole chicken might take 10 or 15 minutes longer, depending on size. Baste frequently.

Colombian-Style Chicken in Rice

Colombian-Style Arroz con Pollo

2 chickens, about 3½ lb each, cut into serving pieces, or 3 lb boneless chicken

2 yellow onions

2 carrots

6 cloves garlic

celery leaves

3 fresh cilantro sprigs

4 fresh parsley sprigs

4 bay leaves

2 green onions

8 cups water

salt to taste

white pepper to taste

2 tbs olive oil

1 tsp dried thyme

½ tsp ground cumin

3 cups white rice

2 cans (15 oz each) tomato sauce

1 can (6 oz) tomato paste

32 green olives

½ lb green peas, shelled and rinsed

8 hard-boiled eggs, sliced

A version of this dish is served throughout the Hispanic world, with every family having their own recipe. This is the Lemos family recipe and the first dish I can remember cooking.

In a large stockpot, combine the chicken, 1 of the yellow onions, 1 of the carrots, 3 of the garlic cloves, the celery leaves, cilantro, parsley, bay leaves, and the green onions. Add the water, salt, and white pepper and bring to a boil. Reduce the heat to low and cook for 10 minutes. Remove from the heat and let stand, tightly covered, for 20 minutes. Then, promptly remove the chicken to prevent overcooking. Strain the broth, refrigerate until the fat congeals on top, then lift off and discard the fat. Set the broth aside. If using boneless chicken pieces, slice into long strips; set the chicken pieces aside.

Finely chop the remaining yellow onion, mince the remaining 3 garlic cloves, and slice the remaining carrot. In another large stockpot, heat the olive oil over medium heat. When it is hot, add the yellow onion, garlic, and carrot and saute until the onion is soft and golden, about 8 minutes. Add the thyme and cumin, stir well, and add the rice. Mix well to coat the rice in the oil. Add 5 cups of the strained broth (reserve the remaining broth for another use), bring to a boil, and season with salt. Add the chicken, tomato sauce, and tomato paste. Mix well, reduce the heat to low, and cook for 5 minutes. Add the green olives and the green peas. Cook until the rice is done, about 15 minutes longer. Garnish with the sliced hard-boiled eggs.

Makes 8 servings.

Shredded Flank Steak

Ropa Vieja

1 flank steak, about 3½ to 4 lb

5 bay leaves

6 whole cloves

2 onions

1 carrot

2 tbs olive oil

4 cloves garlic, minced

2 tsp ground cumin

1 green bell pepper, diced

1 red bell pepper, diced

6 plum tomatoes, peeled and diced

1 tbs capers

2 cans (15 oz) tomato sauce

1 can (6 oz) tomato paste

1 cup beef broth

salt to taste

black pepper to taste

20 pitted green olives, sliced

chopped fresh parsley

This dish is made in Brazil, as well as throughout the Caribbean.

In a large saucepan, combine the flank steak, 2 of the bay leaves, the cloves, 1 of the onions, and the carrot. Add water to cover generously and bring to a boil. Reduce the heat to medium and cook until the flank steak is very tender, about 45 minutes. Remove from the heat and remove the steak from the pan; discard the cooking liquid. Let the steak cool, then shred into small, bite-sized pieces; set aside.

Chop the remaining onion. In a large skillet or saute pan, heat the olive oil over medium heat. When it is hot, add the chopped onion, garlic, and cumin and saute until the onion is soft and golden, about 8 minutes. Add the green and red peppers and cook for 5 minutes, stirring often. Add the tomatoes and cook for another 3 minutes. Add the shredded meat and capers, mix well, and add the tomato sauce, tomato paste, and the broth. Stir well and add the remaining 3 bay leaves. Bring to a boil, reduce the heat to low, and season with salt and pepper. Simmer for 30 minutes to cook the vegetables and blend the flavors.

Stir in the olives and serve garnished with parsley.

Makes 4 servings.

Carne Asada Marinade

Adobo para Carne Asada

2 dried chipotle chilies, soaked in warm water to cover for 15 minutes and drained

1 pasilla chili

2 green jalapeño chilies

1 yellow onion, quartered

8 cloves garlic

2 green onions, cut up

1 cup corn oil

¼ cup red wine vinegar

¼ cup Worcestershire Sauce

½ tsp sugar

1 tsp salt

½ tsp white pepper

This marinade is used to make the meat fillings for tacos and burritos. The recipe yields sufficient marinade for 3 lb skirt steak, flank steak, or similar beef cut, thinly sliced. (An equal amount of chicken or pork can be used in place of the beef.) Marinate for at least 1 hour, then grill over hot coals. For a taco, tuck the grilled meat into a warm corn tortilla with some fresh salsa (page 102); add minced onion and chopped cilantro for extra flavor. For a burrito, stuff a warm large flour tortilla with the meat, some rice, refried beans (page 124), and fresh salsa (page 102); other additions can include guacamole (page 105), sour cream, shredded Monterey jack cheese, or even shredded lettuce and chopped tomato. Experiment with other types of beans and other salsas. Thanks to friends Jorge Sciavon and David Favela for their hints.

In a food processor or blender, combine the chilies, yellow onion, garlic, and green onions. Grind to a paste. Add all the remaining ingredients except the meat and whirl for a few seconds, then use for marinating meat.

Makes about 2 cups.

Chilean Sea Bass with Roasted Red Pepper Sauce

Corvina en Fuente de Barro

2 lb Chilean sea bass steaks or fillets

2 tbs lemon juice

salt to taste

white pepper to taste

2 red bell peppers, roasted (page 227)

6 plum tomatoes, peeled and diced

2 tsp olive oil

½ cup dry white wine or sherry

4 tbs butter

2 shallots, chopped

1 onion, chopped

2 tsp paprika

2 hard-boiled eggs, sliced

croutons

minced fresh parsley

This Chilean dish is best prepared and served in a cazuela, a partially glazed earthenware dish from Spain. You can find cazuelas in well-stocked cookware stores or departments.

Preheat an oven to 350 degrees F.

Season the sea bass with the lemon juice, salt, and pepper. In a blender or food processor, combine the red peppers, tomatoes, olive oil, and wine. Process until smooth. Set aside.

In a skillet, melt the butter over medium heat. Add the shallots and onion and saute until the onion is soft, about 5 minutes. Add the pureed mixture and mix well. Cook for 3 minutes to blend the flavors. Remove from the heat.

In a cazuela or glass baking dish, place the sea bass and cover with the roasted red pepper sauce. Sprinkle with the paprika. Bake until the fish is opaque throughout, about 20 minutes. To serve, top with hard-boiled eggs and croutons and sprinkle with parsley.

Makes 4 servings.

Plain White Rice

Arroz Blanco

2 cups water

1 tsp olive oil

1 green onion

2 cloves garlic

salt to taste

1 cup long-grain white rice, rinsed

Plain white rice is a staple throughout most of Latin America. It is served daily as part of the main meal. Local cooks take great pride in cooking flavorful nonsticky rice.

In a saucepan, combine the water, olive oil, green onion, and garlic cloves. Bring to a boil and add the salt and rice. Bring back to a boil and then reduce the heat to low. Cover partially and cook until the liquid is absorbed and the rice is tender, 15 to 20 minutes.

Makes 4 servings.

Cha Cha Cha's Cajun Shrimp

Cajun spice mix:

½ cup sweet paprika

2½ tbs cayenne pepper

2½ tbs garlic powder

2½ tbs onion powder

1½ tbs black pepper

1½ tbs white pepper

1 tbs dried thyme

1 tbs dried oregano

1 tbs salt

1½ cups dark beer

2 cups (1 pint) heavy cream

1 lb medium shrimp, peeled and deveined

½ tsp red pepper flakes

At Cha Cha Cha, a hip Caribbean restaurant in San Francisco's Haight-Ashbury, this spicy dish is served in individual cast-iron skillets to allow plenty of room for swabbing up the delectable cream sauce. This is not a dish for the faint of heart. To cool it off, add more cream.

To make the spice mix, in a small bowl, stir together all the ingredients until well mixed. You will have about 1⅓ cups. Set aside ½ cup to use for the shrimp, and transfer the remaining mix to an airtight container. Store in a cool, dry place and use with other foods such as fish fillets.

In a large, heavy saucepan, mix together the ½ cup spice mix and the beer. Bring to a simmer over medium heat, whisking constantly to form a thick paste. Do not allow the mixture to burn.

Gradually stir in the cream, stirring constantly to form a smooth sauce. Cook over medium heat, stirring occasionally, until the sauce thickens slightly and turns a rich rust color, 8 to 10 minutes.

Add the shrimp and red pepper flakes, reduce the heat to low, and cook until the shrimp turn pink and begin to curl, 2 to 3 minutes. Taste and adjust the seasonings, then serve.

Makes 4 or 5 servings.

Coconut Rice

Arroz con Coco

1 cup water

1 can (14 fl oz) coconut milk

salt to taste

1 cup long-grain white rice, rinsed

This recipe hails from the Caribbean coast of Colombia, but versions exist throughout coastal Latin America. The rice is most often served alongside fried fish.

In a saucepan, combine the water, coconut milk, and salt and bring to a boil. Add the rice and return to a boil, stirring occasionally. Reduce the heat to low and cover partially. Stir every few minutes until the rice is tender, 15 to 20 minutes.

Makes 4 servings.

Rice with Coca-Cola

Arroz con Coca-Cola

1 can (12 oz) Coca-Cola

½ cup water

1 tsp corn oil

salt to taste

1 cup long-grain white rice

½ cup raisins

Most people are shocked when they find out that this rice is cooked in Coca-Cola. It is slightly sweet and is usually served with a grilled meat. This is a Lemos family recipe.

In a medium saucepan, combine the cola, water, and corn oil, and salt and bring to a boil. Add the rice and return to a boil, stirring occasionally. Add the raisins, stir well, and reduce the heat to low. Cover partially and cook until the rice is tender, 15 to 20 minutes.

Makes 4 servings.

Baked Rice with Cheese

Arroz Asado con Queso

2 recipes Plain White Rice (page 120), kept warm

1 cup milk

½ cup (¼ lb) butter

2 eggs, lightly beaten

½ lb Fontina or Muenster cheese, shredded

3 tsp fine dried bread crumbs

1 tbs grated Parmesan cheese

1 tsp paprika

Preheat an oven to 350 degrees F. Butter a 2-quart souffle dish or other baking dish.

In a metal bowl, combine the warm rice, milk, butter, and eggs. Stir to mix well. The butter will melt into the rice, so it is important to mix it thoroughly. Add the shredded cheese and mix well again. Transfer to the prepared dish.

In a small bowl, combine the bread crumbs, Parmesan, and paprika. Sprinkle over the top of the rice. Bake until piping hot and the top is browned, about 25 minutes.

Makes 8 to 10 servings.

Basic Quinoa

1 cup quinoa

2½ cups water

1 tsp olive oil

1 green onion

salt to taste

Although it resembles and is cooked like a grain, quinoa is actually a seed native to the high Andes. It has a nutty flavor and a slightly grainy texture. In addition to being nutritious, quinoa makes a nice alternative to rice and adds authenticity to Andean meals. Serve it with Peruvian Spicy Chicken (page 114) or Chilean Sea Bass (page 119).

Rinse the quinoa well under running cold water. In a saucepan, combine the water, olive oil, green onion, and salt and bring to a boil. Add the quinoa and return to a boil. Reduce the heat to low, cover, and cook until the liquid is absorbed and the quinoa is tender, about 25 minutes.

Makes 4 servings.

Quinoa with Walnut Sauce

Ocopa de Quinoa

1 cup quinoa

2½ cups water

1 tsp olive oil

1 tsp ground palillo or turmeric

1 green onion

salt to taste

1 cup walnut

2 serrano chilies, seeded

½ cup ricotta cheese

1 cup cottage cheese

paprika

One of my favorites for any Andean dinner. Sometimes I serve the quinoa in hollowed-out tomatoes and decorate the tops with walnuts.

Preheat an oven to 350 degrees F.

Rinse the quinoa well under running cold water. In a saucepan, combine the water, oil, palillo or turmeric, green onion, and salt and bring to a boil. Add the quinoa and return to a boil. Reduce the heat to low, cover, and cook until the liquid is absorbed and the quinoa is tender, about 25 minutes.

Meanwhile, in a food processor or blender, combine the walnuts, chilies, and ricotta and cottage cheeses.

When the quinoa is cooked, transfer to a deep baking dish. Stir in the walnut sauce and mix well. Bake until the sauce is bubbling, about 20 minutes. Sprinkle with paprika and serve.

Makes 4 servings.

Basic Amaranth

2½ cups water

1 cup amaranth

Amaranth is a highly nutritious grain, rich in protein and amino acids. It was the grain of the Aztecs and the Mayas, but sadly it has fallen into disuse. It is even ignored in most Mexican cookbooks. I first had amaranth porridge on a trip to the Yucatán, where it was served in milk with honey as a breakfast food. Later on the same trip I had it in a casserole with corn and beans. The latter is the recipe given here following this basic preparation.

I have never had amaranth plain; instead, it is cooked first and then mixed with various flavorings. There is also an amaranth flour. You might search vegetarian cookbooks for other recipes. Given the small size of the grain, it is best not to try to rinse it.

In a saucepan, bring the water to a boil and add the amaranth. Return to a boil and then reduce the heat to low. Cover loosely and cook until tender, 20 to 25 minutes. If the amaranth sticks to the bottom, add ½ cup more water. You can also cook amaranth in broth, but under no circumstances should you add any salt. This will prevent the amaranth from absorbing water. The amaranth will be slightly runny and is best served in a small bowl.

Makes 4 servings.

Amaranth with Corn and Beans

Amaranta con Maíz y Fríjol

2½ cups water

1 cup amaranth

2 tbs corn oil

2 shallots, chopped

1 onion, chopped

2 cloves garlic, minced

2 serrano chilies, seeded and chopped

1 cup drained cooked red beans

1 cup drained cooked corn

3 tomatoes, peeled and chopped

1 red bell pepper, chopped

10 fresh cilantro sprigs, chopped

This dish, in addition to being delicious, is a visual delight: the brown amaranth, bright red pepper, yellow corn, and earthy beans make a festive combination.

Using the water and amaranth, cook the amaranth as directed for Basic Amaranth, preceding.

Meanwhile, in a large skillet, heat the corn oil over medium heat. When it is hot, add the shallots, onion, garlic, and chilies and saute until the onion is soft, about 5 minutes. Add the cooked beans and corn, stir well, and cook for another 5 minutes. Add the tomatoes and cook for another 3 minutes to blend the flavors. Remove from the heat.

Stir in the cooked amaranth, the bell pepper, and the cilantro. Mix well and serve.

Makes 6 servings.

Venezuelan Black Beans

Caraotas

1 rounded cup dried black beans

3 tbs olive oil

6 cloves garlic, minced

2 shallots, chopped

2 onions, finely chopped

2 tsp ground cumin

½ tsp ground turmeric

2 tsp dried oregano

1 tsp dried chervil

1 tsp dried marjoram

1 green bell pepper, chopped

8 cups chicken broth or water

4 bay leaves

salt to taste

black pepper to taste

My Venezuelan friend Robert Fleischman taught me this dish. It can be served as a side dish or a main. In the latter case, serve over white rice accompanied with avocado slices, hot sauce, sour cream, and a salad of quartered tomatoes, green onions, and cilantro. A side of plantains would also go well.

Rinse the beans and place in a bowl with water to cover by 1 inch. Let stand overnight.

In a stockpot, heat the olive oil over medium heat. When it is hot, add the garlic, shallots, onions, cumin, turmeric, oregano, chervil, and marjoram. Saute until the onion is soft, about 5 minutes. Add the bell pepper and cook for 3 minutes, stirring often. Drain the beans, add to the pot, and mix well with the onion mixture. Add the chicken broth or water, bay leaves, salt, and pepper. Bring to a boil, reduce the heat to low, cover partially, and cook for about 1 hour and 20 minutes. The beans should be soft and tender at this point; if they are not, cook them a little longer until they are done.

Makes 6 servings.

Mexican Refried Beans

Frijoles Refritos

1 rounded cup dried pinto beans

¼ cup olive oil

6 cloves garlic, minced

1 onion, finely chopped

2 shallots, chopped

4 jalapeño chilies, seeded

2 tsp ground cumin

2 tsp dried oregano

½ tsp ground turmeric

8 cups chicken broth or water

4 bay leaves

salt to taste

black pepper to taste

1 cup corn or olive oil

Rinse the beans and place in a bowl with water to cover by 1 inch. Let stand overnight.

In a stockpot, heat the ¼ cup olive oil over medium heat. When it is hot, add the garlic, onion, shallots, jalapeños, cumin, oregano, and turmeric and saute until the onion is soft, about 5 minutes. Drain the beans, add to the pot, and mix well with the onion mixture. Add the broth or water, bay leaves, salt, and pepper and bring to a boil. Reduce the heat to low, cover partially, and cook for 1½ hours. At this point, the beans should be soft and tender; if they are not, cook them a little longer until they are done.

Remove from the heat and let cool. In a food processor, puree the beans in batches, adding a little of the cooking liquid and corn or olive oil as needed to facilitate the blending.

Place a large skillet over medium heat and add the remaining oil. When it is hot, add the pureed beans and fry, stirring to prevent sticking, until smooth and hot.

Makes 6 to 8 servings.

Potatoes and Tubers

Life in the Andes would have been impossible without the humble yet noble potato. The potato and other tubers are the only edible plants that grow in the higher elevations. Quite early on, the native Andeans learned to make *chuno,* a freeze-dried potato dish that kept for years. This formed a key part of the Incan diet. Potatoes were first encountered by the Spanish explorer Gonzalo Jimenez de Quesada in about 1530, although certainly other expeditions had already seen the potato's Caribbean cousin, the yam.

If you should go to the Andes, you will find dozens of different kinds of potatoes and tubers in the markets. You will see purple ones, little speckled ones the size of marbles, red ones with yellow flesh, long, thin ones similar in shape to carrots, and, of course, ones that look just like those in your neighborhood market. I have always found it hard to cook with only two or three kinds of potatoes available. Luckily some Colombian and Peruvian potatoes can occasionally be found in Latin American markets. Foremost among these is the papa criolla, the tiniest potato. It has grainy yellow flesh that some compare to eating an egg yolk, and is delicious quick fried and sprinkled with salt. Another potato that can occasionally be found fresh or canned is the Peruvian blue potato. A deep blue, almost purple, it is wonderful in soups. Yet another class of tubers are the ullucos, which are long and thin and have pink to red-purple skin and white firm flesh. They are found most often canned, imported from Peru, and are also good quick fried and sprinkled with salt.

Unlike chilies or peanuts, the potato at first did not meet with acceptance in the Old World. But given its nutritional value and ease of cultivation, it was only a matter of time before it was an established part of the global diet.

It was actually war that helped potatoes become a pantry staple. During the religious wars of the mid-seventeenth century that devastated central Europe, the potato was the one crop that armies could not trample upon and destroy. This led to its wide distribution in the cuisines of Germany, France, Switzerland, and Poland. The myth of the potato being Irish is probably due to the Irish potato famine of 1846 to 1848. The potato arrived in Ireland during the mid-seventeenth century at about the time the English succeeded in subduing the last of the clans. How it made its way to the island is still a matter of debate, but its value as an easy-to-grow and practically indestructible crop was soon recognized. Slowly but surely, the potato became a staple of the Irish peasantry until it replaced just about everything else grown in the country. Hence, when the crop failed in the late 1840s, the consequences were devastating. Ireland starved, forcing about one-third of the island's population to emigrate.

Fried Ullucos
....
Ullucos Fritos

3 tbs olive oil

1 onion, chopped

2 cloves garlic, minced

2 cans (20 oz each) ullucos, drained and rinsed

1 tomato, peeled and chopped

In a skillet, heat the olive oil over medium heat. When it is hot, add the onion and garlic and saute until soft and golden, about 8 minutes. Add the ullucos and tomato and continue cooking until the ullucos and onion brown, 4 to 5 minutes longer.

Makes 4 to 6 servings.

Ecuadorean Potato Cakes

Llapingachos

2 lb white potatoes, peeled

salt to taste

white pepper to taste

2 tbs olive oil

3 shallots, chopped

2 onions, grated

½ tsp dried marjoram

½ cup butter

2 cups shredded Muenster or
   havarti cheese

½ cup milk or heavy cream

corn oil for frying

Andean Spicy Peanut Sauce (page
   104)

Cook the potatoes in boiling salted water until tender, about 25 minutes. Drain and place in a bowl, then mash to a puree. Season with salt and white pepper. Set aside.

In a nonstick skillet, heat the olive oil over medium heat. When it is hot, add the shallots, onions, and marjoram and saute until soft, about 5 minutes. Remove from the heat.

Mix the cooked onion mixture into the mashed potatoes and add the butter, shredded cheese, and the milk or cream. Mix well. Form the mixture into pancakes about 2½ inches in diameter.

Pour corn oil to a depth of ¼ inch into a large skillet, and place over medium-high heat. When it is hot, add the pancakes and fry, turning once, until golden brown on both sides, 3 to 4 minutes on each side. Serve with the peanut sauce.

Makes 6 servings.

Peruvian Blue Potatoes with Spicy Tomato Sauce

Papas Azules con Ají de Tomate

10 Peruvian blue potatoes, peeled

2 tbs olive oil

1 yellow onion, chopped

3 cloves garlic, minced

2 serrano chilies, seeded and diced

6 tomatoes, peeled and pureed, or
   1 can (15 oz) tomato sauce

4 fresh cilantro sprigs, chopped

3 green onions, sliced

salt to taste

black pepper to taste

Cook the potatoes in boiling salted water until tender, 20 to 25 minutes.

Meanwhile, in a skillet, heat the olive oil over medium heat. When it is hot, add the yellow onion, garlic, and chilies and saute until the onion is soft, about 5 minutes. Add the pureed tomatoes or tomato sauce, cilantro, and green onions and season with salt and pepper. Bring to a boil, reduce the heat to low, and simmer for 5 minutes.

Meanwhile, drain the potatoes and, when cool enough to handle, slice them and arrange on a platter. Smother with the tomato sauce and serve.

Makes 6 to 8 servings.

Peruvian Potatoes in a Spicy Cheese Sauce

Papa a la Huancaina

10 white potatoes, peeled

2 tbs olive oil

2 onions, quartered

2 shallots, chopped

6 cloves garlic, cut in half

1 green bell pepper, diced

1 red bell pepper, diced

2 dried ajis amarillos (see headnote)

1 habanero chili, seeded

2 tsp ground palillo or 1 tbs ground turmeric

½ tsp paprika

1 lb cottage cheese

½ cup ricotta cheese

½ cup lemon juice

½ cup half-and-half

butter lettuce leaves

4 hard-boiled eggs, sliced

sliced roasted pimientos

If you wish this to be milder, use a jalapeño or serrano instead of a habanero. It is difficult to find fresh yellow chili peppers (ajís amarillos), but you can use dried ones. Soak them in water for 20 minutes. Pickled ones are fairly common and can be used. You might even find them frozen. Also, a ground paste is available; use about 2 tsp, adding it when you add the palillo.

Cook the potatoes in boiling salted water until tender, about 25 minutes. Drain and set aside.

In a large skillet, heat the olive oil over medium heat. When it is hot, add the onions, shallots, garlic, bell peppers, and chilies and saute until the onions are soft, about 5 minutes. Add the palillo or turmeric and continue cooking, stirring often, until the peppers and chilies start to blacken. Remove from the heat. When the peppers and chilies are cool enough to handle, peel off the blackened parts of the skins and return the chilies to the pan.

Add the paprika, cheeses, and lemon juice. Mix well and transfer to a blender or food processor. Process until smooth. Return to the skillet and reheat, adding the half-and-half to smooth out the sauce.

Make a bed of lettuce leaves on a platter. Slice the potatoes and place them on the lettuce. Pour the warm sauce over the slices, covering them completely. Decorate with the eggs and pimientos.

Makes 6 to 8 appetizer servings.

Swiss Chard with Onion and Tomato

....

Acelgas con Cebolla y Tomate

2 tbs olive oil

1 onion, chopped

2 cloves garlic, minced

1 shallot, chopped

4 tomatoes, peeled and chopped

½ tsp ground cumin

½ tsp ground coriander

1 bunch Swiss chard, well rinsed and finely chopped

salt to taste

white pepper to taste

In a skillet, heat the olive oil over medium heat. When it is hot, add the onion, garlic, and shallot and saute until soft, about 5 minutes. Add the tomatoes, cumin, and coriander, stir well, and add the Swiss chard. Season with salt and pepper and cook until the greens are tender, about 10 minutes.

Makes 4 servings.

Cuban Yuca in Lemon-Garlic Sauce

....

Yuca al Mojo de Ajo

2 lb yuca

3 tbs olive oil

salt to taste

white pepper to taste

2 heads garlic, minced

½ cup lemon juice

2 tsp distilled white vinegar

3 tbs naranja agría

10 fresh parsley sprigs, chopped

Although yuca is available both fresh and frozen in many Latin American markets and some supermarkets, I generally buy it frozen, because it comes already peeled.

Prepare the yuca as directed in Sidebar on facing page. Drain and place in a bowl. Add 1 tbs of the olive oil and season with salt and white pepper. In a small bowl, combine the garlic, lemon juice, vinegar, the remaining 2 tbs oil, and the naranja agría.

In a saucepan or skillet over medium heat, quickly saute the yuca for 1 minute. Add the garlic-lemon mixture and bring to a boil. Reduce the heat to low and simmer until the yuca is heated through. Sprinkle with the parsley and serve.

Makes 6 servings as a side dish.

Peruvian Spicy Yuca

Picante de Yuca

2 lb yuca

½ head green cabbage, shredded

1 habanero chili, seeded and finely diced

1 green jalapeño or serrano chili, seeded and finely diced

2 tbs olive oil

juice of 6 limes

8 fresh cilantro sprigs, chopped

5 fresh parsley sprigs, chopped

3 green onions, sliced

2 plum tomatoes, peeled and diced

1 tsp distilled white vinegar

½ tsp sugar

corn or safflower oil for frying

The sauce, which is slightly reminiscent of Southeast Asian cuisine, is quite spicy. To make it milder, omit the habanero.

Prepare the yuca as directed below. Drain and place in a bowl.

Line a serving dish with the cabbage. In a small bowl, combine the chilies, oil, lime juice, cilantro, parsley, green onions, tomatoes, vinegar, and sugar. Mix well.

In a skillet or deep fryer, heat oil to a depth of ½ inch over medium-high heat. Add the yuca and fry until golden and crispy on all sides, about 5 minutes. Using a slotted spoon, transfer to paper towel to drain. Arrange the yuca on top of the cabbage. Pour the sauce over the yuca and serve warm.

Makes 6 to 8 servings as a side dish.

Preparing Yuca for Use

Yuca is available both fresh and frozen in many Latin American markets and some supermarkets. The latter comes already peeled. Peeling fresh yuca requires a sharp vegetable peeler or knife and a bit of patience: Using a heavy chef's knife, cut off the top and bottom, then run the knife or peeler down the side from the skinny bottom to the wider top. Starting from the slit and using your fingers, peel away the tough skin. Sever the yuca in half lengthwise and remove the stringy vein that runs down the middle.

Whether purchased fresh or frozen, yuca must be boiled first until tender before it can be used. Cut into chunks, place in a saucepan with water to cover, the juice of ½ lemon, and salt to taste, then boil until tender, about 30 minutes. The only exception to this would be if you plan to use the yuca in soups, in which case it should be rinsed first and then parboiled for only 10 minutes before adding it to the soup pot. This parboiling step removes some toxins present in the root.

Fried Ripe Plantain

· ·

Tajadas de Platano Frito

ripe plantains (allow ½ plantain per person)

corn oil for frying

The plantains must be ripe for this recipe, which means they must be black and soft (a little mold is even okay). If no ripe plantains are available at the market, buy green ones and allow them to ripen at room temperature. It will take about a week. Central Americans serve plantains with crema, a sour cream; Colombians serve them as part of a meal.

Peel the plantains by running a knife down the outside spine of the fruit. With your thumb, lift off the skin, separating it from the fruit. Cut the plantain on the diagonal into slices ⅓ inch thick.

In a skillet, heat corn oil to a depth of ¼ inch over medium-high heat. When it is hot, gently drop the plantain slices into the oil. Fry, turning once, until golden brown, 2 to 3 minutes on each side. Using a slotted spoon, transfer to paper towels to drain. Serve warm.

Fried Green Plantain

· ·

Tostones de Platano Verde

3 unripe plantains (allow ½ plantain per person)

corn oil for frying

1 cup water

1 tsp lemon juice

salt

These must be fried twice.

Peel the plantains by running a knife down the outside spine of the fruit. With your thumb, lift off the skin, separating it from the fruit. Cut the plantain into 1-inch chunks.

In a skillet with a lid, heat oil to a depth of ½ inch over medium-high heat. When the oil is hot, reduce the heat to medium and gently drop the plantain chunks into the pan. Fry, turning as necessary to cook evenly, until the plantains are yellowish, about 4 minutes total. Using a slotted spoon, transfer to paper towels to drain. Reduce the heat to low.

Using the bottom of a glass, your hand, or a mallet, squash each plantain chunk into a flat pancakelike round; it's best to keep the plantains wrapped in paper towels, a paper bag, or plastic wrap when you flatten them. In a bowl, combine the water and lemon juice. Reheat the oil. Dip the squashed plantains in the water mixture for just a second and then add to the oil. Fry a second time over medium heat, turning to cook evenly, until the plantains are a nice golden color, about 3 minutes total. Sprinkle liberally with salt and serve warm.

Baked Ripe Plantains

* *

Platano Maduro Asado

4 ripe plantains

¼ lb cotija cheese, sliced

Cotija is a crumbly, salty cheese that complements the sweetness of ripe plantains; you can also bake the plantains without it. The plantains must be ripe for this recipe, that is, black and soft (a little mold is even okay). Green ones will ripen at room temperature in about a week.

Preheat an oven to 375 degrees F.

Peel the plantains by running a knife down the outside spine of each one. With your thumb, lift off the skin, separating it from the fruit. Cut a slit down the middle of each plantain, and stuff each slit with the cheese slices.

Bake on a lightly greased baking sheet until the cheese is melted and browned and the plantains are easily pierced, about 50 minutes. Serve warm from the oven.

Makes 8 servings.

Sweet Mamey

* *

Dulce de Mamey

2 cups water

4 cups sugar

juice of 2 lemons

1 cinnamon stick

3 whole cloves

2 packages (1 lb each) frozen mamey flesh, thawed

Mamey is a large brown fruit with orange flesh and a flavor that is akin to a sweet pumpkin. It is widely used in desserts and milk shakes in the Caribbean. This recipe calls for the more common frozen pulp, but if you should find fresh or whole frozen mamey, you will need to peel and pit them, then cut into slices (allow 3 lb whole mamey).

In a saucepan, combine the water, sugar, and lemon juice. Bring to a boil, stirring to dissolve the sugar. Add the cinnamon, cloves, and thawed mamey. Reduce the heat to low and simmer for 15 minutes. The sauce will become thick and syrupy.

Remove from the heat, let cool, and transfer to a bowl. Cover and chill overnight before serving.

Makes 8 servings.

Flán

••

Flán de Leche

1 can (14 fl oz) condensed milk

1¾ cups whole milk

5 eggs

1 tsp pure vanilla extract

1 cup sugar

Preheat an oven to 375 degrees F. In a blender, combine the condensed milk and whole milk. Mix briefly, then add the eggs and vanilla. Blend well and set aside.

Place the sugar in a heavy saucepan over medium heat. Shake the pan gently to stir the sugar as it melts and caramelizes. Adjust the temperature to medium-high as the sugar begins to caramelize. If some sugar has formed a pocket, break it with a wooden spoon. Continue to shake the pan as needed. Once the sugar has taken on a deep caramel color, carefully pour it into a 9-inch pie plate, tilting the pie plate to cover the bottom and halfway up the sides. Let set, then pour in the egg mixture. Set the pie plate in a baking pan and pour hot water into the pan to reach halfway up the sides of the plate.

Bake for 50 minutes. Insert a knife into the center; if it comes out clean, it is done. If not, continue baking for another 10 minutes. Remove from the oven and let cool for 20 to 30 minutes, then run a knife around the edge of the pan, and invert pan onto a serving plate. Serve warm or at room temperature.

Makes 8 servings.

Variations: Add 2 bananas, peeled and chopped, after you add the eggs. Or add ¼ cup cold coffee and 1 tbs coffee liqueur after you add the eggs.

Middle East

The Middle East is the cradle of Western civilization, and many of our culinary traditions stem from these ancient lands. Today, this region offers a cuisine that is varied, healthy, and light.

While the Middle East encompasses a large geographic area, its food can be described as a variation on a theme. The differences among Greek, Turkish, Iranian, and Armenian versions of the same dish are often subtle ones. From the Peloponnesus through the Anatolian Plateau, from the Caucasus to the shores of the Gulf (Persian or Arabian, depending on which bank you stand), and from the Levant to Mesopotamia, many of the same ingredients are used similarly.

Middle Easterners have a penchant for tart and tangy tastes. All over the region, astringent agents such as pomegranate seeds, sour cherry syrup, mahlab (cherry pits), lemons, and tamarind are used. Pulses, including fava beans, lentils, and chickpeas, are also popular ingredients. Among vegetables, the eggplant reigns supreme, and it is prepared in hundreds of different ways. Raw fresh vegetables and fruits are also emphasized, especially tomatoes and cucumbers, while various nuts—almonds, hazelnuts, pine nuts, pistachios, walnuts—figure prominently in many dishes, both savory and sweet.

Grains play a large role as well. Many food scholars believe that man first cultivated wheat in Mesopotamia some six or seven thousand years ago, and since then this region has produced some of the world's finest breads. Pita is perhaps the best known, but try lahvosh, a flat bread common from Armenia through Iran. Wheat is also prepared in a dried, cracked form called bulgur, which is used in pilafs, kibbeh, and salads, and the Egyptians use a green wheat called frik in various preparations. Rice is yet another important staple, with Iranians, in particular, boasting a number of interesting preparations. Rice pilafs are found throughout the region, arguably reaching their apex in the Turkish kitchen.

Sweet desserts show up on tables throughout the Middle East. Baklava and halvah, made from sesame seeds and honey, are two of the best known. The latter must be bought in stores, since most modern homes do not come equipped with the large stone grinders necessary for grinding the seeds, and baklava, although more easily made at home, can be purchased with good results. Many bakeries and most Middle Eastern markets make acceptable versions. Look for Middle Eastern breads, such as pita, lahvosh, and various flat griddle breads, in these same shops.

Suggested Menus

Mezze for 10

Mezze are a Middle Eastern smorgasbord of hors d'oeuvres and salads. Generally a large number of dishes are prepared in relatively small amounts. With the current craze for Spanish tapas, this style of service should be familiar. Most of the dishes on this menu can be made in advance. Only the Greek shrimp, phyllo triangles, and grilled eggplant call for last-minute cooking. You will need to double the Greek shrimp recipe to serve 10 people. The Kalamata olives and Greek pepperocini are store-bought, as is the baklava. The menu also includes various spreads or dips, so be sure to serve ample bread (Middle Eastern or French), as well as some raw vegetables such as carrots, celery, peppers, and broccoli (allow a total of about 4 cups vegetables for this menu).

Dolmas

Baba Ghanoush

Greek Shrimp with Feta and Herbs

Hummus with Carrots, Celery, and Pita

Red Pepper, Walnut, and Pomegranate Spread (Muhammara)

Georgian Cucumber and Nut Salad

Armenian Lentil Balls

Cucumber Yogurt Sauce (Tzatziki)

Marinated Greek Kalamata Olives

Greek Pepperocini

Grilled Eggplant with Pomegranate Sauce

Greek Spinach and Feta Triangles (Tiropeta)

Baklava

A Caucasus Winter Supper for Six

Do note that before you can start the lamb you will need an hour to drain the bitter juices from the eggplant. You will also need to boil some leeks. But most important, you should start cooking the lamb. The soup will take 1½ hours, so it should be started as soon as you get the other things going. You can then go back to the Kurdish lamb. The salad is quick and can be made in about 20 minutes. The chickpeas and spinach is another quick dish, as is the pilaf. The bulgur for the pilaf, however, must be soaked for 20 minutes beforehand. The compote can be made the day before. Serve this meal with Armenian lahvosh. With the main course, I recommend any robust wine, such as a cabernet sauvignon or a rioja.

Lentil Soup

Georgian Nut-and-Cucumber Salad

Kurdish Lamb with Eggplant

Armenian Chickpeas and Spinach

Wheat Pilaf

Dried Fruit Compote

A Levant Lunch for Four

This is a simple lunch that can be prepared the day before. It also makes a nice afternoon nibble for any sit-down meetings. Lemonade or iced tea with mint will do quite nicely as a beverage.

Baba Ghanoush

Hummus

Tabbouleh

Carrots, Celery, Cucumbers

Pita Bread

Cheese in Syrup

Lemonade

Iced Mint Tea

A Turkish Feast for Eight

This is an uncomplicated menu with several items that can be prepared in advance. If you wish to serve the dessert cold, it should be made the day before. If you wish to serve it warm, you will have to allow about 1¼ hours for it. You have the same choice with the chicken. It can be served cold and therefore made the day before or earlier in the day. If you wish to serve it warm, it will take about an hour. Definitely make the spread the day before and serve with any good bread. For a Middle Eastern bread, try a lahvosh or flat griddle bread; I generally serve a country loaf from my favorite bakery, Grace Baking in Oakland. As for the pilaf, you will need to drain the bitter juices from the eggplant for a half hour before you start, and for the Turlu, you will need to soak the okra in vinegar for a half hour as well. Beyond these presoaking necessities, both dishes will take about 35 minutes to prepare. If you like white wine, try a chardonnay. Since I prefer red wines, I would serve a cabernet sauvignon.

Red Pepper, Walnut, and Pomegranate Spread (Muhammara)

Turkish Cucumber-Tomato Salad

Turkish Chicken with Walnuts

Eggplant Rice Pilaf

Mixed Braised Vegetables (Turlu)

Almond Custard

A Late Persian Summer Sampler for Six

This menu is a good introduction to the food of Iran. The soup must be started first, as it will need to chill for 2 hours. The fruit dessert will also need to chill for an hour. Everything else can be prepared quickly. I find India's Mango Lassi (page 46) goes well with this menu, but you could also serve iced tea, lemonade, or, if you prefer something alcoholic, a light wine such as a sauvignon blanc or Chablis.

Cold Yogurt Soup

Pomegranate Chicken

Rice with Fruit and Sumac

Persian Cucumber-Tomato Salad

Kharbozeh and Peaches

Mango Lassi

Baba Ghanoush

Eggplant and Tahini Dip

2 eggplants, halved lengthwise

8 cloves garlic

6 tbs olive oil

juice of 2 lemons

¼ cup tahini

salt to taste

white pepper to taste

For best results, the eggplant should be roasted over an open fire until the skin is charred. For convenience, however, I normally bake the eggplant in a hot oven.

Preheat an oven to 450 degrees F.

Place the halved eggplants, cut sides up, in a baking dish and score the flesh in a crisscross fashion. Finely mince 4 of the garlic cloves and mix with 4 tbs of the oil. Rub one-fourth of the mixture on the cut surface of each eggplant half, letting it soak into the meat.

Bake the eggplants until very tender, about 30 minutes. Remove from the oven and, when cool enough to handle, scoop the pulp into a bowl. Discard the skin and squeeze out any juice from the eggplant pulp. In a food processor or blender, combine the remaining 2 tbs olive oil, the remaining 4 garlic cloves, and the lemon juice. Pulse several times to chop the garlic coarsely. Add the eggplant pulp, salt, pepper, and the tahini. Puree until smooth, adding a few tablespoons water if the mixture is too thick.

Makes about 2 cups.

Hummus

Chickpea and Tahini Dip

6 cloves garlic

4 cups drained cooked chickpeas

1 cup lemon juice

1 cup tahini paste

salt to taste

paprika

4 fresh parsley sprigs, finely chopped

carrot or celery sticks and/or pita bread

2 lemons, cut into wedges

Hummus takes me back to my high-school years in Colombia. I would stop off at Los Turcos restaurant almost nightly for a plate of hummus and some sweet apple soda. While Colombia has seen very little immigration, Lebanese, Syrian, and Turkish Christians have moved there. Luckily they brought hummus with them. It's a snap to make if you use canned chickpeas, although I prefer the flavor of freshly cooked chickpeas.

In a food processor or blender, combine the garlic, chickpeas, and lemon juice. Puree coarsely, then add the tahini paste and salt. Puree until well blended and smooth. Transfer to a serving dish and sprinkle with paprika and parsley. Serve with carrot or celery sticks and/or pita bread and lemon wedges.

Makes about 2 cups.

Red Pepper, Walnut, and Pomegranate Spread

Muhammara

6 red bell peppers

2 Fresno chilies (optional)

1 tsp cumin seeds

1 tsp black cumin seeds (optional)

1 cup walnuts

1 tsp lemon juice

3 tbs pomegranate molasses

1 tsp honey

2 tbs olive oil (optional)

I am addicted to this spread. I serve it with pita bread, French bread, and as a dip for crudités. Over time I have made this basic recipe with a number of variations. Sometimes I will use sour cherry syrup, other times a combination of pomegranate and sour cherry. I have substituted almonds and pistachios for the walnuts, but I prefer the walnuts. Sometimes I will make it really hot by using a habanero chili instead of the Fresnos. Rarely will I add the olive oil, but most people prefer it with the oil. The flavors improve if the spread is allowed to sit.

Preheat an oven to 500 degrees F.

Place the bell peppers on a baking sheet and roast in the oven (covering the baking sheet with aluminum foil makes cleaning up easier). Turn the peppers as necessary to char evenly on all sides. If you wish the spread to be hot and spicy, toss in the Fresno chilies when you turn the red peppers for the last time. The chilies will roast much more quickly than the bell peppers. Once the peppers are blackened on all sides (after anywhere between 20 and 40 minutes, depending on the oven), place them in a plastic or paper bag and seal tightly. The steam created by the peppers will cause the skins to loosen. Leave sealed for 20 minutes. Open the bag and peel away the skins from the meat of the bell peppers and chilies. Discard the stems, inner membranes, and all the seeds. Place the flesh of the peppers and chilies in a small bowl and set aside.

In a small dry skillet, toast the cumin seeds and the black cumin seeds, if using, over medium heat for 3 minutes. Remove from the heat. In a food processor, coarsely chop the walnuts and then add the roasted cumin. Pulse a few times and wipe down the bowl sides with a spatula. Add the lemon juice, pomegranate molasses, and honey. Pulse a few more times and then wipe down the sides again. Add the bell peppers and the chilies, if used, and run the processor until the peppers have been absorbed into the spread. If you choose to add the olive oil, do so after adding the peppers and do so with the processor running. Transfer to a serving bowl.

Makes about 2 cups.

Dolmas

....

Greek Stuffed Grape Leaves

1 cup olive oil

2 onions, diced

2 cloves garlic, minced

1 tsp salt

½ tsp black pepper

½ lb ground lamb

1 cup long-grain white rice

2 tablespoons minced fresh dill

12 fresh parsley sprigs, finely
    chopped

2 tbs pine nuts

1 tbs minced fresh mint

6 green onions, finely chopped

1 cup lemon juice

1 jar (8 oz) grape leaves in brine

about 2½ cups water

lemon wedges

In a large skillet, heat ½ cup of the oil over medium heat. When it is hot, add the onions and garlic and saute for 1 minute. Add the salt, pepper, and lamb and brown the meat evenly, stirring often, about 5 minutes. Add the rice, reduce the heat to medium-low, and simmer for 10 minutes, stirring often. Add the dill, parsley, pine nuts, mint, green onions, and 1/2 cup of the lemon juice. Mix well and continue to simmer until all the liquid has been absorbed, about 15 minutes longer. Remove from the heat.

Remove the grape leaves from the jar and rinse carefully under cold running water. Place a leaf, shiny side down, on a work surface. Place 1 tsp of the rice filling near the stem of the leaf. Fold in the sides and then roll up the leaf, tucking in the edges. Repeat until you have used up all the filling.

In a large skillet or saute pan, combine the remaining ½ cup each of oil and lemon juice. Gently slip the stuffed leaves into the pan, stacking them if necessary. Add just enough water to cover. Place a plate on top of the stuffed leaves to anchor them. Simmer over medium-low heat to cook the filling fully and blend the flavors, about 30 minutes. Remove from the heat and let cool.

Serve at room temperature with lemon wedges.

Makes 8 servings.

Greek Cucumber Yogurt Sauce

....

Tzatziki

1 English cucumber, peeled and
    diced

2 cups plain yogurt

¼ cup fresh mint leaves, finely
    chopped

2 cloves garlic, minced

1 tbs olive oil

1 tsp paprika

I serve this sauce as a dip for bread, raw or blanched vegetables, or the preceding dolmas. I like the English cucumber because it has very few seeds and is not as watery as a regular cucumber. If you need to use the latter, remove the seeds, sprinkle it with salt—preferably kosher—and let drain in a colander for at least 15 minutes, then rinse.

Combine all ingredients in a bowl, mixing well. Cover with plastic wrap and refrigerate for 1 hour before serving.

Makes about 2 cups.

Armenian Lentil Balls

Vospov Kufta

1 cup orange lentils (masoor dal)

1 small red onion, grated

3 cups water

1 cup bulgur

4 tbs butter, at room temperature

1 egg, lightly beaten

1 tsp Aleppo pepper (substitute any Middle Eastern chili powder or paprika)

salt to taste

4 green onions, thinly sliced

6 fresh parsley sprigs, finely minced

Serve these with Tzatziki (page 139), Tahini with Yogurt Sauce (following), or a simple blend of 1 cup plain yogurt spiked with 2 tbs lemon juice.

In a small saucepan, combine the lentils, grated onion, and water. Bring to a simmer and cook for 20 minutes. Add the bulgur, mix well, and cook for 5 minutes longer. Remove from the heat. Cover and let stand for 10 minutes. The water should be completely absorbed.

Stir the lentil mixture well and transfer to a bowl. Add the butter, egg, Aleppo pepper or substitute, and salt. Mix well. Combine the green onions and parsley on a plate. Form the lentil mixture into 1-inch balls and roll them in the green onion mixture. Serve at room temperature.

Makes 6 servings.

Tahini with Yogurt Sauce

1½ cups plain yogurt

1 cup tahini

2 cloves garlic, minced

½ cup lemon juice

juice of 1 lime

¼ cup water

1 tsp ground cumin

6 fresh parsley sprigs, finely chopped

Use as a sauce for vegetables or panfried or grilled fish dishes.

Scoop the yogurt into a fine-mesh sieve placed over a bowl and let drain for 30 minutes.

In a food processor or blender, combine the tahini, garlic, lemon juice, and lime juice. Process until well blended and add the water. Process again until smooth. Transfer to a bowl.

Add the drained yogurt in the sieve to the tahini mixture and whisk thoroughly. Whisk in the cumin until well mixed. Sprinkle with the parsley before serving.

Makes about 2 cups.

Greek Spinach and Feta Triangles

··

Tiropeta

2 packages (10 oz each) frozen
   chopped spinach

⅓ cup olive oil

6 green onions, thinly sliced

8 fresh parsley sprigs, finely
   minced

1 tsp white pepper

½ tsp ground nutmeg

½ lb feta cheese, crumbled

3 eggs, lightly beaten

1 lb butter

1 lb phyllo dough, thawed if frozen

The filling for these pastry triangles is very similar to the better-known spanakopita, which is baked in a single, large pie. The small packets, however, are easier to serve.

Thaw the frozen spinach and squeeze to press out all excess water. In a large saute pan or skillet, heat the olive oil over medium heat. When it is hot, add the green onions and saute until soft, about 3 minutes. Add the spinach, mix well, and allow the spinach to wilt, about 2 minutes. Remove from the heat and drain off all but 2 tbs of the liquid.

Transfer the contents of the pan to a bowl. Add the parsley, white pepper, nutmeg, and feta. Mix well. Add the eggs and mix well again. Refrigerate until ready to use.

Melt the butter. Allow to cool for 5 minutes before using. Place 1 sheet of phyllo on a lightly floured flat surface. (As you work, cover the unused phyllo sheets with waxed paper and a damp towel to prevent them from drying out.) Brush lightly with butter. Place a second sheet of phyllo on top and again brush with butter. Repeat once more. Using a serrated knife, cut the stack of sheets in half lengthwise. Then cut each half lengthwise into strips about 2 inches wide. Place a heaping teaspoon of the filling onto the end of a strip. Bring the right edge over and fold at 45 degrees to make a triangle. Bring the bottom of the triangle up against the straight edge. Continue in this manner, forming a triangle with each fold (it is similar to the way in which flags are folded), until you reach the end of the strip. A little tab of phyllo will be visible at the end. Gently tuck it in and brush with butter to secure. Place in a buttered glass baking dish. Repeat with the remaining phyllo and filling, using a second buttered dish if needed to accommodate all the triangles.

When all the triangles have been made, cover the dish(es) with plastic wrap and place in the freezer for at least 1 hour or preferably overnight.

Preheat an oven to 400 degrees F. Remove the dish(es) from the freezer 15 minutes before putting them in the oven. Bake until golden brown, 10 to 12 minutes. Serve hot.

Makes 40 to 45 triangles.

Greek Shrimp with Feta and Herbs

3 tbs olive oil

1 onion, finely chopped

4 cloves garlic, minced

10 fresh parsley sprigs, minced, plus chopped parsley for garnish (optional)

3 tablespoons fresh oregano leaves

¼ cup fresh basil leaves, minced

¼ teaspoon sugar

6 plum tomatoes, peeled and chopped

½ cup tomato sauce

¼ cup lemon juice

1 lb shrimp, peeled and deveined

½ lb feta cheese, crumbled

Preheat an oven to 400 degrees F.

In a large skillet, heat the olive oil over medium heat. When it is hot, add the onion and garlic and saute for 1 minute. Add all the herbs and the sugar, mix well, and add the tomatoes, tomato sauce, and lemon juice. Stir to combine, reduce the heat to low, and simmer, stirring occasionally, until thickened, about 20 minutes.

Add the shrimp to the pan and cook, stirring constantly, for 1 minute. Remove from the heat and transfer to a 1½-quart baking dish. Mix in about three-fourths of the feta and sprinkle the remainder on top.

Bake until the cheese melts and the shrimp are cooked through, about 12 minutes. Just before serving, garnish with chopped parsley, if desired.

Makes 4 servings.

Persian Cucumber-Tomato Salad

9 firm, ripe plum tomatoes

3 cucumbers, peeled and seeded

juice of 1 lemon

4 green onions, thinly sliced

¼ cup olive oil

2 tsp chopped fresh mint

2 tsp chopped fresh parsley

salt to taste

white pepper to taste

1 tsp sumac

Finely dice the tomatoes and the cucumbers. Combine them in a bowl and pour in the lemon juice. Mix in the green onions and olive oil. Cover and chill for 20 minutes.

Just before serving, add the mint and parsley. Season with salt and white pepper and stir in the sumac.

Makes 6 to 8 servings.

Turkish Cucumber-Tomato Salad

5 firm, ripe tomatoes, sliced

2 cucumbers, peeled and sliced

juice of 3 lemons

1 tbs distilled white vinegar

⅓ cup olive oil

2 tsp chopped fresh mint

2 tsp chopped fresh parsley

24 black olives

salt to taste

black pepper to taste

Arrange the tomatoes and cucumbers on a platter. In a small bowl, combine the lemon juice, vinegar, olive oil, mint, and parsley. Mix well and pour over the tomatoes and cucumbers. Arrange the olives around the edge of the platter. Sprinkle with salt and pepper.

Makes 6 to 8 servings.

Dilled Cucumbers in Yogurt

1 cucumber, peeled and thinly sliced

⅔ cup plain yogurt

1 tsp balsamic vinegar

1 tsp lemon juice

2 tbs chopped fresh dill

dash of salt

Combine all the ingredients. Chill for at least 15 minutes before serving.

Makes 4 servings.

Georgian Nut-and-Cucumber Salad

½ cup blanched almonds, toasted (page 227)

½ cup walnuts, toasted (page 227)

½ tsp ground cumin

½ tsp black pepper

2 cucumbers, peeled and thinly sliced

¼ cup distilled white vinegar

1 head butter lettuce

½ bunch spinach, stemmed

1 red onion, thinly sliced

2 red bell peppers, roasted and cut into long, narrow strips (page 227)

½ cup cured black olives

⅓ cup chopped fresh parsley

Pomegranate Dressing:

⅔ cup olive oil

4 tbs balsamic vinegar

juice of 1 lemon

3 tbs pomegranate molasses

1 tsp sugar

1 tsp dried oregano

seeds from ½ pomegranate (optional, page 148)

Preheat an oven to 375 degrees F.

Place the toasted nuts on a cutting board. Sprinkle the cumin and black pepper over the top, then chop coarsely. Set aside.

In a small bowl, combine the cucumber and vinegar and let stand for 5 minutes. Drain and set aside. Carefully rinse the lettuce and the spinach leaves. Be sure to pat them thoroughly dry.

On a large platter, mix the lettuce and the spinach leaves to form a bed. Arrange the cucumbers in a circular fashion in the center atop the bed. The lettuce and spinach should be mostly covered with the cucumber slices except for the outside edges. Place the red onion slices over the cucumber. Divide the red pepper slices into 6 uniform mounds, and place them around the outside edge of the platter atop the lettuce and spinach. Next to each mound, place a couple of black olives. Sprinkle the chopped nuts over the red onion slices. Finally, sprinkle the parsley over the nuts.

To make the pomegranate dressing, in a bowl, combine all the ingredients except the pomegranate seeds, if using. Whisk well. Gently stir in the seeds.

Pass the pomegranate dressing at the table.

Makes 6 servings.

Cold Yogurt Soup

2 English cucumbers, peeled

4 cups plain yogurt

4 green onions, thinly sliced

12 fresh parsley sprigs, chopped

¼ cup chopped fresh dill or 2 tsp dried dill

8 fresh cilantro sprigs, chopped

½ cup pistachios

½ cup chicken broth, chilled

salt to taste

An English cucumber works best because it has very few seeds and is not as watery as a regular cucumber. If only regular cucumbers are available, seed them, sprinkle with salt—preferably kosher—and let drain in a colander for at least 15 minutes, then rinse. This soup can be prepared up to 8 hours in advance.

Grate the cucumbers or puree in a food processor or blender. Transfer to a bowl, add the yogurt, and mix well. Add the green onions, parsley, dill, and cilantro, stirring to distribute evenly.

In a small food processor or clean blender, grind the pistachios coarsely. Reserve 3 tbs for garnish. Continue to grind the remaining pistachios to a fine powder. Stir the finely ground pistachios into the yogurt mixture, then stir in the broth, mixing thoroughly. Cover and chill well, at least 2 hours.

Just before serving, season the soup with salt. Ladle into chilled bowls and garnish with the coarsely ground pistachios.

Makes 6 servings.

Lentil Soup

8 cups lamb or chicken broth

¼ cup olive oil

2 onions, finely chopped

1 carrot, shredded

2 celery stalks, thinly sliced

1 tsp ground coriander

2 tsp dried thyme

1 tsp dried oregano

2 cups red lentils (masoor dal)

1 tbs Aleppo pepper (substitute any Middle Eastern chili powder or paprika)

2 shallots, sliced and fried in butter until brown

Pour the broth into a saucepan and bring to a gentle simmer. Meanwhile, in a large saucepan, heat the olive oil over medium heat. When it is hot, add the onions and saute until soft, about 5 minutes. Add the carrot, celery, coriander, thyme, and oregano; mix well and cook for 5 minutes.

Add the lentils and the Aleppo pepper or substitute and mix thoroughly to coat the lentils with the onion mixture. Add 1 cup of the hot stock and cook, stirring, until the lentils absorb it, about 5 minutes. Then add the rest of the stock and bring to a boil. Reduce the heat to low and simmer, uncovered, until the lentils are tender, about 1 hour. Serve in warmed bowls garnished with the fried shallots.

Makes 6 servings.

Kurdish Lamb with Eggplant and Leeks

3 eggplants, sliced

4 tbs salt, plus extra to taste

3 tbs olive oil

2 onions, quartered

4 cloves garlic, minced

1 tsp cumin seeds

2 tsp ground coriander

1 tsp ground allspice

3 lb boneless lamb from leg, cut into 1-inch cubes

2 cups lamb or chicken broth, or water

1/3 cup sumac

1/4 cup water

2 thin leeks, poached in water until tender, about 5 minutes

1 cup tomato sauce

2 tbs tomato paste

juice of 2 lemons

I got this recipe during a political discussion with Kurt Ugar, owner of Café Pro Bono, a nice little Italian restaurant in Palo Alto, California.

Place the eggplant slices in a colander in a sink, sprinkling each slice with a little of the 4 tbs salt. Let stand for about 1 hour to drain away the bitter juices. Then rinse the eggplant and set aside.

Meanwhile, in a large pot, heat the olive oil over medium heat. When it is hot, add the onions and garlic and saute until the onions are soft, about 6 minutes. Add the cumin seeds, coriander, and allspice and mix well. Add the cubed lamb and brown the meat evenly on all sides. Pour in the broth or water and salt to taste. Bring to a boil, then reduce the heat to low and cover. Simmer until the lamb is tender and the flavors are blended, about 15 minutes.

Using a slotted spoon, remove the lamb from its sauce. Scoop out 1/2 cup of the sauce and combine it with the sumac and water. Mix well and set aside.

Preheat an oven to 350 degrees F. Grease a large baking dish with olive oil.

Place a layer of eggplant slices on the bottom of the prepared dish and then add all the lamb. Cut the poached leeks in long, thin slices and place atop the lamb. Cover the leeks with rest of the eggplant slices. In a small bowl, mix together the tomato sauce, tomato paste, and lemon juice. Mix well and pour the over the eggplant. Now pour the reserved sumac mixture over the top.

Bake until the eggplant is tender, about 35 minutes.

Makes 6 to 8 servings.

Georgian Lamb Kabobs

2½ lb boneless lamb from leg, cut into 1-inch cubes

5 tbs sour cherry syrup

½ cup plus ⅓ cup water

3 tbs olive oil

2 cloves garlic, minced

½ red onion, minced

1 tsp salt

1 tsp white pepper

¼ tsp sugar

Place the lamb in a large bowl. In a small bowl, combine 3 tbs of the sour cherry syrup with the ½ cup water. Mix well. Add to the lamb and stir to coat the lamb evenly. Cover with plastic wrap and refrigerate overnight.

In the morning, in a bowl, combine the olive oil, garlic, red onion, salt, pepper, and sugar. Add to the lamb and mix well to coat the lamb. Re-cover, return to the refrigerator, and continue marinating until the evening.

Light a fire in a charcoal grill.

Thread the lamb onto greased metal skewers. In a small bowl, combine the remaining 2 tbs sour cherry syrup with the ⅓ cup water. Place the lamb over hot coals and grill, turning once and basting with the syrup mixture, until done to your liking, 7 to 8 minutes on each side for medium-well.

Makes 6 to 8 servings.

Turkish Chicken with Walnut Sauce

1 chicken, about 3½ lb, cut into serving pieces

1 carrot

1 onion, peeled and studded with 20 cloves

3 bay leaves

2 celery stalks, halved

about 8 fresh parsley sprigs

3 quarts water

salt to taste

a few black peppercorns

6 slices white bread, crusts removed

3 cups walnuts

An interesting dish that can be served cold or warm, accompanied with couscous or rice pilaf.

Place the chicken pieces in a stockpot with the carrot, the clove-studded onion, bay leaves, celery, 5 of the parsley sprigs, and water. Season with salt and peppercorns and bring to a boil. Boil for 20 minutes and then cover tightly. Reduce the heat to low and simmer for 10 more minutes, then remove from the heat. Let stand, covered, for 20 minutes.

Remove and discard the carrot, the clove-studded onion, bay leaves, celery, and parsley. Reserve 2 cups of the broth to make the walnut sauce (the rest you can either freeze for future use or use instead of water to make your couscous or rice). Transfer the chicken pieces to a platter.

Tear the bread into small pieces and place in a blender. Add the 2 cups broth and puree. Then add the walnuts and the remaining 3 parsley sprigs. Blend well. Pour over the chicken, completely covering it.

Makes 4 servings.

Pomegranate Chicken

6 boneless, skinless chicken breast
  halves

2 tsp Worcestershire Sauce

7 tbs pomegranate molasses

juice of 1 lemon

1 tsp sumac

2 tbs olive oil

2 onions, sliced

1 cup water

½ tsp arrowroot

seeds from 2 pomegranates
  (below)

Although this dish is still delicious when made without the pomegranate seeds, I only make it when I have them. Sadly this means only in August, September, and October. The seeds not only provide a nice tangy crunch but also make the dish a visual delight.

Place the chicken breasts in a shallow dish. In a small bowl, stir together the Worcestershire sauce, 3 tbs of the pomegranate molasses, lemon juice, and sumac. Pour over the chicken breasts and let marinate for 30 minutes.

In a large skillet, heat the olive oil over medium heat. When it is hot, add the onions. Saute until the onions are soft, about 6 minutes. Add the chicken breasts and their marinade and brown the chicken evenly on both sides.

Meanwhile, in a cup or bowl, stir together the water and the remaining 4 tbs pomegranate molasses to make pomegranate juice. When the chicken is browned, pour in the pomegranate juice and bring to a boil. Reduce the heat to low and simmer until the chicken is cooked through, about 10 minutes.

Using tongs or a slotted spatula, transfer the breasts to a warmed platter; keep warm. Scoop out ¼ cup of the pomegranate juice and dissolve the arrowroot in it. Return to the pan, stirring well, and raise the heat slightly. Cook, stirring occasionally, until the sauce thickens slightly, a few minutes. Pour over the breasts and sprinkle the pomegranate seeds over them. Serve at once.

Makes 6 servings.

Removing Seeds From A Pomegranate

Using a sharp knife, cut the fruit into halves or quarters. Using the tip of a spoon, dig out clusters of the seeds, dropping them into a bowl. Then, using your fingertips, separate the seeds from the bitter membrane, freeing them from the small pockets in which they are lodged.

YaYa's Perdaplow

1 chicken, about 3½ lb

2 onions, coarsely chopped

3 cloves garlic, minced

1 tbs salt

1½ tsp black pepper

2 tbs olive oil

2 tbs ground cardamom

4 cups cooked white rice

1 cup almonds, toasted (page 227) and coarsely chopped

1 egg

1 cup golden raisins

1 cup (½ lb) unsalted butter

18 to 24 sheets phyllo dough, about 10 oz, thawed if frozen

Raspberry sauce:

1 pint raspberries

2 tbs unsalted butter

½ tsp minced garlic

2 cups heavy cream

salt to taste

black pepper to taste

confectioners' sugar and ground cinnamon

Chef Yayah Salih serves this adaptation of a Middle Eastern dish in his charming YaYa restaurant.

In a large pot, place the chicken with water to cover. Bring to a boil and cook at a gentle boil for 15 minutes. Remove from the heat and remove the chicken from the water. Set aside to cool. The chicken will not be fully cooked.

In a food processor, blender, or mortar, combine the onions and garlic and grind to a paste. Mix in the salt and pepper. In a large skillet or saute pan, heat the oil over medium heat. When it is hot, add the onion mixture and cook, stirring frequently, until it is dry. (The mixture will release a fair amount of liquid.)

While the onion is cooking, bone the chicken and shred the meat into long strips. When the onion mixture is ready, add the chicken to it and continue to cook, stirring often, until the chicken is visibly cooked, 5 to 7 minutes. Remove from the heat and transfer to a bowl. Add the cardamom, rice, almonds, egg, and raisins. Mix thoroughly and set aside.

In a skillet over low heat, slowly melt the butter. When it is fully melted, skim off any foam from the surface, then carefully pour the clear golden liquid into a bowl, leaving the milky residue behind in the pan. The clear liquid is clarified butter. Let cool.

Preheat an oven to 375 degrees F. Using a pastry brush, coat the bottom of a 9-by-13-by-2-inch baking dish or pan with some of the clarified butter. (You may instead use a round dish or pan 12 inches in diameter and 3 inches deep or 2 round dishes or pans 6 inches in diameter and 2 inches deep.) Place a phyllo sheet into the prepared dish or pan, pressing it into the corners. (Keep the phyllo sheets you are not immediately working with well covered with plastic wrap and a damp towel so they don't dry out.) The sheets should be roughly twice the size of the dish or pan so that they will cover the top once the vessel is full. Brush the sheet with the clarified butter. Top with a second sheet, pushing it gently into the corners, and again brush with the butter. Repeat this process until all the sheets are used. Spoon in the chicken-rice mixture; do not pack it too tightly. Fold the overhang of the phyllo sheets over the mixture, and lightly butter the edges to seal. (The dish may be cooked now or set aside for several hours). Bake until the top is golden brown and the filling is piping hot, 40 to 50 minutes.

Meanwhile, make the sauce: In a blender or food processor, puree the raspberries. Transfer the puree to a fine-mesh sieve placed over a bowl, and press it through with the back of a spoon. Set aside. In a saucepan, melt the butter over high heat. When it foams, add the garlic and saute until translucent, about 1 minute. Pour in the cream and boil vigorously to reduce by one-half. Add the raspberry puree, salt, and pepper and return to a boil. Reduce the heat to medium-low and simmer until the sauce has a nice creamy appearance and texture, 1 to 2 minutes. Do not overcook the sauce or it will separate; if it does, add more cream, remove from the heat, and whisk until smooth.

When the perdaplow is ready, remove from the oven and let stand for a few minutes, then carefully invert it onto a platter. Garnish with a dusting of confectioners' sugar and cinnamon. Pour the sauce around—not over—the perdaplow.

Makes 6 servings.

Rice Pilaf, Wheat Pilaf, and Tabbouleh

Rice pilaf is common throughout the Middle East and Central Asia. There are countless variations, probably as many as there are cooks. Basically they always include rice and often some kind of wheat pasta (orzo, a rice-shaped pasta, is common) and are usually cooked in chicken broth. Nuts and fruits are also typical ingredients. There is a boxed mix made by Near East that is quite nice. Follow the instructions on the package and you can't go wrong. You can also easily make your own rice pilafs, however. One of my favorite recipes follows.

Wheat pilaf is an Armenian dish made from ground rolled wheat. It is available in boxes in most supermarkets. Near East brand sells a good blend. Wheat pilaf can also be made from bulgur. Again, it is a simply wonderful dish and especially delightful as a change of pace. Again, a recipe follows.

Tabbouleh is also made from bulgur wheat. In this case the wheat is mixed with olive oil, mint, parsley, and lemon juice and then studded with cucumber slices and tomatoes. You can buy regular bulgur or you can buy a package mix and then add lemon juice, fresh mint and parsley, tomato wedges, and cucumber slices. I have included a tabbouleh recipe as well.

Basic Rice Pilaf

3 tbs olive oil

1 onion, finely chopped

4 cups light chicken broth or water

salt to taste

½ cup orzo

2 cups basmati rice, rinsed

In a medium saucepan, heat the olive oil over medium heat. When it is hot, add the onion and saute until it begins to soften, about 3 minutes. Then add the broth or water and bring to a boil. Add the salt and orzo and boil for 1 minute. Add the rice and bring to a boil again. Reduce the heat to low, cover, and simmer until the liquid is absorbed and the rice is tender, about 20 minutes. Remove from the heat and let stand, covered, for another 5 minutes before serving.

Makes 6 to 8 servings.

Eggplant Rice Pilaf

2 large eggplants, cut into 1-inch cubes

3 tbs salt, plus extra to taste

¼ cup olive oil

1 onion, finely chopped

2 cloves garlic, minced

1 tsp ground cumin

1 tsp ground coriander

4 cups light chicken broth or water

2 cups basmati rice, rinsed

Place the eggplant cubes in a colander, sprinkling them with the 3 tbs salt as you add the cubes. Rub together gently, then let stand for 30 minutes to drain away the bitter juices. Rinse well and set aside.

In a medium saucepan, heat the olive oil over medium heat. When it is hot, add the onion and garlic and saute until the onion begins to soften, about 3 minutes. Add the eggplant cubes, cumin, and coriander and brown the eggplant cubes evenly, stirring often, about 10 minutes. Then add the broth or water and salt to taste and bring to a boil. Add the rice and bring to a boil again. Reduce the heat to low, cover, and simmer until the liquid is absorbed and the rice is tender, about 20 minutes. Remove from the heat and let stand, covered, for another 5 minutes, before serving.

Makes 6 to 8 servings.

Rice with Dried Fruit and Sumac

∙∙

¼ cup dried Mission figs

¼ cup dried apricots

¼ cup dried pitted dates

¼ cup dried apples

3 tbs olive oil

1 onion, finely chopped

2 cloves garlic, minced

1 tsp ground cumin

1 tsp ground coriander

2 cups basmati rice, rinsed

4 cups light chicken broth or water

salt to taste

white pepper to taste

1 tsp grated orange zest

1 tsp grated lemon zest

2 tbs sumac

In a bowl, combine the figs, apricots, dates, and apples. Add water to cover and let stand for at least 30 minutes to soften.

In a medium saucepan, heat the olive oil over medium heat. When it is hot, add the onion and garlic and saute until the onion begins to soften, about 3 minutes. Add the cumin and coriander, stir well, and cook for another minute. Add the basmati rice and mix well to coat the rice. Add the broth or water, salt, and white pepper. Bring to a boil.

Meanwhile, drain off any moisture from the dried fruits and chop coarsely. As soon as the rice is boiling, add the dried fruits. Reduce the heat to low, cover partially, and simmer until the liquid is absorbed and the rice is tender, about 20 minutes. Remove from heat and let stand, covered, for another 5 minutes. Sprinkle the citrus zests and the sumac over the top and serve.

Makes 6 to 8 servings.

Tabbouleh

∙∙

1 cup bulgur

3 cups water

4 green onions, finely chopped

1 cup chopped flat-leaf parsley

1 tsp salt

1 tsp white pepper

½ tsp cayenne pepper

½ cup olive oil

juice of 2 lemons

4 plum tomatoes, sliced

⅓ cucumber, peeled and thinly sliced

In a bowl, combine the bulgur and water. Let stand for 30 minutes. Pour into a fine-mesh sieve and press out any excess moisture.

Place the bulgur in a large bowl and add the green onions. Leave for 10 minutes so that the bulgur absorbs the flavor. Add the parsley, salt, white pepper, and cayenne pepper. Mix well and add the oil and lemon juice. Mix well again. Add the tomatoes and the cucumber just before serving.

Makes 4 servings.

Wheat Pilaf

2 cups bulgur

2 cups water

2 tbs olive oil

1 tsp ground cumin

½ tsp ground coriander

½ yellow onion, finely chopped

3 cloves garlic, minced

¼ cup dried apricots, chopped

2 cups light chicken broth or water

salt to taste

½ cup orzo

2 green onions, finely chopped

4 fresh parsley sprigs, finely chopped

4 fresh cilantro sprigs, finely chopped

In a bowl, combine the bulgur and water. Let stand for 20 minutes. Pour into a fine-mesh sieve and press out any excess moisture. Set aside.

In a medium saucepan, heat the olive oil over medium heat. When it is hot, add the cumin and coriander, stir well, and add the yellow onion and garlic. Saute until the onion begins to soften, about 3 minutes. Add the apricots, stir well, and add the broth or water. Bring to a boil and add the salt and orzo. Boil for 2 minutes and add the bulgur. Reduce the heat to low and simmer for 3 minutes, stirring occasionally. Turn the pilaf onto a serving platter. Mix together the green onions, parsley, and cilantro, then sprinkle on top of the pilaf and serve.

Makes 6 servings.

Grilled Eggplant with Pomegranate Sauce

½ cucumber, peeled, seeded, and diced

1 tomato, diced

2 green onions, thinly sliced

¼ cup chopped fresh mint

6 Japanese eggplants

½ cup pomegranate molasses

¼ cup heavy cream

This is one of my favorite ways to prepare eggplant. It is an adaptation of a dish made by chef Yayah Salih at his charming YaYa Cuisine restaurant in San Francisco.

Light a fire in a charcoal grill. Oil the grill rack.

In a small bowl, combine the cucumber and tomato. Mix in the green onions and mint. Set aside.

Make 4 long cuts in each eggplant, turning them into fans. Do not cut off the ends. Grill the eggplants over hot coals, turning them once, about 3 minutes on each side.

Meanwhile, in a saucepan, stir together the pomegranate molasses and the cream. Heat slightly and pour over the eggplants. Top with the diced cucumber garnish.

Makes 6 servings.

Armenian Chickpeas and Spinach

2 tbs olive oil

1 onion, finely chopped

4 cloves garlic, minced

1 tsp aniseeds

2 cans (15½ oz each) chickpeas, drained

2 tbs tomato paste

1 bunch spinach, stems trimmed and carefully washed

½ cup water

minced fresh parsley

black pepper to taste

My good friend Shaké Keshkekian prepared this dish for me. This is her recipe. With canned chickpeas, it is quick and easy to prepare.

In a large saucepan, heat the olive oil over medium heat. Add the onion and garlic and saute until the onion is soft, about 5 minutes. Add the aniseeds and the chickpeas. Stir well and add the tomato paste. Again stir well and add the spinach. Add the water and cook until the spinach is tender, 7 to 10 minutes. Remove from the heat and sprinkle with the parsley and pepper.

Makes 6 servings.

Mixed Braised Vegetables

Turlu

8 okras pods

¼ cup white vinegar

¼ cup olive oil

2 Japanese eggplants, sliced

2 onions, sliced

4 cloves garlic, minced

1 tsp cumin seeds

1 tsp aniseeds

½ tsp ground allspice

1 tsp ground coriander

2 green bell peppers, diced

16 green beans, ends trimmed

4 tomatoes, diced

2 zucchini, sliced

2 yellow summer squashes, sliced

1 cup water

8 fresh parsley sprigs, finely chopped

salt to taste

white pepper to taste

This dish is traditionally cooked in a clay pot roaster, although this recipe is adapted for stove-top cooking.

In a bowl, douse the okra pods with the white vinegar, tossing them gently to evenly coat them. Set aside for 30 minutes.

Meanwhile, in a large saucepan, heat the olive oil over medium heat. Add the eggplants and fry until browned, about 5 minutes. Using a slotted spoon, transfer to a platter.

In the same oil, saute the onions, garlic, cumin, aniseeds, allspice, and coriander. As soon as the onion is soft, after about 5 minutes, add the bell peppers. Saute for 2 minutes, stirring constantly. Add the green beans and the tomatoes. Cook for 1 minute. Drain the okra, add to the pan, and mix well. Add the fried eggplant, zucchini, and yellow squash. Mix well, cook for 1 minute, and add the water. Bring to a boil and add the parsley, salt, and white pepper. Reduce the heat to very low and simmer gently until all the vegetables are tender, 20 to 25 minutes.

Makes 8 servings.

Almond Pudding

• •

1 cup blanched almonds

5 cups milk

¼ cup basmati rice

¼ tsp salt

⅓ cup sugar

2 tsp orange blossom water

¼ tsp almond extract or orgeat

ground nutmeg

This dessert can be served warm or cold.

Grind the almonds in a food processor or blender (if using a blender, add ¼ cup water). The almonds should be as fine as possible. Pass through a fine-mesh sieve and mash what goes through the sieve into a paste by hand.

In a small saucepan, heat 1 cup of the milk almost to a boil. Add the almonds and stir well to blend. Remove from the heat and let stand for 20 minutes. Grind the rice in a food processor or blender along with ¼ cup of the remaining milk. Pour into a bowl. Heat the remaining 3¾ cups milk in a large, heavy saucepan. As soon as it boils, add it to the ground rice. Mix well and return the mixture to the saucepan. Bring to a boil and add the salt, sugar, and orange blossom water. Reduce the heat to low. Cook for 15 minutes.

Meanwhile, strain the almonds into a fine-mesh sieve placed over a bowl, pressing all the liquid from them. Pour this liquid into the simmering pudding. When the 15 minutes are up, gently stir in the almond extract or orgeat. Simmer for another 10 minutes. Pour into individual dessert bowls. Sprinkle with nutmeg.

Makes 8 servings.

Dried Fruit Compote

• •

1 cup pitted prunes

1 cup dried Mission figs

1 cup dried apricots

1 cup golden raisins

⅓ cup sugar

2 tbs honey

1 tsp grated lemon zest

1 tsp grated orange zest

1 cinnamon stick

2 whole cloves

½ tsp ground nutmeg

2 tbs orange blossom water

fresh mint leaves

An easy dessert for those dark winter days.

Place all the dried fruits in a medium saucepan with water to cover. Bring to a boil and mix in the sugar, a little at a time. Reduce the heat to low and add the honey, lemon zest, orange zest, cinnamon stick, and cloves. Simmer for 15 minutes. Add the nutmeg and the orange blossom water. Simmer for another 5 minutes. Remove and discard the cinnamon and the cloves. Allow to cool and decorate with mint before serving.

Makes 6 servings.

Cheese in Syrup

3 cups sugar

2 cups water

½ lb mozzarella cheese, cut into ¼-inch-thick slices

2 whole cloves

1 cinnamon stick

1-inch-piece lemon zest

juice of 1 lemon

2 tsp rose water

The Lebanese community in Colombia makes this with Colombian farmer cheese. Here I use mozzarella.

In a medium saucepan, make a syrup by combining the sugar and water over medium heat. Stir well to dissolve the sugar, then bring to a boil. Allow the syrup to thicken.

Drop the cheese slices into the hot syrup and add the cloves, cinnamon, lemon zest, lemon juice, and rose water. Bring to a boil again and remove from the heat. Allow to cool.

Makes 6 servings.

Kharbozeh and Peaches

1 kharbozeh

4 peaches

½ cup sugar

juice of 2 lemons

3 tbs rose water

Kharbozeh is a small Persian melon occasionally found in Middle Eastern markets. If you can not find one, substitute a honeydew melon.

Peel and seed the kharbozeh, then dice into small cubes. Peel, pit, and dice the peaches and add them to the melon. In a small bowl, dissolve the sugar in the lemon juice and rose water. Pour over the fruit. Mix well to coat the fruit. Cover and chill for 1 hour before serving.

Makes 6 servings.

Morocco

Of all the cuisines covered in this book, Moroccan food is probably the least well known. There are few cookbooks on the subject, and Moroccan restaurants are a rare commodity in the Bay Area. When I first arrived in Palo Alto, there was an excellent Moroccan restaurant downtown. Sadly, this charming hole-in-the-wall was one of the casualties of Palo Alto's glitzy boom.

I was still a teenager when I first encountered Moroccan food. On a trip to Spain, I crossed over from Tarifa and spent a weekend in Tangiers. This whetted my appetite, and I returned for a longer stay immediately after college. Morocco is an enchanting land, with some of the world's most vibrant markets. The variety and color of spices for sale is truly the highlight of any market visit. Each vendor places large baskets of spices at the front of his stall, with a prominent place reserved for the special blend known as ras el hanout.

A good Moroccan dinner should consist of four basic components: a stewed meat or chicken, couscous, a few small salads, and the ubiquitous harissa, the Moroccan hot sauce that accompanies almost everything. The stews are remarkably easy and quick to make, and couscous is as simple as boiling water. The salads are also wonderfully uncomplicated. Moroccan food, therefore, lends itself to life on the run.

In this chapter, you will find recipes for traditional Moroccan spice blends and preserved lemons, a few salads, three stews, foolproof instructions on how to make couscous, a couple of desserts, and a few other treats.

Suggested Menus

An Easy Moroccan Dinner

This menu is a wonderful introduction to Moroccan food. From start to finish, it should take no more than about 1¼ hours to prepare. The hummus (page 137) is from the Levant (see the Middle Eastern chapter), but it makes a nice appetizer for any Moroccan dinner. So does baba ghanoush (page 137).

Hummus with Carrots, Cucumbers, and Pita
Moroccan Chicken Stew (Tagine)
Couscous
Cucumber and Tomato Salad with Yogurt Dressing
Harissa
Green Apple Sorbet
Mint Tea

A Special-Occasion Moroccan Dinner

This menu is an elaborate multicourse Moroccan feast. The bastilla makes a nice start to any meal, and the trio of salads that follows acts as a light palate freshener. The bastilla can be made in advance and frozen. Just remove from the freezer 2 hours before baking. Finally, the main course contains preserved lemons, which should be made at least a week in advance. Dessert is a simple preparation of oranges macerated in Cointreau.

Chicken Phyllo Pie (Bastilla)

Spicy Carrot Salad

Lentil Salad

Eggplant Salad

Pita Bread

Moroccan Lamb Stew in Citrus Juice (Tagine)

Couscous Pilaf with Dried Apricots, Raisins, and Dried Mission Figs

Harissa

Preserved Lemons

Macerated Oranges

Mint Tea

Ras el Hanout

1 tsp ground cumin

1 tsp ground turmeric

1 tsp ground coriander

½ tsp ground cinnamon

½ tsp ground cloves

½ tsp ground nutmeg

¼ tsp ground ginger

¼ tsp ground allspice

¼ tsp ground mace

¼ tsp galangal powder

¼ tsp white pepper

¼ tsp ground cardamom

In Moroccan markets, each vendor makes his or her own special blend of ras el hanout and places it in a prominent spot in the front of the stall or shop. Ras el hanout, in fact, means "head of the shop."

Each blend usually contains a score or more ingredients. Some of the ingredients are quite exotic, and I have yet to find them in any market outside of Morocco. Perhaps thankfully, for many blends in Morocco would not be complete without that joy of Berber food, the green Spanish fly beetle. According to Moroccan friends, it is an aphrodisiac that every good ras el hanout should include. Oh well. Here, however, is a more typical blend. You may also be able to buy a ready-made blend—probably without Spanish fly—although not easily. In the Bay Area, Draeger's supermarket sells one.

Combine all ingredients and store in a glass jar.

Makes a scant 2 tablespoons.

Zahtar

2 parts sesame seeds

1 part dried thyme

1 part sumac

A mixture common throughout North Africa, used on meats and vegetables. Various blends are available in Middle Eastern markets, although it is easy to make.

In a small dry skillet, toast the sesame seeds over low heat for 2 to 3 minutes, shaking the pan frequently to prevent burning any seeds. Cool, then mix with the thyme and sumac. Store in a glass jar. The mixture keeps well for a few months.

Preserved Lemons

2 lemons, well washed and dried

⅓ cup kosher salt

½ cup lemon juice

olive oil to cover

Preserved lemons are an acquired taste, and few people I know like them. They are briny and bitter, but they go well with many Moroccan dishes; you eat both the pulp and the rind. Preserved lemons are used both as a relish and as an ingredient in Tagines. Traditional methods call for a month-long process, but Paula Wolfert, a noted authority on Moroccan cooking, offers a week-long preparation.

Cut each lemon into 8 wedges. Toss with the salt and place in a sterilized half-pint canning jar. Pour in the lemon juice. Seal tightly and allow to sit in a warm place for 1 week. Shake the jar twice daily to distribute the salt and juice evenly. To store after a week, add olive oil to cover. Refrigerate and use within 6 months.

Harissa

12 dried red chilies or 10 fresh Fresno chilies

4 cloves garlic

salt to taste

1 tbs coriander seeds

1 tsp caraway seeds

2 tsp ground cumin

black pepper

2 tbs olive oil

Harissa is the classic Moroccan hot sauce, used both in cooking and as a table condiment. Although available at fine food shops in small tins and tubes imported from France, Tunisia, or Morocco, harissa is actually simple to make.

If using dried chilies, soften them by soaking in water to cover for 30 minutes, then drain. Remove the stems and place the chilies in a mortar. Add the garlic and salt and pound into a paste. Then add the rest of the ingredients except the olive oil. Blend well and add the oil. If using fresh chilies, discard the stems, slice the chilies into small pieces, and grind with the rest of the ingredients except the olive oil. When well blended, add the oil. Store in a tightly covered jar in the refrigerator.

Makes about ½ cup.

Spicy Carrot Salad

3 carrots, shredded

¼ cup olive oil

1 tbs distilled white vinegar

3 cloves garlic, minced

1 tsp harissa, homemade (page 161) or purchased

A simple salad that makes a nice appetizer or side dish.

In a bowl, combine all the ingredients and mix well. Cover and chill before serving.

Makes 6 servings.

Lentil Salad

2 tablespoons olive oil

1 yellow onion, finely diced

4 cloves garlic, minced

2 tsp ground cumin

1 rounded cup dried lentils, rinsed

4 cups water

4 plum tomatoes, sliced

2 celery stalks, thinly sliced

¼ cup chopped fresh mint

2 red chilies (Fresno, serrano, or similar), thinly sliced

3 green onions, chopped

6 fresh cilantro sprigs, chopped

1 cup plain yogurt

In a medium saucepan, heat the olive oil over medium heat. When it is hot, add the yellow onion, garlic, and cumin and saute until soft, about 5 minutes. Add the lentils, stir well, and then add the water. Bring to a boil, reduce the heat to low, and simmer, loosely covered, until the lentils are tender, 35 to 40 minutes. If the water begins to cook away before the lentils are tender, add more water, a little at a time, as needed. Remove from the heat, drain well, and let cool.

In a bowl, combine the tomatoes, celery, mint, chilies, green onions, and cilantro. Mix well. Add the yogurt and cooked lentils. Mix well and serve.

Makes 4 to 6 servings.

Cucumber and Tomato Salad with Yogurt Dressing

1 cucumber, peeled and sliced

10 plum tomatoes, sliced

½ cup olive oil

5 cloves garlic

6 fresh cilantro sprigs, plus chopped cilantro for garnish

juice of 1 lemon

2 cups plain yogurt

1 tbs zahtar, homemade (page 160) or purchased, or 1 tsp sesame seeds and 1 tsp dried thyme

Combine the cucumber and tomato slices in a shallow dish. Drizzle the olive oil over them.

In a blender, combine the garlic, cilantro sprigs, and lemon juice. Grind to a paste. Add the yogurt and the zahtar or sesame seeds and thyme and blend well. Pour over the cucumber and tomatoes and sprinkle with some chopped cilantro.

Makes 6 to 8 servings.

Chickpea Salad

2 cans (15½ oz each) chickpeas, drained and rinsed

1 red onion, finely chopped

10 fresh mint leaves, coarsely chopped

1 tsp ground cumin or ras el hanout, homemade (page 160) or purchased

⅓ cup olive oil

1 tbs distilled white vinegar

⅔ cup pitted black olives

1 tsp harissa, homemade (page 161) or purchased

For those on the run, this is a nice salad, as it uses canned chickpeas.

In a bowl, combine the chickpeas, onion, mint, cumin or ras el hanout, olive oil, vinegar, olives, and harissa. Mix well, cover, and chill before serving.

Makes 4 to 6 servings.

Eggplant Salad

2 eggplants, halved lengthwise

4 tbs plus ⅓ cup olive oil

3 tsp sumac

2 tsp dried thyme

6 cloves garlic, minced

1 shallot, finely chopped

4 tomatoes, cut into quarters

juice of 1 lemon

2 tsp capers

⅓ cup pitted black olives

6 fresh parsley sprigs, finely chopped

6 fresh cilantro sprigs, finely chopped

1 head butter lettuce, leaves separated

Preheat an oven to 400 degrees F.

Place the eggplant halves, cut sides up, in a glass baking dish. Cut deep diagonal slits into the eggplant flesh. Drizzle 1 tablespoon of the olive oil onto each eggplant half, allowing the oil to penetrate the slits. In a small bowl, stir together 1 tsp each sumac and thyme. Sprinkle the tops of the eggplants with the sumac mixture.

Bake until soft, about 30 minutes. Remove from the oven and let cool. Scoop the flesh onto a cutting board; discard the skins. Coarsely dice the flesh.

In a medium saucepan, heat the remaining ⅓ cup oil over medium heat. When it is hot, add the garlic and shallot and cook for 2 minutes. Stir together the remaining 1 tsp thyme and 1 tsp of the remaining sumac and add to the pan. Mix well and add the diced eggplant along with any juices. Continue to cook for 5 minutes, stirring often. Reduce the heat to low and add the tomatoes and lemon juice. Mix well and cook for another 5 minutes. Add the capers and black olives. Cook for 2 minutes, stirring constantly. Remove from the heat and mix in the parsley and cilantro. Serve spooned over the lettuce leaves. Sprinkle with the remaining 1 tsp sumac.

Makes 4 to 6 servings.

Chicken Phyllo Pie

Bastilla

2 tbs olive oil

½ onion, finely chopped

1 shallot, finely diced

2 cloves garlic, minced

2 tsp ras el hanout, homemade
(page 160) or purchased

3 leeks, including about two-thirds
of the green tops, thinly sliced

3 lb boneless chicken, cut into
small pieces

1 tsp ground nutmeg

1 tbs ground cinnamon, plus
extra for topping

2 cups chicken broth

1 tbs arrowroot or 1/4 cup
cornstarch

½ cup slivered blanched almonds

1 lb butter, melted

about 16 phyllo sheets, thawed

confectioners' sugar

harissa, homemade (page 161) or
purchased

I don't know why I don't make this dish more often. It is absolutely wonderful and relatively easy to make. I serve it both as an appetizer and as a main dish. In Morocco, bastilla is made from pigeons, although chicken or quail works just as well. The only down side is the copious amount of butter needed. Also, be sure to carefully wash the leeks.

To make the filling, in a saute pan or skillet, heat the olive oil over medium heat. Add the onion, shallot, and garlic and saute until the onion is soft and golden, about 6 minutes. Add the ras el hanout, stirring well to mix. Add the leeks, stir well, and cook for about 5 minutes. Add the chicken, sprinkle with the nutmeg and 1 tbs cinnamon, and continue to cook until the chicken starts to brown. Pour in the broth, reduce the heat to low, and simmer gently until the chicken is cooked, about 20 minutes.

Ladle out ½ cup of the liquid and stir the arrowroot or cornstarch into it until dissolved. Return to the pan, bring to a boil, and stir until the liquid thickens, just a few minutes. Remove from the heat and add the almonds.

Preheat an oven to 350 degrees F.

To assemble the pie, brush a 9-by-13-inch glass baking dish with butter. Fit a sheet of the phyllo dough into the glass dish, with the edges overhanging the rim. (As you work, cover the unused phyllo sheets with waxed paper and a damp towel to prevent them from drying out.) Brush the phyllo sheet with butter and top with another phyllo sheet. Repeat until you have built a nice base of 8 to 12 sheets. Pour the chicken mixture into the dish and spread evenly. Fold the overhanging phyllo over the pie and then place a sheet of phyllo over the top to cover the whole pie. I find that a phyllo sheet folded in half works well, instead of trimming the phyllo sheet to size. Repeat until you have 3 or 4 phyllo sheets on the top, again buttering each sheet.

Bake the pie until golden brown, about 20 minutes. Remove the pie from the oven and sprinkle alternating lines of ground cinnamon and confectioners' sugar over the top. Serve with harissa.

Makes 8 to 10 servings.

Couscous

Couscous is simply so quick to cook that it is unbeatable. The proportion is 2 cups water to 1 cup couscous. Like rice, a cup of uncooked couscous should feed 3 or 4 people. The method is easy: bring the water to a boil with salt to taste and 1 tablespoon butter, margarine, or oil. Once it is boiling, add the couscous, stir, and cover immediately. Turn off the heat and let stand, covered, for 5 minutes before serving.

Traditionally, couscous is prepared in a couscousière, a two-part pot similar to a double boiler made of either glazed clay earthenware or aluminum. The stew of meats or vegetables is cooked in the bottom part, while the top part holds the couscous, which is cooked by the steam rising from the stew. The lid has a number of small holes that allow the steam to escape. Couscousières are rarely, if ever, found in cookware stores. You might try to find one in a Middle Eastern market, although this, too, is unlikely. Luckily, you don't need one to prepare couscous.

Any number of things can be added to couscous, but my favorites are raisins, chopped dried apricots, chopped dried figs, chopped dried apples, and almonds. Add any or all of these with the salt and butter at the beginning before you put the water on to boil. Here I have included a recipe for a couscous pilaf that calls for briefly soaking the dried fruit in rose water. Another possibility is mixing cooked couscous with sauteed sliced carrots and zucchini. Sprinkle with cilantro and parsley before serving.

Couscous Pilaf with Dried Apricots, Raisins, and Dried Mission Figs

⅓ cup dried apricots, sliced

⅓ cup raisins

⅓ cup dried Mission figs, sliced

½ cup rose water

4 cups water

2 tbs butter

2 tsp salt

2 cups couscous

¼ cup chopped fresh parsley

In a bowl, soak the apricots, raisins, and figs in the ½ cup rose water for 15 minutes. In a saucepan, combine the water, butter, and salt and bring to a boil. As soon as the water boils, add the soaked fruits and unabsorbed rose water. Add the couscous, cover immediately, and remove from the heat. Let stand, covered, for 5 minutes before serving. Sprinkle with the parsley.

Makes 8 servings.

Tagines

A tagine is a Moroccan stew. I had a fair number of these when I was in Morocco and Mauritania, but basically they were all cooked in either tomato sauce, broth, or citrus juice. I've included one of each style here. You can substitute different meats in all of these. Since Moroccans are primarily Moslems, they would never use pork, but goat is fairly common. The tagine cooked in broth calls for beef (I do not recall ever eating beef in Morocco), but lamb or chicken will do just as well. A note on the Moroccan chicken stew that suggests omitting the chicken and just cooking the vegetables produces a tasty dish and is something that I've done often. You might also add broccoli or cauliflower; they are not traditional but go quite well in the stew. In every case, the tagine should be served over couscous.

Finally, ras el hanout is essential for making these stews, but if you have none on hand and don't have all the ingredients to make your own (page 160), you can substitute cumin, turmeric, and whatever other spices common to the blend you might have in your pantry. Traditionally, tagines are cooked in cone-shaped earthenware vessels. The vessels can be found in selected cookware shops and kitchen catalogs. Williams-Sonoma mail order sells them

Moroccan Chicken Stew

Chicken Tagine

3 tbs olive oil

1 onion, finely chopped

2 shallots, finely chopped

6 cloves garlic, minced

2 tsp ras el hanout, homemade (page 160) or purchased

1 green bell pepper, chopped

2 carrots, sliced

1 eggplant, peeled and cut into small cubes

1 can (14½ oz) stewed tomatoes

2 cans (15 oz each) tomato sauce

3 bay leaves

6 boneless chicken breast halves, cut into bite-sized strips

1 zucchini, thinly sliced

1 can (15½ oz) chickpeas, drained and rinsed

1⅓ cups pitted black olives

8 fresh cilantro sprigs, chopped

You can omit the chicken and just cook the vegetables to make a delicious vegetarian dish.

In a stockpot, heat the olive oil over medium heat. When it is hot, add the onion, shallots, garlic, and ras el hanout and saute until the onion is soft, about 5 minutes. Add the bell pepper, stir well, and add the carrots. Cook for 3 to 5 minutes, then add the eggplant. Stir well and add the tomatoes and their juices, the tomato sauce, and the bay leaves. Stir well and cook for 5 minutes.

Add the chicken breasts and simmer for 15 minutes. Add the zucchini and continue to simmer until the chicken is cooked, about 10 minutes.

Add the chickpeas and olives and heat through. Top with the cilantro just before serving.

Makes 6 to 8 servings.

Moroccan Beef Stew with Vegetables in Broth

Beef Tagine

4 lb beef stew meat, cut into small
   pieces

salt to taste

white pepper to taste

3 tsp ras el hanout, homemade
   (page 160) or purchased

2 tbs Dijon mustard

2 tablespoons olive oil

2 onions, coarsely chopped

8 cloves garlic, minced

2 shallots, finely chopped

1 red bell pepper, chopped

1 green bell pepper, chopped

4 carrots, sliced

4 cups beef or chicken broth

1 cup dry red wine (optional)

4 bay leaves

2 tsp arrowroot or 2 tbs
   cornstarch

1⅓ cups pitted black olives

1 can (15½ oz) chickpeas, drained
   and rinsed

Sprinkle the stew beef with salt and pepper. Then rub 1 tsp of the ras el hanout and the Dijon mustard into the meat. In a stockpot, heat the olive oil over medium heat. When it is hot, add the onions, garlic, and shallots and saute until soft, about 5 minutes. Add the remaining 2 tsp ras el hanout, stir well, and add the bell peppers, carrots, and beef. Cook until the beef is browned on all sides. Add the broth, wine (if using), bay leaves, salt, and white pepper (remember, if your stock has salt in it, not much more if any is needed). Simmer until the meat is tender, about 50 minutes.

Ladle out ½ cup of the liquid and stir the arrowroot or cornstarch into it until dissolved. Add to the stew and stir until the liquid thickens, just a few minutes. (If it is still very thin, repeat the step with more arrowroot or cornstarch.) Add the olives and chickpeas and heat through before serving.

Makes 8 servings.

Moroccan Lamb Stew
in Citrus Juice

Lamb Tagine

4 lb lamb stew meat, cut into
  small pieces

salt to taste

white pepper to taste

¼ cup Worcestershire sauce

1 tbs ras el hanout, homemade
  (page 160) or purchased

¼ cup Dijon mustard

2 tbs fresh thyme leaves

1 tsp sumac

20 pitted prunes

⅓ cup rose water

3 tbs olive oil

3 onions, coarsely chopped

8 cloves garlic, minced

2 shallots, finely chopped

4 carrots, sliced

4 cups orange juice

1 cup lemon juice

½ cup lime juice

1 eggplant, peeled and cut into
  small cubes

3 zucchini, sliced

2 tsp arrowroot or 2 tbs
  cornstarch

Season the lamb with salt and pepper. Rub the Worcestershire sauce, 1 tsp of the ras el hanout, the mustard, thyme, and sumac into the meat. In a bowl, soak the prunes in the rose water for at least 15 minutes.

In a stockpot, heat the olive oil over medium heat. When it is hot, add the onions, garlic, and shallots and saute until the onions are soft and golden, about 7 minutes. Add the remaining 2 tsp ras el hanout, stir well, and add the lamb. Cook until the meat is browned on all sides. Add the carrots, the citrus juices, salt, and white pepper and bring to a boil. Add the eggplant, reduce the heat to low, and simmer until the lamb is tender, about 35 minutes.

Add the zucchini and the prunes and any unabsorbed rose water and simmer for another 5 minutes. Ladle out ½ cup of the liquid and stir the arrowroot or cornstarch into it until dissolved. Add to the stew and stir until the liquid thickens, just a few minutes. (If it is still very thin, repeat the step with more arrowroot or cornstarch.)

Makes 8 servings.

Green Apple Sorbet

6 Granny Smith apples, peeled,
   cored, and thinly sliced

1/3 cup lemon juice

2 cups confectioners' sugar

1 tsp rose water

1/4 cup apple juice

When I was in Morocco, I never saw a sorbet on any menu (then again everything was in Arabic), but once in a Moroccan restaurant in Strasbourg I ate a wonderful green apple sorbet at the close of a meal. It was a refreshing touch after some fairly hot food. I can't remember the name of the restaurant but I'll never forget the sorbet.

In a food processor, combine all the ingredients. Process until smooth. Transfer the mixture to an ice cream maker and freeze according to the manufacturer's directions.

Makes 6 servings.

Macerated Oranges

6 oranges

6 tbs superfine sugar

grated zest of 1/2 lemon

1/3 cup Cointreau

1/4 cup lemon juice

This is not a traditional Moroccan dessert, but it goes well at the end of a Moroccan meal.

Forming long, narrow strips, remove enough zest from the oranges to yield 24 strips. Set the strips aside. Peel all the oranges, removing as much white pith as possible. Section the oranges and then cut each orange section in half; remove any seeds. Place the halved sections in a bowl.

Sprinkle the sugar over the orange sections. Add the grated lemon zest and orange zest strips and toss gently. Pour in the Cointreau and lemon juice. Let stand for at least 30 minutes before serving. Cover and refrigerate if keeping for more than a couple of hours.

Makes 6 servings.

Southeast Asia

I'd be hard-pressed to name my favorite cuisine, but I can easily say that I enjoy cooking Southeast Asian food more than any other. I first tasted this tropical table on a childhood trip to Amsterdam with my mom, but I truly came to appreciate it, if not revel in it, when I arrived at Stanford.

What I enjoy about it are the rich and tantalizing tastes and aromas, the varied textures and flavors, and the insistence on the freshness of comment Perhaps my favorite comment on the latter comes from Sri Owen, a well-known Indonesian cook and author from Padang, Sumatra, who once observed that frozen food is dead food. Southeast Asian food comes alive in your mouth in large part because of this uncompromising attitude toward the quality of its components.

Another plus is that many of the region's recipes are simple and quick to prepare. Some dishes take less than a half hour from start to finish. Additional time can be saved by making extra batches of sauces or curries and storing them in the refrigerator to use for another night's dinner. Then when you come home from work, all you do is put some rice on, dice some vegetables, cut up some chicken or peel some shrimp, make a quick gado-gado salad, and cook the curry. Everything should be ready by the time your rice is done—twenty-five minutes tops. By varying the vegetables and meats, you can create a different meal nightly, despite using the same curry paste or sauce. Unbeatable.

In terms of dinner parties, Southeast Asian food lends itself well to both spontaneous and plan-ahead entertainment. You can make the sauces and curry pastes a day or two in advance, and perhaps even make the sticky rice with mangoes the night before, then come home to cook the curries and rice at the last minute.

This chapter embraces the cuisines of Burma, Thailand, Laos, Cambodia, Vietnam, Malaysia, Singapore, and Indonesia. Generally for dinner parties, I stick to one ethnicity if there will be only a few people and one or two dishes from a variety of countries if the gathering will be large. At the same time, Thai soups and curries, Indonesian peanut sauces, and Khmer appetizers are part of my everyday fare. Such culinary luxury is possible because the Bay Area offers easy accessibility to all the necessary ingredients, which, for me, is one of the sheer pleasures of living here. Also, don't overlook your local Southeast Asian restaurants for ideas and sources. Ask your waiter or the chef how a dish is made, what goes in it, and where to get the ingredients. Then go home and experiment.

Various kinds of chilies are suitable for use in Southeast Asian food. Serranos, lomboks, Thais, habañeros, Fresnos, and jalapeños are probably the most useful. Refer to the Chili Pepper Glossary to decide which chili best suits your taste buds.

Suggested Menus

Thai Curry Dinner

This menu works well both for small groups of four and larger groups of eight. For eight, you'll need to double both the squid salad and the soup. The curry pastes can be made in advance, although you should cook the curries at the last minute. The pad Thai should also be prepared about an hour before serving. The sticky rice dessert must be prepared in advance.

Squid Salad
Chicken, Lemongrass, and Coconut Milk Soup (Tom Kha Kai)
Red Curry with Chicken
Green Curry with Vegetables
Jasmine Rice
Pad Thai
Mangoes with Sticky Rice

A Simple Vietnamese Dinner

While the chicken needs to be marinated for an hour, it cooks quickly. The shrimp toast must be fried just before serving, but the batter can be prepared ahead of time. The soup is extremely straightforward and takes about 40 minutes to prepare.

Shrimp Toast
Coconut Curry Soup
Lemongrass Chicken
Jasmine Rice
French Vanilla Ice Cream

An Indonesian Rijstaffel

This dinner party is a favorite of mine. It is, however, a time-consuming affair. While the sauces and the relish can be prepared in advance, most of the items need to be made the day of the party. Still, your efforts will be rewarded by your guests' utter delight at the variety of the dishes. This menu makes an excellent buffet.

Balinese Minced Pork Sate

Peanut Chicken Sate (Sauc Kacang Sate)

Indonesian Layered Salad with Peanut Dressing (Gado-Gado)

West Sumatran Beef Cooked in Coconut Milk

Fried Noodles

Spicy Pepper Salad with Sesame Seeds

Curried Vegetables

Festive Rice

Tempe in Candlenut Sauce

Pickled Cucumber Relish

Bananas in Coconut Milk

A Khmer Sampler

Cambodian food is not as spicy as Thai food, yet the two cuisines share a love of tart flavors and fish sauces. This is a simple menu to make. The noodles can be made in advance. You should also prepare the curry paste ahead of time. Cambodians will curry just about anything, but they have a particular fondness for fish curries. Try a catfish curry.

Cold Khmer Noodles

Sweet Khmer Curry

Jasmine Rice

Stir-fried Vegetables

Bananas in Coconut Milk

Indonesian Sweet Soy Sauce

Kecap Manis

1 cup soy sauce

½ cup molasses

2 tbs palm sugar or 3 tbs brown
    sugar

4 star anise

Although bottled kecap manis is available in many Asian markets, it is easy to make your own at home.

In a small saucepan, combine all the ingredients and bring to a boil over medium heat. Reduce the heat to low and stir until dark and thickened, about 5 minutes. Remove and discard the star anise. Cool and refrigerate until needed.

Makes about 1½ cups.

Indonesian Soy-Chili Sauce

Sambal Kecap

2 tbs soy sauce

2 shallots, thinly sliced

1 garlic clove, minced

juice of 1 lime

3 Thai chilies, thinly sliced

dash of fish sauce

1 tbs water

This quick-and-easy sauce is used as a marinade for grilled pork, chicken, and beef. Marinate them for at least 15 minutes or, preferably, up to overnight before grilling, then skewer the meats just before they are placed over the hot coals. Reserve some of the sauce as a condiment with dinner.

In a bowl, combine all the ingredients, mixing well.

Makes about ⅓ cup.

Khmer Spicy Lime Sauce

juice of 5 limes

1 tsp palm sugar or 2 tbs brown
    sugar

3 green serrano chilies, seeded
    and finely chopped

2 tbs tamarind water (page 186)

2 tbs fish sauce or Thai Shrimp
    Sauce (page 175)

4 fresh cilantro sprigs, chopped

I serve this spicy tart-sauce with hot and cold noodles (see Cold Khmer Noodles, page 197). It is also used in several Cambodian dishes. I generally try to keep some in the refrigerator but without the cilantro, which I add as needed.

In a bowl, combine all the ingredients. Stir well to dissolve the sugar. If you are not serving the sauce within a few hours, wait and add the cilantro just before serving.

Makes about ⅔ cup.

Vietnamese Chili-Fish Sauce

Nước Châm

2 red chilies (Fresno, serrano, or similar), coarsely chopped

2 cloves garlic

1 tsp sugar

1 lemon or 2 limes

1 tbs distilled white vinegar

1 tbs water

¼ cup fish sauce

1 carrot, shredded

sliced chilies (optional)

The Vietnamese are devoted to this sauce, and the highest compliment one can pay a Vietnamese cook is to praise his or her version. No Vietnamese meal is complete without generous helpings of it, and it is added to just about everything. I am sure this recipe pales in comparison to those found in Vietnam.

In a small food processor or blender, combine the chopped chilies, garlic, and sugar. Grind to a coarse pulp. Peel the lemon or limes, removing all the white pith, then slice and remove all the seeds. Add the slices to the coarse pulp and mix vigorously to incorporate well. Stir in the vinegar, water, and fish sauce. Garnish with the shredded carrot and with sliced chilies, if desired.

Makes about ½ cup.

Thai Shrimp Sauce

Nam Prik

2 tbs dried shrimp

3 tbs warm water

3 Fresno chilies, chopped

4 cloves garlic

½-inch-piece blachan, grilled, or 1 tsp anchovy paste

2 tbs lemon juice

2 tbs tamarind water (page 186)

2 tsp palm sugar, or 1 tbs brown sugar

1 tbs soy sauce

The Thai use this sauce in almost everything, so it's a good idea to make a large batch so that you always have some on hand. Outside the Thai table, try it as a dip for raw vegetables or tortilla chips and as a marinade for shrimp or chicken. The only downer is that you must use tiny dried shrimp to make it, and they have a powerful odor. They are sold in huge bags, and one bag lasts me over a year, so you might consider buying a bag and splitting it among a few households. Just keep the shrimp well sealed in a glass jar in the cupboard.

In a bowl, soak the dried shrimp in the warm water for 20 minutes to soften. Transfer the softened shrimp and the soaking water to a small food processor or blender and add all the remaining ingredients. Blend well.

You can use sambal ulek instead of chilies. I also have added a few sprigs of fresh cilantro and parsley, a green onion or two, and a teaspoon of grated fresh ginger to this sauce. Store refrigerated.

Makes ½ cup.

Basic Peanut Sauce

Saus Kacang

5 fresh cilantro sprigs

3 fresh parsley sprigs

2 green onions, cut into thirds

1-inch-piece fresh ginger, peeled and coarsely chopped

2 Fresno chilies, halved and seeded

1 habanero chili, halved and seeded

3 tbs brown sugar

¼ cup lemon juice

½ cup soy sauce

2 tbs fish sauce

½ tsp sambal ulek

few drops of Tabasco sauce (optional)

2 cups peanut butter

½ tsp Asian sesame oil

I use this sauce to make peanut chicken sates (the taste is somewhat different than the Indonesian Peanut Sate recipe below): Marinate the chicken strips for at least an hour but preferably overnight, using a ratio of about 1½ cups sauce to 1 lb chicken. Skewer right before grilling. It is a nice base for other sauces, too, so be sure to reserve some to use elsewhere. A word of caution on the chilies: I like the habanero, which is extremely hot, so if you want a milder sauce, use a jalapeño or serrano instead. Also, add 4 cloves garlic, 2 shallots, or 1 tsp dried galangal powder (or ½-inch-piece fresh galangal) for variety if you like.

In a food processor or blender, combine the cilantro, parsley, green onions, ginger, and chilies. Process until coarsely chopped. Add the brown sugar, lemon juice, soy sauce, fish sauce, and sambal ulek. Add the Tabasco sauce if you want an extra kick and whirl for a few seconds. Add the peanut butter in two batches, processing each time until fully incorporated. (Add additional lemon juice and soy sauce if the sauce is too thick.) Finally, add the sesame oil and whirl a few seconds. Use immediately, or transfer to a tightly covered jar and store in the refrigerator for up to 1 week.

Makes about 3 cups.

Indonesian Peanut Sate

Saus Kacang Sate

1 recipe Basic Peanut Sauce (above)

¼ cup tamarind water (page 186)

1 cup coconut milk

sambal ulek to taste (if you want it hotter)

¾ cup crunchy peanut butter

½ cup crushed peanuts (optional)

Use this sauce for marinating fish, pork, chicken, or beef for grilling, using a ratio of about 1½ cups sauce to 1 lb flesh. For fish, use a firm type such as swordfish and marinate for at least 15 minutes but for no more than 30 minutes. For pork, buy pork tenderloin and cut it into rounds for marinating. Marinate pork, chicken, or beef for at least 15 minutes or, preferably, up to overnight before grilling. In every case, do not skewer the fish, meat, or poultry until just before grilling. Reserve some of the sauce to serve as a condiment.

This sauce is also absolutely heavenly with Asian noodles, particularly somen. Add the noodles to rapidly boiling water and cook for 3 minutes. Drain (add any cooked vegetables or boiled shrimp) and mix with some of the warmed sauce. It's a great quick lunch.

In a food processor or blender, combine all the ingredients. Whirl until well blended. Use immediately, or transfer to a tightly covered jar and store in the refrigerator for up to 1 week.

Makes about 5 cups.

Indonesian Tomato-Chili Sauce

Sambal Ulek Tomat

3 tbs peanut or olive oil

3 shallots, coarsely chopped

4 cloves garlic, minced

6 to 10 Fresno chilies, seeded and finely chopped

2 green serrano chilies, seeded and finely chopped

1 tsp sambal ulek

1-inch-piece fresh ginger, peeled and grated

10 plum tomatoes, peeled and coarsely chopped

2 dashes of fish sauce

2 tbs tamarind water (page 186)

I picked this sauce up in Moni, on the island of Flores, when I was there with my friend Tom Frangione. Our innkeeper used it for just about everything. I especially like it for potatoes, eggplant, and tempe. The sauce is really spicy and hot, but you can cut back on the number of chilies and omit the sambal. Store it in the refrigerator.

In a skillet, heat the oil over medium-high heat. When it is hot, add the shallots and cook, stirring, until browned. Using a slotted spoon, remove the shallots from the pan and reserve. In the same oil, saute the garlic, chilies, sambal, and ginger until softened. Add the tomatoes, fish sauce, tamarind water, and the browned shallots. Reduce the heat to low and cook, stirring often, until the mixture thickens and the flavors are blended, about 10 minutes. Puree the sauce in a blender or food processor. Be careful not to overprocess, as the sauce should retain a thick consistency.

Makes about 2 cups.

Sates

I've already covered two basic peanut sates with the Basic Peanut Sauce (page 176) and Indonesian Peanut Sate (page 176). Throughout Southeast Asia, however, there are various grilled sates apart from the peanut-sauced ones. Here is one from Bali.

Balinese Minced Pork Sate

Sate Pentul

4 shallots, diced

4 cloves garlic

thin slice blachan or terasi

1 tsp sambal ulek

9 lemongrass stalks, cut in half

1-inch-piece fresh ginger, peeled and coarsely chopped

1 tsp galangal powder or 1-inch-piece fresh galangal, peeled and coarsely chopped

1 tsp ground coriander

2 Thai chilies

2 tsp kecap manis, homemade (page 174) or purchased

1 tbs palm sugar or 2 tbs brown sugar

¼ cup tamarind water (page 186)

1 can (14 fl oz) coconut milk

1 lb ground pork

1 egg

salt to taste

black pepper to taste

sambal ulek for serving (optional)

1 cup Basic Peanut Sauce (page 176) diluted with ½ cup coconut milk for serving (optional)

I ate this sate in Ubud at a street stall near the market. Through an interpreter, the vendor gave me the recipe in exchange for taking his picture.

Light a fire in a charcoal grill.

In a food processor or blender, combine the shallots, garlic, blachan or terasi, sambal, 1 lemongrass stalk (cut into ½-inch pieces), ginger, galangal, coriander, chilies, kecap manis, palm or brown sugar, and tamarind water and grind to a paste. Mix 1 tbs of the paste into the coconut milk and set aside. Mix the rest of the paste into the pork. Beat the egg well and mix into the pork. Season with salt and black pepper. Mix well.

Shape about 2 tablespoons of the pork mixture into a ball and press firmly onto a stalk of lemongrass (this will be your skewer). Continue adding meatballs to lemongrass stalks until all the pork is used. Drizzle a few tablespoons of the seasoned coconut milk over the pork sate.

Grill immediately over a medium-hot fire, turning as needed. It should take about 5 minutes, perhaps 7. Baste with the seasoned coconut milk often, if not constantly. Serve with any leftover coconut milk mixture, sambal, or, if you prefer, some diluted peanut sauce.

Makes 4 servings.

Khmer Spinach Leaves with Sweet-Spicy Lime Sauce

about 64 spinach leaves

2 cups Khmer Spicy Lime Sauce (page 174)

1 tbs palm sugar or 2 tbs brown sugar

2-inch-piece ginger, peeled and cut into ⅛-inch cubes

3 red serrano or Fresno chilies, thinly sliced

2 tbs dried shrimp

½ cup dry roasted peanuts

1 lime, thinly sliced and slices quartered

6 fresh cilantro sprigs, coarsely chopped

This dish is my interpretation of a wonderful appetizer served at Angkor Borei Khmer Restaurant in San Francisco's Mission district.

Wash the spinach leaves well and pat dry. Add the palm or brown sugar to the spicy lime sauce and stir well to dissolve. Place the ginger, chilies, dried shrimp, peanuts, lime quarters, and cilantro in separate small bowls. Place the spinach leaves in a large bowl, and arrange all the small bowls around it. Let each guest create his or her own packet by choosing ingredients to wrap in individual leaves.

Makes 8 servings.

Vietnamese Shrimp Toast

1 lb shrimp, peeled and deveined

2 green onions, chopped

1 tbs fish sauce

white pepper to taste

2 baguettes, preferably day old

corn or peanut oil for frying

In a food processor, combine the shrimp, green onions, fish sauce, and white pepper and process to a paste. Cut baguettes into slices about ½ inch thick. Spread the paste about ¼ inch thick on each baguette slice.

In a skillet, pour in oil to a depth of 1 inch. Place over medium-high heat. When the oil is hot, add 2 or 3 of the shrimp toasts, shrimp side down, and fry until golden brown, about a minute or so. Turn and cook for another 45 seconds or so. Using a slotted spoon, lift the toasts out of the oil and place on paper towels to drain. Repeat until all the shrimp toasts are cooked, adding more oil and adjusting the heat as needed. Serve immediately after cooling for a minute or two.

Makes 50 to 60 toasts, about 8 servings.

Spicy Indonesian Pepper Salad

Timor Achar

½ lb snow peas, ends trimmed

1 green bell pepper

1 red bell pepper

1 orange bell pepper

1 yellow bell pepper

½ red onion

3 tomatoes

1 tsp sugar

1 tbs sambal ulek

¼ cup rice vinegar

6 fresh cilantro sprigs, chopped

3 Fresno chilies, thinly sliced

juice of 1 lime

2 tbs sesame seeds

Parboil the snow peas in boiling water for 2 to 3 minutes. Drain well, place under cold running water to halt the cooking, and drain again. Halve all the bell peppers, remove the stems and seeds, and cut into long, narrow strips. Slice the red onion, and cut the tomatoes into wedges. Combine all the vegetables in a bowl and mix well.

In a small bowl, stir together the sugar, sambal, rice vinegar, cilantro, chilies, and lime juice. Dress the salad with this mixture. Sprinkle with sesame seeds and serve.

Makes 8 servings.

Thai Squid Salad

Yum Pla Muek

1 lb squid

2 tbs peanut or olive oil

4 cloves garlic, minced

3 shallots, chopped

2 tbs fish sauce

⅓ cup tamarind water (page 186)

juice of 6 limes

1 tbs palm sugar or 2 tbs brown sugar

6 fresh cilantro sprigs, chopped

½ small red onion, chopped

3 serrano chilies

butter lettuce leaves

I ate this dish during my recovery from an all-night party in Kos Samui. Quite refreshing. You can save a lot of time by buying cleaned squid; you'll need about ¾ lb.

Clean the squid (page 227). Cut the bodies into rings about ½ inch wide; leave the tentacles whole. Drop the squid into rapidly boiling water and boil until just cooked, about 2 minutes. Remove and rinse in cold water to stop the cooking. Set aside to cool.

Meanwhile, in a skillet, heat the oil over medium-high heat. When it is hot, add the garlic and shallots and cook, stirring, until soft and golden. Remove from the heat and pour into a bowl. Add the fish sauce, tamarind water, lime juice, palm or brown sugar, and cilantro and mix well to form a dressing.

Place the squid in a bowl and add the red onion. Slice the chilies into easy-to-see pieces and add to the squid as well. Pour in the dressing and toss to distribute evenly. Serve the squid on a lettuce-lined platter.

Makes 4 to 6 servings.

Gado-Gado

Indonesian Layered Salad with Peanut Dressing

2 white potatoes

4 eggs

32 green beans, ends trimmed

2 tbs peanut or olive oil

1 onion, finely chopped

4 cloves garlic, minced

1 tsp ground turmeric

2 tsp ground cumin

1-inch-piece fresh ginger, peeled and grated

1 tsp galangal powder or 1-inch-piece fresh galangal, peeled and grated

½ head green cabbage or 1 small Chinese cabbage, sliced and separated

1 cup water

2 carrots, sliced

1 bunch Swiss chard, coarsely chopped

2½ cups Basic Peanut Sauce (page 176)

1 can (14 fl oz) coconut milk

1 tbs sambal ulek (optional)

1 cucumber, scored and thinly sliced

chopped fresh cilantro

½ cup peanuts

Tom Frangione and I had the best gado-gado in a little truck stop called Wolowaru between Maumere and Moni, on Flores. The peanut sauce was dark and rich yet not overwhelming. After eating my way across the archipelago, I've concluded that gado-gado must include potatoes, cabbage, and green beans. After that, carrots and Swiss chard make nice additions, but basically Indonesians cook up whatever vegetables are on hand and smother them with a deep coconut-peanut sauce. Don't be put off by the long list of ingredients here. You can trim them back to a more manageable number and still end up with a great salad. And remember, if you ever go to Flores, stop off in Wolowaru just for the gado-gado.

First, cook the potatoes in boiling salted water until tender, 20 to 25 minutes, then drain well and cool. Meanwhile, hard-boil the eggs (7 to 8 minutes should suffice), and steam the green beans until they turn a bright green but are still crisp. Set these ingredients aside to cool.

In a large skillet, heat the oil over medium-high heat. When it is hot, add the onion, garlic, turmeric, cumin, ginger, and galangal and cook, stirring, until the onion is soft, about 5 minutes. Add the cabbage and the water. When the cabbage begins to wilt, after just a minute or so, add the carrots. Continue to cook until the cabbage is almost tender, 8 to 10 minutes. Add the Swiss chard and cook for 5 more minutes until tender, then remove from the heat and let cool.

Meanwhile, make the bumbu (Indonesian dressing): In a saucepan, heat the peanut sauce with the coconut milk. Bring to a simmer but do not allow to boil. If a spicy dressing is desired, add the sambal ulek; keep warm.

Once the vegetables are cooked, you can start to assemble the salad. Peel the potatoes and cut into thin slices. Place on a platter and cover with the cabbage mixture. Place the green beans on top. Peel and halve the hard-boiled eggs and arrange along the sides. Arrange the cucumber slices around the edge of the platter. Pour the warm peanut sauce over the top. Garnish with chopped cilantro and peanuts.

Makes 8 servings.

Note: You can add cubed tofu or tempe to this salad, mixing them in with the Swiss chard. For extra flavor, marinate the tofu or tempe in a ½ cup Basic Peanut Sauce (page 176) diluted with 2 tbs coconut milk and 1 tbs fish sauce.

Vietnamese Coconut Curry Soup with Shrimp and Rice Noodles

Bun Nuoc Ken

2 tbs peanut or olive oil

1 onion, chopped

2 cloves garlic, minced

2 shallots, diced

1 tsp ground cumin

1 tsp ground turmeric

2 tsp curry powder

4 cups chicken broth

2 cans (14 fl oz each) coconut milk

½ lb rice vermicelli

1 lb shrimp, peeled and deveined

6 fresh cilantro sprigs, chopped

I first had this soup at the Little Garden Restaurant in Palo Alto, California, a gem of an eatery.

In a large saucepan, heat the oil over medium-high heat. When it is hot, add the onion, garlic, and shallots and saute until the onion is soft, about 3 minutes. Add the cumin, turmeric, and curry powder and cook, stirring, for 3 minutes. Add the chicken broth and bring to a boil. Add the coconut milk, reduce the heat to low, and simmer for 10 minutes.

Meanwhile, soak the rice vermicelli in very hot water to cover for 10 minutes until the noodles are soft. Drain and rinse well in a colander. Add the shrimp to the soup and cook for 3 minutes. Remove from the heat. Divide the noodles among soup bowls and ladle the soup over the top. Garnish with the cilantro. Serve immediately.

Makes 4 to 6 servings.

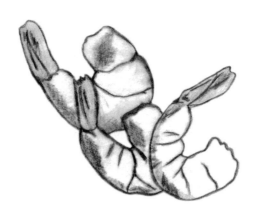

Tom Kha Kai

Thai Chicken, Lemongrass, and Coconut Milk Soup

2 tbs peanut or olive oil

3 cloves garlic, minced

1 onion, finely chopped

1 shallot, finely chopped

3 red serranos or Fresno chilies, sliced in easy-to-see pieces

¾-inch-piece fresh ginger, peeled and finely grated

2 lemongrass stalks, cut in 1-inch segments and bruised

2 tsp galangal powder, or 2-inch-piece fresh galangal, peeled and cut into 12 equal slices

4 cups chicken broth

3 boneless chicken breast halves, cut into long, narrow strips

2 cans (14 fl oz each) coconut milk

20 shrimp, peeled and deveined

1 can (15 oz) straw mushrooms, drained

chopped fresh cilantro

I am indebted to Kitirat Panupong, my good Thai friend, for sharing his invaluable culinary tricks with me.

In a large saucepan or small stockpot, heat the oil over medium-high heat. When it is hot, add the garlic, onion, shallot, chilies, ginger, and lemongrass and saute until the onion is soft. Add the galangal and broth and bring to a boil. Add the chicken, reduce the heat to a simmer, and cook for 15 minutes. Then add the coconut milk and simmer for 5 more minutes. Add the shrimp and straw mushrooms during the last 3 minutes of simmering. Sprinkle with the cilantro just before serving.

Makes 4 servings.

Curries

Many people think of curry as the Indian powder available in the spice section of the supermarket. That is curry, of course, and since it is Indian in origin, it almost always includes turmeric and cumin. But curry is also a catch-all English term for a wide variety of spiced sauces and essences that are used as a base for cooking beef, pork, poultry, and vegetables. Southeast Asian curries are different than Indian curries in the use of such non-Indian ingredients as lemongrass and galangal. In India, the sauce is more often made with yogurt, but in Southeast Asia coconut milk is the common liquid. If you are concerned about the effect on your health of using so much coconut milk, you can substitute chicken broth, yogurt, or a combination of these with a lesser amount of coconut milk or even a "lite" coconut milk. The taste will not be the same, but you will avoid the saturated fat of coconut milk.

Always make more curry paste than needed, for the pastes keep in the refrigerator for a few weeks. I have included both traditional and nontraditional pastes here. Traditional pastes are those that were made before the arrival of the chili pepper. (Chilies, which are now standard in Southeast Asian curries, were introduced by Portuguese and Spanish traders in the sixteenth-century and any curry paste that calls for them is nontraditional.) You will find the yellow musaman curry, a traditional paste from Thailand and Burma, to be quite mild.

You can adjust the hotness of any dish to your taste. My own taste runs to hot, and the paste recipes that follow reflect that. The Thai green curry paste is particularly fiery. Since much of the heat from chilies comes from the seeds, you can increase the heat by including the seeds or decrease it by excluding them. Traditional curries depend on the heavy use of peppercorns and Sichuan pepper for their heat. I have included a traditional mild green curry that is wonderful with poultry, especially duck.

Lastly, a question that I am often asked is to explain the difference between a red and a green curry. Well, red curries are generally made with only ripe red chilies and do not include herbs, and green curries can be made with either red or green chilies and always have some herbs, usually parsley, cilantro, and green onion.

For making curries, you will find a small food processor, blender, or a mortar and pestle essential. All of the curry pastes that follow yield enough to make two curry dishes that will each serve four people. Directions how to turn the various curry pastes into curry dishes are provided in the section Cooking Curries on page 190.

Thai Red Curry Paste

10 Fresno chilies, coarsely chopped

3 shallots

4 cloves garlic

1-inch-piece fresh ginger, peeled and coarsely chopped

½ stalk lemongrass, thinly sliced

1 tsp galangal powder or ½-inch-piece fresh galangal, peeled and coarsely chopped

1 tsp coriander seeds

½ tsp caraway seeds

½ tsp cumin seeds

3 tbs tamarind water (page 186)

3 tbs fish sauce

juice of ½ lemon or lime

black pepper to taste

1 tsp sambal ulek (optional)

This is a sizzlingly hot mixture. For a milder version, substitute 3 red serranos for the Fresno chilies and omit the sambal.

In a small food processor or blender, combine the chilies, shallots, garlic, ginger, and the lemongrass; if using fresh galangal, add it at this point as well. Grind finely. Add the galangal powder and coriander, caraway, and cumin seeds. Whirl or grind for a few seconds and then add the tamarind water, fish sauce, lemon or lime juice, pepper, and, if more heat is desired, the sambal. Mix well.

Burmese Red Curry Paste

¼ cup Asian sesame oil

2 onions, chopped

8 cloves garlic, minced

½-inch-piece fresh ginger, peeled and finely grated

1 tsp ground turmeric

2 tbs fish sauce

4 Fresno or 5 red serrano chilies, cut into thirds and seeded

2 tbs tamarind water (page 186)

2 tbs dried shrimp

1 tsp sambal ulek

2 fresh cilantro sprigs

juice of 1 lemon or lime

Here is a medium-hot curry that can be cooled down by using only 1 Fresno or 1 red serrano.

In a medium skillet, heat the sesame oil over medium heat. When it is hot, add the onions, garlic, ginger, and turmeric and cook until the onion is soft, about 5 minutes. Add the fish sauce, chilies, and tamarind water. Cook for 2 to 3 minutes, then add the dried shrimp. Stir well and cook for another minute. Remove from the heat. Add the sambal, cilantro, and lemon or lime juice. Transfer to a food processor or blender and blend well.

Thai Green Curry Paste

8 green Thai chilies, coarsely chopped

3 shallots

4 cloves garlic

1-inch-piece ginger, peeled and coarsely chopped

½ lemongrass stalk, thinly sliced

1 green onion, cut into large pieces

6 fresh cilantro sprigs

6 fresh parsley sprigs

1 tsp galangal powder or ½-inch-piece fresh galangal, peeled and coarsely chopped

1 tsp coriander seeds

1 tsp cumin seeds

2 tbs tamarind water (page 186)

1 tbs fish sauce

juice of ½ lemon or lime

black pepper to taste

1 tsp sambal (optional)

This is a very hot curry paste. To temper its heat, substitute 3 green serranos for the Thai chilies and omit the sambal.

In a small food processor, blender, or mortar, combine the chilies, shallots, garlic, and ginger; if using fresh galangal, add it at this point as well. Grind coarsely. Add the lemongrass, green onion, cilantro, and parsley and grind finely. Add the galangal powder, coriander seeds, and cumin seeds. Whirl or grind for a few seconds and then add the tamarind water, fish sauce, lime or lemon juice, pepper, and, if more heat is desired, the sambal. Mix well.

Preparing Tamarind Water

Place a 1-inch-lump of tamarind paste in about ½ cup hot water and leave to soak for 10 to 15 minutes. Then, using your fingers, work the lump to release its essence fully into the water. Pour the liquid through a fine-mesh sieve to remove any fibers and seeds. The water can now be used, or it can be stored in the refrigerator in a tightly covered jar for up to 2 weeks. Scale the amount of tamarind paste and water to suit your needs.

Musaman Yellow Curry Paste

3 shallots

8 cloves garlic

1 lemongrass stalk, thinly sliced

½-inch-piece fresh ginger, peeled and grated

seeds from 5 cardamom pods

2 tsp coriander seeds

8 whole cloves, crushed to a powder (about ½ tsp ground clove)

1 tsp galangal powder or ½-inch-piece fresh galangal, peeled and coarsely chopped

2 tsp ground cumin

1 tbs ground turmeric

1 tsp fennel seeds

1 tsp caraway seeds

½ tsp ground cinnamon

1 tbs cracked white peppercorns

1 tsp cracked or ground Sichuan peppercorns (optional)

1 tbs fish sauce

A traditionally mild curry paste that goes well with beef, often married with potatoes. Musaman translates as Muslim, as this curry recipe was ferried across Southeast Asia by Muslim traders.

In a small food processor, blender, or mortar, combine the shallots, garlic, lemongrass, and ginger; if using fresh galangal, add it at this point as well. Grind to a paste. Add the cardamom seeds, coriander seeds, crushed cloves, galangal powder, cumin, turmeric, fennel seeds, caraway seeds, and cinnamon. Grind to incorporate well into the paste. Add the cracked white peppercorns and the Sichuan pepper, if using. Moisten with the fish sauce. Mix well.

Green Pepper Curry Paste

3 shallots

8 cloves garlic

2 tbs green peppercorns

1 lemongrass stalk, thinly sliced

1-inch-piece ginger, peeled and coarsely chopped

seeds from 5 cardamom pods

1 tsp cumin seeds

2 tsp ground turmeric

8 whole cloves, crushed to a powder (about ½ tsp ground clove)

2 tbs coriander seeds

1 tsp caraway seeds

1 tsp fennel seeds

1 tsp galangal powder or ½-inch-piece fresh galangal, peeled and coarsely chopped

4 fresh cilantro sprigs, coarsely chopped

1 tbs fish sauce

A mild traditional curry.

In a small food processor or blender, combine the shallots, garlic, green peppercorns, lemongrass, and ginger; if using fresh galangal, add it at this point as well. Grind to a thick paste. Add the cardamom seeds, cumin seeds, turmeric, the crushed cloves, coriander seeds, caraway seeds, fennel seeds, galangal powder, and the cilantro. Grind to incorporate well into the paste. Moisten with the fish sauce. Mix well.

Khmer Sweet Curry Paste

1 tbs dried shrimp

1 tbs fish sauce

5 cloves garlic, coarsely chopped

½ onion, diced

2 shallots, cut into thirds

1-inch-piece ginger, peeled and coarsely chopped

1 lemongrass stalk, thinly sliced

2 tsp fennel seeds

seeds from 7 cardamom pods

2 tbs coriander seeds

1 tsp galangal powder or ½-inch-piece fresh galangal, peeled and coarsely chopped

1 tsp cumin seeds

1 tsp ground turmeric

1 tbs white peppercorns

2 tbs palm sugar or 4 tbs brown sugar

juice of 1 lemon or lime

This is another mild traditional curry.

Soak the dried shrimp in the fish sauce and warm water to cover for 15 minutes. Meanwhile, in a small food processor or blender, combine the garlic, onion, shallots, ginger, lemongrass, fennel seeds, cardamom seeds, coriander seeds, galangal, cumin seeds, turmeric, and peppercorns (preferably white but black or green will do). Grind to a thick paste. Add the palm or brown sugar, the lemon or lime juice, and the dried shrimp and its soaking liquid. Blend well.

Thai Curry Paste for Grilling

8 to 10 dried red chilies

6 shallots, chopped

6 cloves garlic, chopped

1 lemongrass stalk, thinly sliced

½ tsp galangal powder or ½-inch-piece fresh galangal, peeled and coarsely chopped

1 tbs tamarind water (page 186)

4 thin strips lemon or lime zest

3 fresh cilantro sprigs

1 tbs black peppercorns

½ cup coconut milk

1 tsp fish sauce

Simply put, this paste is hot as hell. Use it for grilling meats.

Soak the dried chilies in warm water to cover for 20 minutes to soften them. Drain and remove and discard the stems.

In a small food processor or blender, combine the chilies, shallots, garlic, and lemongrass; if using fresh galangal, add it at this point as well. Whirl to a thick paste. Add the galangal powder, tamarind water, citrus strips, cilantro, peppercorns, coconut milk, and fish sauce. Blend well.

This sauce is great for marinating pork loin or fish for the grill. Marinate the meat for at least 1 hour and the fish for about 20 minutes. Use a white soft fish such as sole or catfish. Makes enough paste for marinating 3½ to 5 pounds meat or fish

Cooking Curries

Once you have made one of the curry pastes, you are ready to make the curry. The following recipe for chicken curry is a general outline that can be followed to create your own curry dishes. See the variations below for some of my favorite combinations.

Curry pastes also make great rubs for meats, chicken, or fish headed for the grill. In particular, try the Thai Curry Paste for Grilling (page 189). Just rub it on generously, perhaps first dousing the item with some Worcestershire sauce. Marinate the meat for at least an hour and the fish for 20 minutes.

Chicken Curry

2 tbs peanut or olive oil

1 onion, coarsely chopped

4 to 5 tbs curry paste of choice (pages 185 to 189)

3 boneless chicken breast halves, cut into 1-inch dice

1 carrot, thinly sliced on the diagonal

½ red bell pepper, diced

½ green bell pepper, diced

about 1 cup broccoli florets

⅞ cup coconut milk

In a large skillet, heat the oil over medium-high heat. When it is hot, add the onion and saute until soft and golden, 5 to 8 minutes. Add the curry paste and stir it fully into the onion. Add the chicken and stir well again. Then add the carrot, bell peppers, and broccoli and cook, stirring often, until the chicken just loses its pink color, 7 to 10 minutes.

Add the coconut milk and continue to cook, stirring to prevent sticking, until the chicken is fully cooked, just a few minutes longer, then serve.

Makes 4 to 6 servings.

Variations

Duck Curry: Use 4 boneless duck breasts, cut into 1-inch dice, in place of the chicken. Proceed as directed.

Beef or Pork Curry: Use 2 lb boneless beef or pork, cut into 1-inch cubes, in place of the chicken. Proceed as directed, but after you have added the vegetables, pour in ½ cup to 1 cup water and simmer, stirring occasionally, until the meat is almost tender, 15 to 20 minutes. Then add the coconut milk, increasing it to 1 to 1¼ cups, and continue to simmer until the meat is cooked through, about 10 minutes longer.

Fish or Shrimp Curry: Use 2 lb soft white-fleshed fish fillets (tilapia, sole, flounder, or catfish), cut into 1-inch dice, or 2 lb shrimp, peeled and deveined, in place of the chicken. Substitute about 2 oz snow peas for the broccoli. Proceed as directed, but add the vegetables to the onion and curry paste mixture and cook for 5 minutes, stirring often, before adding the fish or shrimp. Immediately add the ⅞ cup coconut milk and cook, stirring constantly, until the fish or shrimp are done. The fish should take no more than 5 to 7 minutes and the shrimp perhaps 3 minutes.

West Sumatran Beef Cooked in Coconut Milk

•••

Rendang

4 lb beef brisket or flank steak

10 shallots

5 cloves garlic

20 serrano chilies or 15 Thai chilies

2 tsp ground turmeric

1 tsp galangal powder or ½-inch-piece fresh galangal, peeled and finely minced

1-inch-piece fresh ginger, peeled and finely minced

8 cans (14 fl oz each) coconut milk

2 to 3 tablespoons olive oil

2 cups water

4 bay leaves

salt to taste

black pepper to taste

A hot and spicy dish from Padang in western Sumatra. It requires long, slow cooking, but it is worth the wait.

Cut the meat into large chunks, each about 2 inches wide and 4 or 5 inches long. In a small food processor or blender, combine the shallots, garlic, chilies, turmeric, galangal, and ginger. Grind to a paste. Divide the paste in half. Stir half of it into the coconut milk, mixing well.

In a large saucepan, heat the olive oil over medium-high heat. When it is hot, add the meat and the remaining paste and brown the meat well. Add the water and the coconut milk mixture along with the bay leaves. Season with salt and pepper. Bring to a boil, reduce the heat to low, and cook, uncovered, at a very gentle simmer for 2 to 2½ hours, stirring every 15 minutes to prevent the meat from sticking. The sauce will reduce slowly and after 2 hours or so not much will be left. Reduce the heat to the lowest possible setting and continue to cook, stirring often (every 3 or 4 minutes), until all the sauce has been absorbed by the meat. This should take another 30 to 45 minutes. Serve hot.

Makes 8 servings.

Vietnamese Lemongrass Chicken

3 lb boneless chicken, cut into bite-sized pieces

salt to taste

black pepper to taste

¼ cup Vietnamese Chili-Fish Sauce (page 175) or 3 tbs fish sauce mixed with 1 tsp chili-garlic sauce

6 green onions, sliced

3 cloves garlic, minced

3 lemongrass stalks, cut into 1-inch pieces

2 tbs olive or peanut oil

1 yellow onion, chopped

4 green jalapeño or serrano chilies, seeded and chopped

2 tbs fish sauce

½ cup fresh basil leaves, chopped

½ cup fresh mint leaves, chopped

This is a wonderfully aromatic combination. The success of this dish depends on fresh lemongrass, basil, and mint. If they are not available, don't even attempt it.

In a large bowl, place the chicken and sprinkle with salt and pepper. Add the chili-fish sauce or fish sauce chili-garlic sauce combination, green onions, garlic, and lemongrass. Stir to coat evenly, then cover and marinate for at least 1 hour. (If you have time, marinate the mixture overnight, but refrigerate it.)

In a large skillet or wok, heat the oil over medium-high heat. When it is hot, add the yellow onion and chilies and cook, stirring, until the onion is soft. Add the marinated chicken and the 2 tablespoons fish sauce. Stir-fry until the chicken is cooked through, 10 to 12 minutes, adding the basil and mint just before the chicken is ready. Serve hot.

Makes 6 servings.

Straits Café's Whole Fish Grilled in a Banana Leaf

Ikan Panggang

Spice mixture:

2 candlenuts (keminri), soaked in cold water to cover for 10 minutes and drained; or blanched almonds

1 lemongrass stalk, sliced

6 shallots or 1 large onion, sliced

1 teaspoon blachan

2 red jalapeño chilies or 6 serrano chilies

3 kaffir lime leaves

1½ tsp sugar

1½ tsp salt

2 whole pomfrets or trout, 10 oz each, or 1 salmon trout, about 1½ lb, cleaned

salt to taste

2 pieces banana leaf or heavy-duty aluminum foil, 4 inches longer than and twice the width of the fish (1 piece if using salmon trout)

2 limes, cut into wedges

1 cucumber, cut into ½-inch cubes

Cooking fish in a banana leaf is like baking it in foil—it keeps the fish succulent. But the leaf also infuses the fish with a herbaceous scent and flavor. This recipe is from Chris Yeo, chef-owner of Straits Cafe, a popular Singaporean restaurant in San Francisco.

To make the spice mixture, in a blender or food processor, combine the nuts, lemongrass, shallots, blachan, and chilies. Grind to a smooth paste. If needed, add 1 tbs or more water to facilitate the grinding. Transfer the mixture to a bowl. Split the lime leaves in half lengthwise, tear off and discard the spines, and cut the leaves into fine slivers. Stir the leaves, sugar, and salt into the spice mixture. Set aside.

Prepare a fire in a charcoal grill.

If not already done, scale the fish, rinse well with water, and pat dry with paper towels. Cut off and discard the fins. Lay a fish flat on a cutting board with the tail toward you. Cut a 1½-inch-deep slit along the backbone, following the curve of the back from head to tail, to expose the backbone. Turn the fish over and repeat on the other side. If the fish has a thin backbone, like trout, one slit will do. Repeat with the second fish, if using.

Season the fish with salt. Fill the slit and the cavity of each fish (or the single fish) with the spice mixture. To make the banana leaves pliable, immerse them in hot water for about 1 minute until they are soft enough to fold, then wipe dry. For each fish, place a leaf shiny side down on a countertop, place a fish on it, and fold the leaf over the fish. Seal the ends with bamboo skewers. If using aluminum foil, fold as directed and crimp ends to seal.

When the coals are glowing white, place the packets (or packet) over them on an oiled grill rack. Cook, turning once, until the fish are fully cooked, 3 to 5 minutes on each side. Remove the packets from the grill and unwrap the fish. Serve hot with lime wedges and cucumber cubes.

Makes 2 servings, or 4 to 6 servings with other dishes.

Malaysian Fried Fish with Coconut

....

Sambal Goreng Ikan

4 fish steaks such as swordfish, tuna, or sea bass

juice of 1 lime

salt to taste

black pepper to taste

4 cloves garlic

4 Thai chilies

6 candlenuts (kemiri) or macadamia nuts

1 lemongrass stalk, cut into ¼-inch pieces

1-inch-piece fresh ginger, peeled and coarsely chopped

1 tsp galangal powder or 1-inch-piece fresh galangal, peeled and coarsely chopped

¼ cup water or coconut milk

1 tbs fish sauce or Thai Shrimp Sauce (page 175)

2 tbs peanut oil

1 onion, chopped

thin slice terasi or blachan

1 can (14 fl oz) coconut milk

Season the fish steaks with the lime juice, salt, and pepper. In a small food processor or blender, combine the garlic, chilies, candlenuts or macadamia nuts, lemongrass, the ginger, and the fresh galangal, if using. Grind to a paste. Add the ¼ cup water or coconut milk to assist in the grinding. Stir in the galangal powder, if using, and add the fish sauce or shrimp sauce to moisten. Mix well.

In a skillet, heat the oil over medium-high heat. When it is hot, add the onion, the paste, and the blachan or terasi and cook, stirring, until the onion is soft. Add the fish steaks and cook for about 1 minute, flip, and cook the second side for about 1 minute. Repeat several times until the fish is almost cooked (you'll probably flip a 1-inch-thick steak six times per side). Remove the steaks and set aside.

Add the can of coconut milk and bring to a boil. Return the fish steaks to the pan and cook for 3 more minutes, turning as needed.

Makes 4 servings.

Pad Thai

· ·

1 package (1 lb) dried thin, flat rice noodles

¼ cup rice vinegar

3 tbs fish sauce or Thai Shrimp Sauce (page 175)

¼ cup tomato paste

sambal ulek to taste

2 tbs peanut or olive oil

1 yellow onion, finely chopped

2 shallots, chopped

3 cloves garlic, minced

1-inch-piece fresh ginger, peeled and grated

2 tsp galangal powder or ½-inch-piece fresh galangal, peeled and grated

1 lemongrass stalk, finely chopped

1 lb boneless chicken, cut into bite-sized pieces

16 shrimp, peeled and deveined

3 eggs, lightly beaten

½ cup peanuts, coarsely ground

8 fresh cilantro sprigs, chopped

3 green onions, sliced

2 cups bean sprouts

4 limes, cut into wedges

Pad Thai remains one of the most popular dishes served in Bay Area Thai restaurants. I picked up this recipe in a fishing village near Kiri Kan on the Gulf of Thailand. There are a couple of variations possible: one substitutes ground pork for the chicken; the other drops the shrimp and chicken altogether and adds 1 broccoli stalk, 1 Japanese eggplant, 2 carrots, and ½ Chinese cabbage. The vegetable pad Thai cooks quickly, in no more than 10 minutes. I generally omit the bean sprouts, but that is not traditional.

Soak the noodles in hot water to cover for 10 to 15 minutes to soften. In a small bowl, combine the rice vinegar, fish sauce or shrimp sauce, tomato paste, and sambal; mix well and set aside.

Meanwhile, in a medium saucepan, heat the oil over medium-high heat. When it is hot, add the yellow onion, shallots, garlic, ginger, galangal, and lemongrass and saute until the onion is soft, about 5 minutes. Add the chicken and stir well. Add the vinegar mixture and continue to cook until the chicken is tender, about 15 minutes.

Drain the noodles and add to the saucepan along with the shrimp. Cook, stirring, for another 3 minutes. Push everything to the sides of the pan, creating a small opening in the center of the pan. Gently drop the lightly beaten eggs into this opening and quickly stir them. As they begin to cook, mix them into the noodles.

Remove from the heat and add the peanuts, cilantro, green onions, and bean sprouts. Serve with the lime wedges.

Makes 6 servings.

Peanut Noodles

2 cups Basic Peanut Sauce (page 176)

¼ cup tamarind water (page 186)

⅞ cup coconut milk

sambal ulek to taste (optional)

¾ cup crunchy peanut butter

½ cup crushed peanuts (optional)

3 bundles (3.2 oz each) somen noodles

2 tbs ground or crushed peanuts

One of my favorite creations. You can use soba or rice vermicelli, if your prefer, or even plain old spaghetti or vermicelli in a pinch. It can be served hot or cold. This version has lots of sauce, making it deliciously soupy. If you like it drier, add more noodles to taste.

Using the peanut sauce for a base, add the tamarind water, coconut milk (well stirred), sambal (if you want it hotter), crunchy peanut butter, and, if desired, the ½ cup crushed peanuts. Whirl in a food processor or blender or blend by hand until well mixed.

Cook the somen noodles in boiling water until tender, about 5 minutes. Drain and rinse well (use warm water to serve hot, cold water to serve cold). Add the sauce to the noodles and top with the 2 tbs peanuts.

Makes 4 servings.

Indonesian Fried Noodles

Mie Goreng

1 package (1 lb) thin, flat dried rice noodles

1 to 2 tbs peanut or olive oil

1 onion, finely chopped

2 shallots, finely chopped

2 cloves garlic, minced

½-inch-piece fresh ginger, peeled and finely grated

2 carrots, sliced

1 broccoli stalk, cut into bite-sized florets

sambal ulek to taste

1 tbs kecap manis, homemade (page 174) or purchased

4 tomatoes, cut into wedges

No matter where you go in Indonesia, mie goreng is available, ready to provide a satisfying breakfast, lunch, or dinner. Generally, I found that any vegetable was acceptable, but broccoli, carrot, and tomato were the most common, with eggplant and cabbage less frequently encountered. A leafy vegetable similar to Swiss chard or spinach almost always appeared in the mix, an addition that I found to be too much. Lastly, Indonesians put a fried egg (telur goreng) on top. I also found this unnecessary. Should you wish to add more vegetables, however, try a Japanese eggplant, Swiss chard, or Chinese cabbage. Add these when you add the broccoli and carrots. You might also substitute Asian eggplant for the broccoli. This dish can also be made with wheat noodles (mein), although they will need to be cooked appropriately (follow package directions).

Soak the noodles in hot water to cover for 10 to 15 minutes.

Meanwhile, in a large saucepan, heat the oil over medium-high heat. When it is hot, add the onion, shallots, garlic, and ginger and cook, stirring, until the onion is soft. Add the carrots and broccoli, stir well, and add the sambal and kecap manis. Cook, stirring and tossing, for a minute or two. Add the tomatoes and mix well. Drain the noodles and add to the pan. Continue to toss and stir until warmed through, about 3 minutes, then serve.

Makes 8 servings.

Cold Khmer Noodles

3 bundles (3.2 oz each) somen
   noodles

2 carrots, shredded

1 cucumber, thinly sliced

2 limes, cut into wedges

1 cup peanuts

2 cups Khmer Spicy Lime Sauce
   (page 174)

A very easy dish to prepare. This is perfectly refreshing on hot days.

Cook the somen noodles in boiling water until tender, about 5 minutes. Drain and rinse well. Let cool.

Grab a handful of noodles and press into a flat, pancakelike mound. Repeat until all the noodles are all used up. Arrange the noodle mounds in the center of a large platter. Put the carrots, cucumber, limes, and peanuts in separate piles around the noodles. Pour the lime sauce into a bowl. Let guests help themselves to the noodles, condiments, and sauce.

Makes 4 servings.

Indonesian Festive Rice

Nasi Kuning

2 tbs peanut oil

½ tsp ground cumin

1 yellow onion, chopped

2 shallots, minced

½-inch-piece fresh ginger, peeled
   and grated

1 tbs ground turmeric

2 cups jasmine rice

4 cups water or 2 cups each
   chicken broth and water

1 lemongrass stalk, bruised

1 green onion

salt to taste

One of my early favorites. I've been cooking this dish since the first time I attempted Indonesian and Southeast Asian food for one of my mother's dinner parties in New York. I still love to make it.

In a medium saucepan, heat the peanut oil over medium-high heat. When it is hot, add the cumin, yellow onion, shallots, and ginger and cook, stirring, until the onion is soft and golden, 5 to 8 minutes. Add the turmeric and mix well. Stir in the rice and coat with the onion-turmeric mixture. Add the water or broth and water, lemongrass, and green onion. Season with salt. Bring to a boil, reduce the heat to low, cover, and cook until the rice has absorbed the liquid and is tender, about 20 minutes. Remove and discard the lemongrass and green onion before serving.

Makes 8 servings.

Stir-fried Vegetables

6 dried shiitake mushrooms

½ cup hot water

5 tbs soy sauce

1 tsp Asian sesame oil

1 tsp fish sauce

1 tsp palm sugar or 2 tsp brown sugar

3 tbs peanut oil

1 yellow onion, chopped into large pieces

3 cloves garlic, minced

1-inch-piece fresh ginger, peeled and freshly grated

1 carrot, sliced on the diagonal

1 stalk broccoli, cut into bite-sized florets

¼ head Chinese cabbage, cut into strips

½ cup cold water

1 tsp cornstarch

2 green onions, sliced

In a bowl, soak the shiitake mushrooms in the hot water for 30 minutes.

Meanwhile, in another bowl, combine 3 tbs of the soy sauce, the sesame oil, fish sauce, and sugar. When the mushrooms are rehydrated, drain them and cut off and discard their stems. Slice each mushroom cap in quarters and add to the soy-sesame mixture. Allow to soak for 10 minutes, then transfer to a small saucepan. Cook over low-medium heat until a little of the liquid has been absorbed. Remove from the heat and set aside.

In a wok or large skillet, heat the peanut oil over medium-high heat. When it is hot, add the yellow onion, garlic, and ginger and cook, stirring, until the onion starts to soften. Then add the carrot slices and the mushrooms along with their remaining liquid. Reduce the heat to medium and cook for 3 minutes. Add the broccoli and cabbage, mix well, and add the remaining 2 tablespoons soy sauce. Cook for another minute and add the cold water. Bring to a boil and scoop out a little of the liquid. Stir the cornstarch into the removed liquid and then pour back into the vegetables. Cook until the sauce thickens, 2 to 3 minutes. Top with the green onions and serve.

Makes 4 servings.

Indonesian Curried Vegetables

Sayur Lodeh

2 shallots

3 cloves garlic

4 candlenuts (kemiri) or macadamia nuts

2 Thai chilies

½-inch-piece fresh ginger, peeled and coarsely chopped

1 tsp galangal powder or ½-inch-piece fresh galangal, peeled and grated

2 tbs fish sauce

thin slice blachan or terasi or 1 tsp anchovy paste

1 tsp ground turmeric

1 tsp ground cumin

3 tbs peanut oil

1 onion, finely chopped

2 carrots, sliced

1 green bell pepper, cut into long, narrow strips

1 red bell pepper, cut into long, narrow strips

2 Japanese eggplants, thinly sliced and lightly salted

1 broccoli stalk, cut into bite-sized florets

1 small head cauliflower, cut into bite-sized florets

16 green beans, ends trimmed and cut in half

2 cans (14 fl oz each) coconut milk

1 can (15 oz) straw mushrooms, drained

1 can (7 oz) baby corn, drained

Don't be intimidated by the long list of vegetables. You can use as few or as many as you'd like (or are in season), as well as make your own substitutions. Other than a little chopping, this is a fast and easy stir-fry.

In a food processor or blender, combine the shallots, garlic, candlenuts or macadamia nuts, chilies, ginger, fresh galangal, if using, fish sauce, and blachan, terasi, or anchovy paste. Grind to a paste. Stir in the turmeric, galangal powder, if using, and cumin. Mix well.

Have your vegetables all cut into bite-sized pieces and ready to go. In a large wok or saucepan, heat the peanut oil over medium-high heat. When it is hot, add the onion and cook, stirring, until soft and golden. Add the paste and cook for 2 minutes. Add the carrots and the bell peppers and stir-fry constantly for 2 minutes longer. Add the eggplants and cook for 2 minutes, stirring often. Add the broccoli and the cauliflower, cook for 2 minutes, and then add the green beans and the coconut milk. Bring to a boil, then immediately reduce the heat to low. Cook, continuing to stir often, until the vegetables are tender, a few minutes longer. Add the straw mushrooms and the baby corn and cook for a minute to heat through, then serve.

Makes 8 servings.

Eggplant-Tempe
Sambal Ulek Tomat

· ·

2 tbs olive oil

1 shallot, minced

2 cloves garlic, minced

1 onion, finely chopped

½-inch-piece fresh ginger, peeled
and minced

1 tsp galangal powder, or ½-inch-
piece fresh galangal, peeled and
minced

2 Japanese eggplants, thinly sliced

½ cup water

1 package (11 oz) tempe, sliced

2 cups Indonesian Tomato-Chili
Sauce, Sambal Ulek Tomat,
(page 177)

1 to 2 tbs chopped fresh cilantro
leaves

*This dish goes well with plain white rice or somen noodles. For variety, add a few spoonfuls
of peanuts or candlenuts just before you add the tempe.*

In a large skillet, heat the oil over medium-high heat. When it is hot, add the
shallot, garlic, onion, ginger, and galangal and saute, stirring often, until the
onion is soft and golden, 6 to 8 minutes. Add the eggplants and water and
continue to cook, stirring often, until the eggplants begin to soften, 4 to 5
minutes.

Add the tempe and the sauce and simmer over medium heat, stirring as
necessary to coat the eggplant and tempe. The tempe should be heated
through and the flavors blended in about 10 minutes. Transfer to a serving
dish, garnish with the cilantro, and serve.

Makes 4 to 6 servings.

Panfried Tempe

· ·
Tempe Goreng

2 shallots

½-inch-piece fresh ginger, peeled
and grated

4 cloves garlic

1 tsp galangal powder or ½-inch-
piece fresh galangal, peeled and
grated

2 tbs tamarind water (page 186)

2 tsp fish sauce

½ lb tempe, sliced

2 tbs peanut, corn, or safflower oil

In a small food processor or a blender, combine the shallots, ginger, garlic,
galangal, tamarind water, and fish sauce. Grind to a paste. Transfer to a bowl,
add the tempe, and marinate for 1 hour or longer, turning the slices
occasionally.

In a skillet, heat the oil over medium-high heat. When it is hot, add the
tempe and fry until it is crisp and browned evenly on both sides. Serve hot.

Makes 4 servings.

Tempe with Vegetables

....

Tempe Sayur

3 shallots

6 cloves garlic

2 Thai chilies, diced

2 tbs tamarind water (page 186)

1-inch-piece fresh ginger, peeled
    and coarsely chopped

1 tsp galangal powder or ½-inch-
    piece fresh galangal, peeled and
    coarsely chopped

1 tbs peanut oil

1 onion, chopped

1 carrot, sliced

1 Japanese eggplant, sliced

1 red bell pepper, sliced

1 tsp sambal ulek (optional)

1 broccoli stalk, cut into bite-
    sized florets

1 lb tempe, sliced

1 can (14 fl oz) coconut milk

In a small food processor, combine the shallots, garlic, chilies along with the tamarind water, ginger, and galangal. Grind to a paste.

In a large skillet or wok, heat the peanut oil over medium-high heat. When it is hot, add the onion and the paste and cook, stirring, until the onion is soft. Add the carrot, eggplant, red bell pepper, and, if a spicier dish is desired, stir in the sambal. Mix well. Stir-fry for 5 minutes. Add the broccoli and tempe and cook, stirring, for another 3 minutes. Pour in the coconut milk and simmer, stirring often, until the vegetables are tender and the flavors are blended, about 5 minutes longer.

Makes 6 servings.

Tofu and Tempe

Tofu is common throughout East Asia, while tempe is a purely Javanese creation. The latter is basically an enzyme-fermented soybean cake that is pressed. Here in California, it is primarily associated with the tempe burgers that were common at Dead shows. I never cared for tempe burgers, but after tasting what the Javanese do with tempe, I have a new found love. I am still experimenting, but these three recipes are a nice start.

Tempe in Candlenut Sauce

Terik Tempe

3 shallots

6 cloves garlic

1-inch-piece fresh ginger, peeled
   and coarsely chopped

½ lb (1⅔ cups) candlenuts
   (kemiri) or macadamia nuts

1 tbs fish sauce

1 tsp ground turmeric

2 tsp ground cumin

1 tsp ground coriander

1 tbs peanut oil

1 onion, chopped

1 lb tempe, sliced

2 cans (14 fl oz each) coconut milk

In Indonesia, cooks use candlenuts, which are hard to find, but macadamia nuts do nicely.

In a small food processor or blender, combine the shallots, garlic, ginger, and nuts. Grind to a paste. Moisten with the fish sauce. Add the turmeric, cumin, and coriander (if you wish to use coriander seed, add ½ tsp coriander seed along with the shallots and garlic).

In a skillet or wok, heat the peanut oil over medium-high heat. When it is hot, add the onion and cook, stirring, until soft and golden. Add the paste and cook, continuing to stir, for 2 minutes. Add the tempe, mix well to coat it on all sides, and pour in the coconut milk. Reduce the heat to low and cook, stirring occasionally, for 10 minutes to blend the flavors.

Makes 6 servings.

Thai Fried Tofu with Sweet Peanut Sauce

Tauhu Taud

1 package (14 oz) soft tofu,
   drained

1⅔ cups tamarind water (page 186)

2 tbs fish sauce

2 tbs Thai Red Curry Paste (page
   185)

1 tbs olive or peanut oil

2 cups roasted peanuts, coarsely
   ground

⅞ cup coconut milk

1 cup brown sugar

3 to 4 tbs peanut oil for frying

Cut the drained tofu into strips about 3 inches long and 1 inch wide. In a bowl, combine the tofu, ½ cup of the tamarind water, and the fish sauce. Let stand for 30 minutes.

Meanwhile, make the peanut sauce: In a saucepan, combine the red curry paste, 1 tbs oil, peanuts, and coconut milk. Bring to a boil and add the brown sugar and the remaining 1 cup tamarind water. Stir well to dissolve the sugar and then simmer for 5 minutes.

Meanwhile, in a large skillet, heat the oil for frying over medium-high heat. When it is hot, add the tofu and fry quickly, about 5 minutes, flipping gently with a spatula. Serve with the warm peanut sauce.

Makes 4 to 6 servings.

Malaysian Pickled Vegetables

Acar Kuning

15 serrano chilies, finely diced

2 carrots, cut into sticks

24 green beans, ends trimmed

1 cucumber, thinly sliced

1 red onion, finely chopped

2 tbs peanut oil

4 cloves garlic

2 shallots

½-inch-piece fresh ginger, peeled and coarsely chopped

6 macadamia nuts

1 tsp galangal powder or ½-inch-piece fresh galangal, peeled and coarsely chopped

2 tsp sugar

⅔ cup rice vinegar

½ cup water

⅓ cup tamarind water (page 186)

In a glass bowl, combine the chilies, carrot sticks, green beans, cucumber, onion, and peanut oil. Toss well.

In a small food processor or blender, combine the garlic, the shallots, ginger, nuts, and galangal, if using fresh. Grind to a paste. If using galangal powder, stir it in at this point. Dissolve the sugar in the rice vinegar and water. Stir well and add to the paste. Mix well and add the tamarind water.

Pour the marinade over the vegetables. Cover and marinate in the refrigerator overnight.

Makes 4 servings.

Indonesian Pickled Cucumber Relish

1 cup rice vinegar

1 tbs palm sugar or 2 tbs brown sugar

5 Fresno chilies, diced

1 cucumber, sliced paper-thin

In a small bowl, combine the vinegar, sugar, and chilies. Stir to dissolve the sugar. Pour over the sliced cucumber in a glass bowl. Cover and refrigerate overnight.

Makes about 2 cups, enough for 8 servings.

Thai Mangoes with Sticky Rice

Khao Niew Mamuang

I have made this two different ways, and both have come out well. So here are both recipes.

My incorrect but not so bad way

2 cups glutinous rice

2 cups water

3 cans (14 fl oz each) coconut milk

1 tbs palm sugar or 2 tbs brown sugar

½ cup granulated sugar

2 or 3 mangoes, peeled, pitted, and sliced

Wash the rice carefully and soak overnight in water to cover. Drain well. In a saucepan, combine the water, coconut milk, and both sugars. Stir well and bring to a boil. Add the rice and return to a boil, stirring occasionally to prevent sticking. Reduce the heat to low and cook, stirring occasionally, until the rice is done, 20 to 25 minutes. Remove from the heat, let cool, and serve on individual plates with the mango slices.

Makes 8 servings.

The correct way

5 cans (14 fl oz each) coconut milk

3 tbs palm sugar or 6 tbs brown sugar

¼ cup granulated sugar

4 cups cooked glutinous rice

2 or 3 mangoes, peeled, pitted, and sliced

In a saucepan, combine the coconut milk and both sugars. Bring to a boil. Add the cooked rice and reduce the heat to low. Simmer, stirring constantly to prevent sticking, until the rice has absorbed the coconut milk, 20 to 25 minutes. Remove from the heat, let cool, and serve on individual plates with the mango slices.

Makes 12 servings.

Thai Bananas in Coconut Milk

Kuay Namuan

2 cans (14 fl oz each) coconut milk

3 tbs sugar

6 bananas, peeled and thinly sliced

In a saucepan, heat the coconut milk, bringing it to a simmer; do not allow it to boil. Simmer gently until thickened slightly, 2 to 3 minutes. Add the sugar and stir to dissolve. Add the bananas and cook for 5 minutes until slightly softened. Serve warm.

Makes 6 servings.

Spain

With its long coastline, the Iberian Peninsula is home to some of the world's finest seafood. *Paella a la valenciana,* of course, stands out as one of the most popular dishes of this southwestern corner of Europe. But there are numerous other specialties that deserve attention as well.

My favorite Spanish food tradition is tapas. Spaniards eat late, often after ten or eleven at night. But around four or five in the afternoon, they begin heading to their local bars for a glass of sherry and a few small bites, or tapas. The word comes from *tapar,* which means "to cover," and is derived from the practice of covering one's sherry glass with a small plate of food. In this chapter you'll find a score of recipes for tapas. I find that a tapas buffet is a wonderful way to host a larger number of people than will comfortably fit around the dinner table.

Spanish food has strong regional distinctions. Still, common threads exist: olives and their oil in almost everything; the use of sherry and red wines for cooking; copious amounts of garlic, shallots, and onions; a love of deep, rich sauces to accompany dishes; an abundance of sausages and cured meats; the appreciation of ripe cheeses; and the use of saffron, the world's most expensive spice. I've tried to include a dish from just about every corner of Spain to give you an idea of the variety and richness of the cuisine.

The majority of Iberian ingredients are fairly easy to locate where I live. But there are a few hard-to-find items, such as certain cheeses and hams. Recently, however, Spanish cheeses have become quite trendy in San Francisco, making them more widely available in cheese shops and upmarket food stores. Nevertheless, they remain generally pricy.

Finally, red wine goes well with most Spanish food, and while tapas traditionally call for a dry sherry, you might try a nice bottle of cava (sparkling wine). I like Cordiniu Brut as an inexpensive bottle; or try Cordiniu Napa, their California label. Also, don't use the finer ports and sherries for cooking. Inexpensive California ports or sherries are fine. Another wine you might want to keep on hand is Madeira, which is similar to Marsala.

Suggested Menu

Tapas for Twenty

The idea here is to serve a buffet and allow your guests to grab small bites while they mingle. Generally I will place different dishes throughout the house and allow people to explore with plate and beverage in hand. I have also served tapas for a sit-down dinner and I find they work well. This menu lends itself to outdoor entertaining, too. Some of the items can be prepared in the days preceding the event, while others need last-minute attention. The dessert is a creamy lemon pudding; you'll need to triple the recipe to serve 20. There is a recipe for flán (page 132) in the Latin American chapter that would also complement this menu.

Tapas:
Seville-Style Marinated Olives
Lamb Meatballs in a Serrano Ham Sauce
Prune and Bacon Skewers
Asturian Eggplant
Fried Squid
Marinated Mushrooms
Chickpea Salad with Roasted Red Peppers and Capers
Asparagus and Blue Cheese Rolls
Spicy Mussels in Tomato Broth
Open-faced Sandwiches with Serrano Ham
Open-faced Sandwiches with Pork Loin
Open-faced Sandwiches with Sardines in Oil
Tortilla Española (Egg and Potato Omelet)

Sauces and Spreads:
Catalan Garlic Mayonnaise (Alioli)
Roasted Red Pepper Puree (Romesco)
Catalan Chili, Tomato, and Almond Sauce
Black Olive and Anchovy Paste

Lemon Yogurt Pudding
Cava
Amontillado Sherry

Basic Sauces

These sauces are good additions to any tapas party. The roasted pepper and romesco sauces go with almost everything, from tortilla española to vegetables to bread. The alioli is also good for vegetables—raw or cooked—or can be served with bread or roasted potatoes. You'll find homemade mayonnaise much better than purchased, and it goes especially well with vegetables. The black olive paste is wonderful with bread. They all are delicious on montaditos.

Catalan Chili, Tomato, and Almond Sauce

···

Romesco Sauce

1 dried morron or ñoras chili

1 tsp dry sherry

¼ cup olive oil

2 red serrano chilies

6 cloves garlic

2 shallots

10 plum tomatoes

6 fresh parsley sprigs

1 cup blanched almonds, toasted (page 227)

One of my favorite sauces for just about everything, from asparagus to boiled shrimp to roast potatoes to bread. You can also make this sauce with hazelnuts. This recipe is quite nutty; if you find the almond flavor too much, cut back to ¾ cup almonds.

Morrones and ñoras are the best Spanish dried chilies, but they are difficult to find. Use dried New Mexico, negro, guajillo, or dark pasilla (a little milder) as a substitute. I also like to add a fresh pasilla or anaheim chili pepper; add it with the serranos.

In a bowl, combine the dried chili, sherry, and warm water to cover. Let stand for 20 minutes.

In a large skillet, heat the olive oil over medium-high heat. Add the serrano chilies, garlic, shallots, and tomatoes and cook, shaking the pan occasionally to prevent sticking, until the chilies and tomatoes are nice and browned. Remove from the heat. Slip the chilies and tomatoes into a plastic bag, close tightly, and let stand for 20 minutes.

Remove the serranos and tomatoes from the bag and peel away and discard the skins. Place the serranos, tomatoes, garlic, shallots, parsley, half of the almonds, the softened dried chili and its soaking liquid, and any juices from the skillet in a food processor. Process to form a coarse mixture. Add the remaining almonds and grind to a coarse paste. Use immediately or store in a tightly covered jar in the refrigerator for up to 1 month.

Makes about 1½ cups.

Mayonnaise

Mayonesa

1 whole egg

1 egg yolk

½ tsp Dijon mustard

2 tsp lemon juice

salt to taste

white pepper to taste

1 cup olive oil

Few people realize that mayonnaise is actually a Spanish sauce. But yes, it hails from the town of Mahon in the Balearic Islands. Homemade mayonnaise is much better than store-bought. It tastes great with vegetables, boiled shrimp, or montaditos and is good as a spread on bread.

In a blender, combine the egg, egg yolk, mustard, lemon juice, salt, and white pepper. Process until blended. With the motor running, add the oil in a slow continuous flow. Continue blending until the mayonnaise is thick and smooth.

Makes about 1 cup.

Alioli

Catalan Garlic Mayonnaise

7 cloves garlic

¼ teaspoon salt

up to 1 cup extra-virgin olive oil

You need a mortar and pestle to make this sauce. Otherwise, it will not emulsify. Because it lacks an egg, it won't work in a blender or food processor. Also, the use of extra-virgin olive oil is essential for smoothness.

In a mortar, mash the garlic with the salt into a thick paste. Add the oil very slowly, no more than a few drops at a time, while continuing to mash and stir. Continue in this manner until the sauce is a creamy white emulsion. Do not add any more oil after this point. Should the emulsion break, you can remedy the situation by adding 1 egg yolk, lightly beaten, and mixing it until it emulsifies once again.

Makes about 1 cup.

Roasted Red Pepper Puree

5 red bell peppers

4 cloves garlic

1 tsp dried thyme

1 tbs olive oil

Preheat an oven to 500 degrees F.

Place the whole bell peppers in a metal pan (covering the bottom of the pan with aluminum foil makes cleaning up easier). The skins of the red peppers will start to char and turn black. Turn the peppers as necessary to char evenly on all sides. When the peppers are about half charred, add the garlic cloves to the pan. When the peppers are completely blackened, which could take anywhere from 20 to 40 minutes, depending on the oven, remove from the oven. Set the garlic aside and place the peppers in a plastic bag, sealing it tightly closed. Let stand for 20 minutes. Remove from the bag and peel away the skins. Discard the stems, seeds, and inner membranes.

Place the peppers and roasted garlic in a small food processor or blender. Puree until smooth. Add the thyme and olive oil and mix well.

Makes about 1 cup.

Black Olive and Anchovy Paste

Garúm

6 anchovy fillets in olive oil, drained

1 slice white bread, crusts removed

1 cup black olives, pitted

1 tbs capers

1 tsp dried thyme

2 cloves garlic, minced

3 tbs olive oil

½ tsp black pepper

chopped fresh parsley (optional)

This is the Spanish version of French tapenade. Serve with bread, crackers, or montaditos.

Place the anchovy fillets in a small bowl with water to cover for 15 minutes. Remove the anchovy fillets from the water, and place the bread in the water to soak up some of it.

In a food processor or blender, combine all of the ingredients except the parsley. Process until smooth. Transfer to a bowl and garnish with parsley, if desired.

Makes about 1½ cups.

Lemon Olives

∙∙

Aceitunas al Limón

2 jars (10 oz each) pimiento-stuffed green olives

2 lemons, quartered

3 fresh oregano sprigs

12 black peppercorns

3 fresh thyme sprigs

¼ cup sherry vinegar

3 cloves garlic, crushed (with a mallet or the edge of a knife, not in a garlic press)

¼ cup lemon juice

You'll need a large canning jar for this recipe. The olives should marinate for at least a week before using. You can serve them as a tapa or add them to other dishes. They're great in lemon Absolut martinis.

Drain the olives, but do not discard the liquid. Rinse the olives under cold water. Pat dry with paper towels. In a 1-pint canning jar, combine the olives, lemon quarters, oregano sprigs, peppercorns, thyme sprigs, vinegar, garlic, and lemon juice. Add enough of the reserved olive brine to fill the jar. Seal tightly. Shake the jar. Place in the refrigerator and allow to marinate for 1 week. The jar should be shaken daily.

After 1 week, remove and discard the garlic, lemon quarters, and peppercorns. The olives will keep indefinitely as long as they are stored in the refrigerator. Serve cold.

Makes about 1½ cups.

Seville-Style Marinated Olives

∙∙

Aceitunas Sevillanas

2 cups pimiento-stuffed green olives

1 tsp dried oregano

1 tsp dried thyme

1 tsp dried marjoram

4 bay leaves

8 cloves garlic, sliced

½ tsp fennel seeds, crushed

½ tsp ground cumin

½ cup distilled white vinegar

2 fresh rosemary sprigs

The olives need to be started at least 2 days before you plan to serve them.

Place the green olives in a bowl. In a small cup, stir together the oregano, thyme, and marjoram. Sprinkle over the olives, coating them gently. Transfer the olives to a good-sized glass jar and add the bay leaves, garlic, fennel seeds, cumin, vinegar, and rosemary. Fill the jar with cold water and seal. Shake well, then allow the olives to marinate in a cool, dark place for 48 hours. After 48 hours, store them in the refrigerator. Serve at room temperature.

Makes about 2 cups.

Marinated Mushrooms

Champiñones Adobados

½ cup olive oil

1 onion, finely chopped

6 cloves garlic, minced

2 shallots, finely chopped

1 tsp fresh thyme leaves

2 tsp fresh oregano leaves

2 tbs tomato paste

½ cup dry white wine

1 cup water

2 bay leaves

salt to taste

white pepper to taste

2 lb small button mushrooms

In a saucepan, heat the olive oil over medium-high heat. When it is hot, add the onion, garlic, and shallots and saute, stirring occasionally, until the onion begins to soften, about 3 minutes. Add the thyme and oregano, mix well, and add the tomato paste and white wine. Again mix well to dissolve the tomato paste. Add the water and the bay leaves and bring to a boil. Add the salt and pepper, reduce the heat to low, and simmer for 20 minutes. Add the mushrooms and cook for 5 minutes. Remove from the heat, cover, and let cool.

Pour the cooled mushrooms into a bowl and cover tightly with plastic wrap. Shake to distribute the spices and juices. Refrigerate for 24 hours before serving. Serve at room temperature.

Makes 20 servings as a tapa.

Vegetable Pickles

Escabeche de Verduras

3 carrots, thinly sliced on the
  diagonal

32 green beans, ends trimmed

1 head cauliflower, broken into
  florets

1 cup distilled white vinegar

1 cup water

¼ cup sugar

3 fresh thyme sprigs

2 cloves garlic

2 tbs capers

Spanish pickle dishes are quick and easy.

Blanch the vegetables separately in rapidly boiling water. The carrots will take 2 minutes, the green beans will take 1½ minutes, and the cauliflower will take 2 minutes. Once each vegetable has been blanched, immediately plunge it into an ice water bath for 5 minutes, then drain.

In a medium saucepan, combine the white vinegar, water, and sugar. Bring to a boil, add the blanched vegetables, and return to a boil. Cook for 1 minute. Cover and remove from the heat. Allow the vegetables to cool in the pot for 30 minutes, then transfer them with their liquid to a glass container (bowl or jars). Add the thyme, garlic, and capers. Cover and refrigerate overnight before serving.

Makes 8 servings as a tapa.

Thirsty Bear's
Pisto Manchego

3 large tomatoes

1 to 2 tbs olive oil

1 large onion, sliced

2 cloves garlic, chopped

2 green bell peppers, roasted and
  cut into long strips (page 227)

2 zucchini, sliced

salt and black pepper to taste

sherry vinegar to taste

1 or 2 thin slices manchego cheese

Thirsty Bear restaurant, located in San Francisco's trendy SoMa (South of Market) district, uniquely combines two popular culinary trends in a single restaurant: a brewpub that serves Spanish food. It's not just a gimmick, the tapas are delicious, particularly this light mixture of vegetables in a tangy vinaigrette topped with creamy melted manchego cheese.

Preheat an oven to 500 degrees F. Place the tomatoes on a baking sheet and slip into the oven until the skins are nicely charred, about 10 minutes. Remove from the oven and, when cool enough to handle, peel, seed, and chop. Set aside.

In a flameproof skillet, heat the oil over medium-high heat. When it is hot, add the onion and garlic and saute until soft, about 5 minutes. Add the bell peppers, reduce the heat to medium, and cook, stirring, until the peppers are soft, about 5 minutes. Stir in the tomatoes and zucchini and season with salt, pepper, and vinegar. Cover, reduce the heat to low, and cook until all the vegetables are tender, about 10 minutes.

Meanwhile, preheat a broiler. When the vegetables are ready, lay the cheese on top of the vegetable mixture. Slip under the broiler until the cheese melts, then serve at once.

Makes 4 servings.

Paprika Oven-Roasted Potatoes

Patatas Bravas al Horno

2 lb new potatoes, quartered

salt to taste

½ cup olive oil

6 tbs butter

1 onion, chopped

6 cloves garlic, minced

2 tsp fresh oregano leaves

2 tsp fresh thyme leaves

2 tbs paprika

½ tsp white pepper

2 tbs all-purpose flour

½ cup hot chicken broth or water

Serve with a selection of sauces (pages 208 to 210).

Preheat an oven to 400 degrees F. Bring a large saucepan filled with water to a boil. Add the potatoes and salt and return to a rolling boil. Boil for 10 minutes. Remove from the heat, drain, and set aside.

In a large saute pan or wide saucepan , combine the olive oil and butter and melt over medium-low heat. Do not allow the butter to brown. Once the butter is melted, add the onion and the garlic. Raise the heat to medium-high and cook until the onions are soft and golden, about 7 minutes. Add the oregano, thyme, paprika, and white pepper. Mix well and add the potatoes. Mix well to coat the potatoes with the mixture. Cook over medium-high heat for 2 minutes, stirring often to prevent sticking and burning.

Meanwhile, stir the flour into the hot chicken broth until well dissolved. Add to the potatoes and cook until the sauce thickens, about 3 minutes longer. Remove from the heat.

Transfer the potatoes to an ovenproof earthenware dish (cazuela) or glass or ceramic baking dish. Bake for 15 minutes. Serve hot.

Makes 8 servings as a tapa.

Sangría

2 bottles inexpensive red wine

5 cups orange juice

2 oranges, sliced

1 cup lemon juice

2 lemons, sliced

juice of 8 limes

2 limes, sliced

1 cinnamon stick

superfine sugar to taste (about ¾ cup suits me)

Sangría hits the spot on a hot summer day.

In a large pitcher, mix together all the ingredients. Chill well before serving.

Makes 3 quarts.

Tortilla Española de Patatas

Egg and Potato Omelet

4 large russet potatoes, peeled and
thinly sliced

1 cup olive or corn oil

1 onion, thinly sliced

salt to taste

white pepper to taste

6 eggs, lightly beaten

To the Spanish, a tortilla is an egg dish similar to an omelet. When the Spanish conquered Mexico, they found that the native corn cakes reminded them of Spanish tortas and tortillas. Thus the corn cakes came to be known as tortillas as well. Given that potatoes are a New World product, this dish is obviously a post-Columbian one. Tortillas españolas are wonderful for breakfast, lunch, or dinner. Serve with a selection of sauces (pages 208 to 210).

Cover the potato slices with water to prevent discoloration while you ready the remaining ingredients. Then, just before using, drain and pat dry.

In a large nonstick skillet, heat the olive oil over high heat. When it is hot, add the potato slices one at a time. Then add the onion slices. Fry over high heat until both the potatoes and onion are lightly colored, about 5 minutes, lowering the heat as needed to prevent burning. They must not become crispy at the edges. They must also remain separated; do not allow them to cake together. Once cooked, remove from the oil with a slotted spoon. Do not discard the oil, but do strain out any particles.

Divide the strained oil into 2 equal portions. Season the potatoes and onion with salt and pepper and add to the beaten eggs. Mix well and let stand for 15 minutes.

In a medium nonstick skillet, reheat one part of the oil over medium-high heat and pour in the potato-egg mixture. Reduce the heat to medium and shake the pan frequently to prevent sticking. Cook until the underside is firm, 12 to 15 minutes. Carefully invert a plate over the skillet, then carefully invert the skillet and plate together. Lift off the skillet. Reheat the second part of the oil in the skillet and slide the tortilla (uncooked side down) back into the skillet. Lower the heat and again shake the pan frequently to prevent sticking. Cook until the tortilla is firm and golden, 8 to 10 minutes. Slide onto a serving platter. Let cool slightly, slice into thin wedges, and serve warm or at room temperature.

Makes 10 servings as a tapa.

Spanish Garlic Shrimp

···

Gambas al Ajillo

24 large or medium shrimp,
  peeled and deveined with last
  tail segment intact

salt to taste

white pepper to taste

¼ cup olive oil

1 tbs paprika

6 cloves garlic, minced

chopped fresh parsley

This is an incredibly easy dish to prepare, and quite delicious. Serve with bread for dipping in the oil.

Season the shrimp with salt and white pepper. In a saucepan, heat the olive oil over high heat. Add the paprika and the garlic. Let sizzle for 1 minute, then add the shrimp. Cook until the shrimp are completely pink, about 3 minutes, stirring often to ensure even cooking. Sprinkle parsley over the top and serve warm.

Makes 4 servings.

Spicy Mussels in Tomato Broth

···

Mejillones Orense

4 lb mussels, scrubbed and debearded

1 onion, cut up

2 shallots

8 cloves garlic

2 red serrano chilies, seeded

¼ cup olive oil

1 tbs dried thyme

½ tsp cayenne pepper

1 tsp paprika

2 tomatoes, peeled and diced

1 cup chicken broth

2 cans (15 oz each) tomato sauce

salt to taste

10 fresh parsley sprigs, finely chopped

Serve with warm French bread.

Discard any mussels that fail to close to the touch.

In a food processor, combine the onion, shallots, garlic, and chilies. Process until a smooth paste forms.

In a large stockpot, heat the oil over high heat. When it is hot, add the onion puree and saute for 30 seconds. Add the thyme, cayenne, and paprika, mix well, and saute for 30 seconds. Add the tomatoes and mix well. Saute for 1 minute and add the broth, tomato sauce, and salt. Bring to a boil, then add the mussels to the pot. Reduce the heat to low, cover, and cook for 15 minutes. Remove from the heat and discard any mussels that have not opened. Serve immediately with warm French bread.

Makes 12 servings as a tapa.

Herb-Marinated Mussels

3 lb mussels, scrubbed and
  debearded

1 cup dry sherry

1 onion, chopped

2 shallots, chopped

¼ cup olive oil

8 cloves garlic, minced

2 tbs fresh thyme leaves

2 tsp fresh marjoram leaves

2 tsp fresh oregano leaves

3 bay leaves

10 fresh parsley sprigs, finely
  chopped

2 tsp paprika

salt to taste

¼ tsp cayenne pepper

lemon wedges

Serve with warm French bread.

Discard any mussels that fail to close to the touch.

In a large saucepan, bring the sherry to a boil. Add the onion, shallots, and mussels. Cover, reduce the heat to medium-low and cook until the mussels open, about 7 minutes. Remove from heat and discard any mussels that have not opened. Using a slotted spoon, transfer the mussels to a bowl and remove them from their shells. Discard half of the shells; divide the reserved shells into halves for presentation. Reserve the liquid in the saucepan.

In a large skillet, heat the olive oil over medium heat. When it is hot, add the garlic and saute for 1 minute. Add the thyme, marjoram, oregano, and bay leaves and saute for another minute. Add the reserved cooking liquid and bring to a boil. Add the parsley, paprika, salt, and cayenne pepper, mix well, and remove from the heat. Pour the liquid over the mussels. Cover with plastic wrap and refrigerate overnight.

To serve, arrange the reserved mussel shells on a platter. Place a mussel in each shell. Pour some of the marinade over each mussel. Serve cold with French bread and lemon wedges.

Makes 8 servings as a tapa.

Fried Squid

•••

Calamar Frito

1 lb cleaned squid

2 cups all-purpose flour

1 tsp paprika

½ tsp cayenne pepper

½ tsp salt or to taste

½ tsp white pepper

4 eggs, lightly beaten

corn oil for frying

lemon wedges

This recipe calls for cleaned squid, a real time-saver (although it does cost a bit more). If you clean your own (page 227), you will need to buy more, about 1½ lb, to yield 1 lb after cleaning. Serve the squid with Alioli (page 209), Mayonnaise (page 209), and/or Catalan Chili, Tomato, and Almond Sauce (page 208).

Cut the cleaned squid bodies into rings. Depending on the size of the squid, you should have 4 or 5 rings from each squid. Combine with the tentacles. In a paper bag, combine the flour, paprika, cayenne, salt, and white pepper. Toss in the squid and seal the bag. Shake vigorously to dust the squid evenly. Remove the squid from the bag and pass through the beaten eggs. Toss the squid back into the bag. Seal the bag and shake vigorously.

In a deep skillet, pour in oil to a depth of about 3 inches and heat over high heat. When it is hot, fry the squid in small batches, planning on about 1 minute for each batch. The squid is done when it puffs up. Using a slotted spoon, transfer to paper towels to drain. Keep warm in a low oven while you cook the remaining squid. Serve with lemon wedges and the sauce of your choice.

Makes 6 to 8 servings.

Prune and Bacon Skewers

•••

Banderillas de Ciruelas Pasas con Tocino

40 pitted prunes

½ cup dry sherry

½ cup cream cheese, softened

½ cup blue cheese, softened

14 bacon slices, cut into thirds

An unusual combination, this is an old family concoction.

Preheat an oven to 350 degrees F.

In a bowl, soak the prunes in the sherry for 15 minutes. In another bowl, combine the cheeses and mix well.

Drain the prunes and stuff each one with a bit of the cheese. Wrap a piece of the bacon around each prune. Thread each prune onto a wooden skewer and place on a baking sheet.

Bake until the cheeses melt and the bacon is cooked, about 15 minutes. Serve warm.

Makes 40 skewers.

Asparagus and Blue Cheese Rolls

Envueltos de Esparagos

1 lb cream cheese

¼ lb blue cheese

1 tsp dried chervil or thyme

1½ lb melted butter

1½ loaves sliced white bread,
    crusts removed

1½ lb butter, melted

1 jar (15 oz) asparagus, drained

Perhaps my most sought-after recipe, making it worth the advance planning required (the rolls must sit overnight before cooking). Also, you will need a pastry brush. Asparagus in a jar works fine here: they are very thin, save you time during preparation, and make it easy to serve the dish year-round. If you use purchase fresh ones, be sure they are pencil-thin and parboil them for 4 minutes before using.

Allow the cream cheese and blue cheese to sit at room temperature for 30 minutes. Once they are soft, combine them in a bowl. Add the chervil or thyme and mix well.

Using a pastry brush, coat both sides and the edges of each bread slice completely with the butter. (It is best to melt the butter ½ lb at a time so it doesn't harden while you work.) Place an asparagus spear across a bread slice. Trim off the bottom of the spear so it doesn't extend beyond the end of the bread (you can use the leftover stems in additional rolls). Place a thin strip of the cheese mixture along the spear. Wrap the bread around the asparagus and, using your thumbs and index fingers, pinch the ends closed. Place the roll seam side down in a buttered glass baking dish. Repeat until you have used up all the ingredients. You should have 40 to 45 rolls. Brush the tops with more melted butter. Cut each roll in half crosswise. Cover the baking dish with plastic wrap and freeze overnight.

Remove the rolls from the freezer about 30 minutes before cooking. Preheat an oven to 375 degrees F. Bake until the rolls are golden brown, 15 to 20 minutes. Allow to cool for 5 minutes before serving.

Makes 40 to 45 rolls, 20 servings as a tapa.

Chickpea Salad with Roasted Red Peppers and Capers

Ensalada de Garbanzos con Pimentónes e Alcaparras

2 cups dried chickpeas

2 tbs olive oil

1 onion, finely chopped

3 cloves garlic, minced

2 cups chicken broth

2 cups water

salt to taste

1 or 2 bay leaves (optional)

½ cup fresh mint leaves, chopped

¼ cup capers

¼ cup extra-virgin olive oil

1 tbs balsamic vinegar

1 tsp Dijon mustard

1 tbs dry sherry

2 tbs lemon juice

1 tsp dried thyme

3 red bell peppers, roasted and cut into narrow strips (page 227)

Rinse the chickpeas and place in a bowl. Add water to cover by 2 inches and let stand overnight.

In a saucepan, heat the olive oil over medium heat. When it is hot, add the onion and garlic and saute until the onion is soft and golden, about 8 minutes. Drain the chickpeas and add to the onion and garlic. Mix well and saute for 1 minute, stirring constantly. Add the chicken broth, water, and salt to taste. A bay leaf or two may be added for extra flavor. Bring to a boil, reduce the heat to low, cover partially, and cook until the chickpeas are tender, 1¾ to 2 hours.

Drain the chickpeas and place them in a large bowl. Add the mint and capers and mix well. In a small bowl, whisk together the extra virgin olive oil, vinegar, mustard, sherry, lemon juice, and thyme. Pour over the chickpeas and add the red pepper strips. Let cool for 1 hour. Serve at room temperature.

Makes 12 servings as a tapa.

Chickpeas in an Onion Sauce

Garbanzos en Salsa de Cebolla

2¼ cups dried chickpeas

2 cups chicken broth

4 cups water

6 cloves garlic, 2 left whole and 4 minced

3 onions, 1 thickly sliced and 2 minced

3 bay leaves

2 tsp salt, plus extra to taste

3 tbs olive oil

½ tsp ground cloves

2 tsp dried thyme

1 tsp dried marjoram

1 tsp dried oregano

2 tomatoes, peeled and crushed to a pulp

black pepper to taste

10 fresh parsley sprigs, chopped

Rinse the chickpeas and place in a bowl. Add water to cover by 2 inches and let stand overnight. Drain and set aside.

In a stockpot, bring the chicken broth and water to a boil. Add the chickpeas, 2 whole garlic cloves, the thickly sliced onion, bay leaves, and 2 tsp salt. Bring to a boil again and then reduce the heat to low. Simmer until the chickpeas are tender, 1¾ to 2 hours. Most of the liquid will have evaporated, but there should be about 1 cup remaining. Reserve ½ cup of it and drain off the rest. Discard the garlic cloves, onion, and bay leaves.

In a large saucepan, heat the olive oil over medium-high heat. When it is hot, add the minced garlic and onions and cook until the onions are soft, about 5 minutes. Add the cloves, thyme, marjoram, and oregano and stir to mix well. Cook for 1 minute and add the chickpeas. Again mix well to coat the chickpeas with the oil. Add the crushed tomatoes and the reserved ½ cup chickpea broth. Season with salt and black pepper. Cook, stirring occasionally, until the chickpeas are heated through, 4 to 5 minutes. Serve warm garnished with parsley.

Makes 20 servings as a tapa.

Asturian Eggplant

2 eggplants, halved lengthwise

8 tbs olive oil

8 cloves garlic

3 tsp dried thyme

2 tsp dried oregano

2 tsp dried marjoram

2 tsp dried rosemary

1 tsp plus ½ cup chopped fresh parsley

1 onion, finely chopped

2 shallots, finely chopped

8 tomatoes, peeled and chopped

1 cup pitted black olives, mashed slightly

salt to taste

white pepper to taste

3 tbs capers

Preheat an oven to 400 degrees F. Score the cut side of each eggplant in a crisscross fashion, cutting deeply into the flesh. Place in a baking dish, cut sides up. In a small food processor, blender, or mortar, combine 4 tablespoons of the oil, 4 whole garlic cloves, and 1 tsp each of the thyme, oregano, marjoram, rosemary, and parsley. Blend well. Rub one-fourth the mixture on the cut surface of each eggplant half, letting it soak into the flesh.

Bake the eggplant until soft, about 30 minutes. Remove from the oven and let cool. Scoop out the flesh onto a cutting board; discard the skins. Coarsely chop the flesh.

Mince the remaining 4 garlic cloves. In a large skillet or saute pan, heat the remaining 4 tablespoons oil over medium heat. When it is hot, add the onion and minced garlic and saute for 2 minutes. Add the shallots and continue to cook, stirring occasionally, until the onion is soft, about 1 minute longer. Add the remaining 2 tsp thyme and 1 tsp each oregano, marjoram, and rosemary. Mix well and add the chopped eggplant. Saute for 2 minutes and add the tomatoes. Mix well and reduce the heat to low. Simmer for 15 minutes. Add the olives, salt, white pepper, and capers and cook for another 10 minutes to blend the flavors. Serve warm with the remaining ½ cup parsley sprinkled on top.

Makes about 3½ cups.

Open-faced Sandwiches

Montaditos are little open-faced sandwiches. Generally a number of toppings and saucy spreads are arranged with bread on a platter. You take a piece of bread, dip it in olive oil if you like, spread on the sauce of your preference, and top it off with any of various meats, seafood, or cheeses. Common toppings include serrano ham, boiled octopus in tomato sauce, sardines in oil, squid in its ink, roasted beef or pork, spicy cod, and manchego cheese. I always serve the serrano ham (substitute prosciutto) and the sardines. Have the butcher slice the serrano ham in paper-thin slices. The sardines come right out of tins. Drain some of the excess oil. If the sardines are large, cut them in thirds or in half. You can also buy squid in its ink in cans imported from Spain. They are called chipirones. For a large party, manchego is too costly, but for a small gathering it makes a nice tapa.

The recipe that follows is for roasting a pork loin. The loin can be served warm, but I prefer it cold. Thinly slice it just before serving.

Roast Pork Loin for Montaditos

8 pitted prunes

¼ cup warm water

1 boneless pork loin roast, 2½ to 3 lb

Worcestershire sauce to taste

salt to taste

white pepper to taste

3 cloves garlic

½ tsp coriander seeds

½ tsp cumin seeds

1 tsp paprika

½ tsp cayenne pepper

½ tsp ground cloves

1 tbs Dijon mustard

3 tbs dry sherry

2 tbs olive oil

2 tsp dried rosemary

In a bowl, soak the prunes in the warm water for 15 minutes. Liberally douse the pork with the Worcestershire sauce and season with salt and white pepper. Set aside while you prepare the marinade.

In a small food processor or blender, combine the garlic, coriander, and cumin. Grind to a paste. Add the paprika, cayenne, cloves, and mustard. Grind for a few seconds and add the sherry, olive oil, and rosemary. Grind again for a few seconds, then add the prunes with their water. Grind until the prunes are completely broken down. Pour the marinade over the pork loin, cover, and marinate overnight in the refrigerator.

Preheat an oven to 400 degrees F.

Place the pork loin in a roasting pan with any unabsorbed marinade. Roast until just cooked through, 45 to 50 minutes. To test, cut into the center with a sharp knife. Serve warm or cold with bread slices and various spreads.

Makes 20 servings as a tapa.

Lamb Meatballs in a Serrano Ham Sauce

Albóndigas de Cordero en Salsa de Jamón

2 lb ground lamb

2 eggs, lightly beaten

4 cloves garlic, minced

¼ cup chopped fresh parsley

2 tsp dried thyme

salt to taste (¼ tsp is standard)

white pepper to taste

1 cup fresh bread crumbs

¼ cup milk

¼ cup red wine

2 to 3 tbs olive oil

1 onion, finely chopped

2 shallots, finely chopped

6 slices serrano ham or prosciutto, cut into small strips

¼ cup brandy or dry sherry

2 tsp tomato paste

1 cup beef broth

These should be served with bread for dipping in the pan broth.

In a large bowl, combine the lamb, eggs, garlic, parsley, thyme, salt, and white pepper. Mix well and set aside.

In a small bowl, combine the bread crumbs, milk, and red wine. Add to the lamb mixture and mix well. Cover and chill for 15 minutes. Form into bite-sized meatballs. You should end up with about 60 meatballs. Chill them until you are ready to cook them.

In a skillet, heat the olive oil over medium-high heat. When it is hot, add the onion and shallots and saute until the onion begins to soften, about 3 minutes. Add the meatballs and brown, stirring gently to color evenly, 2 to 3 minutes longer. Once they are browned, add the ham strips. Mix well and add the brandy or sherry. Allow to cook for 2 minutes to burn off the alcohol.

In a small bowl, dissolve the tomato paste in the broth and add the mixture to the meatballs. Cover, reduce the heat to low, and simmer until the meatballs are cooked through, about 35 minutes. Serve warm in the pan broth.

Makes 20 servings as a tapa.

Veal Meatballs in a Spicy Chorizo Sauce

Albóndigas de Ternera en Salsa de Chorizo

2 lb ground veal

3 eggs, lightly beaten

½ cup fresh bread crumbs

4 cloves garlic, minced

¼ cup chopped fresh parsley

⅓ cup blanched hazelnuts, almonds, or walnuts, toasted (page 227)

½ tsp dried thyme

½ tsp dried marjoram

salt to taste

white pepper to taste

3 chorizo sausages, casings removed

2 tbs olive oil

1 onion, finely chopped

1 tsp ground cumin

1 tsp paprika

½ tsp red pepper flakes

1 cup chicken broth

As with the lamb meatballs, serve crusty bread for dipping in the pan broth.

In a bowl, combine the veal, eggs, bread crumbs, garlic, and parsley. Mix well. Cover and chill for 15 minutes.

Meanwhile, grind the nuts finely and combine with the thyme and marjoram. Add to the veal and season with salt and pepper. Mix well and form into bite-sized meatballs. You should end up with about 60 meatballs. Chill them until you are ready to cook them.

Break apart the chorizo into a coarse pulp and set aside. In a skillet, heat the olive oil over medium-high heat. When it is hot, add the chorizo and the onion and season with the cumin and paprika. Cook until the onion is soft, about 5 minutes. Add the meatballs and brown, stirring gently to color evenly, 2 to 3 minutes longer. Once they are browned, add the red pepper flakes and stir to mix well. Add the broth and bring to a boil. Cover, reduce the heat to low, and simmer until the meatballs are cooked through, about 35 minutes. Serve warm in the pan broth.

Makes 20 servings as a tapa.

Cheese Fritters

••

Rosquillas de Queso

1 lb ricotta cheese

4 eggs

1 cup unbleached flour

2 tsp baking powder

1 tsp pure vanilla extract

dash of salt

corn oil for frying

confectioners' sugar and honey

In a large bowl, whisk together the ricotta cheese and eggs, blending well. Set aside.

In another bowl, sift together the flour and the baking powder. Fold gently into the ricotta-egg mixture. Add the vanilla and salt. Mix gently to incorporate all the ingredients.

In a large skillet or deep fryer, heat corn oil to a depth of 3 inches until very hot. When the oil is ready, drop 1 tablespoon of the batter into the pan. Continue adding spoonfuls of batter until pan is full, but don't let the fritters touch one another (8 to 10 per batch). Fry, turning once, until golden brown, about 2 minutes on each side. Using a slotted spoon, transfer to paper towels to drain. Continue frying until all the batter is used up. These are best if you serve them as soon as they are done. Sprinkle the fritters with confectioners' sugar and drizzle with honey. Serve warm.

Makes about 40 fritters; 6 servings.

Lemon Yogurt Pudding

••

Postre Las Delicias

2 cups plain yogurt

1 can (14 fl oz) condensed milk

½ cup lemon juice

2 tsp grated lemon zest

Combine all the ingredients in a bowl, mixing well. Cover and refrigerate overnight to set. Serve chilled.

Makes 6 servings.

Peeling Tomatoes

Bring a saucepan filled with water to a boil. Meanwhile, cut an X through the skin of the blossom end of each tomato. A few at a time, drop the tomatoes into the boiling water and leave for 15 to 20 seconds; at this point, the skins will have loosened. Then promptly transfer the tomatoes to a bowl of cold water until cooled. Using a small knife and starting at the X, peel away the skin. It should come away easily.

Roasting Chili or Bell Peppers

Preheat an oven to 500 degrees F. Place the chili or bell peppers in a pan lined with aluminum foil and slip into the oven. As the skins on the peppers begin to char and darken, turn to expose the uncharred sides until blackened on all sides. The timing will vary, depending on the size of the peppers and your oven. Chilies, however, generally take less time because of their size. When they are nicely charred, remove from the oven and transfer to a plastic bag. Seal closed with a knot and let stand for about 5 minutes for chilies (or longer, depending on size) and up to 20 minutes for bell peppers. The steam created by the peppers will cause the skins to loosen. Open the bag and remove the peppers. Using your fingertips and a small knife, if necessary, peel away and discard the blackened skins. Cut off the stems and discard, then remove and discard the inner membranes and the seeds. Cut the chilies or peppers as indicated in individual recipes. You can also roast chilies or peppers in a broiler, over a charcoal fire, or over the open flame of a gas stove. In all these cases, they will blacken more quickly than in the oven.

Blanching Almonds

When you blanch almonds, you remove their skins. They can be purchased already blanched or you can blanch them yourself. To do so, bring a saucepan filled with water to a boil. Drop in roasted almonds, blanch for 30 seconds, drain, and rinse in cold water. Using an index finger and thumb, squeeze the nut free of the skin.

Toasting Sesame Seeds

Preheat an oven to 350 degrees F. Spread the sesame seeds in a small pan and toast in the oven until golden, 4 or 5 minutes, shaking the pan occasionally. Alternatively, toast the sesame seeds in a dry skillet on the stove top, shaking the pan often, about 1 minute.

Toasting Nuts

Preheat an oven to 350 degrees F. Spread the nuts in a pan or on a baking sheet and toast in the oven, shaking the pan once or twice, until golden and fragrant, 5 to 8 minutes. Smaller nuts, such as pine nuts, will take a shorter amount of time than larger nuts, such as almonds.

Peeling and Deveining Shrimp

Grasp the two sides of the shell on the underside (concave) side of the shrimp, splitting it apart along the row of legs, then carefully peel away. If a recipe instructs to leave the tail fin segment intact, peel away only to that point; otherwise, carefully pull away the fin segment as well. Using a sharp knife, make a shallow slit along the shrimp's back, then, using the tip of the knife or your fingertips, lift up and pull away the dark intestinal track (called the vein) that runs the length of the back.

Cleaning Mussels

Most farm-raised mussels do not have beards, fibrous extensions from the hinge sides of the shells that permit the shellfish to attach to rocks. If your batch of mussels does, firmly grasp the beard and pull it away. Discard any mussels that do not close to the touch, then, using a stiff-bristled brush, scrub each mussel to remove any dirt or other residue from the shells.

Cleaning Squid

First, pulling gently, detach the head and tentacles from the body of the squid. Set the head and tentacles aside and proceed to clean the body. Insert your index finger into the body cavity and remove all the gelatinous materials and the squid's quill, a spinelike length of translucent cartilage. Then carefully peel off the mottled skin covering the body by gently peeling it away. Rinse the body under running cold water, inside and out. To clean the head and tentacles, using a sharp knife, cut off the tentacles just below the eyes. Reserve the tentacles and discard everything else. Cut the body and tentacles as directed in individual recipes.

Preparing Tamarind Water

Place a 1-inch lump of tamarind paste in about ½ cup hot water and leave to soak for 10 to 15 minutes. Then, using your fingers, work the lump to release its essence fully into the water. Pour the liquid through a fine-mesh sieve to remove any fibers and seeds. The water can now be used, or it can be stored in the refrigerator in a tightly covered jar for up to 2 weeks.

Using Banana or Plantain Leaves

Banana and plantain leaves must be made pliable by one of two methods before using. The first is to place them over a charcoal fire, exposing each side of the leaf to the heat for a few seconds. The second is to pour boiling water over them, let them stand in the water for about 2 minutes, and then to transfer them to a basin of cold water.

Removing Seeds from a Pomegranate

Using a sharp knife, cut the fruit into halves or quarters. Using the tip of a spoon, dig out clusters of the seeds, dropping them into a bowl. Then, using your fingertips, separate the seeds from the bitter membrane, freeing them from the small pockets in which they are lodged.

Preparing Yuca for Use

Yuca is available both fresh and frozen in many Latin American markets and some supermarkets. The latter comes already peeled. Peeling fresh yuca requires a sharp vegetable peeler or knife and a bit of patience: Using a heavy chef's knife, cut off the top and bottom, then run the knife or peeler down the side from the skinny bottom to the wider top. Starting from the slit and using your fingers, peel away the tough skin. Sever the yuca in half lengthwise and remove the stringy vein that runs down the middle.

Whether purchased fresh or frozen, yuca must be boiled first until tender before it can be used. Cut into chunks, place in a saucepan with water to cover, the juice of ½ lemon, and salt to taste, then boil until tender, about 30 minutes. The only exception to this would be if you plan to use the yuca in soups, in which case it should be rinsed first and then parboiled for only 10 minutes before adding it to the soup pot. This parboiling step removes some toxins present in the root.

Curing a Chinese Clay Pot

Made of earthenware, the lidded clay pot has an unglazed exterior and a dark glaze interior. It is flameproof, but must always have some liquid in it when it is over the heat, or it will break. Also, never put a hot clay pot on a cold surface. Instead, allow it to cool down on the turned-off burner. Before using a just-purchased clay pot or one that has not been used for a long time, wash carefully, fill with water, and let soak overnight.

Wok or Skillet?

If you do not already own a wok, consider buying one if you have a gas stove. (Woks for electric stoves have flat bottoms, making them virtually a skillet anyway, albeit with deep sides.) A wok's flared sides and rounded bottom make it ideal for stir-frying, as these features serve to distribute the heat evenly, permit ingredients to be stirred and tossed vigorously without spilling them, and allow a minimum of oil to be used. A skillet, in contrast, with its flat bottom, means that more oil is needed because of the greater cooking surface always in contact with the heat. In addition, any added moisture cooks away more quickly in a skillet, again due to the larger cooking surface.

Blender, Food Processor, or Mortar?

Many recipes in this book give you the option of using any one of these kitchen tools. Although all of them will work in those cases, one or the other may function better. A blender is particularly useful for liquefying and pureeing foods, including soups and chilies (especially when a smooth rather than coarse mixture is desired), and for making very liquid items like batters, sauces, and frothy drinks. It can also be used for grinding spice pastes and nuts. Blenders are good for fairly small quantities of food, but the ingredients must amount to enough to cover the lowest hanging blades, or the blades will spin without effect. Generally, when making a spice paste, a blender works best if a small amount of liquid is added. Food processors are particularly good for chopping, shredding, slicing, and mincing foods. Unless you have a processor with a small mixing bowl, however, mixing spice pastes or small amounts of any kind—chopping herbs, grinding nuts, and so on—is difficult, as the ingredients fly beyond the blades. When pureeing, the coarseness of the mixture can be better controlled in a food processor than in a blender because of the pulse function. A mortar and pestle is ideal for grinding small quantities of ingredients, especially spices, herbs, various seeds—Sichuan peppercorns, coriander, fenugreek—garlic, and the like. You must be careful not to fill the mortar more than half full for most productive grinding, and then you must work the pestle around and around until you arrive at the smooth paste, powder, or other consistency desired. A Japanese mortar, or suribachi, is shallow, glazed on the outside only and with ridges on the inside; a wooden pestle is used. This particular mortar is ideal for grinding sesame and other small seeds.

Glossary

Achiote paste: A red paste made from the seeds of the annatto tree and flavored with various spices. Sold in small bricks, it is used in Mexican, Latin American, and Philippine cooking. Dissolve in hot water or broth. There is also a liquid extract. Achiote paste is generally used to impart color rather than flavor to foods. Available in Latin American and some Asian markets. See also annatto.

Agar-agar: A setting agent, similar to gelatin, commonly used in Asian cooking. Made from seaweed, it comes in various forms. The powdered form is the easiest to use, but there is also a dried stick form that dissolves easily. Store in an airtight container. Available in Asian markets and some supermarkets.

Aïoli: A garlic mayonnaise popular in Provence made from eggs, olive oil, and garlic. A similar sauce, called alioli, is made in Catalonia.

Ajowan: A common Indian spice used in flat breads and vegetables dishes. Used mostly as whole seeds, although the seeds are also ground for curry powders. Available in Indian markets. Also spelled ajwain and ajwan. Thyme is a respectable substitute.

Ajvar: A roasted red pepper, garlic, and eggplant spread from the Balkans.

Aleppo pepper: Recommended by esteemed cook and author Paula Wolfert as the Middle Eastern pepper to search out, Aleppo pepper is one of the region's many red pepper grinds. Dean & DeLuca Mail-Order Services in New York City is the only source I know. While each grind is slightly different, they are all basically mildly hot. A good Middle Eastern market will carry various ground peppers from throughout the region. The shopkeepers should be able to point out the differences and recommend one for your palate. Wolfert also suggests storing these grinds in the refrigerator. Any Middle Eastern chili powder is a good substitute.

Allspice: A spice from the Caribbean Basin. It is primarily used in pickling, sausages, soups, ciders, and in certain desserts. Available in berry form or ground in most supermarkets.

Amaranth: A wonderful grain from Mexico, now sadly fallen into obscurity. It is available both as a grain and a flour. The small grains release a starchy liquid when cooked. To prepare them, combine 1 part amaranth to 2½ parts water. Do not add salt, as this prevents the amaranth from absorbing the water. Amaranth is used in peasant cooking from Mexico through the Andean region of South America. Look for it in health-food stores or Latin American markets. It might also be found under the Quechua name kiwicha. Do not confuse the grain with amaranth greens, which are a type of spinach from India.

Amchur: A powder made from dried green mangoes used primarily as a souring agent in north Indian cooking. It is best purchased in small quantities, as it quickly loses its potency. Store in the freezer. Also spelled amchoor. Available in Indian markets.

Anardana: Dried pomegranate seeds. Available in Indian markets. See also pomegranate seeds.

Andouille: A spicy pork sausage from Cajun country. Available in finer butcher shops.

Anise: A licorice-flavored seed widely used in European desserts and as the flavoring in sambuca, ouzo, and Pernod. In the Middle East, it is common in soups and stews. Also used in Indian cooking. Generally available in supermarkets. Also know as Aniseed.

Annatto: A tree native to the Caribbean, southern Mexico, Central America, and northern South America whose seeds are used to make achiote paste. The paste is used as a red food coloring in Mexican, Central American, and the Philippines. The small, reddish seeds are also combined with vegetable oil to make an orange annatto essence. Annatto seeds are mainly available in Latin American or Philippine stores, but I have seen them in some Indian and Middle Eastern markets as well. See also Achiote.

Arborio: A medium-grain white rice from Italy used in the preparation of risotto. It is sold in upscale markets, Italian markets, and many supermarkets.

Arrowroot: A wonderful thickening agent made from the root of a Caribbean plant. Although more expensive than other thickeners such as cornstarch and tapioca starch, the extra cost is worth the result. Available in Asian stores and gourmet shops as well as many supermarket spice sections.

Asafetida: A foul-smelling, potent spice used in Persian and Indian cooking. It is actually a resin extracted from the rhizome of the plant, and is sold powdered, in granules, and as a resin compound. Look for it in small plastic tubs, often bright yellow, sometimes shelved with cosmetics like henna. Store in an airtight container to prevent contamination of your other spices. A little asafetida goes a long way, imparting a garlicky flavor to dishes. Also used to prevent flatulence. Do not eat raw. Available in Indian markets and occasionally in bulk in health-food stores.

Asam: The Indonesian name for tamarind. Assem is the Malay spelling. See also tamarind.

Bacalao: Spanish for dried salted cod. Used in Iberian, Italian, Cuban, Jamaican, and Brazilian cooking. It must be soaked in cold water for a day—or longer if very salty—before using, changing the water every few hours. Available in Latin American, Italian, and Portuguese markets.

Bagna cauda: A hot Piedmontese mixture made with olive oil, butter, anchovies, and garlic, used for dipping raw and/or blanched vegetables. Cooks in Provence make a similar mixture. You can make your own (page 63).

Baharat: A mixture of cardamom, cinnamon, cloves, coriander, cumin, nutmeg, paprika, and hot chilies. Used in the cooking of the Arabian Gulf States and Mesopotamia. Available in Middle Eastern markets, usually in bulk.

Balsamic vinegar: A vinegar made from unfermented grape juice and aged in a series of casks of different woods and gradually diminishing size. The best balsamic vinegar is from Modena in Italy. Available in gourmet shops and most supermarkets.

Bamboo shoots: Available canned in Asian markets and most supermarkets. Common in Japanese and Chinese cooking, bamboo shoots should be rinsed before use.

Banana or plantain leaves: Used in Asian and Latin American cooking for wrapping all sorts of foods. Available frozen in Latin American and Asian markets. They must be made pliable before using, by either grilling them over an open flame or pouring hot water over them in the kitchen sink. They are also a wonderful and ecological alternative to paper plates.

Basil: A leafy green herb, sometimes called sweet basil, available both freeze-dried and fresh in most markets. A purple-green variety, popular in Asian cooking and sometimes labeled Thai basil or bai horapa, is found in some produce markets and in Southeast Asian markets. Although sweet basil is closely identified with Italian cooking, it is used widely throughout southern Europe.

Basmati rice: An aromatic long-grain rice native to the Himalayas. Available in Asian and Indian markets, although better supermarkets often carry it as well. Given its rising popularity, even some larger warehouse stores now carry it.

Bay leaf: The leaf of the bay laurel tree, which grows in various parts of the Bay Area and other areas of California, although native to southern Europe and the Middle East. French bay is considered the finest. Used widely in European, Latin American, Middle Eastern, and Indian cooking in soups, stews, and spice mixtures. Sold in supermarkets.

Bean curd: See tofu.

Bean sprouts: Sprouted mung beans readily available in supermarkets and Asian markets. Common in many eastern Asian dishes.

Bean thread noodles: Made from mung bean starch, these clear, thin noodles are sold in cellophane packages. They are used primarily in soups and stir-fries (soak in hot water first). They can also be dropped into hot oil briefly, at which point they expand to several times their original size. They are then used as a light, crunchy topping or in salads. Available in Asian markets and many supermarkets.

Besan: Chickpea flour used in India primarily for bread doughs and batters for coating vegetables for frying. Available in Indian markets.

Bitter melon: A sharp-flavored vegetable used in Cantonese, Southeast Asian, and Indian cooking. Also known as bitter gourd, it is generally shaped like a very large cucumber with pale green, deeply wrinkled skin. Available in Asian and Indian markets.

Blachan: Dried shrimp paste from Malaysia. Blachan is the Malay version of the Indonesian terasi or trassi, and can be used in its place. Blachan, also sometimes spelled blacan and blachen, is the most readily available of the Southeast Asian dried shrimp pastes. Most Asian markets carry it. It is sold in various bricks, some rectangular, some circular. See also sambal udang and terasi.

Black beans, salted: Soybeans that have been treated with a mold, dried, and then salted. A popular ingredient in the cooking of southern China, salted black beans are most often found in plastic packages on store shelves, stocked along with bean sauces and pastes. Once opened, store in a tightly covered jar in a cool cupboard for up to 1 year.

Black cumin: A rare variety of cumin from Iran, Pakistan, Afghanistan and Kashmir. Given the instability in these regions, black cumin is hard to find in the United States. Sometimes called black caraway, it is also often confused with nigella (kalonji) and caraway. The seeds of black cumin are smaller than regular cumin seeds and have a sweet and mellow herbal taste. The Indian name for black cumin is kala jeera or kala zeera. It is used primarily in the cuisines of northern India, Pakistan, and Afghanistan and can occasionally be found in Indian markets or ordered by mail from spice houses. There is no true substitute.

Black fungus: Also known as cloud ear, wood ear, tree ear, or tree fungus, this dried mushroom variety has a mild flavor and slightly crunchy texture. To rehydrate, place in hot water to cover for at least 30 minutes. Drain, rinse, and remove and discard the tough stems before using. Available in Asian markets and some supermarkets.

Black mushrooms, dried: Dried shiitake mushrooms, sometimes called forest or Chinese mushrooms. To rehydrate, place in hot water to cover for at least 30 minutes. Drain, rinse, and remove and discard the tough stems before using. Available in Asian markets and some supermarkets. See also shiitake.

Black salt: Also known as kala namak, black salt is an ingredient in the Indian spice blend called chat masala. It is generally available in Indian markets.

Bok choy: Common Chinese cabbage with dark green leaves and white stalks. Also known as Chinese white cabbage and pak choy. A frequent addition to Cantonese dishes, it can be found in Chinese markets and many supermarkets.

Bonito flakes, dried: A relative of the mackerel, bonito is a common fish in Japan. Bonito fillets are steamed and dried until hard and then cut into thin flakes that are used in the making of dashi. The same process is used to form a threadlike product that is used as a garnish. (You can also break up the flakes into smaller pieces to use for garnishing.) The flakes look a little like small wood shavings and are usually sold in boxes or clear plastic bags. Keep bonito flakes in an airtight container in a dry place. See also dashi.

Bouquet garni: The French term for an herb bundle dropped into broths, soups, and sauces during cooking as a flavor enhancer. While the herbs do vary from region to region, the main ones are parsley, chervil, oregano, thyme, and bay leaves. These are either tied together with kitchen string or wrapped in a piece of cheesecloth and then tied with string.

Bulgur: A dried cracked wheat used in the cuisines of the Middle East. Available in most supermarkets (usually in the grains section or the imported-foods area) and health-food stores and in Middle Eastern and Indian markets.

Bumbu: Any of various Indonesian or Malaysian dressings.

Burdock root: See gobo.

Cajun seasoning: A spice mixture of garlic, onions, shallots, paprika, black pepper, cumin, thyme, cayenne, and oregano. Available wherever fine spices are sold, or you can make your own (page 120).

Calvados: An apple brandy from Normandy.

Candlenuts: Nuts from Southeast Asia commonly used in Indonesian cuisine. Also known as kemiri. Substitute macadamia nuts, cashews, or blanched almonds. Do not eat raw. Available in selected Asian markets.

Capers: The pickled flower bud of a small bush. Sold in jars in most supermarkets and gourmet stores, they are primarily imported from Spain and are used in Spanish, Italian, southern French, and Latin American dishes. The word *non-pareil* found on many labels simply means "having no equal." How true, because you can never have enough capers.

Carambola: A light green tropical fruit, the slices of which are shaped like stars, thus its alternate name of star fruit. It has a tart, sharp flavor and is used as a garnish in fruit salads. Indigenous to Southeast Asia and India, it is now generally available in produce stores and certain supermarkets.

Caraway: A spice traditionally used in Central and Eastern European cooking. The whole seeds are used in stews, vegetable dishes, breads, cheeses, and sausages; the ground form is less common. Available in most supermarkets.

Cardamom: One of the world's most expensive spices. Originally from southern India and Sri Lanka, cardamom is now grown throughout the tropics. It is essential to the cuisines of India, Southeast Asia, and the Middle East. Buy cardamom seeds still in their pods, if possible; the already ground spice lacks the same intense flavor. Split open the pod and use the dark aromatic seeds inside. Green cardamom, occasionally found in Indian markets, is preferable to white cardamom. In India, cardamom is a main ingredient of both garam masala and curry powder. There is also a rare black cardamom from India. In Southeast Asia, cardamom is also used in curries. The Arabs use it in desserts, tagines, and coffee. Found in most supermarkets, although probably cheaper in Indian markets.

Cassava: See yuca.

Cassia: The bark of the cassia tree. Closely related to cinnamon, cassia is native to Assam, Burma, and southern China and is also known as Chinese cinnamon. You might find it in Asian markets, although much of the cinnamon sold in the United States is actually cassia anyway. Just so you know, ground cassia is reddish brown, while cinnamon is a lighter tan. See also cinnamon.

Cassia buds: The dried flower buds of the cassia tree. Before the revolution in China in 1949, cassia buds were common in the United States, where they were used in baking and as a mulling spice. Today, despite the resurgence of trade with China, cassia buds have not recaptured their lost position in the American pantry.

Cava: A sparkling white wine from Spain. Cavas run one-third to one-half the price of champagnes, making them an excellent value. Frexeinet and Cordiniu are two of the more popular brands.

Celery: Celery as a spice comes in two forms: celery salt and celery seeds. Both are readily available in supermarkets. Other than in bloody Marys, celery seeds are used in Scandinavian and Russian dishes, particularly soups and vegetables.

Celery root: A variety of celery, the root of which is used as a vegetable in European cooking, especially French. Also called celeriac.

Chanterelle mushroom: An off-white to yellow European mushroom. Available both fresh and dried in produce markets and some supermarkets, it is an expensive fungus. Its warm, subtle taste is wonderful in mushroom sautes, soups, and with meats.

Chat masala: A spice blend used mainly for seasoning fruits in India. It consists of various ingredients, including amchur, black salt, cayenne, cumin, fennel, garam masala, and ginger. You can make your own (page 57).

Chayote: A member of the squash family, chayotes are common in the cuisine of Mexico, Central America, and northern South America. They are somewhat pear shaped and have a tough pale green skin that must be peeled before cooking and regularly show up in soups and stews and occasionally stuffed. Chayotes are now readily available in Latin American markets as well as many supermarkets. Choose one that is firm to the touch. Avoid those that are wrinkled and soft.

Cherimoya: An Andean fruit now being grown in California. It is green and has a sweet custardy white flesh surrounding black pits. The Californian-grown fruit is extremely expensive since it must be hand pollinated. In Ecuador and Colombia, the flower is pollinated by a single species of hummingbird. Cherimoyas are wonderful fruits and are especially delicious when combined with tart raspberries. They are closely related to the guanabana.

Chervil: A delicious yet sadly underutilized herb from Europe that is particularly popular in France. Occasionally found fresh in produce markets, although more commonly sold freeze-dried in the spice section of supermarkets.

Chili oil: A chili-infused oil used in Asian cooking. You can buy a bottled version, or you can make your own: In a skillet, combine ½ cup coarsely chopped chilies (arbol or Thai) and 1 cup peanut oil. Heat slowly over low heat and cook for 10 minutes. Remove from the heat. For a truly Asian taste, add 2 tbs Asian sesame oil and a couple of Sichuan peppercorns (fagara). Cover the mixture and let cool for 12 hours or overnight. Strain the oil through cheesecloth into a bottle, preferably of tinted green glass. Store in a dark, cool place.

Chili peppers: See page 242.

Chili sauce: Many chili sauces are available and many are interchangeable. Indonesian sambal ulek, Vietnamese tú óng ót tói Viet-nam, and Chinese Hunan or Sichuan red chili sauce are among the commonly found Asian chili sauces. The latter three sauces generally contain garlic; sambal ulek does not. Be careful, however, for there are many types of sambal. Some of them, such as sambal udang, are mixed with other ingredients. All are hot. Chili sauces are also available from the Caribbean and Latin America. These sauces are used more as a table condiment than as a cooking ingredient, but many recipes will call for hot sauces. Tabasco sauce from Louisiana is the most readily available, although scores of others exist. Experiment and discover your favorite. See also sambal.

Cotija cheese: A farmer cheese from Mexico. Available in some supermarkets and most Latin American markets. It is salty and crumbly.

Chorizo: A sausage flavored with paprika and garlic. There are varieties from Spain, Portugal, and Latin American. Widely available in butcher shops and some supermarkets, as well as in Latin and Portuguese markets.

Cilantro: Arguably the world's most commonly used herb. Native to Asia, it has spread throughout the world. Also known as Chinese parsley or fresh coriander, it is common in Southeast Asian, Indian, Middle Eastern, and Latin American cuisines and, to a lesser extent, Chinese cooking. Available in supermarkets. See also coriander seeds.

Cinnamon: The bark of the cinnamon tree native to Sri Lanka. Now grown throughout the tropics, it is readily available ground or in sticks (quills). Like its cousin cassia, cinnamon is a member of the laurel family. In the West, cinnamon is mainly used in sweets and desserts, but in other parts of the world it is used more extensively. One source of controversy is that much of what is sold as cinnamon in the United States is actually cassia. Cinnamon is a relatively light tan while cassia is a darker reddish brown. Another clue: if the cinnamon hails from Sri Lanka, it is probably the real thing. Otherwise you may be buying a variety of cassia. See also cassia.

Cloud ears: See black fungus.

Cloves: Another fabled spice from the Spice Islands. Cloves are the unopened flower buds of the small clove tree. Today, Indonesia is both the world's largest producer and the largest importer due to their infamous kretek cigarettes. Cloves are an ingredient in Southeast Asian curries and in Indian garam masala. In the United States, they are used in squash dishes, pumpkin pies, mulled cider, and to stud a baked ham. For an offbeat broth, stud an onion with a dozen cloves. Available both whole and ground in the spice section of most supermarkets.

Coconut milk: Not the juice or water poured from a freshly opened coconut, but rather a mixture of the coconut oils with the coconut juice pressed from the white coconut flesh. You can make your own, but it is much easier and cheaper to buy the canned coconut milk imported chiefly from Thailand available in some supermarkets and most Asian markets. I prefer the Thai Chaokoh brand, but many other good brands are on the market. Used in Southeast Asian and Latin American cooking. Do not substitute cream of coconut for coconut milk. The former is a sweetened concoction for mixed drinks.

Coconut sugar: See palm sugar.

Coriander seeds: The seeds of the herb known as cilantro, Chinese parsley, or fresh coriander. It is available both ground and whole in most supermarkets. Used in Chinese, Southeast Asian, Indian, Middle Eastern, European, and Latin American cuisines. There are two main varieties: Moroccan and Indian. Moroccan coriander is a little darker and more common and what is found in most supermarkets. Indian coriander is sweeter and is generally roasted and ground. Indian markets carry it.

Couscous: Tiny pellets made from rolled coarse and fine semolina wheat flour and water. Although they can be made from scratch, a perfectly acceptable precooked version is available, which is combined in a ratio of 1 part couscous to 2 parts boiling water. It takes only 5 minutes to "cook." Couscous is also the generic name for any of a variety of North African dishes that are served over or with the cooked couscous pellets. Berbers traditionally serve couscous with a tagine, or Moroccan stew. Couscous is now widely available in supermarkets and health-food stores. It is even sold in bulk in some produce markets. A whole-wheat version is now on the market as well.

Cream of coconut: A sweetened coconut concoction used to make piña coladas and various desserts. It is not a substitute for coconut milk. Available in supermarkets and liquor stores.

Cubeb: A berry related to pepper from Indonesia. Cubebs are used in ras el hanout and in Indonesian dishes. Mostly found ground, although occasionally seen as whole or split berries in Persian or Southeast Asian markets.

Cumin: One of the world's most commonly used spices, it is called for in the cooking of India, Southeast Asia, the Middle East, Africa, Spain, and Latin America. Cumin is perhaps best known as one of the two key ingredients in curry powder, while in the United States, it is added to chili con carne. It is also an essential addition to many Latin American bean dishes. Cumin is found in most supermarket spice sections and is generally available both as a seed and ground. Both should be in your pantry. See also black cumin.

Curry leaves: The dark green, somewhat narrow leaf of an ornamental Indian tree. Used extensively in Indian cuisine, the leaves have a distinctive curry aroma when bruised. Unfortunately, fresh curry leaves are hard to find, and you have to use a handful of dried ones for any real flavor. Some Bay Area Indian markets have the leaves, usually well wrapped and stored in a refrigerator or freezer case. If you should find fresh ones, store them in the freezer.

Curry powder: Authentic Indian curry powder is a carefully blended mixture of spices, usually made at home. Commercial Western imitators, rich in cumin and turmeric, pale in comparison. Madras-style curry powder is spicier than other types. Available in supermarkets.

Curubas: A fruit grown only at high altitudes in the northern Andes. It is a member of the passion fruit family, and is used only for its juice, which is either drunk or incorporated in various desserts. Curubas is rarely available in the United States as it is extremely delicate and bruises easily.

Daikon: A large white Japanese radish. Grated daikon is always included in a tempura dipping sauce, as it is believed to aid in the digestion of oily foods. Available fresh in Asian markets and in certain supermarkets. Asian markets, especially Japanese ones, will also carry pickled daikon, called takuan.

Dal: The Indian term for all dried legumes and lentils. Indian markets carry a wide variety of dals. Most popular is orange (or salmon-colored) dal, called masoor dal; they turn yellow when cooked. Also spelled daal, dhal, or dahl.

Dashi: The basic broth of Japanese cooking. Dashi is made from dried bonito flakes and konbu. You can make your own (page 85). Asian markets carry packaged dried bonito flakes as well as infusion bags called dashi-no-moto that allow you to brew the broth as you might brew a cup of tea. It is also available as hon-dashi, or instant dashi granules. I prefer the dried bonito flakes for a more flavorful broth, but the granules are the most convenient. See also bonito flakes, dried, and konbu.

Dates: The fruit of the date palm. Generally available sun-dried in most supermarkets, dates can also be found in Middle Eastern and Indian markets. Used extensively in both savory and sweet dishes in the Middle East.

Dill: Used both as an herb and as a spice. Freeze-dried dill and fresh dill are generally available in supermarkets. Dill seeds are also easily found in most markets. Both forms are primarily used in European cuisine, especially in the more northern latitudes. Dill seeds are a major ingredient in pickling-spice mixes. As an herb, it marries well with salmon, potatoes, and in soups and stews.

Dried Shrimp: Dried shrimp are exactly what the name says. Although they vary in size, the most commonly found varieties are quite small. Sold in large cellophane bags, they are commonly found in Asian and Latin American markets (Latin American markets sell the larger shrimp). Dried shrimp have a much milder flavor than dried shrimp pastes like blachan, which are fermented.

Dried Shrimp Paste: There are a number of different versions of dried shrimp paste, most of which are interchangeable in recipes. See blachan, kapi, terasi, or sambal udang. Terasi is Indonesian, while blachan and sambal udang are from Malaysia. Kapi is the Thai version. Blachan, kapi, and terasi are thick, rich dried shrimp pastes.

Sambal udang is a shrimp-and-chili paste. They are all extremely pungent (that is, they stink), so store carefully in a container that seals well. In a pinch you can substitute anchovy paste with a dash of fish sauce.

Eggplant: Several varieties are available in Bay Area markets. Most have a shiny purple—sometimes almost black—skin, although a small greenish white variety used in Thai food is sometimes found in Asian markets and supermarkets. For Mediterranean and Middle Eastern dishes, use the globe-shaped variety, which usually calls for salting the cut eggplant to rid it of its bitter juices before cooking. For Asian dishes, the long, slender dark purple Japanese variety or the similarly shaped lavender Chinese variety is used. Asian eggplants do not require salting. The fairly rare, tiny Southeast Asian pea eggplant is most often used raw in chili sauces or cooked in curried dishes. Eggplants are also sometimes called aubergines.

Epazote: A Mexican herb used in the preparation of various moles and soups. Available in Mexican or Latin American markets, epazote has a strong flavor and should be used sparingly. It is usually only available dried, although I have occasionally found it fresh. Also known as pazote.

Fagara: Another name for Sichuan pepper.

Fennel: A bulbous vegetable with long stems and feathery foliage used primarily in Italian and French cooking. Available from late fall to early spring in supermarkets under the name of fennel, sweet fennel, Italian fennel, or finocchio, the latter the Italian name. It has a slight anise flavor and may be used raw in salads or cooked as a vegetable.

Fennel seeds: Possessing a light anise or licorice flavor, this spice is primarily used as whole seeds, although it is occasionally also used ground. It is included in the pantries of China, India, the Middle East, and Europe and is readily available in seed form wherever spices are sold. See also fennel.

Fenugreek: Used primarily in Indian, Eritrean, and Middle Eastern cuisine, fenugreek seeds are most easily obtained in Indian markets, often sold under the Indian name methi. You may also find it in health-food stores and supermarket spice sections. In India, where it is a common ingredient in curries, both the leaves and seeds are used. Elsewhere only the seeds are used. Impossible to grind in a food processor or spice mill, the seeds must be ground in a mortar. Indian markets sell ground fenugreek, but I find that the flavor diminishes quickly after grinding. Fenugreek leaves, which are occasionally found in Indian markets, are quite bitter and are best cooked in lentil stews.

Fish sauce: A salty extract of fermented fish, most often made from anchovies. It is used extensively in the cuisines of Southeast Asia. In Thailand it is known as nam pla, and several Thai brands are available in Asian markets. Bottles are increasingly available in supermarkets, often in the ethnic-foods section. The Vietnamese version is known as nuoc mam. It is harder to find outside Vietnamese communities, but the Thai sauce works fine in Vietnamese dishes. In fact, I prefer it.

Feta cheese: A crumbly cheese made from the milk of sheep or goats and cured in brine. Three varieties are generally available in Bay Area markets: Bulgarian, French, and Greek. Wonderful in salads and dressings.

Five-spice powder: A ground spice mixture popular in southern China and most commonly consisting of star anise, Sichuan peppercorns, cinnamon, fennel seeds, and cloves. You can make your own mixture, or you can buy ready-made mixtures at some supermarkets and most Asian markets. Some mixtures use cassia instead of cinnamon.

Fumet: Fish stock.

Galangal: A rhizome closely related to ginger and turmeric. More aromatic than ginger, it is used in Southeast Asian cuisines, especially Thai, Indonesian, and Malaysian. In the Bay Area, it is primarily found in dried slices and in powdered form under the name laos. Cost Plus sometimes carries it, as do some Asian markets, especially Vietnamese ones. Occasionally found fresh in Asian markets catering to Southeast Asian customers—it looks like peeled ginger with a fat body, skinny side shoots, and dark stripes—in which case it keeps well in the refrigerator. Galangal is also known as galanga, laos, ka, or kha. It is sometimes confused with kencur, another closely related rhizome.

Garam masala: The main spice blend used in Indian cooking. It consists of cinnamon, bay leaves, cumin, coriander, cardamom, pepper, cloves, and mace. These spices are ground to make a highly aromatic blend, but there are many variations. Garam masala is available in Indian markets and some health-food stores and supermarkets, although you can certainly make your own.

Ghee: A clarified butter used in Indian cooking. You can make your own but it is cheaper and easier to buy. Be sure you get butter ghee, not vegetable ghee, which is vegetable oil. Store it at room temperature for up to a month or in the refrigerator up to several months. Available in Indian and Middle Eastern markets, as well as some health-food stores.

Ginger: One of the world's most commonly used spices. A member of the rhizome family that includes galangal and turmeric, ginger originated in Asia, although the exact location is not clear. By the time of the Roman Empire, it was relatively common in southern Europe. Today ginger is grown throughout the tropics and is used in Chinese, Japanese, Southeast Asian, Indian, Latin American, European, and Middle Eastern cooking. In the Bay Area, ginger is available fresh, ground, crystallized, in syrup, and pickled.

Glutinous rice: Also known as sweet rice or sticky rice, this starchy grain is eaten in Japan, China, and Southeast Asia. When cooked, it has a particularly sticky nature. In northern Thailand and in Laos, it is a staple, eaten at every meal. Elsewhere it is used less frequently with savory foods. It does turn up in many sweets, however, from sweet cakes in the Philippines to the mochi, or pounded rice cakes, of Japan. Glutinous rice is available in Asian markets.

Gobo: Also known as burdock root, this long, slender brown root is a popular Japanese vegetable. Clean well, but do not peel. Once cut, immediately immerse in cold water to prevent discoloration. Gobo is available in Asian markets, especially Japanese markets, and occasionally some supermarket produce sections.

Gorgonzola cheese: A creamy blue-veined Italian cheese made from cow's milk.

Grains of paradise: Related to cardamom, this spice is rarely found in the United States. It is most common in African and Moroccan cooking. Specialty mail-order houses occasionally carry it.

Greek oregano: A variety of oregano used in Greek and Middle Eastern cooking. Although rarely available fresh, you can occasionally find it dried in Middle Eastern markets. More pungent than regular oregano.

Grenadine: A bright red syrup made from pomegranate juice. Available in supermarkets and liquor stores. In addition to its well-known use in tequila sunrises, it is used in the cooking of Iran. Do not substitute pomegranate molasses, which has its own distinctive flavor.

Guanabana: Also known as soursop or custard apple, the guanabana looks and tastes similar to a cherimoya. Both are native to Latin America, but the guanabana is much larger. Goya brand guanabana nectar is readily found in Latin markets. There is also an imported frozen pulp used for making shakes and desserts.

Guascas: An herb from the highland region of Colombia. Rarely found fresh in the Bay Area, but you might ask in Latin markets for a freeze-dried version—try Fiesta Latina market in San Mateo. There is no true substitute, although thyme is probably the best bet. Also spelled huascas.

Guava: Extremely popular in tropical Latin America, guava is perhaps best known as a sweet dessert paste, usually accompanied with cheese. In Spanish the paste is called jalea de guayaba. A jelly called jarabe de guayaba is also stocked in most Latin markets. Guava fruit is sometimes available in supermarkets and produce markets. There are dozens of guava varieties, although in the United States only three varieties are generally available. The most common have a green skin with a yellowish flesh or drab yellow skin with a pinkish flesh. A small green-skinned Brazilian guava called feijoida is now finding its way into American markets. Beyond the numerous desserts and jellies, guavas are used for juice. Both Goya and Kern's make guava nectar.

Halal: Halal refers to the method prescribed in the Koran for killing animals for meat. It is the Islamic equivalent of kosher.

Halvah: A ground paste made from sesame seeds and nuts, usually almonds and pistachios. Halvah is available in many supermarkets and Middle Eastern markets, often in brick form. It is high in calories and is used in the preparation of various desserts.

Harissa: Morocco's spicy chili sauce. You can make your own (page 161) or buy tins imported from North Africa, Lebanon, or France in gourmet stores and Middle Eastern markets.

Hogao: A regional Colombian sofrito made with tomatoes, green and yellow onions, chili peppers, garlic, achiote, and oil (or lard). See also sofrito.

Hoisin sauce: A slightly sweet Chinese sauce made from soybeans, garlic, five-spice powder, and chili. Readily available canned and bottled in supermarkets or Chinese markets.

Horapa: Thai basil. A sweet purple-stalked variety sometimes available in Asian markets and produce markets. Substitute regular basil.

Horseradish: A pungent European root that is added grated to dishes to give them some zest. Sometimes available fresh but always available bottled. See also wasabi.

Jackfruit: Indigenous to India and Southeast Asia, jackfruit is eaten as a fruit when ripe and used as a vegetable in India and Indonesia when underripe. It is available canned in Asian markets. Indian cuisine in particular makes extensive use of jackfruit. It is dry-cooked with various spices and pickled. In Indonesia, where it is called nangka, jackfruit is common in curries and stews.

Jaggery: Several kinds of unrefined sweeteners fall under this Indian term. True Indian jaggery is a dark unrefined sugarcane product. It can also refer to a sugar extract from a palm tree. In India, there are at least two types of palm sugar: gur and tal gur. These sugars are similar to Thai or Indo-Malay palm sugar. Since the term is a catch-all one for sugar, read the label carefully to see whether it is made from palm or sugarcane. Jaggery is usually available in Indian markets, sold in small, hard, dark brown lumps.

Jasmine rice: A fragrant long-grain white rice from Thailand. Available in many Asian, Indian, or Middle Eastern markets, although many supermarkets also carry small boxes of jasmine rice.

Jicama: A tuber from Mexico and Central America. It has pale brown skin and a white, dry, somewhat tart flesh. It is generally available fresh in produce markets. Mostly eaten raw in salads, although it is sometimes cooked as a vegetable.

Kabocha: A Japanese hard-skinned squash generally found in Asian markets. The interesting thing about kabocha is that it is not native to Japan but to the New World. Apparently, it was introduced to Japan and the rest of Asia by Portuguese missionaries. Kabocha is used in tempura, stews, and as a plain vegetable. It can also be prepared as you would any winter squash. It is green, turning orangish as it ripens, and about the size of a honeydew melon.

Kaffir limes and leaves: Formerly rare in the United States due to an FDA ban, the kaffir lime tree is indigenous to Southeast Asia. Luckily, kaffir limes are now being grown domestically. The fruits and leaves are used extensively in Thai and Indonesian cooking. The fruit is small and knobby with a wonderful clean aroma. The leaves are more often available dried than fresh in Asian markets, although still rather scarce (look in the refrigerator or freezer case for fresh leaves). No true substitute exists, but Indian curry leaves are a nice alternative. If you can't find curry leaves, try lime zest mixed with finely chopped fresh lemongrass. The Thai name is makrut.

Kalonji: See nigella.

Kapi: A Thai fermented shrimp paste similar to Malay blachan or Indonesian terasi. Available in some Asian markets, but you can substitute the easier-to-find blachan.

Kecap manis: Indonesian sweet soy sauce. Make your own (page 174) or buy Indonesian or Dutch brands at selected Asian markets.

Kemiri: See candlenuts.

Kencur: The Indonesian name for lesser galangal, which is closely related both to ginger and galangal. Used both as a spice and a vegetable. Generally available in powdered form or shredded and packed in brine in jars in some Asian markets. Called krachai in Thailand. Also spelled kentjur.

Kharbozeh: A Persian melon shaped like a football, usually pale green in color. It is occasionally found in Middle Eastern markets. Substitute honeydew melon.

Kimchi: Any of various Korean pickled vegetable preparations of which cabbage is the best known. Available bottled in Asian markets and some supermarkets or you can make your own. Also spelled kimchee.

Kinome: The leaves of a prickly ash tree. Used primarily as a decorative garnish in Japanese cuisine. Sold in Japanese markets, sometimes under the name sansho leaves. Kinome is a seasonal product, available from spring through summer.

Kiwicha: The Quechua name for amaranth. See amaranth.

Konbu: One of the basic ingredients of dashi, the ubiquitous broth of Japan. Konbu is a deep brown kelp harvested in northern Japan. In addition to its use in dashi, konbu is used as a vegetable. Available dried at Japanese and Korean markets and in health-food stores, usually in plastic bags of varying sizes.

Krachai: See kencur.

Laos: See galangal.

Lemongrass: A tropical grass found throughout Southeast Asia that imparts a nice lemony taste to foods (this is because both lemongrass and lemon peel contain citral). The bulblike base of the plant is used extensively in Thai, Malay, Cambodian, Burmese, and Indonesian dishes. In the Bay Area, it is available fresh, dried, and powdered, usually in Asian markets, but I've seen it fresh in many a Safeway as well. Cost Plus markets often have a pickled version. The powdered form is generally sold under the Indonesian name sereh. To use the stalks, trim off the top, leafy portions and the bulblike base; the remaining stalk should be about 6 inches long. Remove the outer leaves before using. The remaining stalk can then be cut up and added to soups and stews; to use in a curry paste, you will need to chop the base and then pound it to break down its fibrous nature. Lemongrass is also a common ingredient in herbal teas. It is a remarkably easy plant to grow. Just pick a fresh stalk that has a bit of the root still intact and set in a glass of water. Once the roots develop, plant in a large pot. This way you will always have lemongrass available.

Lesser galangal: See kencur.

Long beans: Also known as Chinese long beans and yard-long beans, these slim green beans are usually about 1½ feet long. They are used in China and Southeast Asia and can be found in Asian markets and some supermarkets most times of the year, although they are at their best in the fall.

Lotus root: A large rhizome used as a vegetable in northeast Asia. Available fresh, canned, and dried in Asian markets. The dried lotus root is soaked in hot water for about 30 minutes before use. Once cut, fresh lotus root must be immersed in cold water to which a teaspoon of lemon juice has been added to prevent discoloration. Dried lotus root is mostly used in Chinese and Korean dishes. In China, lotus root is also ground into a starch and used for thickening sauces. In Japan, lotus root is often pickled.

Linguica: A Portuguese sausage now readily available in most Bay Area markets. For fresh linguica, try the Santos Linguica Factory in San Leandro or the Silva Sausage Factory in San Jose.

Lychee: A white-fleshed fruit with reddish brown skin common throughout East Asia. In the United States, it is primarily available canned in Asian markets.

Mace: Mace is a spice made from the aril, or covering, that surrounds the seed of the nutmeg fruit. Originally found only in the exotic Banda Islands of Indonesia, it is today grown in the West Indies, primarily in Grenada. Mace is mostly used in desserts and is mostly found ground. It is carried by any decent supermarket. See also nutmeg.

Madeira: A sweet Portuguese wine from the islands of the same name. Used in cooking, especially in sauces and desserts. Also served as a postdinner drink. Available at most liquor stores and some supermarkets.

Mahlab: The kernel of the black cherry stone. It used in Syrian and Turkish cooking, especially in breads and pastries. Available in Middle Eastern markets. The spice is sold whole and should be ground before using.

Mamey: A brown-skinned fruit with orange flesh about the size of a coconut. Occasionally found fresh or frozen whole, the fruit pulp is more often available frozen in Latin American markets. Used in juices and desserts.

Manchego cheese: The most popular cheese in Spain, made from sheep's milk. It is available semisoft or aged. Available in fine cheese shops and gourmet delis.

Mango: Indigenous to India, the mango is now grown throughout the tropics. Mangoes from Mexico are available in the United States year-round. They can be eaten both green, usually sprinkled liberally with salt, and ripe, when they have succulent yellow meat. The meat is often fibrous, although some varieties have wonderfully silky flesh. In cooking, mangoes are mostly used for desserts, but in India and Latin America they are also made into chutneys and salsas.

Mangosteen: Never seen fresh in the West, the mangosteen is, however, available canned. Native to India and Southeast Asia, it has a deep purple husk that must torn away to reveal a prized white fruit. It is considered one of the world's best fruits. Should you ever get to Asia, seek it out. Beware: the purple husk produces an indelible stain.

Manioc: See yuca.

Marzipan: A paste made from ground almonds, sugar, and egg whites. Common in European desserts, it is often molded into decorative shapes. You can make your own or buy ready-to-use marzipan in gourmet shops.

Marjoram: Related to oregano, marjoram has a more delicate flavor. Occasionally available fresh, it is more readily found freeze-dried in supermarket spice racks. A pantry essential in France and Italy.

Marsala: A fortified Sicilian wine used in sauces and some desserts. Available both dry and sweet, the former makes an excellent aperitif. Carried at most liquor stores and some supermarkets.

Masoor dal: See dal.

Mint: Varieties of mint are found throughout the world. The herb is available fresh and freeze-dried, but the fresh mint is clearly superior. Unfortunately, fresh mint does not keep well for more than a few days. Mint is common in Middle Eastern cooking, but in the West it is primarily used in desserts and drinks.

Mirin: A sweet Japanese rice wine used only for cooking, never for drinking. Mirin is often added to bastes and marinades for grilled foods. Look for it in Asian markets but not liquor stores.

Miso: There are several different kinds of miso, but basically every miso is made from crushed soybeans combined with wheat, rice, or barley and a yeast mold that ferments the mixture slowly over several months. Miso is a common ingredient in Japanese soups. Packages of instant miso soup are readily found in most supermarkets, while Japanese markets offer several different kinds of the fermented product itself. Red and white misos are two popular forms. Health-food stores are also good sources for miso.

Mitsuba: See trefoil.

Molasses: A dark syrup made from sugarcane. Used mostly in cakes, cookies, and other desserts. Available in supermarkets.

Monosodium Glutamate: A highly controversial flavor enhancer commonly used in Asian cooking. Also known as MSG and by its Japanese name, aji-no-moto. It is available in Asian markets, although no recipe in this cookbook calls for it.

Morcilla: A blood sausage from Spain. The Santos Linguica Factory in San Leandro produces an excellent Spanish-style morcilla. Another excellent source is Neto's brand in Santa Clara. In Latin American markets, you might find the occasional Spanish morcilla, but more often you will encounter a blood sausage from Mexico or Colombia.

Morel mushroom: A European mushroom mostly found dried, although finer markets will occasionally carry them fresh in spring. Morels are extremely expensive but a few go a long way. Use in mushroom sautes, sauces, and with roast meats.

Mozzarella cheese: A common Italian cheese. Traditionally made from the milk of the water buffalo, although cow's milk mozzarella is much more common. Most supermarket mozzarellas are rubbery and tasteless. Look for fresh mozzarella, sold immersed in water. It has a more delicate taste and finer texture.

Mustard: An ancient plant used both as a spice and as a condiment. Mustard seeds come in three major types: white, brown, and black. Indian cooks add the whole seeds to many vegetable dishes. Mustard is also available in powdered form (Colman's markets a nice European product). Powdered mustard is mixed with water and vinegar to make the condiment, of which there are hundreds on the market. Dijon mustard refers to a smooth French mustard sometimes flavored with herbs such as tarragon or thyme. German mustards tend to be strong and hot. Chinese mustard is also renown as a hot mustard.

Mustard Oil: A hot oil made from mustard seeds that carries a rather pungent aroma. Available in Indian stores.

Napa cabbage: Also known as Chinese or celery cabbage, napa cabbage is readily available in Asian markets and many supermarkets. It is commonly used in Chinese, Korean, and Japanese cuisines.

Naranja agría: A tart Cuban sauce made from bitter oranges. It is used as a seasoning. Found in Latin American stores.

Nigella: Once fairly common in European cuisine, nigella seeds are now used primarily in the cooking of India (to flavor nan and vegetable dishes, for example) and in some areas of the Middle East. They are sometimes confused with the rare black cumin, but in fact nigella is quite distinctly nutty and not at all pungent like black cumin. They are also sometimes called black onion seeds, despite the fact that the plant is not related to the onion family. The seeds are said to resemble onion seeds, and since they are black, the name has stuck in some areas. Indian markets generally have a supply of nigella, as do some Middle Eastern markets. Indian markets carry it under the name kalonji. And still to add to the confusion, nigella is also known as charnuska, or Russian caraway.

Nopales: Nopales are the leaves of the prickly pear cactus. Available fresh in many Latin American markets, nopales can also be found canned in the Mexican section of many supermarkets. Fresh nopales should be handled with care until you are sure the spines have removed, or until you remove them yourself, usually by shaving them off with a sharp knife or vegetable peeler.

Nori: Dried seaweed sheets used in Japan for rolling sushi. Available in some supermarkets and Asian markets, especially Japanese ones.

Nutmeg: Nutmeg is the kernel of the nutmeg fruit, surrounded by mace. One of the most prized spices of history, it, along with pepper, launched the great expeditions to reach the Spice Islands of Indonesia, the Bandas and the Moluccas. Efforts to control the production of nutmeg led to many wars, pitting the Portuguese, Spanish, Dutch, English, and the Ternate Sultanate against one another. It is now primarily grown in the West Indies, Sri Lanka, Malaysia, and Indonesia. The nutmeg grown in Grenada is particularly prized. While in the United States it is mainly used in desserts and drinks, cooks elsewhere use it for just about everything. The Dutch, in particular, have a great fondness for it. Although it is commonly sold ground, you can buy the kernel and grate your own when needed. Expensive but always available. See also mace.

Oca: A tuber from the high Andes with yellow-gold skin and flesh and a long, odd shape. Imported from Peru, oca is occasionally available canned in Latin American markets. The taste is similar to grainy potatoes.

Okra: A green finger-shaped vegetable native to Africa but commonly used in Cajun, Indian, and Middle Eastern cooking. Its viscid texture turns off many, but okra's slimy nature can be treated by dousing the pods with vinegar: toss gently to evenly coat the pods and set aside for 30 minutes. Drain and rinse. Commonly found frozen in supermarkets, especially those in the southeastern United States. Seasonally available fresh in supermarkets, produce stands, and some Indian and Middle Eastern markets.

Orange blossom water: Also known as orange flower water, it is one of several floral waters used in cooking. Distilled from orange blossoms, it is a strong flavoring that is used in salad dressings, desserts, and confections. Primarily used in the Middle East, especially in the Levant, the fragrant water should be used sparingly. It is available in gourmet shops and Middle Eastern markets.

Oregano: An herb found in the cuisines of Europe, especially Mediterranean ones, the Middle East, and Latin America. Available fresh, freeze-dried, as dried leaves, and dried and ground. See also Greek oregano.

Orgeat: A sweet syrup made from almonds and rose water or orange blossom water. Used as a flavoring in desserts and certain cocktails.

Orris root: A rare spice most commonly found in Moroccan ras el hanout (page 160).

Orzo: A small oval pasta used in Armenian and Middle Eastern cooking, especially in pilafs and soups, as well as in Italian cooking. Available in gourmet shops, some supermarkets, and many bulk-goods stores.

Oyster mushroom: A wonderful whitish mushroom that is widely available fresh in supermarkets and produce markets. Use in mushroom sautes, but do not overcook.

Oyster sauce: Made from dried oysters and common in southern Chinese cooking. Dark, thick, and slightly salty, oyster sauce can be found in most supermarkets and Asian markets.

Palillo: A spice from Peru that gives off a yellow color. Turmeric is an acceptable substitute in terms of color, although the taste will be off. Hard to find, but look for it in Latin American stores that carry South American, especially Peruvian, foods.

Palm sugar: A very sweet substance made from the juice of the sugar palm. It is mostly used in Southeast Asian cuisine. Depending on the country of origin, it will come in different forms. The Thais make a light brown or beige sugary paste that is sold in small jars. The Vietnamese use a similar paste that is easily found in Vietnamese markets. In Malaysia, palm sugar is found both granulated and in brick form. The granulated version is sometimes found in Asian markets. Brown sugar is an acceptable substitute, but it should be noted that palm sugar is sweeter. Palm sugar can also be found under the name coconut sugar.

Palm vinegar: A vinegar made from nipa palm sap. It is used primarily in the Philippines and is available in most Asian markets, especially Philippine ones.

Pancetta: A cured Italian bacon. While it can be eaten as a cold cut, it is primarily used a flavoring agent in Italian dishes, especially sauces. Available in Italian delicatessens and some cheese shops. Substitute bacon for use in recipes in which it is cooked.

Panch phoran: A mixture of whole seeds that includes cumin, fennel, fenugreek, mustard, and nigella, combined in equal proportions. Used in Indian cooking, especially in Bengal. Add to hot oil before adding vegetables or lentils (dal). Available in Indian markets or you can make your own.

Pandanus: A leaf primarily used in the cuisine of Malaysia, Singapore, Thailand, Indonesia, and India. Also called screwpine, fresh pandanus leaves are occasionally found in Asian markets. Store in the freezer. The Thai name is bai toey, while the Indian name is kewra. In India, the leaves are used as an essence.

Paneer cheese: A farmer cheese from India. Used extensively in Indian cuisine, especially in vegetable dishes, it is occasionally found in Indian marekts.

Panocha: An unrefined dark brown sugar from Mexico. Available in Latin American markets, sold in small, hard, dark brown lblocks.

Papa criolla: A marble-sized potato from Colombia. Available frozen or canned in Latin American markets. Essential for *Ajiaco de Pollo* (page 109).

Papaya: A yellow-green fruit with yellow or orange flesh native to Central and northern South America. This versatile fruit is used in salads, sauces, desserts, and, when still green, as a vegetable. The fruit is now grown throughout the tropics. Sadly, in the Bay Area, mostly Hawaiian papayas are available. Compared to Asian or Latin American papayas, the Hawaiian ones have little sweetness or flavor. Latin markets, however, occasionally carry Mexican or Central American papayas. Jump on these for a real treat. Monterey Market stores in Berkeley and Palo Alto are also a good source. The fruit is widely renown for its medicinal purposes. The hundreds of little black seeds found inside the fruit are used in the treatment of parasites and tapeworms. The fruit itself is used to cleanse pores and remove sun spots. The milky juice from a green papaya can be used to treat acne, warts, and psoriasis. Even papaya leaves have a good use. They are used in Latin America to remove tough stains from clothes.

Paprika: A red powder, which can range from quite mild to nicely hot, made from a relatively mild chili. Hungarian paprika is world renown and highly prized. Spanish paprika is slightly more bitter but less expensive. Used in Hungarian, Polish, Balkan, Spanish, and Latin American cooking. The better paprikas are sold in gourmet stores.

Parmigiano-reggiano cheese: A hard, dry, highly prized cheese from Italy. Primarily used for grating over pastas. Most domestically made Parmesan cheeses are poor imitations of the real thing but are a lot less expensive. Look for the finest Italian renditions in good cheese shops and Italian and gourmet delis.

Passion fruit: Sometimes called granadilla, marquisa fruit, or maracuya, this tropical fruit is now fairly common in the Bay Area. Grown on a vine, its flower is thought to resemble the crown of thorns worn by Christ, hence its name. The fruit is extremely tart and is most often made into a juice with water and sugar added. There are several varieties, but the most common in the United States is a small purple one, about the size of Ping-Pong ball. When ripe, the skin of the fruit should be rather wrinkled. The edible part of the fruit is the interior mixture of pulp and seeds. When juiced, strain to remove any remnants of the seeds.

Pepino: A small, greenish yellow melon-like fruit from the Andes. Available in upscale produce markets.

Pepper: Native to India and Myanmar (Burma), pepper no doubt is the most influential spice in the history of the world. Europe's insatiable demand for it spurred the voyages of da Gama and Columbus and thus changed the course of humanity. Once traded ounce for ounce for gold, it remains the most commonly used spice in Western Europe and the United States. Pepper is the unripe berry of a vine. White, green, and black are all from the same plant. The color depends on the stage of maturity at which the berry is picked. There is a closely related vine that produces long pepper, a 1-inch-long berry that is called pipal in India. Long pepper is primarily used in Indian and Southeast Asian cuisine. While long pepper is mostly available in gourmet shops and Indian markets, all other kinds are readily found. You should stock whole mixed peppercorns, whole black peppercorns, whole white peppercorns, and whole green peppercorns, as well as ground black pepper and ground white pepper.

Pesto: A pine nut, basil, garlic, cheese, and olive oil sauce from Genoa. Some bottled versions are available, but it is easy to make your own (page 73).

Phyllo dough: A very thin pastry dough used in Middle Eastern cooking. Available frozen in many supermarkets and Middle Eastern markets. Thaw in the refrigerator. Also spelled filo or fillo. Hun-I-Nut Company in San Jose makes a pre-buttered phyllo dough that is a great timesaver; it comes in 8-sheet layers, so you don't have to melt butter and brush it on individual sheets.

Pickled ginger: Ginger knobs that have been marinated in a mixture of vinegar, sugar, and water and then thinly sliced. The marinade turns the ginger a pale pink. The ginger slices accompany sushi. Known as *gari* in sushi shops. Available in jars or plastic tubs in Japanese shops and some supermarkets. Sometimes sold under the name shoga.

Pilaf: A pilaf is a grain dish that combines any of several grains with various other ingredients, principally seasonings. Rice and bulgur are the most commonly used grains. In India, lentils, although legumes rather than a grain, are a common base. Less traditional pilafs use amaranth or quinoa. Pilafs find their highest culinary heights in the cuisines of Central Asia, India, the Caucasus, and the Middle East. While a growing number of ready-made mixes are available, you can make your own (pages 50, 150-152, and 166).

Pimiento: The Spanish word for a mild red pepper. Used to make paprika and to stuff green olives, bottled pimientos are available in most supermarkets. They make wonderful sauces and decorative garnishes.

Pine nut: A small nut from the Mediterranean used in Middle Eastern, Balkan, Mexican, Italian, and Chinese cooking. Readily available in supermarkets and health-food stores. The Italians call them pinoli, while Hispanics refer to them as piñones.

Pita bread: A round flat bread from the Middle East. Readily available in supermarkets.

Plantain: A member of the banana family, the plantain is large and starchy. Unlike bananas, however, it cannot be eaten raw. Supermarkets occasionally carry plantains, but Latin American markets almost always have them. Primarily imported from Colombia, they are available green and in various stages of ripeness. The green ones are used to make tostones (page 130) and in soups and stews. The ripe ones are sweet and used to make tajadas (page 130) and baked plantains. Don't be afraid to buy black, soft, mushy plantains. They are at their ripest and sweetest at that stage. If you buy a green one, it will take about a week to ripen completely. The most common variety available is the macho, but occasionally you'll encounter guinea plantains.

Pomegranate molasses: A thick, tart pomegranate syrup used in Near Eastern cooking, especially in Lebanese, Syrian, Assyrian, and Turkish cuisines. Available in Middle Eastern markets. Do not substitute grenadine, which, although also made from pomegranates, is nonetheless quite different.

Pomegranate seeds: Used both fresh and dried in the cuisines of the Middle East and India. Fresh pomegranate seeds are a popular garnish in the Middle East, Turkey, and Iran. Dried pomegranate seeds are used in Persian and north Indian cuisines as an astringent, that is, a souring agent. Dried pomegranate seeds are available in Indian and Middle Eastern stores. Fresh pomegranate seeds must be removed from fresh pomegranates, which are generally available in supermarkets and produce stands at the end of the summer into fall. The seeds freeze well. In Indian markets dried pomegranate seeds might be found under the name anardana.

Poppy seeds: The seeds of an opium poppy. Used primarily in Indian and Middle Eastern cooking, although in the West they are common in cakes, desserts, and bagels. Poppy seeds do not have any narcotic properties despite being from the same plant. Widely available in supermarkets.

Port: A fortified wine from the Porto region of northern Portugal. Port wines are normally drunk after dinner, sometimes with a cheese course. There are three main types: white, bottle-aged red, and cask-aged red. Vintage Portuguese ports should be aged 12 or more years to develop their full flavor. Normally shipped 2 years after bottling, a vintage port will have its date clearly imprinted on the bottle. Cheaper ports are usually a blend of various tawny or ruby ports. For cooking use an inexpensive California port.

Poudre de colombo: A currylike blend of spices common in the West Indies, especially in the French Caribbean and Trinidad and Tobago.

Pozole: Mexican hominy. Available in some Latin American markets as well as certain supermarkets.

Prosciutto: A cured ham that originated in the Parma region of Italy. Only in recent years has imported Italian prosciutto been available in the United States. Delicatessens here, however, have long hung their own hams, although not with results to match the Italian product.

Pulse: Pulses are the edible seeds of leguminous plants. Lentils, split peas, masoor dal, mung beans, chickpeas (also called garbanzo beans or ceci beans), kidney beans, navy beans, and black-eyed peas are but a handful of the many kinds of pulses. Many kinds are widely available, although Indian markets carry a dazzling selection.

Queso fresco: A crumbly, soft, somewhat salty cheese from Mexico that is similar to other Latin American cheeses. It can be bought in most Latin American markets and many supermarkets.

Quinoa: Despite regularly being termed a grain, quinoa is actually a seed native to the high Andes. Today it is imported from Peru and Bolivia, although a California company, Ancient Harvest, is attempting to grow it in Colorado in an effort to save one of the "lost grains" of the world. Quinoa is one of the most nutritious foods known to man, containing all eight essential amino acids. Rinse well before cooking, then cook at a ratio of 2½ parts water to 1 part quinoa. Ancient Harvest also produces quinoa flour and a variety of pastas made from it. Available at some Latin American markets, health-food stores, and selected gourmet shops.

Rambutan: A sweet and juicy Southeast Asian fruit similar to a lychee. The white fruit is enclosed in a spiked reddish skin. Rarely found fresh in the United States, it is available canned from Thailand and Singapore. It can be found in Asian markets.

Ras el hanout: A Moroccan blend of several different spices. It normally consists of over 20 different elements, including several rather exotic ones. Among the most common inclusions are cardamom, pepper, cubeb, turmeric, cumin, cinnamon, mace, nutmeg, and galangal. Among the more exotic ones are Spanish fly beetle, orris root, grains of paradise, and nigella. Rarely available in the United States outside of mail order spice houses—try Dean and DeLuca. In the Bay Area, Draeger's supermarket sells its own blend. You can also make your own (page 160).

Rice vermicelli: Dried thin rice noodles sold in cellophane packages. Like bean thread noodles, they are soaked in hot water and then added to soups and stir-fries, or they are fried briefly in hot oil until light and crisp. Available in Asian stores and many supermarkets.

Rice vinegar: Although there are many different rice vinegars used in Asia, from red to black to amber, Japanese or Chinese white rice vinegar should be used in the recipes in this book. Available in many supermarkets.

Ricotta cheese: A fresh, white cow's milk cheese. In Italy, it is generally made from the whey that remains from the making of other cheeses. In the United States, it is made from a combination of milk and whey. Available in most supermarkets as well as Italian delis.

Romano cheese: A hard, dry, sharp-flavored cheese. In Italy, most commonly made from sheep's milk. In the United States, most commonly made from cow's milk, sometimes combined with sheep's milk. Available in most supermarkets, especially American kinds.

Romesco sauce: A Catalan sauce made with almonds, tomatoes, olive oil, and roasted peppers. Trader Joe's carries a bottled version, but I would advise you to make your own (page 208).

Rose water: One of several floral waters used in cooking as an aromatic flavoring. Rose water is particularly common in the cuisine of Turkey, the Levant, India, and France. Available in gourmet shops and Indian and Middle Eastern markets.

Rosemary: An herb snipped from the rosemary bush, which grows throughout the Bay Area. The leaf actually looks like a pine needle. Wonderful for roasting meats and in vegetable dishes. Readily available fresh or freeze-dried wherever herbs are sold.

Safflower: Used both to produce an oil and a spice. The spice, which is often used as a cheap alternative to saffron, is available in Indian, Middle Eastern, and Latin American markets. Beware of vendors who try to pass off safflower for the pricy saffron.

Saffron: The world's most expensive spice is actually the dried stigmas of a crocus flower. Spanish Mancha saffron is superior to all other kinds, although a number of serious cooks rave about a saffron produced in Kashmir. Saffron is used primarily in Mediterranean and Latin American cooking, but many Indian and Middle Eastern recipes also call for it as well. Spanish Mancha (so-called because it is grown in the Spanish province of La Mancha) saffron is available in gourmet shops and many supermarkets. Or, if you know anyone headed for Spain, give them ten bucks and ask him or her to bring some back. It will keep in a cool, dry, dark place for up to a year. Never buy ground saffron, as it may be cut with turmeric; always buy the threads. See also safflower.

Sake: Japanese rice wine. Available in Asian markets, supermarkets, and liquor stores. Sake is generally served warm, although it is sometimes served cold in special boxes that store the ice.

Sambal: See sambal ulek.

Sambal assem: An Indonesian and Malaysian chili-and-tamarind sauce. Available in some Asian markets.

Sambal udang: A thick Malaysian paste made from shrimp and chilies. Similar to terasi or trassi but not as pasty and definitely more spicy. Still a decent substitute for terasi if blachan is unavailable. There is also a Malay shrimp dish with the same name. Available in some Asian markets. See also blachan and terasi.

Sambal ulek: An Indonesian and Malaysian hot sauce made from chilies. Sometimes referred to simply as sambal and also spelled sambal oolek. Indonesian or Malaysian sambals are

available at Asian markets. Dutch brands, such as Cominex, are available at Cost Plus. See also chili sauces.

Sambuca: An Italian liqueur with an anise flavor. Available in Italian delis and liquor stores.

Sansho: Closely related to fagara or Sichuan pepper, sansho is the berry of a prickly ash bush. The berry is dried and ground and generally available as a powder in Japanese markets. It is one of the most common spices used in Japan.

Sansho leaves: See kinome.

Screwpine: See pandanus.

Sereh: The Indonesian word for lemongrass. See lemongrass.

Serrano: A Spanish cured ham. Occasionally found in gourmet delis and Latin American markets. Substitute prosciutto.

Sesame: An old and venerable spice used in cooking throughout Asia and the Middle East. Asians, in particular the Chinese, have long toasted sesame seeds in the making of sesame oil. The seeds come in white, brown, and black. White sesame seeds are available in most supermarkets, as are both Asian sesame oil and cold-pressed sesame oil. Black sesame seeds can be found in Japanese or Chinese markets. An Asian sesame paste is used to make dressings for noodles and rice. In the Middle East, sesame seeds are ground into a paste called tahini. Sesame seeds are also common in Persian and African cuisine, and they have a limited use in Mexican and Central American dishes.

Sesame oil, Asian: Nutty-tasting amber oil extracted from roasted sesame seeds. Used by Chinese, Japanese, and Korean cooks mainly as a flavoring, as it burns easily over high heat. Available in most supermarkets.

Shallots: A small, reddish white multicloved bulb that is a relative of the onion and garlic. Available in most supermarkets.

Shaoxing wine: Amber-colored rice wine traditionally made in Shaoxing in China's Zhejiang province. Available in Chinese and other Asian markets. A good-quality dry sherry can be substituted.

Sherry: A fortified wine from the Spanish region of Jérez de la Frontera. There are four kinds of sherry: amontillado, manzanilla, fino, and cream. Cream sherry is an after-dinner drink, while the others

are dry aperitif drinks. Amontillado is the most commonly used in cooking; cream sherry is often added to desserts. For cooking, you can use inexpensive California varieties.

Shichimi: Japanese seven-spice mixture. Made from crushed red pepper (togarashi), sansho, mandarin orange peel, black hemp seeds, crushed dried nori, white sesame seeds, and poppy seeds. A popular table seasoning for udon noodles in broth. Available in Japanese markets and in some supermarkets.

Shiitake: An Asian mushroom available fresh and dried. Japanese and Korean cooks use them in both forms, while Chinese cooks prefer them dried. There are four grades that define size and quality. To rehydrate dried shiitakes, see black mushrooms, dried. Available in most Asian markets and many gourmet stores, as well as some supermarkets.

Shoga: See pickled ginger.

Sichuan pepper: Also known as fagara or Sichuan wild pepper, this mildly pungent spice, despite its name, is not related to pepper at all. It is instead the berry of a prickly ash bush, although it vaguely resembles a reddish brown peppercorn. Available in Asian markets or wherever fine spices are sold.

Soba noodles: Japanese buckwheat noodles. Available in Asian markets as well as many supermarkets.

Somen noodles: A fine white Japanese noodle made from hard-wheat dough. Available in Asian markets as well as many supermarkets. Sold in packages which contain multiple, neatly tied bundles of noodles.

Sorbet: A fruit or vegetable ice served between courses or at the end of a meal to cleanse the palate.

Sour cherry syrup: A tart and sour syrup made from cherries. It is used in Middle Eastern cooking, in particular the cuisines of Turkey, Syria, and Georgia. Available in Middle Eastern markets.

Soy sauce: There are various kinds of soy sauce. The main differences are between Japanese and Chinese soy sauces. Chinese soy sauce is saltier and therefore heavier. Japanese soy sauce uses more wheat in the brewing process, resulting in a sweeter, lighter sauce. Never buy a synthetic soy sauce under any condition. You will find that certain recipes call for light soy sauce, while others just call for soy sauce. The latter refers to regular dark soy sauce. If a recipe calls for light soy sauce, you can use the dark type, but you will change the taste. In this case, omit or lessen the salt content of the dish and perhaps add a teaspoon of sugar. Kikkoman is my favorite brand of soy sauce. Kikkoman produces both dark and light soy sauces; the light soy sauce is imported from Japan and the dark one is made at Kikkoman plants in the United States. Indonesian soy sauce is called kecap and there are two varieties, asin (salty) and manis (sweet). Kecap asin is a regular dark soy sauce while kecap manis is unique. Make your own (page 174) or buy a bottle. The main Indonesian brand is ABC, and it is outstanding. Kikkoman soy sauces are widely available, while ABC is only found in selected Asian markets.

Squash flower blossoms: Used in Mexican and Central American cuisine in various dishes, especially in a well-known Oaxacan soup. Squash flower blossoms are available in finer produce markets and Latin American markets.

Star anise: It is a staple spice of Chinese cooking and a key ingredient in Chinese five-spice powder. Although not related to anise, this brown, star-shaped spice shares a licoricelike taste. It is also found in the Vietnamese pantry, and Indonesians employ it in the making of kecap manis. Available in Chinese and other Asian markets and in many supermarkets.

Straw mushrooms: A small Asian mushroom generally available canned. Used extensively in Chinese and Southeast Asian cooking, they take their name from the fact that they are cultivated on straw mats.

Sumac: Native to the Middle East, sumac is common in Moroccan, Turkish, and Persian dishes. The sumac bush produces a brick red berry that is then ground. The powder is available at many Middle Eastern markets. Sumac is sprinkled liberally on rice, grilled fish, salads, and dressings. In Morocco, a blend of spices called zahtar includes sumac.

Szechwan pepper: See Sichuan pepper.

Tabasco sauce: A hot sauce from Louisiana. Readily available.

Tagine: A Moroccan stew.

Tahini: A Middle Eastern paste made from sesame seeds. Tahini is used to make hummus and baba ghanoush as well as various dressings and marinades. Be sure to mix the oil that forms on top into the paste before using. Available in many supermarkets, health-food stores, and Middle Eastern markets. See also sesame.

Takuan: A yellow Japanese pickle made from the daikon radish. Available in Japanese markets.

Tamari: A thick and very dark soy-based Japanese sauce. It is sold in some supermarkets as well as many health-food stores and most Asian markets, especially Japanese ones. True tamari is brewed without wheat. It is mainly used as a dipping sauce.

Tamarillo: A tropical fruit also know as a tree tomato. It takes its name from its resemblance to regular tomatoes. Tamarillos can be found in selected produce markets and supermarkets. In Latin America, tamarillos are mostly used in juices and in desserts. They are poached lightly to remove toxins from their skin.

Tamarind: Originally from India but now common throughout the tropics. Tamarind is used in Indian, Latin American, and Southeast Asian cuisine. The fruit resembles a hard, brown pea pod with dark flesh surrounding a pit. It is quite tart and acidic. The main ingredient of Worcestershire sauce, tamarind is wonderful in marinades and sauces. In the Bay Area, tamarind can be found in Latin American, Indian, Middle Eastern, and Asian markets. Usually in the form of a paste sold in small bricks. Slice off a piece ½ inch wide by 2 inches long and place in warm water to cover. Let sit for 5 minutes and then begin to squeeze the tamarind mass to extract the essence. Use the water to impart a sour flavor. Also sometimes available fresh (especially in Latin American markets) and in a liquid concentrate (common in Indian markets).

Tandoori: An Indian mix of various spices used as a rub for meats. Sharwood makes a nice blend that is available in most supermarkets. Tandoori mix normally includes garam masala, cardamom, chilies, turmeric, and saffron. You can easily make your own.

Tapénade: A sauce common to Spain and Provence made with black olives, garlic, olive oil, capers, and anchovies. The Spanish version is called garúm.

Tarka: A cooking technique used in India to infuse a spice flavoring into hot oil.

Tarragon: Indigenous to Central Asia, the herb is closely identified with French and Mediterranean cooking. Available both fresh and freeze-dried. Also a common flavoring in vinegar.

Tempe: A Javanese fermented soybean cake (page 201). Wonderful and under-utilized outside Indonesia, tempe is rich in protein and vitamins. It is sold both plain and in such flavored varieties as sun-dried tomato tempe. Available in health-food stores and certain upscale markets such as Whole Foods.

Tempura: A Japanese batter-fried dish that has its origins with the Jesuit missionaries from Spain and Portugal who established themselves in Japan in the late sixteenth century. The Japanese dip shrimp, fish, and numerous vegetables into a thin, lumpy batter and then deep-fry them. It is served with a dipping sauce that includes freshly grated daikon. Packaged tempura batters are available in Asian markets and many supermarkets.

Terasi: A thick, pungent Indonesian paste made from dried salted shrimp. Also spelled trassi. If terasi is to be included with other ingredients and sauteed, use as is. Otherwise, to prepare terasi for use, first wrap a small piece in foil and grill over a burner or coals for a minute or two. You can also fry in a teaspoon of oil or roast for 5 minutes in an oven set at 325 degrees F. Generally available in Asian markets. There are several similar dried shrimp pastes from other parts of Southeast Asia. In Thailand, it is known as kapi; in Vietnam, as mam tom; and in Malaysia, as blachan or blachen. Of these, the Malaysian is perhaps the easiest to find in the shops. It must be stored tightly wrapped in an airtight container. See also blachan and sambal udang.

Thyme: One of the world's most common herbs. Available both fresh and freeze-dried. It goes well in most dishes, but it is absolutely perfect with roasted meats and stewed vegetables.

Tofu: Made from soybean milk, tofu (also known as bean curd) is common in the cooking of eastern, central, and Southeast Asia. Given its wide geographic distribution, tofu is available in slightly different forms. The two main forms available in the United States are Chinese firm tofu and Japanese soft tofu. All tofu, however, is protein-rich soybean curd made from crushed soybeans that have been separated into pulp and soy milk. The soy milk is mixed with a coagulant that separates the milk into curd and whey. The curd is poured into molds, and then when set is transferred to water to keep it fresh. In the United States, tofu can bought in supermarkets and Asian markets. The brands sold in supermarkets include sell-by dates, while some tofu available in Asian markets is freshly made. Store immersed in water in the refrigerator.

Togarashi: Small, red Japanese chilies. Available in Japanese markets both dried and powdered. Used in shichimi, the seven-spice Japanese mix. Substitute Thai chilies or cayenne.

Tomatillo: A husk-sheathed green tomatolike fruit native to Mexico. Peel away the husk and cook or roast the tomatillos for salsa. In addition to salsa, tomatillos are used in various sauces. Generally available in most supermarkets but always found in Latin American markets.

Trefoil: A member of the parsley family—it looks like a large, long-stemmed flat parsley—trefoil is used primarily in Japanese and Korean cooking. It is available in Asian markets. Also known as mitsuba.

Truffles: The king of fungi, truffles are found growing near the base of European oak trees. Extremely expensive and occasionally found in gourmet shops, they are shaved into pâtés, sauces, and other dishes.

Tú óng ót tói Viet-nam: A Vietnamese chili-garlic sauce. Widely available in supermarkets and Asian markets. See also chili sauce.

Turbinado: A partially refined sugar that is at least 15 percent molasses. Available in health-food stores and many supermarkets.

Turmeric: A rhizome related to ginger and galangal. Originally from Southeast Asia but now common throughout the world in its powdered form. Used in curries, both Indian and Southeast Asian, and as a yellow coloring in food. In Latin America, turmeric is called color and is often used as a substitute for saffron and palillo. In the United States, ground turmeric is readily available in supermarkets. Fresh turmeric is occasionally found in Indian and Asian markets; it resembles a dark, miniature ginger root.

Udon noodles: A thick, white Japanese wheat noodle. Used primarily in soups and broth. Soba noodles can be substituted for udon noodles in many recipes. More often than not, udon is available fresh in the grocer's dairy case, sealed in plastic vacuum packs; it sometimes is sold frozen as well. Available in Asian markets as well as many supermarkets.

Ulluco: A tuber from the Andes. Available canned or frozen in some Latin American markets. Ullucos range in color from pinkish red to a deep purple. Ecuadoreans call them mellocos.

Vanilla: One of the world's most expensive spices, vanilla is native to Mexico and Central America. There is an artificial substitute, but it is an inferior product. Vanilla beans and the true extract are available in gourmet shops and selected supermarkets. A real money saver is to buy vanilla bean or the extract during a trip to Mexico, where it is substantially cheaper. Keep your vanilla beans well stored in an airtight container in a dry place. Flavor a jar of sugar with a vanilla bean for use in special desserts. Just bury the vanilla bean in the sugar, replacing with regular sugar as you use it up. The vanilla bean will impart its flavor to the sugar for about a year, depending on use.

Vindaloo: A fiery spice blend from southern India, especially popular in the area around the former Portuguese colony of Goa. Vindaloo is made from black pepper, cardamom, cayenne, chili peppers, cinnamon, cloves, coriander, garlic, ginger, and mustard seeds. The blend is used to marinate meats and is available in jars in most Indian markets.

Wakame: A seaweed used in Japanese cooking, primarily in the preparation of soups and salads. It is available dried in Japanese and Korean markets and some Asian markets and health-food stores. Before using, soak in warm water for 15 to 20 minutes and cut away any tough parts.

Wasabi: Also called Japanese horseradish, although the wasabi plant is not related to horseradish. The plant grows only in Japan on the edges of cold mountain streams or rice terraces. In the United States, fresh wasabi is generally not available. It can be found ready to use in small tubes or powdered in small tins. Both are imported from Japan. To make the wasabi paste from the powder, mix 1 tablespoon with an equal amount of lukewarm water. Stir well until smooth, adding more powder or water if necessary. Allow it to stand for a few minutes to develop its full flavor. Wasabi paste is used in sushi and sashimi. It is eye-watering hot, so use in moderation. It is available in Asian markets and many supermarkets.

Water chestnut: Not long ago only canned water chestnuts imported from Taiwan were available in the United States, but now you'll find fresh water chestnuts in many Asian markets and some supermarkets. Used commonly in Chinese cuisine, they impart a nice sweet crunch. If you find them fresh, rinse well, cut off the top, and then pare off the skin. Place in a bowl of cold water to prevent discoloration.

Wheat pilaf: A wheat dish from Armenia. Near East markets a ready-to-cook wheat pilaf. It is readily available in supermarkets. Wheat pilaf can also be made from bulgur wheat (page 152). See also pilaf.

Worcestershire sauce: A seasoning sauce made by Lea & Perrins, among others. Made from tamarind, vinegar, molasses, anchovies, and spices, it is available in the condiment section of supermarkets.

Yuca: Also known as cassava, mandioca, or manioc. This is not the desert cactus, but rather a tropical root native to the Amazon Basin. Also adding to the confusion is the fact that there are two main types: sweet and bitter. Sweet yuca is usually referred to as yuca, while bitter yuca is called manioc. Today yuca is found throughout the tropics, where it is used in soups, stews, and as a flour (yuca harina) for bread. Tapioca is also made from yuca. Yuca is available both fresh and frozen. Latin American markets, Pacific Islander markets, and Asian grocers usually carry it. Occasionally, even supermarkets will have it fresh. As for bitter yuca, it is slightly toxic and must be boiled before consuming. See also Techniques (page 227).

Zahtar: A North African spice mixture of thyme, sesame seeds, and sumac. Although available in Middle Eastern markets, it is easy to mix your own (page 160).

Zedoary: A rhizome closely related to ginger and turmeric, it is believed to be native to Indonesia. More bitter than its close relatives, it is used in Indian as well as Indonesian cooking. Use as you would ginger or turmeric but more sparingly. It is rarely found, however; Asian or Indian markets occasionally carry it in powdered form.

Chili Peppers

Peppers, both sweet bell and hot chili, are indigenous to the New World. By 1600, their distribution had spanned the globe courtesy of Spanish and Portuguese explorers and traders. In the Caribbean and South America, hot peppers are called by the Arawak word ají. In the rest of the world, the Nahuatl or Aztec word, chili, is used for these fiery fruits.

All chilies are members of the capsicum family, which is named for the oil, capsaicin, that gives them their hot bite. Today there are a bewildering number of species and varieties, ranging from the innocent and ubiquitous green bell pepper to the devilishly hot habanero. What follows is list of the most common peppers available in the Bay Area, along with a commonly used rating of them on a heat scale of 1 (no heat) to 10 (fiery). You'll find that over time you will build up a tolerance for heat and an almost surreal addiction that will tempt you to test ever-increasing doses of fire.

Dried chilies keep well if stored in a dry place. The process of drying, as well as roasting, intensifies the flavor of a chili, so you will want to preserve it. Don't buy broken or spotty dried pods. Check for depth and evenness of color. Fresh chilies should be crisp, firm, smooth, and free of blemishes. A green chili is unripe, while a red or orange one indicates maturity. Store in the refrigerator, preferably in an open glass container. Do not leave them in a plastic bag, as that will only insure their rapid decay. Properly stored chilies will keep for up to 3 weeks in the refrigerator.

A few words of warning and advice: wear rubber gloves when working with hot chilies. The capsaicin oil that gives the chili its heat is concentrated in the seed and in the inner whitish membranes, so be especially careful when handling these. (When cooking, leave the seeds out of a recipe if you want it milder, include them if you want it hotter.) Wash your hands and utensils carefully after working with chilies. Be especially careful not to wipe your eyes or other sensitive areas with unwashed hands. When blending chilies in a sambal or other spicy sauce, don't put your face over the food processor or blender once you uncover it, as the fumes will likely burn your eyes and nasal membranes. Lastly, capsaicin oil is fat soluble, which means drinking water to dissipate the burning won't do you any good. Try a glass of milk or other dairy product, such as yogurt.

Sweet Bell　　　　**Heat Factor: 0**
Comes in a variety of colors: green, red, yellow, orange, and purple.

Sweet Banana　　　**Heat Factor: 0**
Available only fresh, they resemble wax peppers but have no heat.

Pimentón　　　　　**Heat Factor: 1**
Its two primary purposes are for stuffing green olives and for making paprika. Hungarian paprika has more zest than Spanish paprika. Don't even think of buying any other kinds. Pimentones also come roasted as red pimientos, usually from Spain. Use for sauces or for decorating dishes.

Morrón　　　　　　**Heat Factor: 1**
Available only dried, this chili hails from Spain, where it is used in making romesco sauce. It is rarely found in the Bay Area.

New Mexico　　　　**Heat Factor: 2**
Also known as chile colorado, the New Mexico is a rather mild pepper available fresh or dried. It is primarily used in chili powder; also good for roasted salsas, chili con carne, and most Southwestern dishes. Dried New Mexicos are a nice substitute for dried Spanish chilies (morrones or ñoras).

Anaheim　　　　　**Heat Factor: 2**
A light green, mild chili. Long and thin, the Anaheim is a wonderful chili for roasting and for use in mild tomatillo salsas. Allow one to ripen for use in sweeter salsas or chutneys.

Poblano　　　　　**Heat Factor: 3**
The poblano is a mild pepper available fresh or dried. It is best known as the chili in chiles rellenos. Poblanos are wonderful for milder sauces and salsas. The ancho, the poblano's dried version, is the most commonly used dried chili in Mexico. Anchos have a dark red, almost black skin. This makes them a good choice for use in roasted salsas. In California and northern Mexico, anchos are mistakenly called dried pasillas. Both chilies are mild and darkish, but the dried ancho is triangular, while the pasilla is longer and fingerlike. There is also another closely related dried chili called the mulato, which is a bit more rounded than the ancho and dark brown rather than dark red. Occasionally you will find fresh poblanos in supermarkets, but you will almost always find them in a

Mexican or Latin American market. Use a roasted poblano or ancho in tomatillo salsas.

Pasilla　　　　　　**Heat Factor: 3**
This mild chili is available fresh and dried. It is mostly used to make salsas and mole sauces. The dried pasilla makes a nice substitute for dried Spanish chilies (morrones or ñoras). Should you find it fresh, use it as you would a poblano.

Cascabel　　　　　**Heat Factor: 4**
Occasionally found fresh, but mostly encountered dried. Its name translates as "rattlesnake," and it does have a bite.

Ñora　　　　　　　**Heat Factor: 4**
Another dried Spanish chili occasionally found in Bay Area markets.

Chipotle　　　　　**Heat Factor: 5**
A dried Mexican chili, usually a smoked dried jalapeño. Easily found in Bay Area markets.

Pepperoncini　　　**Heat Factor: 5**
Mostly found pickled. They are imported from Italy and Greece and are used in salads. Readily available in the pickle section or in the import section of supermarkets.

Negro　　　　　　**Heat Factor: 5**
A black-red chili available only dried. Perhaps the hottest of the large dried chilies. It is a must for hot roasted salsas. Easily found in most Latin markets, although there is some confusion between negro chilies and dried pasillas. Both are long and dark but the former is a shiny black, while the latter is dark red.

Guajillo　　　　　**Heat Factor: 5**
A Mexican chili now beginning to make its way into Bay Area markets. It is available in Latin American markets, both fresh and dried. It is most commonly used in *pollo al guajillo*, chicken sauced with sour cream and chilies, but you can use it for salsas and Latin dishes, too. More often than not, it is roasted first to develop its full flavor.

Jalapeño　　　　　**Heat Factor: 6**
Green or greenish black, jalapeños are feared for their heat. In the United States, jalapeños are the most common and readily available chili and are great

for roasting, making salsas, and for cooking Southwestern and Latin American dishes. Use for Asian dishes such as green curries, although serranos or Thais would preferable. Jalapeños are also available pickled and canned. Should you find a red ripe one or allow one to ripen, it will be slightly sweet and primed for use in salsas.

Togarashi   Heat Factor 6.5
Small red Japanese chilies available fresh, dried, and powdered. Available in Japanese markets. Substitute cayenne for dried and powdered, Thai chilies for fresh.

Fresno   Heat Factor: 6.5
One of my favorite chilies, Fresnos are only available fresh. Readily found in most markets. They have the size and shape of a jalapeño, and are usually bright red. Use to make red curry pastes and salsas.

Ají Amarillo   Heat Factor: 7
A Peruvian chili available dried whole, frozen, or in powdered form in many Latin American markets. Rarely found fresh in Bay Area markets, this South American import is a shiny yellow. I have also seen pickled ones in Latin markets. Also known as ají mirasol or mirasol, it is a prime component in *ají de gallina* and *papa a la Huancaina*. Also use it in ceviches and Latin American chili sauces. The pepper is quite hot and thus should be used sparingly.

Hungarian Wax   Heat Factor: 7
Usually yellow but sometimes found red. It is available fresh or pickled.

Serrano   Heat Factor: 7.5
The most versatile of chilies. You can use it in Asian, Latin, or Moroccan dishes without worry. In markets, you'll find mostly green (unripe) ones, but let them ripen to their full red-orange for use in red curries, sambals, and salsas. Mexican markets sometimes carry dried or pickled serranos. I love this chili!

Lombok   Heat Factor: 7.5
An Indonesian chili, somewhere between a serrano and jalapeño in size. I've only seen them fresh and always bright red in local Asian markets. Should you find them, use for sambals and any Southeast Asian dish.

Rocotillo   Heat Factor: 8
A Caribbean and South American chili occasionally found fresh in Bay Area markets. Most often found frozen or pickled in Latin American markets.

Cayenne   Heat Factor: 8
In addition to being increasingly seen fresh in the Bay Area, cayenne pepper is one of the few chilies available in a powdered form; many markets also carry them dried. Since it is also one of the few chilies commonly found (at least in its powdered form) throughout the world, you'll find it called for in French, Latin, and Asian recipes. Should you find it fresh, use it as you would a serrano or jalapeño.

Thai   Heat Factor: 8.5
Also known as bird chilies or bird's-eye chilies. These little devils pack a punch, so a few go a long way. They are available green and ripe. Increasingly avail-

able dried at places like Cost Plus, over the last few years fresh ones have become a staple in many markets, especially Indian and Southeast Asian ones. Thai chilies can be used in curries, sambals, and even salsas.

Habanero   Heat Factor: 10
The king of heat. A cousin of the Jamaican Scotch bonnet, this monster of a pepper is available both fresh and dried. It has about a hundred times the heat of a jalapeño. Given its scorching bite, one or two peppers usually suffice in a recipe. Habaneros are most often found already ripened to a bright yellowy orange, although occasionally I have seen red ones. I have found green ones only rarely. They are most readily identified by their lantern shape. In Colombia, I knew them as farolitos, literally "little lanterns." While I like them for their heat in almost any dish, they go especially well in fruit chutneys and salsas. I also use habaneros for South American chili sauces and for dishes like *papa a la Huancaina* or *papa ocopeña*.

Mail Order Sources for Specialty Ingredients

The Blazing Chile Brothers
PO Box 19023
Aptos, CA 95001
(800) 473-9040
Mail-order house specializing in spicy hot sauces, salsas, condiments, and other gourmet specialty items. Free catalog.

Culinary Alchemy
PO Box 393
Palo Alto, CA 94302
(650) 367-1455
Mail-order house specializing in Indian spices and products. Culinary Alchemy sells various kits, including one with 26 ingredients and another with 9 of the more exotic spices, including amchur, asafetida, black cumin, fenugreek, and nigella.

Dean & DeLuca
Mail Order Department
560 Broadway
New York, NY 10012
(212) 431-1691
(800) 221-7714
For those who prefer to shop by mail, Dean & Deluca is perhaps the most complete food purveyor in the United States, covering goods from India, Latin America, Morocco, the Middle East, China, and Southeast Asia. Call or write for catalog.

Foods of India
121 Lexington Ave.
New York, NY 10016
(212) 683-4419
Indian spices and other products.

G.B. Ratto and Company
821 Washington St.
Oakland, CA 94607
(800) 228-3515 in California
(800) 324-3483 outside California
A good source for international ingredients, from the spices of India to the seaweeds of Japan.

India Spice and Gift Shop
3295 Fairfield Ave.
Bridgeport, CT 06605
(203) 384-0666
Indian spices and other products. Send or call for catalog.

Mo' Hotta Mo'Betta
PO Box 4136
San Luis Obispo, CA 93404
(800) 462-3220
Good source for Latin American, Southeast Asian, and Southwestern ingredients.

Penzeys Spice House
PO Box 1448
Waukesha, WI 53187
(414) 574-0277
The best spice house in the United States. Penzeys is a family-owned and -operated business that stocks wonderful spices and dried herbs from all over the world, including such exotic items as Chinese cassia buds, Indian nigella (kalonji), Kashmiri saffron, Madagascar bourbon vanilla, Jamaican ginger, and Grenadan nutmeg and mace. Their philosophy of being not just a business but also a place to learn about other cultures makes Penzeys an extraordinary institution.

Shallah's Middle Eastern Importing Company
290 White St.
Danbury, CT 06810
(203) 743-4181
Source of Indian, Middle Eastern, and Moroccan ingredients.

Guide to Bay Area
Specialty Food Stores

The Bay Area grocery scene is dominated by Safeway (megachain Lucky Foods also has a local presence but less so in the city). The stores vary in size and selection; for instance, the Marina Safeway is upscale, while the Fillmore Safeway, situated between Japantown and the Fillmore, offers many Asian vegetables as well as traditional Southern fare. In addition to the giants, Cala Foods, Bell Market, and Andronico's are local chains; Cala and Bell are mainstream, while Andronico's is upscale. Most neighborhoods also have smaller, independent supermarkets, as well as a range of specialty, ethnic, and health-food stores.

As the Bay Area has become more ethnically diverse, the stores have followed suit by tailoring their product selection to their clientele. You never know which so-called specialty ingredients you'll find in your neighborhood grocery store. From lemongrass to pomegranate molasses, it could be there, just waiting for you to look or ask.

San Francisco

San Francisco's ethnic diversity supports an abundance of specialty markets. For Asian produce, sauces, seasonings, fish, and meat, head for Grant Avenue or Stockton Street in Chinatown, or Clement Street in the Richmond District. Farther west on Clement Street you'll find stores jammed with Russian and Mediterranean specialties. The supermarkets in Japantown carry everything you'll need for Japanese cooking or snacking. For Mexican and Central American foods, the Mission District, Twenty-Fourth Street in particular, abounds with grocers selling tortillas, chilies, beans, and Mexican fruits and beverages.

There are also three Farmers' Markets: one at Civic Center Plaza on Sunday and Wednesday mornings (see Union Square/Civic Center section), one at the Embarcadero Ferry Plaza on Saturday, Sunday, and Tuesday mornings (see SoMa/Embarcadero section), and one at Alemany Boulevard on Saturday mornings, just off the ramp from Hwy 101 to I-280 (see Mission/Bernal section).

Chinatown
North Beach

As you would expect in one of the largest Chinese communities outside of China, you can get everything you need for Chinese cooking in the space of a few blocks: vegetables, sauces, seasonings, fish, meats, and cooking equipment from chopsticks to rice makers. In addition, prices are usually absurdly low. How these stores can sell shrimp and asparagus so much cheaper than Safeway is a complete mystery. The down sides of Chinatown shopping are that parking is all but impossible (try the garage under Portsmouth Square at Kearny and Washington streets) and most information is presented in Chinese. If you are looking to grab a few supplies quickly, the narrow aisles crammed full of exotic merchandise with no English labels will be frustrating. On the other hand, if you are willing to spend time exploring, Chinatown can be an exciting shopping experience of picking your way through pungent herbs and dangling Peking ducks, and it's a whole lot cheaper than a flight to Hong Kong.

Most food stores are located on Stockton Street between Clay and Vallejo streets and on Grant Avenue between Pacific and Broadway. While the streets are filled with markets, we've highlighted only a few to get you started (particularly those with a wider selection suitable for one-stop shopping). Plan on exploring further on your own to find personal favorites. One other hint, packaging in Chinatown stores isn't the same as in Safeway: spices are usually in cellophane bags, not jars; preserved vegetables can be in jars, cans, or plastic bags; same for many beans and dried products.

North Beach, the traditional home of San Francisco Italian culture, has little left in the way of specialty food stores, in part because most Italian food items are readily available in supermarkets. A few delis remain, however, purveyors of housemade pastas and sausages, Arborio rice for risotto, polenta and semolina flour, cured meats, cheeses, anchovy paste, and more.

Apple Land
881 Clay St. (Stockton), SF, (415) 399-1817
A medium-sized store that's a little off the main drag and consequently not too frenzied. In addition to the usual selection of dried, bottled, and canned goods, Apple Land offers some fresh produce, a wide selection of dried noodles, especially rice noodles, and some Japanese and Southeast Asian goods (wasabi, nori, fish sauce).

Cheung Hing Meats
1151 Stockton St. (Pacific/Jackson), SF, (415) 951-8628
One of many Chinatown butchers offering such fare as roast duck and pork, fried chicken, and whole roasted pigs in addition to standard cuts of raw meat and poultry.

Chung Hing Produce
1300 Powell St. (Pacific), SF, (415) 693-9634
You'll find a little of everything for Chinese cooking at this medium-sized store: fresh produce, preserved vegetables, noodles, sauces, rice, and frozen and dried fish. They also have a few Southeast Asian sambals and such.

Cost Plus Imports
2552 Taylor St. (Bay/Northpoint), SF, (415) 928-6200
This bargain Mecca offers an eclectic mix of gourmet and international foods. They sell many varieties of olive oil, vinegar, mustard, and pasta, boxed Italian tomatoes, and European cookies and chocolates. They also have a good mix of Asian

sauces and noodles (some Chinese, some Japanese, some southeast Asian), and some Mexican salsas. Their extensive spice collection includes garam masala, fenugreek, and orange peel, all at good prices. Selection varies from store to store and season to season.

Florence Ravioli

1412 Stockton St. (Vallejo/Columbus), SF, (415) 421-6170
An old-fashioned Italian deli with lots of cheese, imported tomatoes, olives and olive oil, cured meats, jams, Nutella, and so forth. As the name implies, they also sell housemade ravioli and other filled pastas.

Four Seas Supermarket

1100 Grant Ave. (Pacific), SF, (415) 788-2532
One of the biggest fish markets in Chinatown with the usual variety of seasonal offerings on ice, in buckets, and in tanks ("no photo please" a sign admonishes tourists). Meats are sold out of another counter. Unusual items include live shrimp, eels, and spiny lobsters.

Gum Shing

774 Pacific Ave. (Stockton/Grant), SF, (415) 989-4836
This small store has the usual produce bins out front. The well-organized interior has a good selection of basics and spices. The small refrigerator shelters wonton wrappers, noodles, and fresh tofu. Employees are unusually friendly and helpful.

S.E. Hong Kong Market

1136 Grant Ave. (Pacific/Broadway), SF, (415) 986-8410
A large butcher and seafood store with an ample supply of roast ducks and pork, lots of tanks and buckets filled with shellfish (live clams, New Zealand green-lipped mussels, crabs, lobsters), and an aggressive attitude toward pricing.

Kowloon Market

1217 Stockton St. (Pacific/Broadway), SF, (415) 788-3668
There's a wealth of products at this large store: noodles, wonton wraps, preserved vegetables, dried fish, spices, sauces, even a butcher. Lots of Japanese teas, wasabi, and nori and hard-to-find shrimp paste are sold here as well.

Lee Yuen

1131 Stockton St. (Pacific/Jackson), SF, (415) 956-0216
A small store with a good selection of canned and dried goods, preserved and pickled vegetables, noodles, dried fish, chili sauces, dried shrimp, and a less-than-frantic atmosphere.

Lien Hing

1112 Stockton St. (Pacific/Jackson), SF, (415) 986-8488
A large general-purpose Chinese market with a full selection of produce, a meat, fish, and poultry department, and a small array of packaged goods such as sauces, dried and preserved vegetables, and noodles. In addition to Chinese staples, you'll find a few sambals.

Little City Meats

1400 Stockton St. (Vallejo), SF, (415) 986-2601
The only surviving meat market from North Beach's Italian days, this old-fashioned shop is the kind of place where you can order special cuts for any recipe. Offerings include lots of veal, lamb, Rocky brand chickens, and fresh sausage. The people behind the counter are happy to offer tips and advice on cooking, plus the gregarious window signs mix education and promotion in a fun-filled way.

Mandarin Delight

1024 Stockton St. (Washington/Jackson), SF, (415) 781-4650
A typical small Chinatown store with standard items—sausage, spices, sauces—plus lots of dried beans, nuts, noodles, and tea. The refrigerator case holds tofu and prepared dumplings, and a close look at the shelves reveals such Japanese items as nori, wasabi, sesame-seed mixtures, and bonito flakes. Friendly service from people obviously used to lots of mystified tourists (they're ready to make a joke in German).

May Wah Trading Co. Shopping Center

1230 Stockton St. (Broadway/Pacific), SF, (415) 433-3095
A highlight of any visit to Chinatown is a stop at this large, bustling Asian market. The Chinese goods run the gamut from wonton wrappers and various rice and wheat noodles—fresh and dried—to black bean sauces, hoisin sauce, and spices. Various sambals and chilies sauces are readily available, and the selection of Indonesian, Thai, and Malaysian canned goods and bottled products is notable for Chinatown, including hard-to-find blachan, palm sugar, kecap manis, plantain leaves, coconut vinegar, palm vinegar, and sugar cane vinegar. Among the Japanese basics on hand are wasabi, dried seaweed, miso paste, and somen and udon noodles. The produce section is well-stocked with all manner of Asian vegetables, and there's a small meat and fish counter. Unfortunately, Chinese cookware and tableware seem to be expanding at the expense of spices and dried and bottled products.

Mayerson Food Company

1101 Grant Ave. (Pacific), SF, (415) 398-4618
A sparse store with a moderately good produce selection and a meat market specializing in organ cuts. Produce includes most staples plus lemongrass. Refrigerator counter looks like a second outlet for New Hong Kong Noodle Company.

Metro Foods Company

641 Broadway (Grant/Stockton), SF, (415) 982-1874
Large, well-organized, and packed with merchandise. One wall is lined with cans and bottles including hoisin, bean, and chili sauces (including sambals), preserved vegetables, and virtually every Asian cooking wine and vinegar known to the Western world (some to drink, too). Dried products include fish, beans, noodles, spices, mushrooms, seaweed (nori), and fruits. Refrigerator cases include noodles, wonton wrappers, miso paste, and lots of premade dumplings. Plenty of cooking supplies, too, including clay pots.

Molinari Delicatessen

373 Columbus Ave. (Vallejo), SF, (415) 421-2337
For the surliest counter staff around, head for this North Beach institution. Molinari offers a full range of pastas (including housemade ravioli); reasonably priced cheeses (predominantly Italian), olive oil, and wines; a deli counter loaded with olives, peppers, cured meats, pasta salads, and housemade sausages; staples such as Arborio rice, polenta, and anchovy paste; hard-to-find salt cod; and sandwiches to go.

The Nature Stop
1336 Grant Ave. (Vallejo/Green), SF, (415) 398-3810
This small natural-foods store doubled in size a few years ago and now has a decent produce department with some fresh and dried chilies. The mostly natural food-type items include bulk nuts, seeds, grains, and spices (asafetida, garam masala, fenugreek, and cardamom are available). Other useful items include small samplings of udon and soba noodles, dried seaweed, wasabi paste, fish sauce, chili oils, and prepackaged Indian and Asian dinners.

New Hong Kong Noodle Company
874 Pacific Ave. (Powell/Stockton), SF, (415) 433-1886
This noodle and wonton wrapper factory has a small retail storefront, but the products are available in most Asian markets around town. Items are available fresh and dried, and most use wheat flour (no rice stick). Some cooks find their products tend to be too doughy and difficult to work with.

Panelli Bros.
1419 Stockton St. (Green/Vallejo), SF, (415) 421-2541
This old time Italian deli has been around since the 1920s. Offerings include lots of pasta (dried, fresh ravioli), Arborio rice, bulk polenta and semolina flour, imported boxed tomatoes, and jars of peppers, caper, and olives. The deli counter is filled with a few cheeses and lots of cured meats, which they use to build hearty sandwiches.

Prudente
1462 Grant Ave. (Union), SF, (415) 421-0757
Better known by its former name, Iacopi Deli (previous owner Leo Rossi retired), this deli continues to sell excellent, pricy housemade sausages, tortas, cold cuts, and cheeses, as well as imported Italian packaged foods such as pasta, Arborio rice, and boxed tomatoes. Great Italian sandwiches.

Sanh Hing
945 Stockton St. (Jackson/Washington), SF, (415) 398-2586
A well-stocked small store with lots of noodles (including somen), dried spices, bottled and canned goods, preserved vegetables, sausages, dried fish, and salted dried beans.

Russian Hill
Polk Street
Although this area sometimes seems like a residential extension of Chinatown, it doesn't have any of the street-market activity. Nevertheless, a few stores with an eclectic mix of goods exist in the neighborhood. And it's just a short trip to Chinatown, the Tenderloin, Japantown, or Whole Foods for those missing ingredients. Since the stores aren't destination places, and the parking can be impossible (Real Foods validates at a nearby lot during peak hours), you'll usually shop here only if you live here.

Better Life Whole Foods
1058 Hyde St. (Pine/California), SF, (415) 474-3053
A small health-food store with a nice mix of items. Bulk spices include cardamom and garam masala. Other shelves have tahini, tofu, dried seaweed, miso, date sugar, fish sauce, and lots of noodles (udon and somen).

Food Warehouse
1732 Polk St. (Clay/Washington), SF, (415) 292-5659
Don't be put off by the small facade, this store, while not a full warehouse, has lots of international staples buried in its random stock. Italian pasta, Arborio rice, boxed tomatoes, and polenta mingle with Middle Eastern sumac, broad beans, grape leaves, and rose water. You'll also discover ghee, bulk grains, beans and lentils, sour cherries, preserved lemons, chutneys, and tamarind paste on the shelves. Cheeses include American staples like cheddar and jack, as well as Greek kasseri and queso blanco fresco. A small selection of produce lies at the front of the store, while a wide variety of bulk olives are hidden in the back.

Grand Meat Market
1806 Polk St. (Washington/Jackson), SF, (415) 885-5030
The very definition of hole-in-the-wall, this motley little store saves Nob and Russian Hill residents a trip over the hill to get Chinese ingredients. Pickled vegetables, tamarind paste, pickled ginger, hoisin sauce, dried mushrooms, red beans, mung beans, rice wine, and all manner of noodles (mein to rice stick) are sold. The tiny selection of meat and fresh produce is forgettable.

Leonard's 2001
2001 Polk St. (Pacific), SF, (415) 921-2001
A great source for gourmet and international ingredients. Best known for the cheese selection, which covers over 150 types, including various fetas, many Bries, numerous cheddars, Manchego, and mascarpone. Prices are low—although they won't usually sell blocks smaller than half a pound—and the staff love to talk cheese. You can also find bulk grains and beans (from amaranth and couscous to quinoa), and all kinds of dried pastas. Gourmet ingredients such as mustards, vinegars, tapenades, and barbecue sauces mix with pomegranate molasses, harissa, tahini, sambals, fish and hoisin sauces, chili oil, soba and somen noodles, dried seaweed, and chutneys.

Real Food Company
2140 Polk St. (Broadway/Vallejo), SF, (415) 673-7420
San Francisco's mini chain of health-food stores, Real Food carries a beautiful selection of organic produce, with some unusual vegetables, dozens of gourmet oils, vinegars, jams, and bulk grains and spices. The Polk Street location has a small, expensive selection of organic meats, fish, and poultry. You can find a small array of dried seaweeds, udon and soba noodles, coconut milk, tofu, tempe, sambals, chutneys, tahini, and bottled and canned curry sauces and mixes. Unfortunately, the prices have earned the chain the name "Really expensive food company," and the emphasis on organic ingredients limits selection of things like chilies, lemongrass, and plantains (if organics aren't available, they usually won't substitute commercial products).

Swan Oyster Depot
1517 Polk St. (Sacramento/California), SF, (415) 673-1101
This small store is half oyster bar, half fish market and has an excellent reputation for high-quality fish. The selection is usually small but fresh, and they can get harder-to-find ingredients like crayfish.

Marina
Pacific Heights
Japantown

Japantown makes for a very focused shopping trip. The three main stores focus almost exclusively on Japanese products, so you should be able to find everything you need to prepare a Japanese meal. There's very little available for other types of cooking, however. Pacific Heights and the Marina are not very ethnically diverse, and the demographics are reflected in the stores: mostly mainstream supermarkets where gourmet products predominate. Nevertheless, the upscale-healthy Whole Foods Market has an incredible array of useful items, and bits and pieces of other ingredients can be found elsewhere.

California Street Creamery

2413 California St. (Fillmore/Steiner), SF, (415) 929-8610
Cheese is the focus at this tiny store. Charcuterie, fresh pastries, and some milk, eggs, and other dairy products round out the selection. If you need advice, ask the knowledgeable staff.

Grand Central Market

2435 California St. (Fillmore/Steiner), SF, (415) 567-4902
A fairly complete grocer with an outstanding deli featuring many imported Italian products. Not much in the way of ethnic goods, but you will find quinoa, a great selection of cheeses, and fresh pastas. Grand Central also boasts a long meat counter with real butchers who will cut and grind to order; across the aisle is an equally long fish and poultry counter. The market was recently taken over the by Mollie Stone's chain, so changes may be coming.

Lucca Delicatessen

2120 Chestnut St. (Steiner/Pierce), SF, (415) 921-7873
Given the dearth of quality provision stores in the Marina, Lucca Delicatessen stands out as an oasis. Their offerings are all high quality. The small selection of cheeses focuses on French, Swiss and Italian varieties; Italian offerings include parmigiano-reggiano, fontina, mascarpone, ricotta, and mozzarella. A nice stock of about a dozen olive oils, olives, marinated peppers, capers, and anchovy paste lines the shelves. The cold cuts, mainly Italian, and fresh sausages are outstanding, and there are fresh pasta (the ravioli are delicious), Arborio rice, and semolina flour. Cooking wines and sherries are also carried.

Maruwa

1737 Post St. (Webster/Buchanan), SF, (415) 563-1901
One of the best Japanese goods stores in the Bay Area. The selection of fresh and frozen fish is superb. Highlights include fresh unagi and saba (which is usually just available frozen elsewhere). Maruwa also has a nice array of roes: salmon, herring, cod, flying fish. Meats include cuts presliced for sukiyaki. The noodle and rice section is extensive, as is the variety of pickled vegetables and tofu products. The prepared foods selection is also impressive, and the produce section has most ingredients for Japanese cooking. Maruwa stocks Japanese beer, sake, and mirin, and a small cookware section has the basics.

Sakai K Uoki Company

1656 Post St. (Laguna/Buchanan), SF, (415) 921-0514
This Japantown market has a complete fish counter, with items for both sushi and cooking. Prices are pretty good, too. The counter also sells meats and poultry. The selection of everything else you'll need for Japanese cooking is excellent, with dried seaweed, pickled vegetables, noodles (fresh and dried), miso, tofu, and snacks galore. There's even a small area with Chinese sauces (bean paste, chili oil) and such. A small produce section rounds out the market.

The Straw, The Jar and The Bean

2047 Fillmore St. (Pine/California), SF, (415) 922-3811
This tiny, trendy shop features a few useful ethnic products, mostly from organic specialty growers and manufacturers. Look for a good variety of dried beans, lentils, grains, and seeds sold in bulk. The bulk spices include cardamom, fenugreek, garam masala, five-spice powder, and asafetida. There's no real produce section, but they do have garlic, ginger, and so forth.

Super Koyama

1790 Sutter St. (Buchanan), SF, (415) 921-6529
A basic shop with all the essentials for Japanese cooking. Super Koyama has both fresh and frozen fish for sushi and sashimi, fish for cooking, nori, wasabi, and shoga. There is a small produce section that has a good selection, including lotus root and burdock root. The canned selection is fairly complete. The shelves also have a few Southeast Asian staples—hot sauces, fish sauce, and the like. A nice pastry shop called Yasukochi's Sweet Stop is on the premises as well.

Whole Foods

1765 California St. (Franklin), SF, (415) 674-0500
The San Francisco location of this gourmet health-food store has been an instant success, providing customers with an abundant variety of organic foods in a soothing shopping environment. Whole Foods is expensive, but their goods are of the highest quality. Although they are mixed in with other items, the selection of ethnic items is topnotch. Among the offerings are excellent produce (lots of chilies, herbs, and occasionally lemongrass), seafood, meats, and poultry. The fantastic spice selection includes asafetida, annatto, garam masala, and cardamom (many in bulk, not jars). Among other bulk items are quinoa, couscous, bulgur, masoor dal, various beans, and dried seaweed, mushrooms, and chilies. Although not equal to Asian markets, they have a reasonable variety of sambals, bean pastes, and other sauces, as well as a variety of Asian noodles. Gourmet items include a full range of mustards, capers, and such, as well as a great selection of cheeses, olives, and other deli items. Whole Foods stocks a fairly complete selection of Indian and Southeast Asian ready-made sauces and marinades. And, of course, they have a complete line of health products. The hundred parking spots is a comforting sight.

Tenderloin
Union Square

The Tenderloin is not typically a big shopping destination, unless you're looking for various and sundry illicit things. But the area's low rents have proven attractive to many new immigrants, and spawned accordingly good ethnic variety in the stores. Most neighborhood stores have useful ingredients for Southeast Asian, Chinese, Indian, Middle Eastern, or Mexican cooking, although market Balkanization means you won't find food from a multitude of regions under one roof.

Heart of the City Farmers' Market
Civic Center Plaza (Grove/Van Ness/Polk), SF, (415) 558-9455
This farmers' market offers what could be the city's best collection of international produce. In addition to the usual fruits and vegetables, offerings include Chinese greens, long beans, and bitter melon, Indian baby eggplant and beans, Thai basil, and lemongrass. Chilies seen here include habanero, serrano, Thai, poblano, pasilla, and wax. Various vendors sell fresh fish and live poultry. The produce is fresh and inexpensive; a great find. Wednesdays and Sundays only.

New Chiu Fong Company
724 Ellis St. (Larkin/Polk), SF, (415) 776-7151
Something of a neighborhood gathering place, this is the neighborhood's biggest source for Southeast Asian and Chinese groceries. The front of the store displays plentiful produce—lemongrass, banana flowers, Thai basil, chilies, yuca, galangal—although quality varies with turnover. A large counter handles meat, fish, and poultry needs. The selection of bottled sauces and vegetables is complete, as is the noodle section (both fresh and dried). Plenty of wrappers (flour and rice), tamarind paste, miso, and dried beans round out the store.

New India Bazaar
1107 Polk St. (Sutter/Post), SF, (415) 928-4553
Although the store is small, it has an excellent selection of dried spices (amchur, asafetida black sesame), tamarind, ghee, coconut milk, and bulk beans, grains, flours, and rice. If you don't feel any culinary inspiration, choose from the many premade curry mixes and Indian snacks and desserts.

Queen of Sheba
1100 Sutter St. (Larkin), SF, (415) 567-4322
Primarily a Middle Eastern market but with a few Indian products. Queen of Sheba stocks a large selection of rices, beans, grains, and lentils, plus other staples, such as bulk dried spices, fava beans, tahini, ghee, pomegranate molasses, grape leaves, phyllo dough, harissa, and tamarind. Also has some cheeses like kasseri and Bulgarian feta.

Thang Xuong Market
724 Larkin St. (Ellis/O'Farrell), SF, (415) 474-4004
This tiny full-service market with narrow aisles packs in most Chinese and Southeast Asian cooking necessities. All the usual canned and jarred items are on hand, plus a wall of dried noodles, palm sugar, tamarind, and dried spices (galangal to zedoary). The small produce selection includes Thai basil, lots of chilies, galangal, yuca, lemongrass, and Chinese greens. The selection of wrappers includes both Chinese and Southeast Asian, and a small counter sells meat (especially pork).

UN Market
900 Post St. (Hyde), SF, (415) 563-4726
In front it looks like any other corner grocer, but in the back row of this helpful market are many basic Indian and Middle Eastern dry goods. A decent selection of spices is displayed, with sumac, asafetida, and zahtar among them. Rices, including basmati, pomegranate molasses, ghee, olive oil, and various dals are all stocked. This is also one of the few places where frik, the Egyptian green wheat, is sold.

Haight
Western Addition
Castro/Noe

Good shopping for ethnic ingredients is pretty slim in these neighborhoods, although European specialty items, cheeses, health foods, and organic produce get a fair commercial shake. Fortunately, the Sunset, Richmond, and Mission are nearby.

Ashbury Market
205 Frederick St. (Ashbury), SF, (415) 566-3134
This huge corner market actually has two entrances: one to the general-supplies market and one to the next door deli, wine, and cheese shop. The connecting corridor holds a great selection of dried noodles, oils, and other specialty items. A fully stocked meat-and-fish counter, a large produce selection, a good selection of fresh-baked goods, and more canned and bottled goods than you can shake a stick at keeps local residents packing the aisles. The staff is friendly and helpful.

Cheese Boutique
666 Chenery St. (Castro/Diamond), SF, (415) 333-3390
Those who seek out health foods will find this specialty store a boon, as will anyone who wants to cook up an Italian meal, especially if pasta or risotto is on the menu. Cheese lovers won't be disappointed either, with such irresistible choices as Italian Gorgonzola dolcelatte or French Morbier.

Country Cheese
415 Divisadero St. (Oak), SF, (415) 621-8130
Country Cheese, with stores in Berkeley and San Francisco, carries about 60 different domestic and imported cheeses. Highlights include mascarpone, manchego, and various fetas including Bulgarian, Greek, and French. They also stock Mexican queso fresco and cotija. In addition to the nice array of cheeses, Country Cheese carries a limited supply of prepackaged meats (good for sandwiches), a number of grains including semolina and quinoa, and nuts and spices in bulk.

Harvest Ranch Market
2285 Market St. (Sanchez/16th St.), SF, (415) 626-0805
This popular and hip Castro specialty shop features most everything necessary for a gourmet meal: fresh organic produce, fresh-baked breads, numerous canned and bottled condiments, high-quality olive oils, and numerous spices in bulk. A superb soup-and-salad bar for takeout and some delicious homemade desserts cleverly placed within reach of the check-out line keep a steady stream of folks coming through the door. Not surprisingly in this neighborhood, prices are quite high.

Real Food Company
1023 Stanyan St. (Carl), SF, (415) 564-2800
3939 24th St. (Noe/Sanchez), SF, (415) 282-9500
See Russian Hill/Polk Street listing. At the Stanyan location

there is also a deli. The 24th Street location is somewhat smaller than the other two in the city, there is no meat or fish, and the cheese selection is not as extensive.

Say Cheese
856 Cole St. (Carl/Frederick), SF, (415) 665-5020
Perhaps the premier cheese shop in the Bay Area, Say Cheese stocks well over a hundred cheeses. Some of the harder-to-find cheeses normally stocked are manchego, majón, and huntsman cheddar.

Tower Market
635 Portola Dr. (O'Shaughnessy /Fowler), SF, (415) 664-1600
With more than 55 years history, this supermarket, one of San Francisco's best known, carries a fine supply of organic products, a slew of cheeses, beautiful olive oils and vinegars, meats handled by a consummate staff of butchers, and neatly stocked shelves of mostly European foods. Many of the city's swells shop here, pushing their carts and toting designer handbags.

Twenty-Fourth Street Cheese
3893 24th St. (Vicksburg/Sanchez), SF, (415) 821-6658
Hundreds of cheeses, prosciutto and pancetta, crackers, breads, olives, anchovies, various bottled sauces, and plenty of wines are sold at this friendly neighborhood shop. A good place to buy fior di latte, fresh mozzarella from the East Coast.

Mission
Bernal Heights

In the Mission district, ethnic diversity runs far and wide. Since it is the center of the city's Latino culture, just about every grocer sells tortillas, chilies, beans, and Mexican spices. You'll find the greatest concentration of goods in the shops along 24th Street between Mission and Harrison. The neighborhood also boasts first-rate outposts for Middle Eastern, Indian, Italian, and Asian goods. Put simply, some of the city's best stores for foods of all kinds are found within walking distance in this food-heavy zone, making the Mission a perfect place for a sunny outing for groceries.

Alemany Farmers' Market
100 Alemany Blvd. (Highway 101/ Nevada St., nr intersection I-280), (415) 647-9423
The market, which has been around since way before farmers' markets became trendy, features an international collection of locally-grown fruits and vegetables—enough to cook any cuisine from Afghanistan to Zanzibar. The selection is highly seasonal, but look for the likes of winter and bitter melons, chayote, sugarcane, taro leaf, Chinese greens, Indian beans, a good variety of chilies, and up to eight kinds of eggplant. Other items include dried fruits, nuts, eggs, herbs, honeys, and jams. Sa 8am-8pm

Bernal Heights Produce Market
800 Cortland Ave. (Ellsworth), SF, (415) 282-7308
Excellent produce selection and a spice section that includes such exotics as achiote and cardamom. Small, quick, and easy.

Bombay Bazaar
548 Valencia St. (16th St./17th St.), SF, (415) 621-1717
A one-stop market for anyone seeking ingredients for an Indian meal. Most of the dried goods here are sold in bulk, arranged in a row of big plastic containers along one wall. Amchur, star anise, sumac, ajowan and cardamom are among the multitude of spices offered. Basmati rice and dal are sold by the pound from massive sacks. There are also bottled and canned specialties like ghee, rose water and asafetida, plus nan and other traditional breads. An ice cream annex next door offers truly unique flavors Tuesdays through Sundays.

Casa Lucas (aka La Hacienda)
3100 16th St. (Valencia), SF, (415) 431-8445
A popular grocery store which was once a bank, it has one of the best selections of chilies in the Mission, plus a small produce aisle, a meat counter, and both bottled and canned goods. Limited cheese selection as well.

Casa Lucas Market
2934 24th St. (Harrison/Florida), SF, (415) 826-4334
If you can go only to one market to fulfill all your Latin American provision needs, Casa Lucas Market should be your destination. You'll find an entire wall of refrigerated items, plus meats, cheeses, spices and canned goods.

Duc Loi
2200 Mission St. (18th St.), SF, (415) 558-9494
One of the better markets in the Mission, Duc Loi has a fine produce section stocked with tomatillos, nopales, fresh tamarind pods, yuca, plantains, taro roots, and fresh chilies. There is also a small meat department. Mexican cheeses, including cotija, are carried. Spices include epazote, dried chilies, and jamaica (hibiscus). Bottled goods such as palm sugar and Terasi are also available.

Fresh Meat Market
2704 Mission St. (23rd St.), SF, (415) 550-8044
A complete meat and poultry market with a limited fish selection. Live turtles, fresh seafood, and goat are available. Also sells jasmine rice, various Mexican spices, and a limited supply of fresh Asian noodles.

Greek American Food Imports
223 Valencia St. (14th St./Duboce), SF, (415) 864-0978
This small store is a good place to stock up for cocktail-party food: Greek olives, wines, olive oil, feta, vine leaves, and baked goods.

Homestead Ravioli
120 14th St. (Folsom/S. Van Ness), SF, (415) 864-2992
This factory has been turning out stuffed pastas since 1917. Ravioli, of course, are the specialty, in big and small sizes. Tortellini are also for sale. Fillings include cheese, beef, a veal sausage mixture, and even pumpkin in season. Ravioli are sold in small flats or large boxes, and prices are low. Homestead products are available in stores around town, too.

Hwa Lei Market
2970A 16th St. (S. Van Ness/Mission), SF, (415) 863-1618
A small market mainly featuring Chinese and Southeast Asian

products. Among the produce are Thai eggplants, bitter melons, plantains, yuca, and kabocha. There is also a small meat department. The dry goods section, packed into very narrow aisles, features coconut milk, lemongrass, galangal in brine, various chili sauces including sambal, and fish sauce. Among the Philippine products are banana sauce, palm vinegar, and coconut vinegar. Plantain leaves and a wide selection of noodles are available in the refrigerator case.

Kim's Market
300 Alemany Blvd. (Crescent), SF, (415) 647-2929
A Philippine market with a good selection of fresh seafood, some fresh produce (lots of peppers, Asian greens, and plantains), and poultry, and a small array of dried and bottle Asian goods.

L & M Produce
2169 Mission St. (17th St./18th St.), SF, (415) 552-8606
A standard Mission produce stand with a good selection of dried chilies and a more limited selection of bottled and canned items.

La Gallinita
2989 24th St. (Harrison), SF, (415) 826-8880
This small, Mexican butcher specializes in pork. You can buy carnitas and chicharrones, freshly rendered pork cracklings, by the pound.

La Palma Mexicatessen
2884 24th St. (Bryant/Florida), SF, (415) 647-1500
This tiny market sells many Latin American specialty items like banana leaves, mamey, chorizo, and achiote. A deli counter in back serves up plenty of deep-fried goodies.

Lucca Ravioli Co., Inc.
1100 Valencia St. (22nd St.), SF, (415) 647-5581
Not to be confused with Lucca Delicatessen in the Marina, this Lucca opened in the 1920s, when the Mission was more European. They sell great homemade ravioli, fresh pasta, Italian cheese, sausages, and sauces, all at reasonable prices.

Mi Rancho Market
3365 20th St. (Shotwell/S. Van Ness), SF, (415) 647-0580
A midsized grocery store with a friendly, helpful staff, Mi Rancho is a good place to pick up Latino food items, especially of the canned and bottled variety. A butcher shop, a bakery, a good-sized produce section, and a wine selection featuring Chilean and Argentinean labels are also under this bountiful roof.

Rainbow Grocery
1745 Folsom St. (13th St.), SF, (415) 863-0620
Rainbow Grocery, which carries many organic foods and health foods, has an eclectic mix of goods. A nice display of produce and herbs doesn't stress the exotic. The bulk-goods section is fantastic. There are various flours and grains including quinoa and millet. The rice selection is good, with basmati and jasmine among the offerings. This is also one of the few places that sells bulk olive oil. The array of dried beans is extensive: lentils, dals, black beans, pinto beans. Several varieties of miso are available, and tempe is stocked.

Samiramis Imports
2990 Mission St. (26th St.), SF, (415) 824-6555
This long-established store caters to Middle Eastern food needs. It stocks five different kinds of imported couscous, which are sold in bulk or packaged. The emphasis is imported Middle Eastern groceries, rather than fresh foods.

San Francisco Herb Company
250 14th St. (S. Van Ness/Mission), SF, (415) 861-3018
This hole-in-the-wall on an industrial-looking street in the Mission sells nothing but dried goods, albeit an incredible variety of such. Spices, extracts, and potpourri are available in plastic bags of varied weights—from 4 ounces up to 20 pounds. A great place to buy in bulk (for long-term usage or to split among fellow cooks) and save lots of money in the process. They also do a strong mail-order business.

Tony's Groceries Market
2146 Mission St. (17th St./18th St.), SF, (415) 553-8627
A relatively large market with a meat-and-poultry department. The produce is standard Mission fare: plantains, yuca, taro roots, tomatillos, and nopales. Dried chilies and epazote are also stocked. Among the Asian products sold are fish sauce, noodles, tamarind, and chili sauces.

Twenty-Third & Mission Produce
2700 Mission St. (23rd St.), SF, (415) 285-7955
A clean and spacious market with fine, inexpensive produce, although much of it is standard fare. Highlights include a nice array of dried chilies, including mulato, guajillo, New Mexico, pasilla, and negro.

SoMa
Potrero
Bay View

Although SoMa and the Embarcadero have become trendy places to live, the food stores servicing the neighborhood have not achieved the variety found in neighborhoods with more residential history. The Ferry Plaza Farmer's Market has become a darling of the gourmet set, but the offerings, while mostly organic, aren't especially international. Further south, San Bruno Supermarket is one of the best places to stock up on ingredients you'll find anywhere.

Ferry Plaza Farmers' Market
Market St. (Embarcadero/California), SF, (415) 981-3004
Located on the waterfront in front of the Ferry Building, this is more of a yuppie gourmet event than a farmers' market. Sip a cappuccino, nibble sandwiches from Rose Pistola or Hayes Street Grill or a sweet roll from Healdsburg's Downtown Bakery, and participate in special events like "Shop with the Chef." If you can fight your way through the crowds to the food stalls, you'll find a nice selection of seasonal produce, with an emphasis on organic producers. Not many ethnic ingredients other than chilies, Asian eggplants, and some greens. Prices rival Whole Foods and Andronico's (at least the money goes to the farmers). Saturday market runs from 7:30am in summer or 8am in winter until about 2pm, at the Ferry Plaza, Embarcadero near Market Street.

Spring through fall, the market runs on Sundays from 9am-1pm. Spring through fall, the Tuesday market runs from 11:30am to 3pm, at edge of Justin Hermann Plaza near the Hyatt Regency (near Market and Spear sts.).

Polarica
3107 Quint St. (3rd St./Cesar Chavez nee Army), SF, (415) 647-1300
Wholesale and retail sales of game and other specialty products from all over the world. This is the place to buy a whole fresh foie gras, smoked quail, smoked sturgeon, caviar—just about anything that is exotic and pricy.

San Bruno Supermarket
2480 San Bruno Ave. (Carl), SF, (415) 468-5788
A supermarket with an excellent assortment of Asian goods and products. The produce section is complete and carries fresh galangal, Thai eggplant, Japanese squash, bitter melon, and various Chinese cabbages. The meat department has a good selection of beef, pork, lamb, chicken, and some fresh fish. Various rice and wheat noodles, sauces, spices, sambals, and chili sauces are readily available, and the selection of Indonesian, Thai and Malaysian canned goods and bottled products is outstanding. A number of Japanese products are stocked as well.

Trader Joe's
555 9th St. (Bryant/Brannan), SF, (415) 863-1292
Various locations throughout Northern California—call 1 (800) 746-7857 for the location and phone number of the store nearest you. A discount gourmet store with a decent assortment of domestic and imported cheeses. Salsas, chutneys, and various sauces are available, as well reasonably priced olives, nuts, and frozen fish. Good cheap wines perfect for cooking.

Richmond
Presidio Heights
The inner Richmond might be the single best place to shop for specialty items for this cookbook. As with Chinatown, you can find an extensive selection of ubiquitous ingredients for Chinese cooking, but you'll also discover stores offering a wide array of ingredients useful in Southeast Asian, Japanese, Indian, and Middle Eastern recipes. Inexpensive fresh produce, meat, seafood, herbs, and spices are all here. Stores are scattered throughout the area, but the greatest concentrations are along Clement Street between 5th and 10th avenues and Clement Street around 25th Avenue. Parking is a little easier here than in Chinatown as well, although Saturdays on Clement Street are pretty hectic.

Bangkok Grocery
3236 Geary Blvd. (Spruce/Parker), SF, (415) 221-5863
One of the few sources around that regularly stocks kaffir lime leaves. All the usual Thai products are also carried, including jasmine rice, galangal (dried), fish sauces, tamarind, chili sauces, coconut milk, and prepared curry sauces. You can usually find fresh lemongrass and chilies hidden in the back refrigerator. A gem of a store and the owner will patiently answer your food questions.

Bryan's
3473 California St. (Laurel/Spruce), SF, (415) 752-3430
Bryan's is a full-service butcher and also has separate counters for fish, poultry, and prepared entrees for those who don't want to cook. Catering unabashedly to neighborhood matrons, this is a high-quality, high-price kind of place. The butchers can cut to order, and the poultry section has a good collection of game (quail, duck, *poussin*). One wall has a bit of fresh produce and a few gourmet staples—oils and vinegars and so forth.

Clement Produce
645 Clement St. (7th Ave./8th Ave.), SF, (415) 221-4101
658 Clement St. (8th Ave.), SF, (415) 221-4101
Although the space is a little spartan looking, the selection includes good-looking lemongrass and lots of varieties of Chinese greens, chilies, and tofu. Other useful items include fresh herbs—basil, mint, cilantro—yuca, nuts, grains, and galangal. A few shelves hold spices, sambals, and other Asian sauces. Prices are very low. Clement Produce II, across the street, offers similar products with cheap cooking oils and sauces.

18th & Geary Produce
5350 Geary Blvd. (18th Ave.), SF, (415) 751-1177
This small corner store carries a little something for everyone in the neighborhood. Outdoor produce bins include all the usual stuff, plus lemongrass, Thai chilies, and plantains. Some Japanese items include seaweed, miso, somen noodles, and yakisoba noodles. The shelves also contain hoisin sauce, sambals, dolmas, tahini, grape leaves, and a variety of oils and vinegars.

El Chico Produce Market
2214 Clement St. (23rd Ave./24th Ave.), SF, (415) 752-7372
A fairly large produce stand with an eclectic mix of goods. The standard selection of produce is cheap. Packaged goods include Mexican, Middle Eastern, and Asian in the mix: masa, rose water, tofu, gourmet oils, mole mix, hoisin sauces and bean pastes, sambals, cane vinegar, tahini, dried chilies, and many beans and grains. The cheese section has every imaginable kind of feta (French, Greek, Bulgarian).

First Korean Market
4625 Geary Blvd. (9th Ave./10th Ave.), SF, (415) 221-2565
A complete Korean grocer with the largest selection of kimchi that you'll ever see. Thanks to culinary overlap, the store is also good for many other Asian items. Highlights include a good selection of rice and noodles (somen, soba, ramen, udon), dried seaweed (wakame and nori) and bottled sauces; lots of beans and grains, bulk sesame seeds, and giant bags of red pepper powder are also available, plus various prepared dishes. A small meat counter has cuts suitable for Korean barbecue, and a small produce section carries cabbages, roots, and chilies.

H K Market
115 Clement St. (2nd Ave./3rd Ave.), SF, (415) 752-2033
Billed as an Asian and American food market, this is a small market that carries just the basics. The selection of Chinese products is good, with various sauces, noodles, and rices stocked. Among the Southeast Asian goods carried are fish

sauces, sambals, and shrimp pastes. Japanese goods include a little nori, some sauces and snacks, and lots of tea.

Haig's Delicacies
642 Clement St. (7th Ave./8th Ave.), SF, (415) 752-6283
A simply wonderful store filled with good things. The selection of Indian goods is outstanding, with such esoteric items as nigella (or kalonji, although Haig's labels them as black seeds), asafetida, fenugreek, and amchur commonly stocked. Dal, garam masala, various vindaloo pastes, pickles, chutneys, and a good selection of ghee are also sold. Middle Eastern goods include fragrant waters including rose water and orange blossom water, tahini, pistachios, pomegranate molasses, sour cherry syrup, and ajvar. Southeast Asian products include various bumbus, sambals, and the Cominex line of spices. A large selection of olives, housemade hummus, and a few cheeses and pastries round out the offerings. Don't be afraid to ask for help in this friendly store.

Happy Supermarket
400 Clement St. (5th Ave.), SF, (415) 221-3195
For pan-Asian groceries, this is arguably the most complete source in the Clement shopping district, with a little of virtually everything you'll need. Happy features a complete butcher and small fish department heavy on shellfish. There is an excellent produce section with galangal, lemongrass, chilies galore, Thai eggplants, bitter melons, fresh turmeric, and Thai basil among the offerings. The variety of Chinese products is complete and the Southeast Asian selection is outstanding. Candlenuts, shrimp paste (blachan or terasi), bumbus, fish sauces, and sambals are commonly carried. Japanese goods include dried seaweed, miso pastes, yakisoba, and wasabi. All this and cookware, too.

Kowloon Market
251 Clement St. (4th Ave.), SF, (415) 386-6918
Another branch of a Chinatown store, Kowloon has a full selection of Chinese cooking staples with lots of noodles (mein, somen, rice stick, udon), sauces, preserved vegetables, cooking wines, and dried mushrooms. Also has small butcher and fresh produce sections, refrigerator cases filled with noodles and wonton wrappers, and fish cakes. More interesting finds include palm sugar, dried shrimp paste, pickled ginger, miso paste, and a little dried seaweed.

May Wah Supermarket
547 Clement St. (6th Ave./7th Ave.), SF, (415) 668-2583
A sister of the May Wah market in Chinatown but even better supplied. This May Wah has a small but useful produce section (regular items include galangal, lemongrass, lots of chilies, and herbs galore), along with a nice butcher and fish department. The Chinese goods selection is excellent. New May Wah stocks various rice and wheat noodles (fresh and dried, Chinese, Japanese, and Southeast Asian), sauces, and spices (from annatto to zedoary). Various sambals and chili sauces are readily available, and the selection of Indonesian, Thai, and Malaysian canned goods and bottled products is outstanding. Tamarind paste, blachan (dried shrimp paste), palm sugar, kecap manis, plantain leaves, pandanus leaves (screwpine), coconut vinegar, palm vinegar, and sugar cane vinegar. A small but fairly complete liquor section with lots of cooking wines. A

few Japanese items in addition to the noodles include dried seaweed, bonito flakes, pickled ginger, and frozen soybeans. Chinese cookware and tableware also available. Chaotic but useful.

Odessa
5427 Geary Blvd. (18th Ave./19th Ave.), SF, (415) 666-3354
A basic Russian deli with a case full of smoked meats, fish, and cheeses. Packed products such as sour cherries and pomegranate molasses, lots of pickles and borscht, farmers cheese, Russian-style yogurt and kefir, and some beans and grains.

Pacific Food Market
2147 Clement St. (22nd Ave./23rd Ave.), SF, (415) 387-6210
Another small market catering primarily to Korean customers but with many ingredients for Japanese, Chinese, and Southeast Asian cooking. In addition to kimchi, there are plenty of noodles (soba, somen, udon), grains and beans, sauces, dried seaweed, oils and vinegars, a little fresh produce (including burdock root), and a small counter with meat cut for Korean barbecue.

Richmond Produce Market
5527 Geary Blvd. (19th Ave./20th Ave.), SF, (415) 387-2515
A busy, fully-stocked market with fairly typical produce but with shelves lined with quite a few Middle Eastern products: tahini, pomegranate molasses, grape leaves, rose water. You can also find many beans, nuts, and grains, some pasta, lots of pickles and pickled vegetables, a few spices, and good lahvosh.

Seafood Center
831 Clement St. (9th Ave./10th Ave.), SF, (415) 752-3496
Probably the nicest seafood market in the neighborhood, featuring an extensive selection both in tanks and on ice. A good shellfish selection includes mussels, Manila clams, and cherrystones, octopus, live spot prawns, and conch. Prices are very reasonable, with frequent good deals on *ahi* tuna.

Sixth Avenue Cheese Shop
311 6th Ave. (Clement/Geary), SF, (415) 387-1436
Imported and domestic cheeses. A small, pleasant shop stocked with dozens of fine cheeses: Spanish Manchego, mascarpone, huntsman cheddar, St. André, Mona Lisa gouda, limburger, sardo dolce, and many varieties of Brie. A small selection of wines is available. All this complemented with a nice selection of prosciutto, pancetta, pâtés, smoked salmon, salamis, dried mushrooms (including porcini), and an excellent array of fine crackers.

T & L Market
339 Clement St. (4th Ave./5th Ave.), SF, (415) 668-2166
A small store with a good mix of Chinese and Southeast Asian ingredients. A full produce section with galangal, lemongrass, and Thai chilies, all kinds of noodles, preserved vegetables, and sauces galore for starters. Other items include lots of wonton wrappers, a well-organized spice section, dried shrimp paste, banana leaves, guanabana, palm sugar, some dried seaweed, and prepared dumplings. Those looking for a shortcut can choose from a wide array of premade curry pastes from India and Southeast Asia.

Thom's Natural Foods

5843 Geary Blvd. (22nd Ave./23rd Ave.), SF, (415) 387-6367
This longtime neighborhood fixture seems pretty dated when compared with today's upscale health-food stores. Still, amid the vitamins and cures you'll find a nice selection of organic produce (not much international, although they have burdock root and many chilies), cheese, fresh chickens, miso paste, and a huge selection of grains, beans, and seeds (including amaranth). The knowledgeable and friendly staff happily offer advice on nutrition, helping customers to choose from among the wide selection of vitamins and herb extracts; sunflower meal, soy flour, and protein powder are also in stock.

Tip Toe Inn

5423 Geary Blvd. (18th Ave./19th Ave.), SF, (415) 221-6422
A Russian deli that gives you a glimpse of what turn-of-the-century New York was like when the first wave of Eastern Europeans Jews arrived. Caviar, pelmini, piroshki, and other fresh and frozen Russian and European delicacies are available. The deli counters are filled with cured meats and luscious baked goods. Phyllo dough is stocked in the freezer case.

Tokyo-Ya

554 Clement St. (7th Ave.), SF, (415) 379-9088
Although it's just a small store, it's the only shop in the Clement District with a complete selection of Japanese products. No fresh produce or fish, but lots of tofu, miso, noodles, dried seaweed, pickled vegetables, and spices and packaged products. Prices are also a little lower than in Japantown.

Trader Joe's

3 Masonic Ave. (Geary), SF, (415) 346-9964
See SoMa listing.

Wing Hing Seafood

2222 Clement St. (23rd Ave./24th Ave.), SF, (415) 668-8986
An inner Richmond branch is unexceptional in an area filled with markets, but this outer Richmond Wing Hing branch is a good deal less hectic, more friendly, and cleaner. Typical of Chinatown markets, lots of fish varieties, both on ice and in tanks, a meat counter heavy on pork and organ meats, and low prices. A few vegetables at the door if you don't want to make another stop.

Sunset

The Sunset is similar to the Richmond in ethnic diversity, but the shopping is less concentrated. You can find some stores offering a good selection of ingredients useful in Chinese, Southeast Asian, Japanese, and Middle Eastern recipes. Stores are scattered throughout the area, but the greatest concentration is along Irving Street between 20th and 26th Avenues. Parking is also a little easier here than in the Richmond.

Andronico's

1200 Irving St. (Funston), SF, (415) 661-3220
With locations throughout the Bay Area, Andronico's is the Bay Area's premier up-scale grocer. There is an excellent selection of fresh seafood and meats, with many fresh sausages. The produce section is among the best for a supermarket, with some organic items and such ethnic goods as lemongrass, Chinese long beans, bok choy, and many chilies. Nearby you'll find miso, fresh wonton wrappers, and noodles (udon, yakisoba, mein). The cheese selection is also outstanding. The gourmet products are as good as you would expect in specialty stores, and the small international section boasts tahini, dried seaweed, wasabi, soba, somen, mein, and some sambals and other Asian sauces. Prices are higher than at ethnic markets, but you won't feel as disoriented.

Cheese Boutique

1298 12th Ave. (Irving), SF, (415) 566-3155
This tiny, friendly store boasts a wide selection of cheese at reasonable prices. The proprietor works to bring in what's high quality and well priced, so the selection varies from visit to visit. Look for a particularly good choice of cheeses from the Alps: Appenzeller, raclette, Gruyere. A few shelves stock such items as tomato paste, mustards, tahini, and rose water.

Irving May Wah Supermarket

2201 Irving St. (23rd St.), SF, (415) 665-4756
Lining the outside walls of this large market are bins filled with fresh, inexpensive produce, mostly Chinese. Inside, once you get past the overpowering smell of dried fish products, you'll find a complete grocer with meat, poultry, and fish counters. The Chinese section is excellent, stocked well with various rice and wheat noodles, sauces, and spices. Various sambals and chili sauces are readily available and the selection of Indonesian, Thai and Malaysian canned goods and bottled products is outstanding. Refrigerator cases hold tofu, lemongrass, galangal, and lots of noodles and wrappers. Hard-to-find blachan, palm sugar, kecap manis, plantain leaves, pandanus leaves (screwpine), coconut vinegar, palm vinegar, and sugar cane vinegar.

Irving Seafood Market

2130 Irving St. (22nd Ave./23rd Ave.), SF, (415) 681-5000
Despite the name, this is actually two stores in one: enter through the seafood market half, with a little produce in bins out front and the usual counters and tanks of fish and shellfish inside, and then move next door to a reasonably stocked collection of packaged goods for Chinese and Southeast Asian cooking. The seafood side also has refrigerated fresh noodles and miso. The dry side has fish sauces, sambals, spices, dried and preserved vegetables, pickled ginger, and a wall of noodles (mostly Southeast Asian).

Tel Aviv Kosher Meats

2495 Irving St. (26th Ave.), SF, (415) 661-7588
The name says it all here: kosher meats, chicken, cold cuts, salads, knishes, piroshki, matzo ball soup, chopped chicken liver—in short, the works. The shelves are well stocked with kosher dry goods.

22 & Irving Market

2101 Irving St. (22nd Ave.), SF, (415) 681-5212
This warehouse-sized market has plenty of produce, although mostly general-purpose stuff (nice herbs), all at good prices. Packaged goods are an odd assortment geared to the neighborhood, with quite a bit of Middle Eastern stuff. Plenty of olive oils, fava beans, flat breads, rose water, pomegranate molasses, grape leaves, pickled vegetables, harissa, and olives. The

refrigerator case has phyllo, feta and kasseri cheeses, kimchi, and wonton wrappers.

Wah Lian Supermarket
1931 Irving St. (20th Ave./21st Ave.), SF, (415) 665-7598
Two stores under one roof. The fresh side has produce—not the best looking—meat, poultry, and seafood (nice-looking live prawns and langoustines), as well as some fresh noodles and wonton wrappers. The packaged side has all the basic Chinese sauces and some miscellaneous Japanese and Southeast Asian items: miso, nori, wakame, sambals, rice paper rounds, prepared curries.

Yum Yum Fish
2181 Irving St. (22nd Ave./23rd Ave.), SF, (415) 566-6433
A fish store geared strictly to the sushi market (at night they do a steady sushi-to-go business). In addition to the impeccably fresh sushi cuts, they have rarer cooked or frozen items (octopus, unagi, saba).

Marin

Marin's food stores reflect the county's population, with plenty of gourmet and health-foods stores but only a few ethnic stores. San Rafael is definitely the place to find markets. There is a little bit of everything there within a couple of miles of downtown.

Andronico's
100 Center Blvd. (Sir Francis Drake), San Anselmo, (415) 453-6774
See San Francisco listing.

Asian Market
5 Mary St. (3rd St./4th St.), San Rafael, (415) 459-7133
Probably the most complete source of Asian ingredients in Marin, with a broad definition of Asian that includes Chinese, Japanese, Southeast Asian, and even some Indian and Middle Eastern goods. Japanese ingredients feature dried bonito flakes, mirin, dried seaweed, sansho pepper, fish cake, and sushi fish on Saturday. Southeast Asian supplies include the more esoteric, such as frozen kaffir lime leaves, fresh Thai basil and chilies, candlenuts, fresh and dried galangal and lemongrass, shrimp paste, and palm sugar, which share space with Indian ghee, curry leaves, and pickles. The noodle selection is adequate, with a good mix of fresh and dried kinds. Fresh Thai eggplants, bitter melons, and a variety of beans and greens are stocked. The freezer case is filled with many kinds of fish, banana leaves, and prepared dumplings. Helpful, friendly service.

Azteca Market
Harbor Center, 555 East Francisco Blvd. (Grand), San Rafael, (415) 459-0669
802 4th St. (Lincoln), San Rafael, (415) 457-2518
A friendly pair of Latin American markets with small produce sections, full pastry cases, and large meat counters. Packaged goods include the usual Mexican spices, sauces, and dried chilies, plus a few South American items: canned ullucos and rocotos, dried ají amarillo and ají panca peppers, palillo, and lots of grains. You'll also find frozen banana leaves, mamey, and rocotos. The 4th Street venue has more South American goods, the Francisco Boulevard one has better produce.

Casa Lucia Market
2240B 4th St. (Hilldale/Forbes), San Rafael, (415) 457-8755
A small, primarily Salvadorean market. Fresh produce like guavas and ripe plantains, a standard array of packaged goods supplemented by cane vinegar and coconut milk, and frozen mamey and rocotos. Unusual ingredients include palillo, ullucos, some Central American sauces, and tasajo (cured meat) from Brazil.

The Cheese Shop
38 Miller Ave. (behind Jennie Low's Chinese Cuisine), Mill Valley, (415) 383-7272
A small store with a large cheese selection, as well as such accompaniments as bread, crackers, and wine.

Cost Plus
2040 Redwood Hwy. (Tamalpais/William), Larkspur, (415) 924-7743
See San Francisco listing.

Dandy Market
100 El Prado Ave. (Merrydale), San Rafael, (415) 479-9111
Outside it looks like a typical country mini mart; inside, however, you'll find many Middle Eastern staples. They have an extensive spice selection, with sumac and zahtar among others. There are plenty of nuts, grains, and beans, plus pomegranate molasses, fragrant waters, and a good selection of flat breads. The small produce section has okra, cucumbers, and eggplants.

David's Finest Produce
341 Corte Madera Town Center (Tamalpais Dr. at Madera Blvd.), Corte Madera, (415) 927-2431
A produce stand with beautiful, if not overly international, produce, and a few gourmet and Mexican items (a taqueria is attached). Nonstandard items include lemongrass, prickly pear cactus, Chinese broccoli, and some nice chilies.

Farmers' Markets
Downtown San Rafael: 4th St. between Lootens and B sts., (415) 457-2266. Th 6-9pm April-October. Features live entertainment, from musicians to clowns.
Marin Civic Center: Civic Center Dr. off Hwy 101, (415) 456-3276. One of the Bay Area's most celebrated farmers' markets. Th 8am-1pm, Su 8am-1pm year-round.
Novato: Sherman Ave. between Grant and De Long aves., (415) 456-3276. Tu 4-8pm May-October.
The Village at Corte Madera: Paradise Dr. and Hwy 101, in the courtyard, (415) 456-3276. W 2pm-7pm May-October.

Hatam
821 B St. (2nd St./3rd St.), San Rafael, (415) 454-8888
A small produce selection of cucumbers, tomatoes, and onions, but the dried goods section is good with sumac, pomegranate

molasses, basmati rice, lentils, ghee, and lahvosh. Formerly located on Third Street in San Rafael, as of winter 1998, Hatam was occupying temporary quarters on B Street while working to move into permanent quarters at 821 B Street. You may want to call to verify the exact address before you go; plans were to keep the same phone number.

Oasis Natural Foods
2021 Novato Blvd. (Regalia), Novato, (415) 897-4706
Hidden behind the vitamins and herbal remedies is a basic selection of natural foods. The spice section includes garam masala and asafetida; the grains and dried beans and lentils section is also decent and includes quinoa. The standard health-foods store items are stocked: miso, dried seaweed, soba, somen, a few Asian sauces.

Oriental Food Connection
650 Irwin St. (Francisco Blvd. West), San Rafael, (415) 453-7509
A decent-sized market with an emphasis on Vietnamese goods. A nice produce section carries lots of greens, fresh galangal, lemongrass, bitter melon, banana buds, and green mangoes. The small meat-and-fish department has live crabs and lobsters and cheap shrimp. There is more seafood frozen. Basic Chinese and Vietnamese sauces, sambals, Siracha chili sauce, lots of dried noodles (plus a few fresh) and preserved vegetables, some spices, and a few curry mixes line the shelves. Japanese basics include dashi concoctions, wasabi, and dried seaweed.

Real Food Company
200 Caledonia St. (Turney), Sausalito, (415) 332-9640
See San Francisco listings.

Trader Joe's
337 3rd St. (Grand/Mary), San Rafael (415) 454-9530
See San Francisco listings.

Ultra Lucca Delicatessen
107 Corte Madera Town Center (Tamalpais Dr. at Madera Blvd.), Corte Madera, (415) 927-4347
The Marin branch of the Berkeley-based chain of gourmet Italian delis. The specialty is pasta, and they have a wide array of pricy fresh and dried varieties, as well as loads of delicious sauces for when you're not up to cooking. The large deli case has plenty of prepared foods and cured meats, plus a small but nice selection of cheeses. A few oils, vinegars, mustards, tomato sauces, and the like round out the merchandise offerings.

Wailey Trading & Market
2240 4th St. (Hilldale/Forbes), San Rafael, (415) 456-2530
A small, pan-Asian market with a useful mix of ingredients. The bulk of the selection is Chinese and Vietnamese, with sauces, dried spices, sausages, and preserved vegetables. One of the few places in the county with dried tangerine peel on the shelf. Southeast Asian sambals, kecap manis, tamarind paste, and prepared curries and Japanese dried bonito flakes, shichimi, and nori and wakame seaweeds are all available, and a good variety of dried noodles and wrappers are part of the picture.

Whole Foods
414 Miller Ave. (Evergreen), Mill Valley, (415) 381-1200
See San Francisco listing.

Wild Oats Community Market
222 Greenfield Ave. (Red Hill), San Anselmo, (415) 258-0660
This location arguably has the best produce and meat departments of any Wild Oats in the Bay Area. Not much in the way of International items, per se, but the health food angle provides plenty of bulk grains and beans, tofu, tempe, gourmet oils, polenta, seaweed, soba, udon, pickled ginger, wasabi, and a surprising amount of miso. Other attractions include a decent produce selection and some Indian and Southeast Asian spice packs.

Woodlands Market
735 College Ave. (Stadium/Sir Francis Drake), Kentfield, (415) 457-8160
A friendly, upscale grocer with gorgeous meat, fish, and poultry and attractive local produce, some organic. Not much in the way of international fresh greens and the like, but plenty of fresh herbs and chilies are on display. The selection of bulk grains and nuts is pretty good, and a small international section with some Mexican sauces and gourmet salsas, some Asian goods (hoisin, mirin, dried seaweed, pickled ginger, soba, somen) and curry mixes is good for the basics. The deli is large, with many cheeses, cured meats, and prepared entrees; a sushi-to-go section keep raw fish lovers happy.

East Bay

Thanks to Chez Panisse, Berkeley has established itself as a gourmet paradise, and with such places as Rockridge market and Andronico's, the town lives up to its reputation. But for this cookbook, it is the East Bay's ethnic diversity that is so wonderful.

In Berkeley, the intersection of University and San Pablo avenues is home to great Indian, Middle Eastern, and Latin American stores. Downtown Oakland boasts a vibrant Chinatown with many markets, which, because they cater to a large Vietnamese population, carry many Southeast Asian goods. Downtown Oakland is also home to G.B. Ratto, one of the best stores around for a diverse collection of spices, cheeses, nuts, grains, and pastas. Heading south through Oakland, San Leandro, Union City, and Fremont, you'll find stores for everybody (and for every section of this book).

Andronico's
1550 Shattuck Ave. (Cedar), Berkeley, (510) 841-7942
2655 Telegraph Ave. (Stuart), Berkeley, (510) 845-1062
1414 University Ave. (California), Berkeley, (510) 548-7061
1850 Solano Ave. (Colusa), Berkeley, (510) 524-1673
See San Francisco listing.

Bazaar of India

1810 University Ave. (Grant), Berkeley, (510) 548-4110
Although small, this is a complete Indian grocer. All the unusual spices are carried, as are various flours, dals, and chutneys. The store also has a selection of Indian goods such as textiles.

Berkeley Bowl

2777 Shattuck Ave. (Ward), Berkeley; meat dept. (510) 841-6346, produce dept. (510) 843-6929, seafood dept. (510) 548-7008.
Berkeley Bowl is crowded and barnlike, housed in a former bowling alley. Despite its pedestrian appearance, it offers an incredible array of exotic produce: purple-spotted dragon-tongue beans, Japanese leeks, lemongrass, galangal, turmeric root, nopales, Thai eggplants, and an inconceivable array of mushrooms and chilies. The fresh herb selection is equally impressive. Bulk foods include dried seaweeds, ample nuts, lentils, pastas, and grains (quinoa included). Fresh seafood features sushi grade ahi and roes. Meats, wines, coffees, cheeses, and packaged Asian foods—especially Japanese—are also specialties. The small spice selection includes Sichuan peppercorns. The overall quality is high and prices are reasonable.

Bombay Spice House

1036 University Ave. (9th St.), Berkeley, (510) 848-1671
A bright, friendly, Indian grocery store with a complete selection. All the basic ingredients fill the well-organized shelves—ajowan to tamarind—with spices, grains, flours, and curry mixes, and a refrigerator unit holds paneer cheese and nan bread. Fresh produce includes chilies, turmeric, jackfruits, and Indian beans.

Chao Thai Market

2445 San Pablo Ave. (Channing), Berkeley, (510) 486-0515
For those who would love to cook Thai food at home, Chao Thai is a gift from the gods. This Berkeley market carries fresh galangal, fresh kaffir lime leaves, kapi (the Thai version of Malaysian blachan), lemongrass, palm sugar paste, ginger, pandanus leaves, and fish sauces. There are numerous canned and bottle products.

Cheese Board

1504 Shattuck Ave. (Vine), Berkeley, (510) 549-3183
A decent cheese shop with all the basics and a number of rarer cheeses, including mascarpone and manchego. A great selection of cheddars from England, New York, and Wisconsin.

Cheung Kong Market

325 10th St. (Webster/Harrison), Oakland, (510) 839-8478
A small but full market with a good selection of produce—lots of chilies and lemongrass—fresh seafood, and a full meat department. They also have one of the better assortments of frozen seafood. A pretty good variety of Chinese and Southeast Asian sauces, with preserved vegetables galore, tamarind, Sichuan peppercorns, dried galangal, and many noodles.

Cho Lon Moi

378 8th St. (Franklin/Webster), Oakland, (510) 451-5808
Similar to next-door neighbor, Sam Yick, but on a smaller scale. Also has a meat counter and more fresh noodles and dried seaweed.

Cost Plus

201 Clay St. (Embarcadero/2nd), Oakland, (510) 834-4440
1301 S. California Blvd. (Botello), Walnut Creek, (510) 256-4077
1975 Diamond Blvd. (Willow Pass), Concord, (510) 827-1100
39177 Farwell Dr. (Mowry), Fremont, (510) 794-9959
5564 Springdale Ave. (Stoneridge), Pleasanton, (510) 460-0606
See San Francisco listing.

Country Cheese

2101 San Pablo Ave. (Addison), Berkeley, (510) 841-0752
Country Cheese has stores in Berkeley and San Francisco. They carry about 60 different domestic and imported cheeses, including such highlights as mascarpone, manchego, and various fetas, including Bulgarian, Greek, and French. They also stock Mexican queso fresco and cotija. In addition to the nice array of cheeses, Country Cheese carries a number of grains, nuts, dried beans, lentils, and spices, all in bulk.

Eastern Market

1106 Meadow Ln. (Monument), Concord, (510) 676-7844
Owned by a very pleasant fellow from Afghanistan, this market focuses on goods from Iran, Afghanistan, Pakistan, and northern India. There is a full butcher featuring beef, chicken, lamb, and goat, all halal. The produce section is small and carries seasonal produce, Iranian and Afghan breads and various rices are stocked, and the spice collection includes three types of cumin, saffron, safflower, ajowan, amchur, sumac, and coriander. Ghee, mustard oil, olive oil, sour cherry syrup, and pomegranate seeds fill the shelves. The owner provides recipes to boot.

Erawan Market

1463 University Ave. (California), Berkeley, (510) 849-9707
A tiny store with almost all the specialty ingredients you'll need for Thai, Southeast Asian, and Chinese cooking. In addition to standard packaged goods—noodles, dried galangal, bamboo shoots, coconut milk—you'll find candlenuts, frozen and dried kaffir lime leaves, tamarind and shrimp pastes, preserved vegetables, and fresh lemongrass, galangal, turmeric, Thai chilies, and eggplants.

European Deli & Middle East Grocer

1500 Monument Blvd., #F13 (I-680/Oak Grove), Concord, (510) 689-1011
This small store is packed with Middle Eastern goods. Highlights include sumac, sour cherry syrup, pomegranate molasses, and various breads. There is a good selection of nuts, Bulgarian and French feta are available, and a few Indian products are carried, including various chutneys, pickles, and teas. Among the spices, amchur, asafetida, and various cumins are stocked. But the true treasures are the occasional shipments of small Persian cucumbers and melons (kharbozeh).

Farmer Joe's Marketplace

3501 MacArthur Blvd. (35th St.), Oakland, (510) 482-8178
This small grocery store has an eclectic mix of health foods, gourmet items, and ethnic offerings. The large produce section has some organic choices, lemongrass, Chinese greens, lots of chilies, and bitter melons. One corner has Mexican dried herbs and spices. One aisle has Asian sauces, sambals, spices, preserved vegetables, and salted black beans; another has many

kinds of Japanese noodles and dried seaweed. The store also has some fresh meat, fish, and poultry, gourmet cheeses, bulk nuts and grains, and fresh Asian noodles and wraps—both Chinese and Southeast Asian.

Farmers' Markets
Hosted by the Ecology Center, Berkeley, (510) 548-3333 Tuesday market: Derby St. between Martin Luther King Jr. Way and Milvia St.; summer 2pm-7pm, winter 1pm-dusk. Saturday market: Center St. between Martin Luther King Jr. Way and Milvia St., behind City Hall; year-round 10am-2pm. Thursday market: University Ave. at 4th St., May-Nov. only.

For the freshest produce and best selection of organic fruits and vegetables, visit one of Berkeley's farmers' markets. California farmers from as far away as Santa Cruz and the Central Valley bring seasonal produce, honey, herbs, and flowers to the open-air stalls.

Fiji India Market
3996 Horner St. (Union City Blvd.), Union City, (510) 441-1755 This small store caters to Fiji Islanders, particularly Indian transplants. The selection of spices and packaged goods is small, but includes nigella, asafetida, mustard oil, ghee, tamarind, and fresh Thai chilies. A butcher cuts lamb and goat to order. Frozen fish also available.

The Food Mill
3033 MacArthur Blvd. (Coolidge/35th), Oakland (510) 482-3848 A fairly standard collection of health foods, including some organic produce, dried seaweed, some Asian sauces and noodles, and a large variety of bulk grains and nuts.

Fourth Street Market Plaza
1784-8 4th St. (Virginia/Hearst), Berkeley, (510) 528-9800 Set up like Rockridge Market Hall, only smaller, this little group of gourmet markets on a walkway off Fourth Street includes a cheese shop with a huge selection, including many varieties from Spain; gourmet items like fresh pasta, olives, olive oil, vinegars, and mustards; and an unpredictable mix of such ethnic ingredients as pickled ginger, somen, soba, udon, pomegranate molasses, sambals, shrimp paste, harissa, and couscous—albeit at prices higher than the ethnic stores. The small produce store offers mostly traditional ingredients and some grains and beans.

G. B. Ratto & Company
821 Washington St. (9th St.), Oakland, (510) 832-6503 One of the treasures in Bay Area cooking, G. B. Ratto has just about everything produced under the sun. The selection of spices is the most complete in the Bay Area. There is a strong Middle Eastern, Latin American, and Indian emphasis. Zahtar, sumac, pomegranate molasses, couscous, cardamom, asafetida, ghee, chutneys, pickles, Sichuan peppercorns, black cumin, capers, and quinoa are all stocked. This is one of the few places in the United States that sells frik, the Egyptian green wheat. Bulgur and tabbouleh are also available. Italian and Spanish saffron are carried at some of the best prices around. The selection of olive oil is outstanding, with varieties from Greece, Italy, France, Spain and Portugal. The vinegar choices are extensive as well. The cheese section is well stocked with mascarpone, parmigiano-reggiano, fetas, Monterey jacks, and provolones.

Various excellent sausages and cold meats are also available. The array of dried beans and lentils is impressive. A helpful, friendly staff makes shopping a pleasure.

Good Luck Supermarket
259 10th St. (Alice/Harrison), Oakland, (510) 208-1944 Good Luck is what you'd get if you took a small Chinatown grocery store and expanded it to the size of a supermarket. The large produce section includes all the basic Chinese beans and greens, lotus root, lemongrass, Thai basil, galangal, and many chili varieties. In the back you'll find a full meat, fish, and poultry section (fish is more on ice than in tanks), and the shelves have a nice mix of Chinese, Japanese, and Southeast Asian products. Basics like bean pastes, misos, noodles, and wrappers, and a few hard-to-find items like blachan, pickled mangoes, and coconut vinegar. Another bonus: a parking lot.

Guru Place
5146 Mowry Ave. (Farwell), Fremont, (510) 791-7410 A small, friendly Indian general store with nigella, asafetida, amchur, ghee, mustard oil, basmati rice, tamarind, rose water, and several dal varieties are stocked. There's also as much chapati flour as you could ever want and plenty of music and clothing.

Housewives' Market
818 Jefferson St. (8th St.), Oakland, (510) 444-8784 Despite the outdated name, this might be called downtown Oakland's answer to Rockridge Market, with a few separate markets under one roof. Moura's Fish Market has a good selection of fish, albeit with a Southern orientation: catfish, buffalo fish, gar, and crawfish galore. Taylor's Sausage and Meat Market lives up to its name, especially the meat half, with a wide selection of cuts, complete with many parts (pigs' tails, hooves, and the like), and a small selection of African spices and goods. Cervantes Produce has a basic supply of produce with many yams, greens, chilies, and plantains. Allan's Ham and Bacon also lives up to its name, with many smoked meats from ham hocks to slab bacon. They also sell Southern and African spices, lentils, and sausages. The dry goods store is big on Southern staples like canned corn and black-eyed peas.

Indus Food Center
1964 San Pablo Ave. (University), Berkeley, (510) 549-3663 Self-described purveyor of "Indo-Pak & Middle Eastern Groceries." In addition to a small but complete selection of grains, lentils, nuts, and canned and bottled goods, you'll find asafetida, ajowan, amchur, sumac, and a butcher counter stocked with goat.

International Market
31840 Alvarado Blvd. (Fair Ranch), Union City, (510) 429-8739 A giant supermarket catering to a mostly pan-Asian audience: Chinese, Japanese, Korean, Vietnamese, even Philippine and Mexican. The store is organized more like a Safeway than most ethnic stores, with orderly shelves, a whole aisle of noodles and wrappers (fresh and dried), all kinds of preserved vegetables, spices, and sauces. Other highlights include pickled ginger, kimchi, dried seaweed (nori, wakame, kombu), dried galangal, tamarind, coconut vinegar, hot sauces in abundance,

miso, meat substitutes, and cheap coconut milk. One aisle has Mexican spices, chilies, and sauces such as adobo and mole. The freezer section is filled with prepared dumplings, fish, cassava, and banana leaves. Produce is abundant, with many chilies, tamarind pods, plantains, bitter melon, lemongrass, and every type of leafy green and herb grown. There is also a full meat, fish, and poultry department with goat, octopus, and lobster.

J. Wiggins
6309 College Ave. (Claremont/Alcatraz), Oakland, (510) 652-4171
This tiny cheese shop features a good range of high-quality cheeses, with such rarer types as Appenzeller and tomme de Savoie. Other offerings include cured meats, oils and vinegars, breads, and crackers, plus fresh pasta, hummus, salads, mustards, and more.

Khanh Phong Supermarket
429 9th St. (Franklin/Broadway), Oakland, (510) 839-9094
Next door to and similar to the New Saigon Market, with similar offerings. Produce includes lemongrass, chilies, galangal, and turmeric. In addition to a complete array of packaged goods, Khanh Phong also has a meat-and-poultry department and some fresh and frozen fish.

Khyber International
114 Center Square, 37070 Fremont Blvd. (Thornton), Fremont, (510) 795-9549
This small Middle Eastern store has all the basics for putting together a feast: grape leaves, rose water, pomegranate molasses, and tahini. In the back, nicely arranged bins are filled with lentils, beans, and grains. The refrigerator has kasseri and feta cheeses, while spices include sumac, dried mint, and more. Audio tapes and cookware round out the selection.

Kyo-Po Market
2370 Telegraph Ave. (24th Ave.), Oakland, (510) 986-1234 or (510) 832-3731
A giant modern Asian supermarket geared mostly to Korean customers. Full bakery, meat, and produce sections are on the premises. Look for Japanese cucumbers and Korean chilies. One of the best noodle sections around, with both fresh and dried choices. All the standard packaged products, and nice cookware and gas burners for tabletop cooking. Although it's in a grim block, the parking lot is filled with Volvos and Lexuses.

Magat's Asian Groceries
31873 Alvarado Blvd. (Dyers), Union City, (510) 487-1900
The Union City branch is small and caters primarily to Filipinos. Produce includes banana buds, some Asian greens, and bitter melons. The fish selection is reasonable with South Pacific species well represented. The shelves stock a small mix of Asian prepared sauces and snacks. The sister store next door sells meat and poultry.

Magnani's Poultry
6317 College Ave. (Alcatraz/Claremont), Oakland, (510) 428-9496
1586 Hopkins St. (N. Capitol), Berkeley, (510) 528-6370
Sure they sell plain chickens and turkeys, but they also sell harder-to-find hens, capons, ducks, quail, squabs, poussins,

and rabbits. If you don't feel like cooking, they do a good business in barbecued chicken, deli salads, bread, and gourmet garnishes.

Mangal's Market
14014 E. 14th St. (140th), San Leandro, (510) 352-3337
This warehouse-type store specializes in goods of the Pacific Islands, which include many Indian ingredients and a few Asian: tamarind, asafetida, rice, dals, grains, curry pastes, rose water, papadams, ghee, coconut milk, garam masala, Fiji masala, canned mutton, and fish sauce. Freezer cases in the back are filled with frozen fish, goat, lamb, and sausages. Mangal's doubles as a meat wholesaler and distributor, doing a large business in goat and lamb.

Mediterranean Bazaar
924 San Pablo Ave. (Solano), Albany, (510) 524-5663
A basic store filled with Middle Eastern staples: sumac, pomegranate molasses, rose water, zahtar, tahini, ghee, olives and olive oil, tamarind, sour cherries, and garam masala. Other ingredients include many beans, grains, and lentils, kasseri and feta cheeses, phyllo dough, and yogurt.

Mi Tierra Foods
2056 San Pablo Ave. (University), Berkeley, (510) 704-1726
Overshadowed by the neighborhood's Indian and Middle Eastern markets, this small Mexican store has a produce section with chilies, yuca, and plantains, as well as a counter with meat, poultry, and fish (a good place for flank steak or tripe). Cheeses include crema and Oaxaca. Dried goods include many chilies, corn husks for tamales, tamarind pods, and hibiscus flowers. The rest of the shelves have beans, rice, hominy, masa, spices (achiote and safflower), and canned peppers and sauces.

Middle East Market
2054 San Pablo Ave. (University), Berkeley, (510) 548-2213
A good source in the East Bay for Middle Eastern goods, including halal meats. The market stocks harissa, couscous, sumac, fragrant waters such as rose and orange blossom, pomegranate molasses, tahini, and sour cherry syrup. There are also a good selection of nuts, including almonds, pistachios, and walnuts, and various kinds of rice. Among the Indian goods carried are ghee, amchur, black cumin, garam masala, bottled chutneys, and pickles. The refrigerator section has a variety of cheeses and phyllo dough.

Milan International
990 University Ave. (9th St.), Berkeley, (510) 843-9600
Probably the best-supplied Indian food store in the Bay Area, this warehouselike room is packed with all manner of goods: giant bags of rice, a huge array of bulk spices and grains, canned and bottled chutneys and curry mixes, cookware, even fresh chilies, beans, and other produce. For Middle Eastern cooking you can find pomegranate molasses, tahini, sumac, and fava beans. Milan also handles mail orders.

Monterey Market
1550 Hopkins St. (California), Berkeley, (510) 526-6042
Simply one of the best produce markets in the area. The selection of fruits and vegetables is varied and of excellent quality:

blood oranges, passion fruits, tamarillos, guavas, Mexican papayas, pepinos, plantains, baby bok choy, and oodles of exotic mushrooms (chanterelles, shiitakes, and porcini). Monterey Market also has a nice array of fresh herbs, bulk nuts, and large bags of basmati and other rices.

New Basement Seafood Market

373-A 8th St. (Franklin/Webster), Oakland, (510) 763-8977
Down a flight of stairs you'll find a fully stocked Chinese fish market with the largest collection of tanks in town (filled with live fish and shellfish). Also the place to go for frozen alligator or armadillo.

New Saigon Supermarket

441 9th St. (Franklin/Broadway), Oakland, (510) 839-4149
Located on the edge of Chinatown, this complete market has a large produce display of Chinese greens, plantains, Thai basil, galangal, some chilies, and banana buds. One side of the store is dedicated to meats, fish, and poultry. The main shelves have all the standard Chinese sauces and spices, sambals, and tamarind. There's a wide array of noodles, fresh and dried, made from wheat, rice, and bean flours, plus spring roll and wonton wrappers.

99 Ranch Market

34444 Fremont Blvd. (Decoto/Paseo Padre),
Fremont, (510) 791-8899
31056 Genstar Rd. (San Louis Obispo/Salmon), Hayward,
(510) 487-8899
338 Barber Ln. (Alviso), Milpitas, (408) 943-6699
See Peninsula listings.

Oakland Market

401 9th St. (Franklin), Oakland, (510) 835-4919
This pan-Asian grocery store has a more modern appearance than its neighbors. The shelves have all the Chinese basics and Japanese dried seaweeds (nori, wakame), wasabi, and miso, along with Southeast Asian sambals and shrimp paste. Noodles come fresh and dried—somen, soba, mein, rice stick, bean thread—and there are rice and wheat wrappers. Other miscellaneous ingredients range from buckets of shrimp to Chinese sausage. Produce is limited but very cheap.

Oakville Grocery

1352 Locust St. (Mt. Diablo), Walnut Creek, (510) 274-7900
See Peninsula listing.

Old Oakland Farmers' Market

9th St. (Washington/Broadway), Oakland, (510) 452-3276
A small farmers' market with a mix of inexpensive Asian produce, organic products, and bakery products (great for snacking along the way). Located next to G. B. Ratto, which makes for a great combination trip. Open Fridays from 8 am-2pm.

Orient Market

337 8th St. (Franklin/Webster), Oakland, (510) 444-1220
The largest store on the block, Orient Market is split in half. One side offers decent produce and dry goods (all the Chinese basics with a good selection of Japanese seaweeds and some Southeast Asian sambals, shrimp pastes, and such). The other half has fresh fish, meat, poultry, and refrigerator and

freezer cases filled with fresh noodles, wonton wrappers, miso paste, and edamame.

Oriental Food Fair

10368 San Pablo Ave. (Stockton), El Cerrito, (510) 526-7444
A small but complete Asian grocer with goods from Japan, Korea, China, Taiwan, Thailand, Malaysia, and Indonesia. A very small selection of fresh and frozen fish and produce but lots of fresh and dried noodles, pickled vegetables, dried mushrooms and seaweed, and miso.

Pamir Food Mart

37422-37436 Fremont Blvd. (Peralta/Central), Fremont,
(510) 790-7015
The friendly Afghan owners have turned this store into a community center, perhaps owing to the steady stream of customers coming to get the delicious fresh-baked bread. The market has both Middle Eastern and Indian ingredients. Spices include sumac, ajowan, asafetida, and zahtar. Other products such as rose water, tahini, phyllo dough, mustard oil, ghee, bulk lentils and grains, fresh baklava, and cookware are also on site. An in-house butcher sells halal meats (including goat) cut to order.

Ramirez Market

37365 Fremont Blvd. (Peralta), Fremont, (510) 797-2999
This small Mexican market has a good produce section with plantains, chayotes, chilies, and cheap avocados. The dried herb, spice, and chili selection is fairly complete, as are dried goods (corn husks, rice, beans, masa, drink mixes). They also have crema, cotija and Oaxaca cheeses, canned chilies and sauces, and many household products.

Rockridge Market Hall

5655 College Ave. (Shafter), Oakland, (510) 655-7748. Pasta Shop, (510) 547-4005; Alan's Meats, (510) 547-5839; Enzo Meat and Poultry, (510) 547-5839; Rockridge Fish, (510) 654-3474; Grace Baking Shop (510) 428-2662
This urban collection of markets under one roof offers it all: pasta and cheese, baked goods, coffee and tea, wine, produce, meats, and fish. All the stores are geared toward the Williams-Sonoma gourmet crowd, with an eye to stimulating your urges to cook. The pasta shop, in addition to its namesake—both fresh and dried kinds available—offers a large selection of prepared and imported foods. Olives in bulk, sausages, smoked fish, cured meats, gourmet oils, and anchovy paste are squeezed into the refrigerator case and onto the shelves. One shelf dedicated to ethnic goods has tamarind, shrimp paste, harissa, and a few Asian sauces and noodles (all for a price). The delightful corner cheese shop is heavy on trendy Spanish cheeses and goat cheeses. The small, high-quality butcher shop carries gorgeous natural beef, free-range chickens, rabbits, and some game. The fish market is equally small but select. Produce is primarily mainstream but fresh, with a good variety of mushrooms and chilies, lemongrass, and bitter melons. Dried goods such as spices, chilies, beans, and nuts complete the store.

Sam Yick

362 8th St. (Webster/Franklin), Oakland, (510) 832-0662
This Chinatown store is packed to bursting with good stuff. The small produce section out front has all the standard

greens and beans and roots, plus many chilies, lemongrass, green papayas, and yuca. Inside has stocks of noodles, wrappers, tofu, dried mushrooms, cookware, salted black beans, seaweed, miso, fish cake, galangal, sambals, beans, flours, shrimp paste, sausage, and more. One corner is dedicated to Indonesian goods, with candlenuts, blachan, coconut vinegar, and bumbus.

San Ramon International Market & Deli

2217-F San Ramon Valley Blvd. (Danville), San Ramon, (510) 820-6611
A complete Middle Eastern market with a produce section and a deli. Among the products are pomegranate molasses, sumac, harissa, rose and orange blossom waters, feta, ghee, lahvosh, various kinds of rices, pistachios, and numerous imported olive oils.

Santos Linguisa Factory

1746 Washington Ave. (Thornton/Williams), San Leandro, (510) 351-9212
Factory being the operative word here. This hole-in-the-wall shop, located in the back of an industrial building, manufactures linguisa and morcella (Portuguese blood sausage) on premises (you can smell the wood from the smokers). They've been doing it since 1921, and the sausages are delicious and nitrite free.

Spice House Co.

29266 Union City Blvd. (Kohoutek), Union City, (510) 489-6857, (510) 489-8110
This warehouse in an industrial area is filled with large bags of basmati rice, flours, nuts, beans, dals, and snacks. You'll find all the regular spices, ghee, coconut and mustard oils, tamarind, rose water, and many curry mixes. They also stock some fresh produce—okra, ginger, Indian eggplant—and lots of cookware and clothing.

Trader Joe's

5700 Christie Ave. (Powell), Emeryville, (510) 658-8091
See San Francisco listings.

Verbrugge Meat and Fish

6321 College Ave. (Claremont/Alcatraz), Oakland, (510) 658-6854
An upscale meat market with choice cuts of meat, a decent fish selection, and poultry (competing with Magnani's next door).

Whole Foods

3000 Telegraph Ave. (Ashbury), Berkeley, (510) 649-1333
See San Francisco listings.

Wild Oats Community Market

1581 University Ave. (Sacramento), Berkeley, (510) 549-1714
Formerly Living Foods, this store was taken over by Wild Oats of Boulder, Colorado. See Marin listing.

Yasai Produce Market

6301 College Ave. (Claremont/Alcatraz), Oakland, (510) 655-4880
At the end of the gourmet strip of College is this small produce store with an Asian slant. The produce is straightforward, but lemongrass can be found, and the dried goods include nori, sambals, hoisin sauce, and fresh and dried noodles.

Yekta Market & Deli

41035 Fremont Blvd. (Washington), Fremont, (510) 440-1111 or (510) 599-0014
A nice market carrying mainly Middle Eastern goods with some Indian products. There is a small produce section that carries Persian cucumbers and melons (in season). Among the goods are sumac, pomegranate molasses, mustard oil, chutneys, pickles, frozen meats, ghee, dal, basmati rice, various olive oils, and feta cheeses. Many beans, grains, and nuts are stocked as well.

Peninsula

Although generally ignored by San Francisco's foodie elite, the Peninsula and South Bay offer an ethnically diverse scene with many markets creatively mixing international cuisines. The opening of Draeger's food palace in San Mateo is a tremendous boon to aspiring cooks. The store boasts the widest array of ingredients under one roof anywhere in the Bay Area, in a comforting supermarket setting with a helpful staff. The disadvantages to shopping here are that prices are generally higher than in the ethnic stores and you miss the excitement of exploring. To the north, Daly City has many Philippine markets, South San Francisco has markets catering to an Hispanic clientele, and San Mateo Avenue in San Bruno has a great mix of markets, including some with hard-to-find South American goods. Millbrae, Burlingame, and San Mateo all deliver a good mix of stores with Chinese, Japanese, and Middle Eastern goods. Redwood City is well known as the place on the mid-Peninsula for Latin American goods, but has other stores as well. Even white-bread Menlo Park and Palo Alto have a few gems of stores, and all the produce money can buy. Mountain View's Castro street is a great one-stop Mecca of diverse stores. The South Bay has many stores equal to task of supplying its large Persian, Indian, Chinese, Vietnamese, Japanese, and Latino populations. The South Bay is also home to 99 Ranch Market, that great southern California institution—part supermarket, part ethnic grocer, and the perfect place to get up to speed on Asian goods as well as similarly outfitted local stores.

Al Manar Market

6331 Mission St. (Hillcrest), Daly City, (650) 756-1133
This small, neat Middle Eastern market has a limited supply of basics. Cheeses include haloumi, feta, and kasseri. Pomegranate molasses, grape leaves, phyllo dough, a few spices, some beans and grains, and nice pastries round out the wares.

Aladdin Market & Deli

224 E. Hillsdale Blvd. (Saratoga Dr./Hwy 101), San Mateo, (650) 574-7288

A small Middle Eastern grocer stocked with the basics: basmati rice, sumac, couscous, pomegranate molasses, various breads. The refrigerator has many cheeses (kasseri, blanco fresco, feta). The spice selection is small, but they do have tamarind, phyllo dough, and lots of olives.

Almar Oriental

15 El Camino Real (Millbrae), Millbrae, (650) 692-5008

This small, dusty market has a good mix of products for Southeast Asian, Chinese, Japanese, and Philippine cooking. Packaged goods include wasabi, bonito flakes, cane vinegar, dried galangal, preserved vegetables, dried orange peel, Chinese sausages, sambals, bean pastes, and more. The noodle selection is extensive, with pancit, bean thread, somen, soba, and imitation egg noodles.

Attari Mini Market

582 S. Murphy Ave. (El Camino), Sunnyvale, (408) 738-3030, (408) 773-0290

A small Middle Eastern market that carries numerous hard to find ingredients including sumac, pomegranate molasses, basmati, flat breads, ghee, and fragrant waters. A limited selection of various dried beans and a nice assortment of nuts are other highlights, but the line of various teas is beyond belief. Lastly, Attari has some interesting Greek jams, as well as French and Bulgarian fetas.

Bahar Market

811 W. Hamilton Ave. (San Tomas), Campbell, (408) 378-7477

A complete Middle Eastern grocer with sumac, fragrant waters, pomegranate molasses, and sour cherry syrup stocked. Fresh Bulgarian and French fetas also carried. Rices include both basmati and jasmine. Frozen phyllo dough is available, as is a wide selection of Arab, Armenian, and Iranian breads. Some Indian products are carried, including dal, curry pastes, and a few spices. A small juice bar and small produce section are also on the premises.

Ban Do Market

503 E. 2nd Ave. (S. Claremont), San Mateo, (650) 347-2928

A small Korean store with a decent selection of goods. In addition to many noodles, Ban Do has lots of dried seaweed and mushrooms, bonito flakes, miso, udon, fish cake, and a few Asian sauces, from hoisin to sambal to mirin.

Belmar Meat Market (La Gallinita No. 2)

612 Linden Ave. (6th), S. San Francisco, (650) 871-9121

A small store with a full meat counter (poultry, shrimp, and some fish, too). Cooked carnitas and chicharrones are offered by the pound, and a little produce, some dried chilies and beans, and a few packaged goods round out the selection.

Carniceria Mi Rancho

39 North B St. (Baldwin/Tilton), San Mateo, (650) 347-7052

A full-service Latin American market with a decent produce section full of plantains, chilies, and nopales and a large meat counter with plenty of tripe and flank steak, as well as poultry and some fish. A modest selection of dried chilies, spices, cheeses, and canned and bottled sauces is offered, plus some fresh baked goods, desserts, and mesquite charcoal.

Castillo Tiene de Todo/Carniceria Tepa

249 Hillside Blvd. (Linden), S. San Francisco, (650) 742-9201, (650) 737-9881

While it looks more like a warehouse than a castle, this store does have most of what you'll need for Latin American cooking. The produce section is full, with cheap avocados, chayotes, cactus, chilies, and more. Large bins dispense bulk beans, rice, and dried chilies, and a standard selection of spices, packaged goods, and a few South American items such as ullucos and ocas are on hand. A big meat department carries every part of the cow, from skirt steak to hooves, plus pork, chicken, and shrimp are available. The household goods section is grand, and there's a taqueria on one wall.

Chapparral Super

1001 E. Santa Clara St. (21st/22nd), San Jose, (408) 998-8028

One of the most complete Latin American grocers in town, with Mexican, Central, and South American products. The meat, fish, and poultry counter is large and loaded. Produce includes all the usual goods and some gems like mamey. Packaged goods cover the basic sauces, spices, and chilies, plus a complete line of South American goods (palillo; ullucos, both canned and frozen; ají amarillo, dried and frozen; even frozen empanada wrappers). To top it off, cheap Mexican beer is available.

Chavez Supermarket

3282 Middlefield Rd. (7th St.), Menlo Park, (650) 365-6510
775 Arguello St. (Brewster/Whipple), Redwood City, (650) 367-8819

A clean, well-organized supermarket with a Latin focus. The produce section is small and carries many Latin American fruits and vegetables, including plantains, tomatillos, and nopales. The dried chilies selection is outstanding and the butcher features meat from Harris Ranch, with cuts aimed at a Mexican and Latin public. The Middlefield branch is much larger, with more produce, chilies, and spices; a bigger fish selection; and a small section with South American goods (palillo, ullucos, ají amarillo).

Cosentino's Vegetable Haven

S. Bascom Ave. and Union Ave., San Jose, (408) 377-6661
3521 Homestead Rd. (Bing), Santa Clara, (408) 243-9005

For South Bay denizens, Cosentino's is the food emporium. In addition to high-quality vegetables, Cosentino's has a great selection of bulk items and gourmet goods. There are a few ethnic items—lemongrass, lots of chilies, a few Asian greens, quinoa, couscous—and a good selection of gourmet mustards and olive oils. The meat, fish, and poultry counter features superior cuts, and many game meats, including quail, ostrich, and rattlesnake, are available.

Cost Plus

785 Serramonte Blvd. (I-280), Daly City, (415) 994-7090
68 Hillsdale Mall (El Camino/Hillsdale), San Mateo, (650) 341-7474
1910 W. El Camino Real (Magdalena), Mountain View, (650) 961-6066

See San Francisco listing.

Country Sun Natural Foods

440 California Ave. (El Camino/Ash), Palo Alto, (650) 324-9190
Natural and wholesome products are featured at this Palo Alto institution. Country Sun carried quinoa, couscous, and millet long before these grains became popular in today's health-conscious society. The produce section is small but heavily organic. Numerous organic flours, oils, and even ghee are sold. Other international items include tahini, some Asian noodles, dried seaweed, miso, and tamarind.

Danya Imports

3087 El Camino Real (Calabazas/Kiely), Santa Clara, (408) 248-5025
A basic Middle Eastern market. The selection of grains, lentils, beans, and nuts is extensive. The usual fragrant waters, tahini, pomegranate molasses, phyllo dough, and desserts are also stocked, as well as some Indian goods like ghee and dal, in an apparent effort to compete with the Indian market next door which carried Middle Eastern goods.

Dobashi Market

240 E. Jackson St. (5th/6th), San Jose, (408) 295-7794
Although primarily Japanese (it is in the heart of Japantown), this small supermarket has a slightly pan-Asian feel to it. They sell produce like burdock root, peas, cucumber, various radishes, and spinach, as well as fish—both for cooking and sashimi—poultry and meat (mostly cuts for shabu shabu and sukiyaki). Japanese staples like dried bonito flakes, sansho pepper, soba, somen, udon, wakame, pickled vegetables, and miso and Chinese sauces, sambals, saifun, 5-spice powder, and Sichuan peppercorns line the shelves.

Draeger's Supermarket

342 1st St. (Main), Los Altos (650) 948-4425
1010 University Dr. (University), Menlo Park, (650) 688-0677
222 S. 4th Ave. (B St.), San Mateo, (650) 685-3730
An upscale food emporium with a full-service butcher (game birds available), an above-average produce department, and an extensive wine section. Draeger's has a wonderful selection of European goods, including a score of olive oils, gourmet mustards, fine vinegars (several brands of balsamic, and a stupendous deli with marinated olives, cold meats, and salads. They also carry an expensive selection of fine domestic and imported cheeses. When Draeger's added its San Mateo gourmet temple, it also made a commitment to serve a multiethnic cooking audience. Among the international offerings are produce such as tamarind pods, lotus roots, lemongrass, burdock roots, nopales, and many chilies and mushrooms; bottled and packaged items such as ghee, mustard oil, rose water, pomegranate molasses, tamarind, mirin, hoisin sauces, bean pastes, kecap manis, tahini, and Thai palm sugar and bottled curry pastes; a full complement of grains and beans; and a wide range of dried seaweeds, Asian noodles, and some wonton wrappers. Most useful of all, Draeger's has a private label line of spices that includes everything from asafetida, ajowan, and panch phoran to Sichuan peppercorns and ras el hanout. The San Mateo store is the most complete, followed by Menlo Park.

Familia Felix de Casa Lucas y Casa Felix

632 San Mateo Ave. (Layne/Angus), San Bruno, (650) 794-1290
Similar to Mexicana Produce down the street, but with even more South American products, a wider range of produce, and better prices. Produce selection is varied, with young coconut, fenugreek leaves, Chinese greens, bitter melons, chayotes, and many chilies. Spices, dried chilies and beans, rice, masa, tamarind pods, dried shrimp, and frozen banana leaves are on hand, plus cheese, salt cod, and a complete range of South American goods: ají amarillo, ají panca, ullucos, papas secas.

Fiesta Latina

1424 Cary Ave. (Norfolk/Patricia), San Mateo, (650) 343-0193
A very complete Latin American produce and dry goods market. Fresh produce includes plantains, yuca, taro roots, and various fruits. A complete meat, fish, and poultry counter and a deli case packed with salt cod, serrano ham, and Latin American cheeses keep local cooks coming back. Hard-to-find items carried here include palillo, ullucos, papas criollas, guascas, and amaranth (kiwicha). Frozen fruit concentrates including tamarind, mora, mamey and guanabana are also stocked and Latin American beers, liquors, and soft drinks can also be found. The selection of dried chilies is good and includes guajillo, pasilla, ancho, and negro. Mustard oil, ghee, pancit, and coconut vinegar are also carried.

Great India Foods

1242 S. Wolfe Rd. (El Camino), Sunnyvale, (408) 720-0522
A nice Indian market with an adequate selection of lentils, grains, and rices, all the basic spices, ghees, oils, and curry mixes. The small produce selection features plantains, yuca, a few kinds of eggplants and melons, and curry leaves. They also have paneer cheese and many kinds of frozen bread (nan, chapati, etc.).

Halal Meats Deli & Grocery

1538 Saratoga-Sunnyvale Rd. (Duckett/Prospect), San Jose, (408) 865-1222
Although the highlight here is the halal butcher with good chicken, lamb, goat, and beef, there is more than meat. Packaged goods mix Indian and Middle Eastern staples. Various breads, some fresh, some frozen: pita, lahvosh, nan, and chapati. Indian spices are well labeled and feature black cumin, nigella, and asafetida. You'll also find grains and nuts, couscous and basmati rice, mustard oil, ghee, sumac, pomegranate molasses, sour cherry syrup, and tahini. The produce section is small and limited mostly to okra, tomatoes, cucumbers, cilantro, and onions.

Hankook Supermarket

1092 E. El Camino Real (Wolfe/Lawrence), Sunnyvale, (408) 244-0871
This modern Korean supermarket has an especially large seafood department, with many cuts of fish for sashimi (not well labeled in English). The aisles are filled with useful items for creating a Japanese meal: dashi, sansho pepper, all kinds of dried seaweeds, miso, fish cake, and lots of noodles. Produce is basic but features some greens, radishes, and chilies.

Hun-I-Nut Company

789 The Alameda (Sunol), San Jose, (408) 286-8202
There is one reason to go to this little deli: prebuttered phyllo dough. They make their own brand of phyllo here, self-proclaimed home of the "finest in strudel pastries." Anyone who

has worked with phyllo can tell you what an incredible time-saver it is not having to butter each layer individually. Suddenly, tiropeta are a snap. They sell their product in a few bay area stores (Whole Foods, Palo Alto) and will handle mail orders.

India Food Mill

650 E. San Bruno Ave. (San Mateo Ave./Hwy 101), San Bruno, (650) 583-6559
460 Persian Dr. #1 (Fair Oaks/Hwy 237), Sunnyvale, (408) 744-0777
A pair of small, well-organized warehouses filled with dried beans and lentils, rice, and flours. The spice selection is complete, with amchur, ajowan, black cumin, and asafetida. Plenty of bottled ghee, mustard oil, and canned mutton, along with a small produce section featuring Indian eggplants, Thai chilies, okra, and hard-to-find curry leaves. Fresh nan, too, along with some cookware.

International Food Bazaar

2052 Curtner Ave. (Union), San Jose, (408) 559-3397
5491 Snell Ave. (Blossom Hill), San Jose, (408) 365-1922
This fully stocked Mideast market has plenty of beans, lentils, rice, pickles, cheeses, and yogurts. There are also spices like sumac and zahtar, tamarind, ghee, teas galore, some cookware, frozen halal meats and sausage, and lots of prepared salads. The bread selection is extensive, and there is even a little bit of basic produce. The Curtner branch is located in a something of an Persian strip mall.

Kyo-Po Market

3379 El Camino Real (Lawrence/Nobili), Santa Clara, (408) 244-1234
See East Bay listing. This store is smaller, but in a much nicer neighborhood.

La Costeña

2078 Old Middlefield Wy. (Rengstorff), Mountain View, (650) 967-0507
Latin American products, especially Mexican and Salvadoran. They also carry Colombian papa criolla and Peruvian ullucos, as well as frozen mamey and guanabana. This is one of the few places that carries palillo and ajís amarillos. La Costeña has an excellent selection of dried chilies and Mexican herbs, including epazote, and a small produce section with fresh yuca and plantains.

La Estrellita Market & Tortilla Factory

2205 Middlefield Rd. (Hwy 84/Douglas), Redwood City, (650) 369-3877
Freshly made masa for tortillas and tamales is the highlight of this Redwood City store. There is a restaurant next door run by the same people, and the store carries a few but varied Mexican and Salvadoran products.

M & M Food Mart (aka Farm Fresh Produce & Persian Grocery)

10021 S. Blaney Ave. (Stevens Creek), Cupertino, (408) 257-3746
The name is in the process of changing to avoid confusion with the Farm Fresh Produce stores that are vegetable markets, not Persian groceries. This small, meticulously organized market has the usual pomegranate molasses, fragrant waters, and

spices. The bread section is large, as is the variety of beans and grains. Produce is limited, but includes eggplants and cukes. The deli cases have various cheeses, olives, and prepared dips (hummus, muhamarra).

Magat's Asian Groceries

1176 N. Capitol Ave. (Berryessa), San Jose, (408) 926-4412
See East Bay listing.

Maharaj Enterprises

850 Willow Rd. (Durham), Menlo Park, (650) 328-9927
Hidden in an obscure strip mall on the way to Hwy 101—look for the faded Indian movie posters in the window—Maharaj sells a small selection of Indian groceries, including all the necessary spices such as amchur, ajowan, and nigella, dal (lentils), ghee, mustard oil, and various curry mixes. They also sell frozen goat and lamb.

Mangal's Market

1620 Palm Ave. (16th Ave./Bovet), San Mateo, (650) 570-6663
See East Bay listings.

Marina Foods

2992 S. Norfolk St. (Hillsdale), San Mateo, (650) 345-6911
10122 Bandley Dr. (Stevens Creek at De Anza), Cupertino, (408) 255-2648
4140 Monterey Hwy. (Senter), San Jose, (408) 224-8786
A large supermarket—Cheerios and all—oriented toward Asian customers. A highlight is the well-labeled produce section filled with yuca, lemongrass, chilies, chives, greens, beans, nopales, and chayotes. A few aisles are dedicated to Chinese goods, with a full range of products. Sections are also given over to Japanese goods such as dashi, fish cakes, and nori; Southeast Asian products such as dried galangal, sambals, and tamarind and shrimp pastes; and Korean and Filipino items. An aisle filled with canned chilies, dried spices, and corn husks keeps Mexican cooks happy. A full meat, poultry, and fish department with many cuts of pork and many kinds of South Pacific deep-sea denizens takes up space. Watch for the great specials on coconut milk.

Mario's Fine Foods

812 Willow St. (Durham), Menlo Park, (650) 321-4902
This medium-sized independent market caters to a diverse neighborhood. Produce includes lots of chilies, young coconuts, plantains, yuca, and many yams and greens. The meat department has ham hocks and skirt steak and other Mexican cuts and some cheeses. The Mexican spice and sauce selection is pretty good, and there's even corned mutton and a small Asian section with dashi, soba noodles, and a few sauces.

Mercadito Latino

1726 El Camino Real (Hwy 84/Oak), Redwood City, (650) 306-0105
After expanding some time ago, this busy store has become quite a complete grocer. The produce section stocks plantains, nopales cactus, coconuts, and chilies. Frozen goods include fruits and fruit pastes (mamey), banana leaves, and salt cod. In addition to a full array of Mexican dried chilies, spices, and packaged goods, there are many South American products: ullucos, flours, and grains. The deli counter has such cheeses as

cotija, queso fresco, and Oaxaca, plus sausages and guava and mango pastes. To top it off, one aisle is lined with cookware.

Mexicana Produce
533 San Mateo Ave. (Angus/San Bruno Ave.), San Bruno, (650) 583-0851
This market is small but packed with Latin American goods, including some hard-to-find South American staples. The extensive produce section has plantains, yuca, good chilies, fresh herbs, chayotes, and guavas. A deli dispenses sausages and cheeses, while a bakery case is filled with pastries. You'll find a large selection of dried chilies, spices, and beans, and many useful frozen goods (cassava, papa amarilla, ají amarillo, ullucos, rocoto peppers, and empanada wrappers). The shelves of packaged goods include cane vinegar, many chili sauces, dulce de leche, palillo, ullucos, quinoa, and mesquite charcoal.

Mi Pueblo
40 S. Rengstorff Ave. (Middlefield), Mountain View, (650) 967-3630
1114 S. King Rd. (Story), San Jose, (408) 272-5370
A clean, well-organized Latin American store. The high-quality produce includes lots of fresh chilies, a few plantain varieties, and nopales and prickly pear cactus, all at good prices. The meat counter is well stocked and even has goat; they also have a good cheese selection, fresh crema, sausages, and housemade salsas. The dried chili and spice sections are extensive, and they have many South American products: canned ullucos, palillo, purple corn, dried potatoes, and beer. A nice bakery case for folks with a sweet tooth occupies some floor space, and a taco truck is parked out front.

Mid-East Market
1776 El Camino Real (Santa Lucia), San Bruno, (650) 875-7100
Small, but it covers the Mideast basics. Pomegranate molasses, tahini, grape leaves, tamarind, and some beans and lentils. Cheeses such as haloumi, kasseri, and feta. Spices are limited.

Middle East Foods
26 Washington St. (Newhall), Santa Clara, (408) 248-5112
A small store with the standard Middle East goods: some lentils, grains, and nuts, a nice variety of bulk spices, aromatic waters, pomegranate molasses, and a few cheeses.

Monterey Market
399 Stanford Shopping Center, (El Camino Real and Quarry Rd.), Palo Alto, (650) 329-1340
Simply one of the best produce markets around. The fruit and vegetable selection is varied and of excellent quality. Monterey Market also has a nice selection of fresh herbs. Among the hard-to-find produce items carried (some only in season) are blood oranges, passion fruits, tamarillos, guavas, Mexican papayas, plantains, baby bok choy, and various kinds of exotic mushrooms (chanterelles, shiitakes, and porcini). Monterey Market also sells bulk nuts and large bags of basmati and rice.

Nak's Oriental Market
1151 Chestnut St. (Santa Cruz/Oak Grove), Menlo Park, (650) 325-2046
This tiny gem of a store is packed with Japanese and other Asian products, even fresh fish for sushi on Wednesdays and Fridays (they also stock frozen saba and unagi). Fresh produce includes galangal, ginger, daikon, Asian mushrooms, lemongrass, and lotus roots. Japanese products include various kinds of miso, seaweed, fresh tofu. Numerous sambals and chilies sauces stocked. Among the esoteric Southeast Asian ingredients regularly stocked by Nak's are candlenuts, blachan, shrimp chips, galangal, and kecap manis. Japanese tableware also available.

Narayan Enterprises
2520 California St. (Showers/San Antonio), Mountain View, (650) 948-4777
Indian, Pakistani, Middle Eastern, and some Southeast Asian groceries. Fresh produce includes curry leaves, eggplant, okra, and beans. Fresh paneer is also available, and an excellent assortment of basmati and other rices. They also stock besan, tamarind, Indian spices (including nigella and ajowan), dal (lentils); Middle Eastern staples like pomegranate seeds and syrup, grape leaves, sumac, rose water, and harissa; and Southeast Asian items such as sambals, coconut milk, curry mixes, and rice sticks. They also have a nice selection of frozen breads: nan and chapati.

Narine Deli & Grocery
1138 Chula Vista Ave. (Broadway/Carmelita), Burlingame, (650) 348-9297
A small, spare shop with some basic Middle Eastern goods, including grape leaves, couscous, bulgur, basmati rice, phyllo, sumac, pomegranate molasses, harissa, and several kinds of feta.

Neelam Pacific Market
492 San Mateo Ave. (Sylvan/Angus), San Bruno, (650) 583-5024
If you can get over the confusion of having a two Neelam markets (they are run completely separately by two brothers), one in San Mateo, the other on San Mateo Avenue in San Bruno, you'll find this one is larger and caters more specifically to an Indian/Fijian/Pacific Island clientele. The food is hidden among the music and videos, cookware, and trinkets, but includes the important spices (nigella, garam masala, ajowan), ghee, beans, nuts, grains, rice, flours, pickles, and chutneys. They also sell canned mutton, dried fish, and frozen goat and lamb.

Neelam Supermarket
150 North B St. (Tilton), San Mateo, (650) 340-8208
Subtitled the Islander's Market, this Neelam offers a combination of Indian and Latin American products. Asafetida, tamarind, mustard oil, corned mutton, and frozen goat share space with plantains and bottled mole. Plenty of beans, pulses, and rice, along with frozen fish and lamb.

Neto's Brand
3499 The Alameda (Harrison), Santa Clara, (408) 296-0818
Spanish and Portuguese Sausages.

New Castro Market
340 Castro St. (California/Dana), Mountain View, (650) 962-8899
One of the better Asian markets in the area. The produce section is decent and offers many choys, long beans, chayote, and lemongrass; the chili selection, however, is limited. The highlight of the store is perhaps the fish and meat department,

which is as complete as any in the Bay Area. There is fresh fish and seafood especially for sushi, including uni (sea urchin) and hamachi (yellowtail), and tanks with live shrimp, abalone, and many clams—all at great prices. The noodle section spans an entire aisle, with selections from Taiwan, Japan, Vietnam, Thailand, and Korea. Other highlights include various chili sauces, several sambals, numerous fish sauces, and many varieties of soy sauce. Japanese goods include fish cake, many kinds of miso, udon and other fresh noodles, dried seaweeds, sansho pepper, and bonito flakes. There are also canned Asian fruits, including mangosteens and lichees, and frozen durian.

New India Bazaar

2644 Alum Rock Ave. (Capitol), San Jose, (408) 272-0202
An Indian market with a full selection of nuts, dals, beans, and rice and an aggressive approach to pricing. They also have frozen breads, fresh vegetables, and curry leaves.

99 Ranch Market

250 Skyline Plaza (Westmoor and Southgate), Daly City, (650) 992-8899
Cupertino Village, 10983 N. Wolfe Rd. (Homestead), Cupertino, (408) 343-3699
1688 Hostetter Rd. (Lundy), San Jose, (408) 436-8899
This Orange County–based chain has really nailed the assimilated Asian-American market with its modern supermarkets mixing traditional American goods with Asian specialty items. The fish department is a highlight, offering Chinatown-style low prices, variety, and live tanks in a comfortably sanitized environment. They even have some sashimi fish. Produce is another highlight, and items are well organized and well labeled in English. Goods include most every Asian green and radish desirable, nice snow peas, green papaya, chayote, lemongrass, galangal, Japanese cucumber, and a variety of chilies and melons. Packaged goods are grouped loosely by country, with Chinese preserved vegetables, dried mushrooms, and bean pastes; Japanese bonito flakes, miso, wasabi, and seaweeds; Southeast Asian sambals, cane vinegar, kecap manis, and dried galangal. They even offer on-line shopping via their web site (www.99ranch.com) and will ship most anywhere (a nice way to get those candlenuts or shrimp paste in remote areas).

Norooz Bazaar

1378 S. Bascom Ave. (Hamilton/Stokes), San Jose, (408) 295-2323
Among the various and sundry goods available at this large, well-stocked Middle Eastern market are sumac, frozen phyllo dough, and couscous. A decent produce section carries a few kinds of eggplant and cucumber. Various fresh fetas and yogurts are in the refrigerator case, and nice pastries, lots of breads (lahvosh, pita), and frozen halal meats are available.

Oakville Grocery

715 Stanford Shopping Center, (El Camino Real and Quarry Rd.), Palo Alto, (650) 328-9000
An upscale food emporium with a nice wine selection. The fine array of domestic and imported cheeses includes mascarpone, manchego, and fresh mozzarella, along with excellent breads and crackers for serving with them. Canned and bottled Indian chutneys and spice pastes, Thai coconut milk, Lebanese pomegranate molasses, and Moroccan harissa and couscous acknowledge the rest of the world, but the emphasis is on European cuisine, especially French and Italian. Well over a dozen olive oils, including Greek ones, other gourmet oils such as walnut and avocado, numerous vinegars, gourmet mustards, and exotic dried mushrooms, flours, and grains are stocked.

Oriental Market

588 San Mateo Ave. (Angus/Sylvan), San Bruno, (650) 588-8079
A small, primarily Korean market with some produce (a few chilies, roots, greens, and radishes), some frozen fish, and most packaged basics: noodles—fresh and dried—fish cake, miso, bonito flakes, dashi, and lots of dried seaweed.

Paak International Gourmet

1614 S. El Camino Real (16th Ave.), San Mateo, (650) 574-3536
Spices, dry goods, and produce needed for Middle Eastern cooking are carried in this small storefront. Pomegranate molasses, sumac, Greek feta, tahini, rose and orange blossom water, marinated olives, dal, and basmati rice are stocked.

Panaderia Hernandez No. 2

401 Grand Ave. (Maple), S. San Francisco, (650) 588-9738
In addition to the large selection of Mexican baked goods (panaderia means bakery), this store has a small, tropically oriented produce section with plantains (including ripe ones), sugarcane, coconuts, Mexican limes, and lots of chilies. The packaged goods include the basic sauces and chilies, as well as many Latin American hot sauces, coffees, and cocoa mixes. The dried chili and spice selection is decent, the deli has chorizo and some cheeses (cotija, crema), and the beer choices feature obscure South American brands like Aguila, Paceña, and Imperial.

Persian Center Bazaar aka Bazaar Iran

398 Saratoga Ave. (Kiely), San Jose, (408) 241-3700
In addition to using two names (the sign says Persian Center Bazaar, the phone book Bazaar Iran), this sprawling store has all the Middle Eastern basics—sumac, tahini, pomegranate molasses—lots of pickles, some cookware, a good variety of flat breads, and cheese and yogurt. Produce is limited to a few cucumbers, tomatoes, and pomegranates.

Philippine Grocery

92 Hill St. (Washington), Daly City, (415) 991-2043
This warehouselike Philippine grocer has a diverse mix of produce, including Chinese greens, plantains, yuca, chilies, and chayote. Noodles include pancit, fresh udon, and mein. There is a full meat, poultry, and fish counter with nice sausages like chorizo. A fairly standard selection of bottled and packaged sauces and goods is on the shelves.

Race Street Fish & Poultry

253 Race St. (Park/W. San Carlos) San Jose, (408) 294-4857
An excellent fish and poultry market, Race Street carries crab, crawfish, shrimp and prawns, squid, octopus, oysters, mussels, live lobsters, chicken, duck, and rabbit. They'll handle special orders for game meats such as pheasant and quail. The attached fast-food restaurant does a booming business in fried and grilled fish.

Ratna Palace

2630 Broadway (Arguello), Redwood City, (650) 365-1832
Indian, Pakistani, and Fijian groceries. A great source in the mid-Peninsula area for ghee, Indian spices, basmati rice, and dals.

Rose International

1060 Castro St. (El Camino), Mountain View, (650) 960-1900
A wide array of Middle Eastern, Balkan, and Indian goods. Rose carries nigella, pomegranate molasses, sumac, harissa, rose and orange blossom waters, and other offbeat items, as well as more common goods such as ghee, various kinds of rices, pistachios, walnuts, and numerous imported olive oils. A butcher and a produce section are on the premises, and various Middle Eastern and Armenian breads are stocked. A deli counter has many cheeses, olives, and prepared salads and entrees. Outdoor grills are fired up for cooking kebabs, and patio furniture offers a place to sit and enjoy your snack hot off the coals.

Santo Market

245 E. Taylor St. (6th), San Jose, (408) 295-5406
Located on the edge of Japantown, this market is similar to Dobashi Market: all the Japanese basics, some fish and meat, and a nice produce section.

Schaub's

The Street Market, Stanford Shopping Center, (El Camino Real and Quarry Rd.), Palo Alto, (650) 325-6328
A complete butcher shop with a great variety of fresh meats, poultry, and fish. Schaub's has wonderful store-made sausages and offers a number of marinated meats. Duck and rabbit are always on hand, while game meats such as pheasant, venison, and quail can be special ordered.

Senter Foods

933 E. Duane Ave. (Lawrence/Fair Oaks), Sunnyvale, (408) 735-7277
2889 Senter Rd. (Lewis), San Jose, (408) 227-8771
A large pan-Asian supermarket, complete with a full meat, fish, and poultry department and Cheerios and Jell-O. Sauces run from hoisin to fish to sambals, with preserved vegetables, dried mushrooms, and regional sections for Philippine and Japanese goods. Fresh produce includes lots of plantains, lemongrass, galangal, Thai eggplants, tamarind pods, banana buds, bitter melons, and many kinds of basil and greens.

Sigona's Farmer Market

2345 Middlefield Rd. (Hwy 84/Douglas), Redwood City, (650) 368-6993
A wonderful produce market with a wide variety of fruits and vegetables, including cherimoya, carambola, lots of chilies, nopales, lemongrass, chayote, pea sprouts, and papayas and mangoes of all stripes. Sigona's boasts a complete selection of grains, dried beans and legumes, nuts, dried fruits and flours in bins. Some products are organic.

Silva Sausage Co.

1266 E. Julian St. (26th/Hwy 101), San Jose, (408) 293-5437
All things Portuguese: Portuguese sausages, cheeses, sweet bread, salt cod, wine, even beer. The sausage selection is more international, and includes chorizo, Italian, Polish, and Cajun varieties, among others.

South Seas Market

612 San Mateo Ave. (Angus/Sylvan), San Bruno, (650) 873-2813
This little market has one of the most eclectic mixes of goods you'll find anywhere. Their card says they carry "Polynesian, West Indian, British, Irish, and African" specialties. And you'll find tamarind, frozen lamb and cassava, ghee, dried beans, and ajowan. You'll also find Jamaican hot sauces, Boddington and Dragon beers (and ginger beer), Vegemite, British jams, malt vinegar, and cocoa beans.

Spark Supermarket

175 W. 25th Ave. (El Camino/Hacienda), San Mateo, (650) 571-8620
A modern little supermarket for Japanese foods. The small sushi fish selection is reasonably priced, as is the meat cut for sukiyaki. Produce includes daikon, burdock root, and assorted chilies, greens, and mushrooms. Of course, you'll find miso, soba, somen, udon, and ramen, as well as fish cake, pickled vegetables, dried seaweeds and beans, and tea and sake. They do have soup stocks such as dashi-no-moto, but don't always have plain bonito flakes. A small kitchen in the back sells simple meals—udon, ramen, donburi, and sushi. The store functions as a Japanese community center; in addition to renting videos, they circulate a flyer showing other businesses of interest to the mid-Peninsula Japanese community (Draeger's description translates to "high-class market").

Spiceland Indian Groceries & Videos

1591 Pomeroy Ave. (El Camino), Santa Clara, (408) 554-1378
Another in the small-warehouse variety of Indian markets, with an extensive selection of lentils, rices, flours, and grains in addition to the normal spices and staples: ajowan, asafetida, ghee, mustard oil, tamarind. The freezer case is stocked with ice cream and breads. Fresh produce includes curry leaves, beans, chilies, and eggplants.

Stevens Deli & Liquor

260 Broadway (La Cruz/Millbrae Ave.), Millbrae, (650) 692-7027
As much a corner liquor store as anything, but it does stock some Middle Eastern basics: pomegranate molasses, rose water, tamarind, tahini, and a few beans, grains, and spices. Falafel sandwiches for those who don't want to cook their own.

Super Mercado Mexico

1098 Park Ave. (Race), San Jose, (408) 297-5659
204 Willow St. (Almaden), San Jose, (408) 278-9380
400 S. King Rd. (Virginia), San Jose, (408) 937-3800
860 S. White Rd. (Story), San Jose, (408) 259-8430
This Mexican market features an above-average meat counter, with nice cuts, cheap shrimp, and even goat. Shelves are compact but well-stocked with basics. Produce is basic but nice, with chayote, nopales, and a few chilies.

Suruki Japanese Foods

71 E. 4th Ave. (San Mateo Dr.), San Mateo, (650) 347-5288
A fairly large, well-equipped Japanese supermarket with a large produce section, a full meat and fish department (with sushi fish), a good little restaurant in a corner (Sozai Corner), and many premade salads. The packaged goods selection is complete, with dried bonito flakes, dried seaweeds, and an extensive noodle collection. In addition to soy, rice vinegar, and

sake, they have some Chinese sauces. Cookware and utensils and plenty of beverages are also on hand.

Taj Mahal Imports

3085 El Camino Real (Calabazas/Kiely), Santa Clara, (408) 247-4507

Although the name implies strictly Indian goods, Taj Mahal offers "Indo/Pak/Mid Eastern" groceries, creating some competition with Danya, the Middle Eastern store next door. Goods include all the Indian spices you'll need, a good selection of dals, rices, and flours and ghee. They also sell tahini, fava beans, halal meats, and a few other Mideast staples.

Takahashi Market

221 S. Claremont St. (3rd/4th), San Mateo, (650) 343-0394

A complete Japanese-Hawaiian market with fresh fish and all the necessary items for sushi. You can special order fresh hamachi and uni. Frozen unagi and saba are carried. Dried seaweeds, dried bonito flakes, mirin, wasabi, rices, vinegars, and tamari are on the shelves. A selection of prepared Hawaiian foods (poi, lau-lau) is carried, and a big section of popular Chinese items—hoisin sauce, plum sauces, fermented black beans, and chili oils—are here for those who favor the foods farther east. Among Southeast Asian goods are fish sauce, dried lemongrass, laos powder, coconut milk, and dried galangal roots. A small selection of Japanese tableware is stocked as well.

Takemura Market (aka Japanese Foods)

1360 Broadway (Capuchino), Burlingame, (650) 344-5004

A small store with most of the basics for Japanese cookery, a tiny produce section, a small selection of packaged fish (for cooking and sushi) and beef sliced for sukiyaki. Other offerings include fish cake, gyoza wrappers, bonito flakes, dried seaweeds, mushrooms, soba, and somen, and vacuum-packed udon and yakisoba.

Thien Thanh Supermarket

455 Keyes St. (10th St.), San Jose, (408) 295-1043

Your standard Vietnamese market with a large produce section and a good variety of dried goods. Produce features chayote, galangal, lemongrass, banana buds, and many kinds of chilies, greens, eggplants, and basil. The fresh noodle section is adequate, but they have a meat, poultry, fish counter, and even sell some Mexican spices, chilies, and sauces.

Tin Tin Oriental Supermarket

10881 S. Blaney Ave. (Bollinger), Cupertino, (408) 255-7804

Similar to 99 Ranch Market, this complete supermarket sells both standard American and Asian specialty goods. Produce is fresh and varied, with pea shoots, bitter melons, galangal, Thai chilies and basil, Japanese cucumbers, lemongrass, plantains, and various choys (all labeled in English). The large meat, poultry, and seafood department has many tanks—lobster and spot prawns—as well as more familiar cello packs, some with sashimi cuts. Packaged goods are not as organized as the competition, but the Indonesian goods selection is extensive, with sambals, shrimp paste, dried zedoary, and various bumbus. Other regional areas hold Philippine, Japanese, and Korean goods (bonito, shichimi, wakame, cane vinegar). The tofu, noodle, and wrapper selections are predictably large.

Valley Produce Market

3380 Middlefield Rd. (8th Ave.), Menlo Park, (650) 368-9226

Owned by a friendly Greek, this produce market specializes in Latin American, Samoan, and Tongan fruits and vegetables: plantains, yuca, nopales, taro roots, and chilies. They also have a full meat counter, some frozen fish and frozen banana leaves, and a few packaged staples for both Asian and Latin American cooking.

Vasquez Market

7369 Mission St. (San Pedro), Daly City, (650) 755-6094

A small Latin American market with a full butcher. In addition to a well-stocked case of meat and poultry, they are happy to cut to your specifications. A small produce section has plantains, nopales, a few chilies, and such. Very basic dry goods like masa, achiote, and bottled mole. The freezer has banana leaves and cassava.

Whole Foods

774 Emerson St. (Homer), Palo Alto, (650) 326-8666

15980 Los Gatos Blvd. (Blossom Hill), Los Gatos, (408) 358-4434

20830 Stevens Creek Blvd. (De Anza/Stelling), Cupertino, (408) 257-7000

1690 S. Bascom Ave. (Hamilton), Campbell, (408) 371-5000

See San Francisco listing.

Yaohan

675 Saratoga Ave. (I-280/Blackford), San Jose, (408) 255-6690, (408) 255-6699

This American branch of a Japanese supermarket is large, modern, and targeted, with almost exclusively Japanese goods, an in-house sushi bar/quick restaurant, and an attached Japanese bookstore. The store has all you'll need for a Japanese meal: somen, soba, udon, and ramen, both fresh and dried; other staples like bonito flakes, dried seaweed, shichimi; and every sauce imaginable. One corner is dedicated to seaweed salads and pickles. Of course, there are fish for cooking and for sashimi, with many kinds of roe and even sea urchin. Meats are primarily specialty cuts for shabu shabu and the like. The produce is nice, and includes eggplants, various mushrooms and chilies, Japanese cucumbers, and trefoil (mitsuba).

Specialty Food Store Indexes

New Chiu Fong Company (SF/Tenderloin) 249
New Saigon Supermarket (Oakland) 260
99 Ranch Market (Fremont, Hayward, Milpitas) 260
99 Ranch Market (Cupertino, Daly City, San Jose) 266
Oakland Market (Oakland) 260
Oriental Food Connection (San Rafael) 256
Pacific Food Market (SF/Richmond) 253
Philippine Grocery (Daly City) 266
Sam Yick (Oakland) 260
San Bruno Supermarket (SF/SoMa) 252
Senter Foods (San Jose, Sunnyvale) 267
T&L Market (SF/Richmond) 253
Thang Xuong Market (SF/Tenderloin) 249
Thien Thanh Supermarket (San Jose) 268
Tin Tin Oriental Supermarket (Cupertino) 268
Tony's Groceries Market (SF/Mission) 251
Wah Lian Supermarket (SF/Sunset) 255
Wailey Trading & Market (San Rafael) 256

Meat/Poultry/Game

Andronico's (Berkeley) 256
Andronico's (San Anselmo) 255
Andronico's (SF/Sunset) 254
Azteca Market (San Rafael) 255
Belmar Meat Market (South San Francisco) 262
Berkeley Bowl (Berkeley.) 257
Bryan's (SF/Richmond) 252
Carniceria Mi Rancho (San Mateo) 262
Castillo Tiene de Todo/Carniceria Tepa (South San
    Francisco) 262
Chavez Supermarket (Menlo Park, Redwood City) 262
Cheung Hing Meats (SF/Chinatown) 245
Cheung Kong Market (Oakland) 257
Cosentino's (San Jose, Santa Clara) 262
Draeger's Supermarket (Los Altos, Menlo Park, San
    Mateo) 263
Eastern Market (Concord) 257
Fiesta Latina (San Mateo) 263
Fiji India Market (Union City) 258
Fresh Meat Market (SF/Mission) 250
Good Luck Supermarket (Oakland) 258
Grand Central Market (SF/Marina) 248
Happy Supermarket (SF/Richmond) 253
Hong Kong Market (SF/Chinatown) 246
Housewives' Market (Oakland) 258
Indus Food Center (Berkeley) 258
International Market (Union City) 258
Irving May Wah Supermarket (SF/Sunset) 254
Irving Seafood Market (SF/Sunset) 254
Kowloon Market (SF/Richmond) 253
La Gallinita (SF/Mission) 251
Lien Hing (SF/Chinatown) 246
Little City Meats (SF/Chinatown) 246
Magnani's Poultry (Berkeley, Oakland) 259
Mangal's Market (San Leandro) 259

Mangal's Market (San Mateo) 264
Marina Foods (Cupertino, San Jose, San Mateo) 264
Mario's Fine Foods (Menlo Park) 264
May Wah Supermarket (SF/Richmond) 253
Mayerson Food Company (SF/Chinatown) 246
Mi Pueblo (Mountain View, San Jose) 265
Mi Rancho Market (SF/Mission) 251
Mi Tierra Foods (Berkeley) 259
Middle East Market (Berkeley) 259
New Basement Seafood Market (Oakland) 260
New Castro Market (Mountain View) 265
New Saigon Supermarket (Oakland) 260
99 Ranch Market (Fremont, Hayward, Milpitas) 260
99 Ranch Market (Cupertino, Daly City, San Jose) 266
Orient Market (Oakland) 260
Pamir Food Mart (Fremont) 260
Polarica (SF/SoMa) 252
Race Street Fish & Poultry (San Jose) 266
Rockridge Market Hall (Oakland) 260
Rose International (Mountain View) 267
San Bruno Supermarket (SF/SoMa) 252
Schaub's (Palo Alto) 267
Senter Foods (San Jose, Sunnyvale) 267
Super Mercado Mexico (San Jose) 267
Tel Aviv Kosher Meats (SF/Sunset) 254
Tin Tin Oriental Supermarket (Cupertino) 268
Tony's Groceries Market (SF/Mission) 251
Tower Market (SF/Haight) 250
Vasquez Market (Daly City) 268
Verbrugge Meat and Fish (Oakland) 261
Wah Lian Supermarket (SF/Sunset) 255
Whole Foods (Berkeley) 261
Whole Foods (Mill Valley) 256
Whole Foods (Campbell, Cupertino, Los Gatos, Palo
    Alto) 268
Whole Foods (SF/Marina) 248
Wing Hing Seafood (SF/Richmond) 254
Woodlands Market (Kentfield) 256

Cheese

Berkeley Bowl (Berkeley.) 257
California Street Creamery (SF/Marina) 248
Cheese Board (Berkeley) 257
Cheese Boutique (SF/Haight, Sunset) 254
Cheese Shop, The (Mill Valley) 255
Country Cheese (Berkeley) 257
Country Cheese (SF/Haight) 249
Draeger's Supermarket (Los Altos, Menlo Park, San
    Mateo) 263
Fourth Street Market Plaza (Berkeley) 258
G. B. Ratto & Company (Oakland) 258
J. Wiggins (Oakland) 259
Leonard's 2001 (SF/Russian Hill) 247
Molinari Delicatessen (SF/Chinatown) 246
Oakville Grocery (Walnut Creek) 260

Oakville Grocery (Palo Alto) 266
Rockridge Market Hall (Oakland) 260
Say Cheese (SF/Haight) 250
Sixth Avenue Cheese Shop (SF/Richmond) 253
Twenty-Fourth Street Cheese (SF/Haight) 250

Chinese

Almar Oriental (Millbrae) 262
Apple Land (SF/Chinatown) 245
Asian Market (San Rafael) 255
Cheung Kong Market (Oakland) 257
Cho Lon Moi (Oakland) 257
Chung Hing Produce (SF/Chinatown) 245
Erawan Market (Bekeley) 257
Farmer Joe's Marketplace (Oakland) 257
Good Luck Supermarket (Oakland) 258
Grand Meat Market (SF/Russian Hill) 247
Gum Shing (SF/Chinatown) 246
H K Market (SF/Richmond) 252
Happy Supermarket (SF/Richmond) 253
Hong Kong Market (SF/Chinatown) 246
Hwa Lei Market (SF/Mission) 250
International Market (Union City) 258
Irving May Wah Supermarket (SF/Sunset) 254
Khanh Phong Supermarket (Oakland) 259
Kowloon Market (SF/Chinatown) 246
Kowloon Market (SF/Richmond) 253
Lee Yuen (SF/Chinatown) 246
Lien Hing (SF/Chinatown) 246
Mandarin Delight (SF/Chinatown) 246
Marina Foods (Cupertino, San Jose, San Mateo) 264
May Wah Supermarket (SF/Richmond) 253
May Wah Trading Co. (SF/Chinatown) 246
Mayerson Food Company (SF/Chinatown) 246
Metro Foods Company (SF/Chinatown) 246
New Castro Market (Mountain View) 265
New Chiu Fong Company (SF/Tenderloin) 249
New Hong Kong Noodle Company (SF/Chinatown) 247
New Saigon Supermarket (Oakland) 260
99 Ranch Market (Fremont, Hayward, Milpitas) 260
99 Ranch Market (Cupertino, Daly City, San Jose) 266
Oakland Market (Oakland) 260
Orient Market (Oakland) 260
Oriental Food Connection (San Rafael) 256
Pacific Food Market (SF/Richmond) 253
Sam Yick (Oakland) 260
San Bruno Supermarket (SF/SoMa) 252
Sanh Hing (SF/Chinatown) 247
Senter Foods (San Jose, Sunnyvale) 267
Takahashi Market (San Mateo) 268
Thang Xuong Market (SF/Tenderloin) 249
Thien Thanh Supermarket (San Jose) 268
Tin Tin Oriental Supermarket (Cupertino) 268
Wah Lian Supermarket (SF/Sunset) 255
Wailey Trading & Market (San Rafael) 256

Fish/Seafood

Andronico's (Berkeley) 256
Andronico's (San Anselmo) 255
Andronico's (SF/Sunset) 254
Berkeley Bowl (Berkeley.) 257
Bryan's (SF/Richmond) 252
Cheung Kong Market (Oakland) 257
Cosentino's (San Jose, Santa Clara) 262
Dobashi Market (San Jose) 263
Draeger's Supermarket (Los Altos, Menlo Park, San Mateo) 263
Four Seas Supermarket (SF/Chinatown) 246
Good Luck Supermarket (Oakland) 258
Grand Central Market (SF/Marina) 248
Hankook Supermarket (Sunnyvale) 263
Happy Supermarket (SF/Richmond) 253
Hong Kong Market (SF/Chinatown) 246
Housewives' Market (Oakland) 258
International Market (Union City) 258
Irving May Wah Supermarket (SF/Sunset) 254
Irving Seafood Market (SF/Sunset) 254
Kim's Market (SF/Mission) 251
Lien Hing (SF/Chinatown) 246
Magat's Asian Groceries (Union City) 259
Marina Foods (Cupertino, San Jose, San Mateo) 264
Maruwa (SF/Marina) 248
May Wah Supermarket (SF/Richmond) 253
New Basement Seafood Market (Oakland) 260
New Castro Market (Mountain View) 265
New Saigon Supermarket (Oakland) 260
99 Ranch Market (Fremont, Hayward, Milpitas) 260
99 Ranch Market (Cupertino, Daly City, San Jose) 266
Orient Market (Oakland) 260
Oriental Food Connection (San Rafael) 256
Oriental Food Fair (El Cerrito) 260
Philippine Grocery (Daly City) 266
Race Street Fish & Poultry (San Jose) 266
Real Food Company (SF/Russian Hill) 247
Rockridge Market Hall (Oakland) 260
Sakai K Uoki Company (SF/Marina) 248
San Bruno Supermarket (SF/SoMa) 252
Schaub's (Palo Alto) 267
Seafood Center (SF/Richmond) 253
Senter Foods (San Jose, Sunnyvale) 267
Spark Supermarket (San Mateo) 267
Super Koyama (SF/Marina) 248
Suruki Japanese Foods (San Mateo) 267
Swan Oyster Depot (SF/Russian Hill) 247
Takahashi Market (San Mateo) 268
Takemura Market (Burlingame) 268
Tin Tin Oriental Supermarket (Cupertino) 268
Verbrugge Meat and Fish (Oakland) 261
Wah Lian Supermarket (SF/Sunset) 255
Whole Foods (Berkeley) 261
Whole Foods (Mill Valley) 256

Whole Foods (Campbell, Cupertino, Los Gatos, Palo Alto) 268
Whole Foods (SF/Marina) 248
Wild Oats (San Anselmo) 256
Wing Hing Seafood (SF/Richmond) 254
Yaohan (San Jose) 268
Yum Yum Fish (SF/Sunset) 255

Gourmet

Andronico's (Berkeley) 256
Andronico's (San Anselmo) 255
Andronico's (SF/Sunset) 254
Ashbury Market (SF/Haight) 249
Cheese Boutique (SF/Haight) 249
Cosentino's (San Jose, Santa Clara) 262
Cost Plus (Concord, Fremont, Oakland, Pleasanton, Walnut Creek) 257
Cost Plus (Larkspur) 255
Cost Plus (Daly City, Mountain View, San Mateo) 262
Cost Plus Imports (SF/Chinatown) 245
Draeger's Supermarket (Los Altos, Menlo Park, San Mateo) 263
Fourth Street Market Plaza (Berkeley) 258
G. B. Ratto & Company (Oakland) 258
Grand Central Market (SF/Marina) 248
Leonard's 2001 (SF/Russian Hill) 247
Oakville Grocery (Walnut Creek) 260
Oakville Grocery (Palo Alto) 266
Polarica (SF/SoMa) 252
Real Food Company (Sausalito) 256
Real Food Company (SF/Haight) 249
Rockridge Market Hall (Oakland) 260
Tower Market (SF/Haight) 250
Trader Joe's (Emeryville) 261
Whole Foods (Berkeley) 261
Whole Foods (Mill Valley) 256
Whole Foods (Campbell, Cupertino, Los Gatos, Palo Alto) 268
Whole Foods (SF/Marina) 248
Woodlands Market (Kentfield) 256

Health/Natural Foods

Better Life Whole Foods (SF/Russian Hill) 247
Cheese Boutique (SF/Haight) 249
Country Sun Natural Foods (Palo Alto) 263
Food Mill, The (Oakland) 258
Harvest Ranch Market (SF/Haight) 249
Nature Stop, The (SF/Chinatown) 247
Oasis Natural Foods (Novato) 256
Rainbow Grocery (SF/Mission) 251
Real Food Company (Sausalito) 256
Real Food Company (SF/Haight, Russian Hill) 247
Straw, The Jar and The Bean, The (SF/Marina) 248
Thom's Natural Foods (SF/Richmond) 254
Trader Joe's (San Rafael) 256

Whole Foods (Berkeley) 261
Whole Foods (Mill Valley) 256
Whole Foods (Campbell, Cupertino, Los Gatos, Palo Alto) 268
Whole Foods (SF/Marina) 248
Wild Oats (Berkeley) 261
Wild Oats (San Anselmo) 256

Indian

Asian Market (San Rafael) 255
Bazaar of India (Berkeley) 257
Bombay Bazar (SF/Mission) 250
Bombay Spice House (Berkeley) 257
Danya Imports (Santa Clara) 263
Draeger's Supermarket (Los Altos, Menlo Park, San Mateo) 263
Eastern Market (Concord) 257
European Deli & Middle East Grocer (Concord) 257
Fiji India Market (Union City) 258
G. B. Ratto & Company (Oakland) 258
Great India Foods (Sunnyvale) 263
Guru Place (Fremont) 258
Haig's Delicacies (SF/Richmond) 253
Halal Meats Deli & Grocery (San Jose) 263
India Food Mill (San Bruno, Sunnyvale) 264
Indus Food Center (Berkeley) 258
Maharaj Enterprises (Menlo Park) 264
Mangal's Market (San Leandro) 259
Mangal's Market (San Mateo) 264
Middle East Market (Berkeley) 259
Milan International (Berkeley) 259
Narayan Enterprises (Mountain View) 265
Neelam Pacific Market (San Bruno) 265
Neelam Supermarket (San Mateo) 265
New India Bazaar (SF/Tenderloin) 249
New India Bazar (San Jose) 266
Pamir Food Mart (Fremont) 260
Ratna Palace (Redwood City) 267
Rose International (Mountain View) 267
South Seas Market (San Bruno) 267
Spice House Co. (Union City) 261
Spiceland Indian Groceries (Santa Clara) 267
Taj Mahal Imports (Santa Clara) 268
UN Market (SF/Tenderloin) 249
Yekta Market & Deli (Fremont) 261

Italian

Florence Ravioli (SF/Chinatown) 246
Food Warehouse (SF/Russian Hill) 247
Fourth Street Market Plaza (Berkeley) 258
Grand Central Market (SF/Marina) 248
Homestead Ravioli (SF/Mission) 250
Lucca Delicatessen (SF/Marina) 248
Lucca Ravioli Co. (SF/Mission) 251
Molinari Delicatessen (SF/Chinatown) 246

Alphabetical

Index